University of Plymouth
Charles Seale Hayne Library
Subject to status this item may be renewed
via your Primo account

http://primo.plymouth.ac.uk
Tel: (01752) 588588

CULTURE, NORTHERN IRELAND, AND THE SECOND WORLD WAR

Culture, Northern Ireland, and the Second World War

GUY WOODWARD

OXFORD
UNIVERSITY PRESS

Great Clarendon Street, Oxford, OX2 6DP,
United Kingdom

Oxford University Press is a department of the University of Oxford.
It furthers the University's objective of excellence in research, scholarship,
and education by publishing worldwide. Oxford is a registered trade mark of
Oxford University Press in the UK and in certain other countries

The moral rights of the author have been asserted

First Edition published in 2015

Impression: 1

Published in the United States of America by Oxford University Press
198 Madison Avenue, New York, NY 10016, United States of America

British Library Cataloguing in Publication Data
Data available

Library of Congress Control Number: 2014942171

ISBN 978–0–19–871685–3

Printed and bound by
CPI Group (UK) Ltd, Croydon, CR0 4YY

To my father

Acknowledgements

This book began as my doctoral thesis, completed at Trinity College Dublin in 2012. First of all I would like to thank my doctoral supervisor Eve Patten for her invaluable help and support over the years. I also thank Gerald Dawe and Peter McDonald, generous examiners at my viva whose suggestions helped this book to develop beyond its original thesis. At Trinity College I also thank Terence Brown and Nicholas Grene for reading and commenting on my work at earlier stages. For generous financial assistance over two years of doctoral study and one year of post-doctoral research I thank the Irish Research Council for the Humanities and Social Sciences and its successor the Irish Research Council, and at Trinity I thank the Trinity Long Room Hub, the Graduate Studies Travel Fund, and the Trinity Trust for providing additional support enabling me to pursue research around Ireland and in Britain.

For all of their help and patience during the research of this book, I thank the staff of the BBC Northern Ireland Archive at the Ulster Folk and Transport Museum, Cultra, Co Down; of the Linen Hall Library, Belfast; of the Mass Observation Archive at the University of Sussex; of the National Library of Ireland; of the Public Records Office of Northern Ireland; of the Special Collections Department of Queen's University Belfast; of the Library of Trinity College Dublin; and of the University of Ulster Special Collections Department.

At OUP I thank Jacqueline Baker and Rachel Platt for all their help during the preparation of this book. I would also like to thank my two anonymous readers for their perceptive contributions.

For their various assistance, generosity, and forbearance during the research and preparation of this book I thank Ríann Coulter, Frank Ferguson, Sarah Ferris, Terence Harrington, Anthony Kennedy, Grania McFadden, Susanna Maybin and family, Eiléan Ní Chuilleanáin, and Deirdre Wildy.

For all her encouragement and support over the years I thank my mother.

Finally I thank Julie, without whom very little of this would have been possible.

Monterrey, Mexico, 2014

Contents

List of Illustrations

Permissions

The author would like to thank the following for permission to quote from copyright material:

The Estate of Maurice James Craig and the Jonathan Williams Literary Agency for permission to quote from 'Easter Tuesday, 1941', by Maurice James Craig.

The Estate of Robert Greacen and the Jonathan Williams Literary Agency for permission to quote from *Collected Poems 1944–1994*.

The Estate of John Hewitt for permission to quote from works by John Hewitt and materials in the John Hewitt Collection, University of Ulster, Coleraine, and the John Hewitt Papers, Public Records Office of Northern Ireland.

The Estate of Roy McFadden for permission to quote from *Collected Poems 1943–1995*.

The Estate of Roy McFadden and the McClay Library, Queen's University Belfast, for permission to quote from materials in the Roy McFadden Papers.

The Estate of Roy McFadden and the Linen Hall Library, Belfast, for permission to quote from materials in the Robert Greacen Collection.

The Estate of Louis MacNeice and David Higham Associates for permission to quote from 'Cushendun'.

The Trustees of the Mass Observation Archive and Curtis Brown Group Ltd, London, for permission to quote from materials in the Mass Observation Archive.

The Estate of Patrick Maybin for permission to quote from materials in the John Hewitt Papers, Public Record Office of Northern Ireland.

The Estate of Colin Middleton and the Irish Visual Artists Rights Organisation for permission to quote from materials in the John Hewitt Papers, Public Records Office of Northern Ireland.

The Estate of Frank Ormsby and the The Random House Group Limited for permission to quote 'Some of Us Stayed Forever' from *Northern Spring* by Frank Ormsby, published by Vintage and reprinted by permission of The Random House Group Limited.

The Deputy Keeper of the Records, Public Records Office of Northern Ireland for permission to quote from the diary of Emma Duffin, and from materials in the Arts Council of Northern Ireland Archive, the John Hewitt Papers, and the W.R. Rodgers Papers.

The Estate of W.R. Rodgers and Gallery Press for permission to quote from *Awake! and Other Poems*.

The Irish Capuchin Franciscans for permission to quote from the *Capuchin Annual*.

Ríann Coulter for permission to quote from her doctoral thesis 'Nationalism, Regionalism and Internationalism: Cultural Identity in Irish Art, 1943–1960' (Courtauld Institute of Art, University of London, 2006).

All reasonable efforts have been made to contact the holders of copyright in materials reproduced in this book. The publisher will be happy to rectify any omissions in future printings.

Introduction

On Friday 8 October 1999 a crowd gathered outside the City Hall in Belfast to witness the unveiling by the Lord Mayor of a memorial to James Magennis, the only serviceman from Northern Ireland to be awarded the Victoria Cross for service during the Second World War. Magennis was Catholic and from the Falls Road area of West Belfast, and the ways in which his wartime story has been celebrated, contested, forgotten, remembered, and, more recently, memorialized in Northern Ireland since 1945 illustrate the strikingly complex relationship, sometimes fraught and often muted, that has existed between the province and the Second World War.[1]

Fifty-four years earlier Magennis, a diver on a midget submarine, had carried out a daring and physically demanding underwater raid on a Japanese heavy cruiser moored off Singapore.[2] His Victoria Cross citation came through from Buckingham Palace on 13 November 1945, while Magennis was stationed at a submarine base in Sydney, Australia, and the news broke in Belfast the same day. The *Belfast Telegraph* carried an interview with Magennis's mother, said to be 'the proudest woman in Ulster today', and the following day 'Heartiest congratulations' were sent to the diver in a telegram by the prime minister of Northern Ireland, Basil Brooke. The celebrations continued on Magennis's return to Belfast on 14 December. The next day he was mobbed by crowds outside the City Hall as he arrived at a reception given by the Lord Mayor and corporation. The Mayor, Sir Crawford McCullagh, told him that he had 'added lustre to the annals of the British Empire', and Magennis was later presented with a gift of £3,066 that had been collected by the people of Northern

---

[1] Throughout this study I use 'province' as a synonym for Northern Ireland, not in its ancient Irish sense (the six counties of Northern Ireland being less than the nine counties of the historic province of Ulster) but in broad terms to describe Northern Ireland as a 'territory, region or subdivision' or 'administrative division' (*Oxford English Dictionary* online edition ([Oxford: Oxford University Press, 2013], <http://www.oed.com/view/Entry/153460?redirectedFrom=province>).

[2] The mission, carried out on 29 July 1945, is recounted in detail in George Fleming's biography *Magennis VC* (Dublin: History Ireland, 1998), pp. 150–160.

Ireland. Sectarian tensions do not seem to have surfaced in these civic responses to the hero's return, but when Magennis visited his old school, the Catholic St Finian's on the Falls Road, children reportedly refused to stand to welcome the uniformed sailor.[3] Magennis's biographer George Fleming claims that:

> It was clear that he was not wanted in Protestant Unionist East Belfast and neither was he wanted in Catholic Nationalist West Belfast. That uneasiness about a former pupil winning a high decoration for bravery in the British armed forces felt even by the teachers and pupils in his old school St Finian's was hardening into something else, as attitudes in Northern Ireland themselves hardened. He was the little guy in the middle caught in a strange religious and political trap.[4]

The revival of interest in James Magennis in the late 1990s seems almost entirely due to Fleming's letter writing campaign for the commemoration of Magennis's achievement, which succeeded in attracting significant interest from newspapers in Northern Ireland. In February 1997 Belfast City Council voted to erect a monument, and the present memorial in bronze and Portland stone was unveiled two years later. Fleming's biography also inspired at least two poems: 'James "Mick" Magennis VC' by Tom Paulin, and Michael Longley's 'Ocean', subtitled 'Homage to James "Mick" Magennis VC', were both published in 2000.

On the day of the unveiling, Lord Fitt, former leader of the SDLP and himself a merchant seaman during the Second World War, told the Belfast *News Letter* that it was a shame that the tribute had taken fifty years to be erected.[5] Sinn Féin councillors and assembly members boycotted the event, and almost all of the politicians present were unionist, but none on record addressed Fitt's implicit claim that it was Magennis's Catholic background that had delayed the civic recognition eventually granted to him. The convoluted post-war response to his story is perhaps symptomatic of an enduring reluctance within Northern Ireland to examine its place in the Second World War or to address the impact of the war on the province, and the physical awkwardness of the original underwater mission is echoed by later historical contortions.

In the aftermath of the Second World War, many in Northern Ireland seemed unwilling to dwell on the significance of the war. Nationalists may have been reluctant to face the probability that but for the province's strategic geopolitical location, within the United Kingdom and on the edge

---

[3] Fleming, *Magennis VC*, p. 170, p. 171, p. 178, p. 13, p. 182.
[4] Fleming, *Magennis VC*, pp. 199–200.
[5] Stephen Dempster, 'In memory of a *hero*', Belfast *News Letter*, 9 October 1999, pp. 24–25.

of the Atlantic, the war in Europe would have had a longer and bloodier course; if unionists were keen to cite the involvement of Northern Ireland in the war as proof of the indissoluble bonds of the union, the fact that significant numbers of Catholics from north and south of the border fought with distinction in the British armed forces during the conflict was problematic. The Second World War occupies a seemingly irresolvable position in relation to the Troubles: Glenn Patterson's novel *Fat Lad* (1993) notes the irony of British regiments who served with distinction in the Normandy landings of 1944 being deployed in far more controversial circumstances in Northern Ireland a quarter of a century later.[6] The postwar silence around James Magennis is demonstrative of a resignation to the probability that the province's position during the war was too difficult either to appropriate or explain.

The subaqueous nature of Magennis's mission also seems relevant when considering the cultural history of Northern Ireland and the war, where the submersion of artefacts and paraphernalia is a pervasive theme of a discourse which itself has often existed in a submerged or sunken state. The most striking monuments to the Second World War in Northern Ireland are out of sight and underwater, and include dozens of German U-boats that litter the sea bed of the Atlantic Ocean off Malin Head.[7] Like the Allied merchant ships and naval vessels they hunted, some sank during the Battle of the Atlantic, but many, following the surrender of their German crews, were deliberately towed from berths at Lisahally on the Foyle out to sea and scuttled.[8] Some of the flying-boats used to hunt these U-boats were also sunk when they became surplus to requirements at the end of the war. On Lough Erne in County Fermanagh in 1947, six Royal Air Force Catalinas were towed into the middle of the lake, where Marine Craft crew opened the sea-cocks and set about the bodies of the aircraft with axes, sending them to the bottom. Local historian Breege McCusker writes that 'they soon disappeared from sight but not from memory'.[9]

This book aims to recover submerged and neglected texts and artefacts which articulate the effect of the war on the province, with the hope of enlarging the sphere of its twentieth-century cultural history. How well

[6] Glenn Patterson, *FAT LAD* (London: Minerva, 1993), p. 120.

[7] These and other underwater wrecks were explored in the BBC One documentary series *Dig WW2 with Dan Snow*, broadcast 14–28 May 2012.

[8] Dermot Francis, Brian Lacey, and Jim Mullen, *Atlantic Memorial: The Foyle and the Western Approaches 1939–1945* (Derry: Derry City Council, Heritage and Museum Service, 2005), pp. 84–90; Derry Heritage Library Oral History Department, *The War Years: Derry 1939–45* (Derry: Guildhall Press, 1992), pp. 55–57.

[9] Breege McCusker, *Castle Archdale and Fermanagh in World War II* (Irvinestown: Necarne, 1993), p. 149.

the war has been remembered in Northern Ireland is less clear than McCusker's view, cited above, would suggest. In 'Some of Us Stayed Forever', the penultimate poem of Frank Ormsby's sequence *A Northern Spring* (1986), the voices of the deceased crew of a crashed United States Air Force bomber that came to rest on the bed of a lough are heard. In its entirety:

> Some of us stayed forever, under the lough
> in the guts of a Flying Fortress,
> sealed in the buckled capsule, or dispersed
> with odds and ends—propellers, dogtags, wings,
> a packet of Lucky Strike, the instructor's gloves –
> through an old world of shells and arrowheads,
> dumped furniture, a blind Viking prow.
> In ten years or a hundred we will rise
> to foul your nets with crushed fuselage.
> Our painted stork, nosing among the reeds
> with a bomb in its beak, will startle you for a day.[10]

Ormsby's imagined sunken bomber is both a time capsule and a tomb, a repository destined to rise in Arthurian fashion from the water at some future date. Wartime artefacts (dog tags, American cigarette packets, a painted nosecone) have here become embedded in a submerged material cultural history of the province, and, in the company of the medieval arrowhead or the Viking ship, have become equally remote from present-day concerns. The juxtaposition of these objects and the deliberately elastic timescale for the aircraft's reappearance suggests that Northern Ireland should be considered in a broader and deeper historical context than its bloody late-twentieth-century history has often allowed.

Another narrative of sub-aquatic awkwardness and survival may be found in James White's bizarre science-fiction novel *The Watch Below* (1966), in which, following a torpedo attack on a merchant ship during the Battle of the Atlantic, five survivors manage to remain alive below deck within an air pocket created in one of the ship's empty tanks. As a result of this, the ship fails to sink completely but moves suspended beneath the waves, unable either to sink or to float to the surface. The tank dwellers manage to adapt to a severely constricted existence (and indeed to reproduce) in this dark, damp, and claustrophobic environment for several generations over a period of one hundred years. One survival technique is known as 'The Game', whereby memory is tested by trying

---

[10] Frank Ormsby, 'Some of Us Stayed Forever', *A Northern Spring* (London: Secker and Warburg; Dublin: Gallery Press, 1986), p. 38.

to remember narratives of culture, history, and science in minute detail through repetition:

> 'And the opening questions and answers in the Children's Catechism,' Jenny broke in. 'I can remember most of them without digging, even. It starts like this. Question: Who made the world...?'
> 'Answer,' said her husband. 'Harland and Wolff...'[11]

Despite the flippancy of this quip (which itself acknowledges Belfast's prodigious wartime industrial output), and the idiosyncrasy of the novel itself, it is clearly possible to read *The Watch Below* as metaphorically resonant of Northern Ireland's cultural remembrance of the war: submerged, suspended, darkened, and surviving by adapting to the pressures of constrained circumstances.

In concluding *Key to Victory* (1995), a short history of Derry at war, Richard Doherty briefly surveys the physical relics of the war around the city, including gun emplacements and aluminium Hawksley bungalows at the Cloughglass estate, produced by aircraft manufacturers to meet the post-war demand for housing and recycled from aeroplanes scrapped by the RAF. He notes that the importance of the city to the progress of the Second World War, in particular to Allied success in the Battle of the Atlantic, has not been recognized locally, and suggests a number of explanations for this, including Derry's peripheral European location, its majority nationalist population, or 'a collective application of what psychologists refer to as the forty-year block, a closing-out of awful experiences from the memory for a period of roughly four decades'.[12] This latter explanation, implying that the corollary of collective memory must be collective amnesia, is clearly problematic in the context of Northern Ireland's post-war history of political violence and sectarian conflict, and it would be simpler to say that other 'awful experiences' day by day in Derry and elsewhere in the province over the decades prior to 1995 served to obscure or outweigh the effects of the Second World War.

If there is a perceptible awkwardness and eccentricity to these diverse literary, historical, and monumental Northern Irish responses to the Second World War, paradoxically such writings might fruitfully be recruited to a dominant and more general critical discourse of awkwardness in cultural or literary criticism of the period. The 1940s are widely, and perhaps over-enthusiastically, acknowledged to be a 'critically

---

[11] James White, *The Watch Below* (London: Ronald Whiting and Wheaton, 1966), p. 109.
[12] Richard Doherty, *Key to Victory: The Maiden City in the Second World War* (Antrim: Greystone, 1995), p. 81.

awkward' phase of twentieth-century writing.[13] As a vast, heavily mecha-
nized conflict encompassing almost the entire globe, which affected both
combatants and civilians almost indiscriminately, the Second World War
has proved resistant to theoretical critical frameworks, presenting difficulties for cultural historians and literary critics examining the period
retrospectively which echo those faced by artists and writers at the time.
Phyllis Lassner has described how modernist and postmodernist distrust
of the 'historical' is challenged by the war, arguing that 'When history
is invoked by both modernists and postmodernists what is meant are
the ideologies that framed, perhaps shaped, and helped define historical events and periods, and rarely the events themselves'—approaches
that have tended to efface the 1940s from such critical attention, since
the Second World War's 'material realities overwhelm any debates about
uncertain hermeneutics or epistemology'.[14] To this end, the opening lines
of Donald Bain's poem 'War Poet' (reading 'We in our haste can only
see the small components of the scene/We cannot tell what incidents
will focus on the final screen') have sometimes been quoted, to illustrate
the tendency of many artists and writers to limit the scope of their work
during the war to that which they had personally experienced, thereby
establishing a path subsequently followed by later commentators.[15] On
the British Home Front at least, much official and unofficial wartime
culture revolved around the recording of personal experience, and the
detailing of the minutiae of life as it was lived day by day. The dominance
of the Mass Observation movement in cultural and social histories of this
period has reinforced the impression that the Second World War created conditions whereby historiography became irrevocably indebted to
personal testimony. The importance accorded these individual accounts
has aided the construction of the idea of the 'People's War' in Britain—a
broad means of describing the dependence of the coalition government
on the cooperation of all parts of society for the successful prosecution of

[13] Marina MacKay and Lyndsey Stonebridge, 'Introduction: British Fiction After
Modernism', in *British Fiction After Modernism: The Novel at Mid-Century*, edited by Marina
MacKay and Lyndsey Stonebridge (Basingstoke and New York: Palgrave Macmillan, 2007),
pp. 1–17 (p. 1).
[14] Phyllis Lassner, 'The Timeless Elsewhere of the Second World War: Rosamond
Lehmann's *The Ballad and the Source* and Kate O'Brien's *The Last of Summer*', in *The Fiction
of the 1940s: Stories of Survival*, edited by Rod Mengham and N.H. Reeve (Basingstoke and
New York: Palgrave Macmillan, 2001), pp. 71–90 (p. 71).
[15] See Angus Calder, *The Myth of the Blitz* (London: Pimlico, 1991), p. 120; Marina
MacKay, 'Introduction', in *The Cambridge Companion to the Literature of World War II*,
edited by Marina MacKay (Cambridge: Cambridge University Press, 2009), pp. 1–9 (p. 1).
The poem has been widely anthologized, notably in *Components of the Scene: Stories, Poems
and Essays of the Second World War*, edited by Ronald Blythe (Harmondsworth: Penguin,
1966), where it is used as an epigraph.

the war, resulting in the fomenting of revolutionary attitudes and move-ments for social change.[16]

Whatever interest such accounts may hold for the historian, a percep-tion that the incontrovertible historical and social importance of the Second World War was not reflected in the quality of its art and literature has per-sisted. As Patrick Deer has noted, many literary critics have tended to adhere to Malcolm Bradbury's observation that: 'The relative artistic silence of the period from 1939 till toward the end of the 1940s seems very comprehensi-ble, until we recall that the First World War, quite as terrible, and with equal restrictions on artistic activity, was a major seedbed of modern artistic inno-vation.'[17] The terms of this perception were set during the war itself, when vocal and repeated demands in the press for war poets in the early years of the Second World War contributed to a lingering sense that its poetry compares unfavourably with that of the First World War. As Marina MacKay argues, little of the literature of the second war has ever 'fully registered on the critical field of vision', whereas the Great War 'set the standard by which the literature of the second war was judged wanting'.[18]

The material I address in this book is variable in quality, but is read with the aim of recovering forgotten ways of describing the place of Northern Ireland in relation to the Second World War, by examining the impact of that war on literature and culture in the province. Since the eccentricity and diversity of much of this material pose such a striking contradiction to the terms of recalcitrance and entrenchment in which Northern Ireland has so often been figured, this book, like others in the field, questions the continued relevance of a discourse of inferiority regarding the literature of the Second World War.

Recent years have seen several attempts to negotiate or overcome the per-ceived limitations and difficulties posed by British literature of the 1940s and the war.[19] I have not tried to impose any of these critical approaches

---

[16] Angus Calder, *The People's War: Britain 1939–1945* (London: Jonathan Cape, 1969; rev. edn. London: Pimlico, 1992), pp. 17–18. Despite the election of a Labour government in 1945 and the subsequent implementation of programmes of nationalisation and social reform, Calder argues that the forces of 'wealth, bureaucracy and privilege survived [the war] with little inconvenience' (p. 18).

[17] Malcolm Bradbury, '"Closing Time in the Gardens": Or, what happened to writing in the 1940s', in *No, Not Bloomsbury* (London: Andre Deutsch, 1987), pp. 67–86 (p. 69), cited in Patrick Deer, *Culture in Camouflage: War, Empire, and Modern British Literature* (Oxford: Oxford University Press, 2009), p. 2.

[18] Marina MacKay, *Modernism and World War II* (Cambridge: Cambridge University Press, 2007), p. 5.

[19] See Kristine A. Miller, *British Literature of the Blitz: Fighting the People's War* (Basingstoke and New York: Palgrave Macmillan, 2009); Adam Piette, *Imagination at War: British Fiction and Poetry 1939–1945* (London: Papermac, 1995); Mark Rawlinson, *British Writing of the Second World War* (Oxford: Clarendon Press, 2000); Victoria Stewart,

on works of art and literature in Northern Ireland, but do explore some of
their concerns within that context. In *Imagination at War: British Fiction
and Poetry 1939–1945* (1995), which charts the impact of the wartime isolation of Britain on the private imagination, Adam Piette seeks to address
a 'guilt complex' or lingering anxiety over the status of British poetry and
fiction of the Second World War in relation to European or world literature of the period.[20] Since Piette, several critical works have considered
British wartime literature and culture. Lyndsey Stonebridge's *The Writing
of Anxiety: Imagining Wartime in Mid-Century British Culture* (2007) also
examines the effect of the war on the mind of the individual but is more
explicitly theoretical in approach, exploring the traumatic impact on writers with reference to developments in post-Freudian psychoanalysis, whilst
Mark Rawlinson's *British Writing of the Second World War* (2000) develops
a politicized argument that writers and artists, by avoiding representations of actual death or injury to the human body in their works, helped
legitimize acts of military violence during the war. Piette's interest in the
transformative effect of Britain's wartime isolation on the private imagina-
tions of its writers and artists is reflected in one of my central concerns:
the tension between the cultural tendency to explore the local and the
regional in Northern Ireland during the war, and the fact that the province
became more susceptible to international pressures and influences at this
time, from its involvement in the war itself, and from the influx of foreign
troops and refugees. Where Piette's conception of the wartime imagination 'hollowed out by the relentless privations of the war' and 'invaded,
dismantled and displaced' is overwhelmingly negative, I hope to show that
despite the comparative isolation of the province, the war provided conditions which encouraged some transgressive and imaginative expressions
of cultural identity in Northern Ireland.[21] Piette's apprehension that the
work of the Welsh writer Alun Lewis was 'complicated by his Welshness'
since Lewis had 'the capacity, reinforced by his culture, to distance himself
from the propaganda of the British wartime government' is important to
my theme in so far as I attempt to show how Northern Ireland's wartime
culture was complicated by its Northern Irishness.[22] Marina MacKay's
claims that 'the nation's minor status is the keynote of both the war's literature and its subsequent discursive construction' and that standing alone
was Britain's 'master narrative' at this time, in part accounting for the continuing cultural significance of the war, also provoke important questions

Narratives of Memory: British Writing of the 1940s (Basingstoke and New York: Palgrave
Macmillan, 2006); Lyndsey Stonebridge, *The Writing of Anxiety: Imagining Wartime in Mid-
Century British Culture* (Basingstoke: Palgrave Macmillan, 2007).
[20] Piette, p. 1.   [21] Piette, pp. 4, 7.   [22] Piette, p. 124.

in a Northern Irish context.[23] If post-imperial Britain was coming to terms with its 'minor status', what were the implications of this shift for the status of Northern Ireland during and after the war? And if culture in Britain followed an isolationist narrative, how did artists and writers in Northern Ireland conceive of the province's place in the war?

The recent flurry of critical studies questions whether it is any longer possible to claim that literature of the Second World War in Britain has been neglected. Cultural historians and literary critics alike have tended to focus on a relatively limited body of work, however. Recurring across these studies are Elizabeth Bowen's wartime short stories and her novel *The Heat of the Day* (1949), T.S. Eliot's *Four Quartets* (1943), Henry Green's *Caught* (1943), the shelter drawings of Henry Moore, the paintings of Graham Sutherland, the poetry of Dylan Thomas, the novels of Evelyn Waugh, and Virginia Woolf's *Between the Acts* (1941). Mark Rawlinson has warned of the 'comforting familiarity' of these names, comparing their recurrence to 'the cast of the post-war British war movie, the literary analogues of John Mills, David Niven, and Kenneth More', but it is also worth remembering that many of these works refer directly only to London's experience of the war, perhaps reflecting a contemporaneous and enduring Anglocentricity of British wartime mythmaking, where 'England' and 'Britain' were used interchangeably.[24] As noted by Angus Calder in *The Myth of the Blitz* (1991), it is striking that London and the south-east of England, geographically closest in Britain to the European theatre of war, also provided the setting for many of the events which dominate British wartime mythology of the early years of the conflict such as the evacuation of Dunkirk, the Blitz in London, and the Battle of Britain.[25] We might also consider the freedom with which Winston Churchill used the terms 'Britain', 'the British Isles', and 'England' in his wartime speeches, or George Orwell's admission, some way into *The Lion and the Unicorn* (1941), of terminological inconsistencies within the essay itself regarding the interchangeability of 'the nation', 'England', and 'Britain', before claiming that 'we call our islands by no less than six different names, England, Britain, Great Britain, the British Isles, the United Kingdom and, in very exalted moments, Albion'.[26] If Scotland, Wales, and

---

[23] MacKay, *Modernism and World War II*, p. 2.

[24] Mark Rawlinson, 'Review of Patrick Deer, *Culture and Camouflage: War, Empire and Modern British Culture*, *Review of English Studies* 62, no. 253 (February 2011), pp. 158–160 (p. 160), doi:10.1093/res/hgq073.

[25] Calder, *Myth of the Blitz*, pp. 1–2.

[26] George Orwell, 'The Lion and the Unicorn: Socialism and the English Genius', in *The Complete Works of George Orwell*, vol. 12, 'A Patriot After All', edited by Peter Davison assisted by Ian Angus and Sheila Davison (London: Secker and Warburg, 1998), pp. 391–434 (p. 398).

the regions of England north and west of London were marginalized in both official and unofficial culture of the war, questions must surely also be asked about the place of Northern Ireland in relation to the British war effort: although the vexed term 'British Isles' would draw the province into such discourse, both 'Great Britain' and certainly 'England' would serve to exclude it.

Apart from Calder's *The Myth of the Blitz*, none of the critical studies to which I have so far referred address Northern Irish writing or culture during the war. Given that their self-defined remit has been 'British' literature and culture there is no reason why they should, but the swiftness with which a consideration of Northern Ireland disturbs or contradicts many of their arguments nevertheless suggests that new ways need to be found of approaching wartime art and literature in marginalized regions of Britain, and in Northern Ireland, where cultural Anglocentrism has had its own repercussions.

Introducing *Irish Poetry of the 1930s* (2005), Alan Gillis argues that Irish literary criticism's neglect of the decade immediately prior to the Second World War reflects the 'apparent Anglocentrism of Thirties literature', and exemplifies a waning delusion that 'Irish history ended in 1922, and did not begin again until either the opening-out of the economy in the late 1950s, or else the resumption of the Troubles'.[27] He writes that:

> It would be absurd to underplay the way in which Irish historical experience, throughout the decade, was distinct from Britain's. But, at the same time, Irish culture does not exist in isolation, and the historical forces that rampaged across the globe could not but be felt in Ireland, albeit in modified forms. Thus, without denigrating the specificity of Irish history, it seems clear that Irish culture can and should be perceived as part of the broader historical environment: a starkly conflictual arena in which pressures borne from drives towards socialism, capitalism, ethnic essentialism, democracy, and despotism mangled and collided.[28]

Gillis explains that his decision to discuss Louis MacNeice first reflects not only the poet's acknowledged status as a 'Thirties poet' but also the fact that 'his work explicitly pulls Irish historical contexts out of their apparent insularity, giving voice to acutely registered themes and circumstances that also affect his "more Irish" peers'.[29] Although Gillis's focus is on the poetry of the preceding decade, his arguments are of clear relevance to literature of the Second World War, especially in the case of MacNeice, whose

[27] Alan Gillis, *Irish Poetry of the 1930s* (Oxford: Oxford University Press, 2005), p. 9.
[28] Gillis, *Irish Poetry of the 1930s*, p. 2.
[29] Gillis, *Irish Poetry of the 1930s*, p. 3.

wartime poetry repeatedly addresses the 'apparent insularity' of neutral Ireland.

This book develops some of these ideas within the specific context of wartime Northern Ireland, itself a 'starkly conflictual' arena, and explores the role of culture in drawing the province into the 'broader historical environment' of the time. It is no coincidence that MacNeice presides over much of the third chapter, which examines the effects of the war on poetry in Northern Ireland. If, as Gillis suggests, MacNeice's work pulls Irish historical contexts away from their 'apparent insularity', this book shows that an exploration of Northern Irish wartime art and literature at this time can similarly encourage a reconsideration of the cultural history of the province in more expansive terms. Here we may apprehend Edna Longley's positive conception of a body of Northern writing that 'over-spills borders and manifests a web of affiliation that stretches beyond any heartland—to the rest of Ireland, Britain, Europe' and of a province that functions as 'a frontier-region, a cultural corridor, a zone where Ireland and Britain permeate one another'.[30] The editorial line taken by the influential Dublin magazine *The Bell* during the war years suggests that Seán Ó Faoláin and others were drawn to consider Northern Ireland for these very reasons. Nicholas Allen has observed that neutrality, censorship, and the stifling effect of the Catholic Church combined to enhance the appeal of Belfast for artists and writers in Éire during the war, but Ó Faoláin's attempts at enunciating an inclusive and mutually beneficial approach to culture north and south were not entirely enamoured of the northern city's cosmopolitan status.[31] Although he wrote that 'the great strength of the North is that she does live and act in the Now. Belfast has immediacy. Ulster has contemporaneity. Our southern curse is that we have never cut off the umbilicus', he also warned that the obverse of 'hyper-nationalism' south of the border was 'hyper-internationalism' in Northern Ireland, and despaired at the diverging paths of literature north and south.[32] It is ironic that these arguments were made in the editorial of a specific 'Special Ulster Number' of *The Bell*, but Ó Faoláin displays a greater willingness to consider and conceptualize north–south cultural relations during the war than many literary critics and historians since.

---

[30] Edna Longley, 'From Cathleen to Anorexia: The Breakdown of Irelands', in *The Living Stream: Literature and Revisionism in Ireland* (Newcastle Upon Tyne: Bloodaxe Books, 1994), pp. 173–195 (p. 195).
[31] Nicholas Allen, 'Out of time: Belfast and the Second World War', in *The Cities of Belfast*, edited by Nicholas Allen and Aaron Kelly (Belfast: Four Courts, 2003), pp. 88–100 (p. 90).
[32] 'An Ulster Issue', *The Bell* 4, no. 4 (July 1942), pp. 229–231 (p. 231); 'Ulster', *The Bell* 2, no. 4 (July 1941), pp. 4–11 (p. 5). Editorials in *The Bell* were unsigned.

Considering the freeness of Orwell's comments regarding the interchangeability of 'England', Britain', and 'the British Isles', it is easy to see how the London-led British war effort fomented peripheral resentment, resulting in some limited support for anti-war nationalist factions in both Scotland and Wales. Sonya O. Rose has described in *Which People's War? National Identity and Citizenship in Britain 1939–1945* (2003) how scenic invocations of the English countryside in wartime propaganda that purported to address Britain as a whole resulted in 'tension between Welsh and Scottish identity, on the one hand, and understandings of Englishness and Britishness, on the other, [which] very overtly complicated the idea that the nation was an organic community even as the multi-nation was threatened from without'.[33] Rose's claim that 'Britain as a nation [was] constituted as both a multiplicity of regions and as a cultural, if not political, "multi-nation" composed of four distinctive "national" cultures: Northern Ireland, Wales, Scotland, and England', contributes to a confused and Anglocentric discourse, however, and she is explicitly reluctant to examine Northern Ireland at all.[34] A footnote to her introduction reads:

> I did not include a discussion of Northern Ireland because of its incredible complexity relative to Wales, Scotland, and England. The Government did not institute conscription in Northern Ireland, although there were recruits. Also the Ministries of Labour and Supply recruited workers from Éire, although Éire was neutral in the war. Complicating the picture as well was that the division of Ireland into the independent Southern Counties and the North, which remained part of Britain, was quite recent. The topic of British nationhood with respect to Ireland during the war is worthy of a book-length study on its own.[35]

After a later reiteration of this, she adds that:

> Because of these complications, especially the potentially explosive issue of Irish nationalism and Roman Catholic-Protestant discord, to have included Ulster in this study of national identity and citizenship in wartime Britain would have meant adding considerable length to an already long and complex chapter.[36]

Rose's reasoning provides a useful illustration of some of the problems and contradictions facing cultural historians. Leaving aside the well-worn misconception that 'Ulster' is equivalent to Northern Ireland, whether 'the North' remained 'part of Britain' is less a question of geography (clearly Northern Ireland is physically detached from the island of Great Britain)

---

[33] Sonya O. Rose, *Which People's War? National Identity and Citizenship in Britain 1939–1945* (Oxford and New York: Oxford University Press, 2003), p. 198.
[34] Rose, p. 197.   [35] Rose, p. 28.   [36] Rose, p. 219.

than a matter of political allegiance. It is undeniable that Northern Ireland was involved in and affected by a war in which the United Kingdom was a leading combatant nation and Éire was not. Rose identifies the lack of conscription and the recruitment of industrial workers from south of the border as complicating factors which have encouraged her avoidance, but Northern Ireland was unavoidably drawn into the British war effort through its military and industrial participation. That the province's involvement in this war effort was fraught is evident from Gillian McIntosh's account of the problems faced by the BBC during the war. Whereas in Britain, broadcast efforts to encourage national unity could be rooted in the supposedly non-controversial past, in Northern Ireland 'there was no common historical past to which BBC NI programme makers could hark back in an effort to create the image of a common cultural heritage', leaving the corporation in an almost impossible position.[37] Indeed, as a British institution it became a focus of anti-English sentiment that characterized much unionist literature of the time.

The problems arising from such inconsistencies and contradictions were clearly felt at the time in Northern Ireland, within and beyond traditional sectarian divisions. One Mass Observer described his anger at the singing of a patriotic song at the conclusion of a concert and variety show at the City Hall in Armagh, in December 1939:

> A man then sang 'There'll always be an England.' This infuriated me—I think it is wrong to sing this song in Ireland. After all, although under British Rule, I and most Ulstermen quite naturally love our own part of the world best of all. Most of us, too, are very irritated by English people, whose manner and outlook seem very overbearing and humourless to us. There were some English soldiers there of course, but I think that the song should be altered to 'There'll always be a Britain'. This should satisfy everyone. Both the 'Marseillaise' and 'The King' were sung at the end.[38]

The song itself exemplifies the problematic equation of England with Britain during the war. Despite the claim made by its title, repeated in the chorus, the song's lyrics also ask 'Red, white and blue/What does it mean to you?' and urges 'Britons awake!/The Empire too/We can depend on you', inconsistently applying the colours of the flag of the whole United Kingdom to England before encouraging Britain and its Empire to rise in

---

[37] Gillian McIntosh, *The Force of Culture: Unionist Identities in Twentieth Century Ireland* (Cork: Cork University Press, 1999), pp. 69–70.

[38] Diary of S.J.C. Harrison, 7 December 1939 (University of Sussex: Mass Observation Archive, MO5102). All material from the Mass Observation Archive is reproduced with permission of Curtis Brown Group Ltd, London on behalf of The Trustees of the Mass Observation Archive. Copyright © The Trustees of the Mass Observation Archive.

some non-specific defence of England and 'Freedom'.[39] Harrison's resentment of the song is also contradictory, as his irritation at the incompatibility of its lyrics with its Northern Irish performance setting and audience and dislike of an 'overbearing' imposition of Englishness are undermined by the scarcely credible assertion that altering 'England' to 'Britain' in the song's title and lyrics 'should satisfy everyone' and his unquestioning acceptance of the singing of the national anthems of both France and the United Kingdom at the end of the night.

Regardless of its contested territorial status, artists and writers in Northern Ireland were clearly subject to many of the same threats and privations as their counterparts in Britain. They were also surrounded by much of the physical paraphernalia which is by now almost indelibly associated with the British war effort, as air raid shelters were dug, barrage balloons raised in the skies, and a blackout imposed, whilst the building of airfields and military bases as thousands of foreign troops poured into Northern Ireland changed its rural landscape forever.[40] The bombing of Belfast on Easter Tuesday 1941 killed 745 people and destroyed hundreds of buildings, and although Dublin also came under attack by the Luftwaffe during the war, the cumulative effect of these experiences inevitably opened up and accentuated differences between Northern Ireland and the southern state. If this study seems critically aligned more with British than Irish cultural history, this is explained by the fact that it charts the impact on literature and culture in Northern Ireland of a war in which Britain, unlike neutral Éire, was directly involved. Unlike in Britain however, in Northern Ireland a significant proportion of the population were implacably opposed to the war. Denis Donoghue wrote in his memoir *Warrenpoint* (1991) that 'I didn't regard myself as at war: as a Catholic my loyalty was to Ireland, not to Britain, and I didn't consider Northern Ireland as a part of Britain'.[41] Many Catholics felt uneasy at the prospect of becoming involved in what was often figured as an exclusively British war effort, thereby implicitly accepting the legitimacy of partition. The novelist Brian Moore, convinced of the need to defeat fascism, nevertheless balked at the prospect of donning British army uniform and in the

---

[39] Stephen Seidenberg, Maurice Sellar, Lou Jones, *You Must Remember This . . . Songs at The Heart of the War* (London: Boxtree, 1995), p. 29.

[40] For an account (and, indeed, an indictment) of these preparations see Brian Barton, *The Blitz: Belfast in the War Years* (Belfast: Blackstaff Press, 1999), pp. 27–41; for a brief summary of the arrival of US troops and the subsequent construction programme see Brian Barton, *Northern Ireland in the Second World War* (Belfast: Ulster Historical Foundation, 1995), pp. 98–101. This latter account should not be confused with John W. Blake's book of the same title (*Northern Ireland in the Second World War*), edited by Barton for its 2000 reprint by the Blackstaff Press.

[41] Denis Donoghue, *Warrenpoint* (London: Jonathan Cape, 1991), p. 145.

end joined Air Raid Precautions.[42] Many nationalists felt that Britain's colonial history made a mockery of claims to be fighting a moral war, and graffiti appearing in West Belfast reading 'England's Difficulty is Ireland's Opportunity' revived memories of the Easter Rising during the First World War.[43] Mr Burke in Moore's novel *The Emperor of Ice Cream* (1965) sums up these feelings, saying that 'when it comes to grinding down minorities, the German jackboot isn't half as hard as the heel of John Bull'.[44] A more extreme example of anti-British nationalist feeling is that of Your Man Gallagher in the same novel, a former member of the IRA attempting to make an active contribution to a German war against Britain by keeping a flashlight in his overcoat to signal to Luftwaffe aircraft above Belfast. Gallagher 'no longer had great hopes of the IRA as a force to overthrow the British. He put his money on Hitler. When Hitler won the war, Ireland would be whole again, thirty two counties, free and clear'.[45] The tone of much unionist rhetoric during the war years was also stridently myopic, exemplified by Prime Minister Lord Craigavon's wireless broadcast in 1940 declaring that 'We Are King's Men', which animated many other attempts to figure the war as demonstrative both of Northern Ireland's fidelity to the British crown and separateness from the southern state.[46] In these ways the possibility of a People's War on British lines was either supplanted by loyalist dogma or fatally compromised by nationalist dissent.

For the most part the artists and writers examined here worked outside this environment, and their concerns and debates challenge and contradict both unionist political hegemony and the anti-partitionist and isolationist nationalist rhetoric prevalent at the time. Relative to the status of filmmakers, painters, and poets in Britain in relation to the war effort, the lack of an established cultural infrastructure and a long-standing resistance within Northern Ireland to many forms of artistic expression prevented artists and writers from entering mainstream political discourse, had they wanted to do so. Despite this eccentricity, it is clear that the terms of political debate in Northern Ireland were significantly enlarged beyond traditional sectarian boundaries both during the war and in the years that

---

[42] Patricia Craig, *Brian Moore: A Biography* (London: Bloomsbury, 2002), p. 75.

[43] Paddy Devlin, *Straight Left: An Autobiography* (Belfast: Blackstaff Press, 1993), p. 26.

[44] Brian Moore, *The Emperor of Ice Cream* (London: Andre Deutsch, 1965; repr. London: Paladin, 1987), p. 36. All subsequent references to 'Moore, *Emperor*' are to the Paladin reprint.

[45] Moore, *Emperor*, p. 61.

[46] James Craig, 'We Are King's Men', in *The Field Day Anthology of Irish Writing*, vol. 3, edited by Seamus Deane (Cork: Cork University Press, 1991), pp. 363–365 (p. 365). Originally broadcast 5 February 1940.

immediately followed. The war drew the province into an international context against which broadly socialist ideas were briefly able to prosper, both at the ballot box in elections to Stormont in 1945, and in a number of regular, irregular, and one-off publications, demonstrative of the inter-penetration of political, poetic, and artistic spheres in Belfast at this time. The lack of cultural and political infrastructure, the dependence on unreliable or maverick figures, and the hostility of both nationalist and unionist discourse to internationalist or socialist ideas served as impediments to a lasting impact being made by these developments.

The awkwardness of Northern Ireland's position in relation to the war may explain the relative lack of manifesto-making by artists and writers in the province at this time, and may also account for their inability or reluctance to move in a concerted artistic direction, despite the strength of their personal friendships. Attempts were made, but in retrospect John Hewitt's regionalism can hardly be said to have resulted in the body of work he hoped for, and although Robert Greacen's attempts to promote New Apocalyptic verse enable important if overlooked links to be drawn between the wartime literary worlds of Belfast, Dublin, and London, today the poetry itself seems overwrought and overladen with symbolism. These efforts might be contrasted with the brief success in Dublin during the war of the White Stag Group of painters in articulating a cohesive and distinctively modernist body of work, or, conversely, with the huge number of artists and writers recruited to the British war effort, who produced propaganda material, wrote for the BBC, or worked as official war artists.[47] The paths taken by artists and writers in Northern Ireland at the time seem, in comparison, eccentric and non-conformist. The Ulster Unit group of artists formed in Belfast in 1934 to evangelize a modernist aesthetic quickly fell apart after one exhibition, and the subsequent path taken by its leading painter Colin Middleton, as he switched between divergent themes and styles, simply defies categorization or explanation.[48] Politically speaking, the writings of the Protestant nationalist Denis Ireland, a former Captain in the British army who served in the First World War, also exemplify the maverick tendency which was able to prosper in Northern Ireland during the war.

In acknowledging and exploring these eccentricities, this book explores a diverse body of work encompassing literary writing in poetry and prose, as well as historical, political, and journalistic writing and pictorial and graphic works of art. In their introduction to *Across a Roaring Hill: The Protestant Imagination*

---

[47] S.B. Kennedy, *The White Stag Group* (Dublin: Irish Museum of Modern Art, 2005).
[48] S.B. Kennedy, *Irish Art and Modernism: 1880–1950* (Belfast: Institute of Irish Studies, The Queen's University of Belfast, 1991), p. 77.

in Modern Ireland (1985) Gerald Dawe and Edna Longley claim that 'the Ulster Protestant voice in prose often sounds most natural in less evolved structures, and in Belfast working-class accents', citing the anecdotal writings of Sam McAughtry and the 'more studied wit' of John Morrow.[49] Although I have not limited myself to writers of Protestant backgrounds, it does seem as though the predilection for unofficial or non-literary forms and modes detected by Dawe and Longley coincided successfully with a wartime cultural atmosphere which encouraged 'less evolved structures' to emerge and gain acceptance. The impact of the Second World War in both practical and psychological terms on literary form, encouraging short fiction and poetry, and discouraging the writing of novels, has been much noted, and is discernible in the emergence in Northern Ireland as in Britain at this time of various little magazines and one-off publications.[50] Mengham and Reeve have described the 1940s as a time when much writing in Britain at least understood itself to be 'raw material to which later construction would bring a necessary finish', and to this end I have considered the 'raw material' of artists and writers—documents including unpublished diaries, letters, and other literary and non-literary drafts and ephemera—alongside their work in the public domain.[51]

* * *

Due to the contradictions I have outlined, and attendant antagonisms and divisions of longer standing, the cultural and social history of Northern Ireland during the Second World War has remained relatively unexplored. In their studies of the Home Front in Britain, neither Angus Calder nor Arthur Marwick devote any attention to the Northern Irish experience of the Second World War, not do they consider the implications for the province of the election in 1945 of a Labour government in Britain. Marwick omits Northern Ireland altogether from his illustrated history *The Home Front: the British and the Second World War* (1976), and Calder affords less than two pages in his vast account *The People's War* (1969, rev. edn. 1992) to what he describes as 'a limb lopped off Éire in the aftermath of the Irish revolution and run ever since by a species of Protestant Mafia'.[52] Calder's

[49] Gerald Dawe and Edna Longley, 'Introduction', in *Across a Roaring Hill: The Protestant Imagination in Modern Ireland. Essays in Honour of John Hewitt*, edited by Gerald Dawe and Edna Longley (Belfast: Blackstaff Press, 1985), pp. i–xii (p. x).
[50] Rod Mengham, 'British Fiction of the War', in MacKay (ed.), *Cambridge Companion to the Literature of World War II*, pp. 26–42 (p. 26); Woodrow Wyatt, 'Introduction', in *The Way We Lived Then: The English Story in the 1940s*, edited by Woodrow Wyatt (London: Flamingo, 1990), pp. 7–9.
[51] Rod Mengham and N.H. Reeve, 'Introduction', in Mengham and Reeve (eds.), *The Fiction of the 1940s*, pp. xi–xiii (p. xi).
[52] Arthur Marwick, *The Home Front: the British and the Second World War* (London: Thames and Hudson, 1976); Calder, *People's War*, p. 413.

brief summary of events, cribbed, it seems, from John W. Blake's official history *Northern Ireland in the Second World War* (1956), serves only to remove Northern Ireland from his arguments and conclusion, and the flippancy of his final assertion that 'Ulster' had 'a decidedly Irish sort of war' is indicative of an unwillingness to engage with the Northern Irish experience of the war, even while acknowledging its singularity.[53] In *The Myth of the Blitz*, however, Calder co-opts Northern Ireland into his debunking of wartime myths, writing that 'No inhabitant of Ulster, surely, can now believe that the Second World War had any healing effect on that society'.[54] The suggestion that Northern Ireland's violent post-war history contradicts notions that the war had any lasting effect on the province, positive or otherwise, is important, and shows how the Troubles have displaced the Second World War in public, cultural, and historical consciousnesses within and outside Northern Ireland, complicating the ability of historians to write the province into British or European narratives of the period. In this respect, Juliet Gardiner's recent volumes of social and cultural history are notable for her decision to consider Northern Ireland's experiences alongside those of wartime Britain.[55]

   In accounts of Ireland and the Second World War, Northern Ireland has suffered marginalization in discussions which focus on Irish neutrality: the wartime equation of England with Britain might, indeed, be compared with the tendency to disregard or avoid making explicit the separate experiences of the war north and south of the border. This reticence, alluded to by Alan Gillis, derives in part from political and academic allegiances that have pervaded since partition. Edna Longley's attack on Seamus Deane's *Field Day* project provides a more vivid illustration of this, when she addresses the omission of both nineteenth-century Ulster liberalism and twentieth-century Ulster socialism from the anthology. Deane's problem, she suggests, is:

> How to divide the century without dividing the country? British anthologies and literary histories generally take a break, whether justifiable or not, at the Second World War, but only Northern Ireland officially joined in that skirmish. Deane's autobiographical section, despite its martial emphases, includes memoirs of neither World War.[56]

[53] Calder, *People's War*, p. 414.   [54] Calder, *Myth of the Blitz*, p. xiv.
[55] Juliet Gardiner, *Wartime: Britain 1939–1945* (London: Headline, 2004, repr. London: Headline Review, 2005); *The Blitz: The British Under Attack* (London: HarperPress, 2010).
[56] Edna Longley, 'Introduction: Revising "Irish Literature"', *Living Stream*, pp. 9–68 (p. 43).

Paradoxically, such omissions may also have been encouraged by the power and resonance of Louis MacNeice's indictment of 'The neutral island' in the poem 'Neutrality' written in 1942.[57] If Churchill and others were able to use Great Britain's island status as a powerful metaphor of defiance and separateness during the war, the island of Ireland could conversely be conceived of as a symbol of isolation and introversion. Bernard Share uses 'Neutrality' (wrongly credited as 'The Closing Album') as the epigraph for his intermittently whimsical and evasive account *The Emergency: Neutral Ireland, 1939–45* (1978), and MacNeice's phrase was adapted by Clair Wills for the title of her landmark 2007 cultural history of Ireland at war, *That Neutral Island*.

In earlier accounts, such as Joseph T. Carroll's *Ireland in the War Years* (1975) and Tony Gray's *The Lost Years: The Emergency in Ireland, 1939–45* (1997), the preoccupation with the question of neutrality and even the use of the term 'the Emergency' serve to emphasize the experiences of the southern state at the expense of Northern Ireland. The contentious and divisive involvement of Ireland in the First World War may also be considered as a contributory factor in the awkwardness of historians and others in accounting for its experience of the Second. Despite his claim that the outcome of the Second World War 'had an important bearing on the post-war development of the Irish state, politics and society', Geoffrey Roberts suggested in 2000 that 'challenges to Irish identities' had yet to be fully worked through, given that 'the diversity of responses to the identity question produced a series of political and cultural contradictions and tensions which are still evident 60 years later'.[58]

The observations and anecdotes of Belfast journalist and raconteur Sam McAughtry relating to the differing perceptions of the war north and south of the border are particularly interesting in this respect. In *On the Outside Looking In: A Memoir* (2003) he recalls a sharply critical *Irish Times* review of his earlier book *The Sinking of the Kenbane Head* (1977), written as a tribute to his brother Mart, who died when the freighter on which he was serving was sunk by a German battleship during the Battle of the Atlantic. The reviewer, Eileen O'Brien, wrote that 'Mr McAughtry writes as well as the Belfast people talk, and that is very well indeed', but added that joining the Royal Air Force as McAughtry had done was 'a waste of a young man who could have done great things in his own country instead'—comments

---

[57] Louis MacNeice, 'Neutrality', *Collected Poems*, edited by Peter McDonald (London: Faber and Faber, 2007), p. 224.

[58] Geoffrey Roberts, 'Neutrality, Identity and the Challenge of the "Irish Volunteers"', in *Ireland in World War Two: Neutrality and Survival*, edited by Dermot Keogh and Mervyn O'Driscoll (Cork: Mercier Press, 2000), pp. 274–284 (p. 274).

that clearly angered the author.[59] He also recalls an appearance on the *Late Late Show* on RTÉ television in Dublin, when he is struck by:

> ...the realisation that these people belonged to a different society from the one in which I had been reared. This was their television station, in their capital city. It was like being outside my Ireland, in another country . . . For them there had been no war, no Luftwaffe obliteration of city centres. Hitler had even compensated them for an accidental bombing by a Luftwaffe plane.[60]

McAughtry's actual involvement in the Second World War enabled him to discover hitherto unacknowledged or unexplored versions of Irishness, but here he identifies the war as an instrumental factor in the post-war divergence of north and south.

In addressing Northern Ireland's specific experience of the war, works by Brian Barton (in *The Blitz: Belfast in the War Years* [1989] and *Northern Ireland in the Second World War* [1995]) and Robert Fisk (*In Time of War: Ireland, Ulster and the Price of Neutrality 1939–1945* [1983]) remain unsurpassed. It is significant that both writers draw on a work of fiction—Brian Moore's novel *The Emperor of Ice Cream*—in their accounts of the traumatic aftermath of the Belfast Blitz, reproducing passages of description as though historical fact. Angus Calder's only sustained exploration of Northern Ireland and the war in *The Myth of the Blitz* also stems from a reading of Moore's novel, which has become the province's urtext for the war: the repeated recourse to Moore's novel in these works of cultural and social history and the growing body of literary critical engagements with the book certainly highlight the relative scarcity of post-war fiction addressing Northern Ireland's war years. Barton and Fisk aside, independent researchers and local historians have perhaps been most active in describing the province's experience of the war. Over the past decade, websites produced by the BBC and the Second World War Online Learning Resource for Northern Ireland have collated first-hand memories of the war years, developing valuable, if potentially unreliable, sources for future researchers.[61] The recreational nature of the pursuit of much local and family history and the anecdotal nature of the material offer further resistance to theoretical examinations of Northern Ireland's place in the war, as the gathering of such stories returns the study of the Home Front to a

---

[59] Sam McAughtry, *On the Outside Looking In: A Memoir* (Belfast: Blackstaff Press, 2003), p. 35; Eileen O'Brien, 'Home From Sea', *Irish Times*, 26 November 1977.

[60] McAughtry, *On the Outside Looking In*, p. 54.

[61] BBC 'WW2 People's War' website, accessed 23 February 2014, <http://www.bbc.co.uk/history/ww2peopleswar/categories/c1103/>, Second World War Online Learning Resource for Northern Ireland, accessed 23 February 2014, <http://www.secondworldwarni.org/>.

matter of personal testimony—a retrospective, haphazard form of Mass Observation.

One source on which Brian Barton is particularly reliant in *Northern Ireland in the Second World War* is the Mass Observation diary of Moya Woodside, a surgeon's wife living in south Belfast during the war, and one of three Mass Observation diarists in Northern Ireland at this time.[62] The space and status accorded to her diary is comparable with the historians' reverential treatment of *The Emperor of Ice Cream*, and the use of the diary and the novel together in such social histories (and, indeed, in this volume) is demonstrative of the extent to which literary and non-literary, fictional and factual accounts of the Second World War can be seen to overlap. Quoting extensively from Woodside's diary and from an account of a visit to Northern Ireland by the founder of Mass Observation Tom Harrisson, Barton draws the province into the contested 'People's War' narrative of the British Home Front, prevalent since the publication of Calder's study of the same name which similarly relied heavily on the work of Mass Observers. Moya Woodside's diary is a valuable resource, and highlights many of the concerns that figure repeatedly in writing during and since the war: she served on a committee organizing welfare for refugees, so was acutely aware of the influx of émigrés, and she also travelled between Belfast and Dublin, providing vivid descriptions of her impressions of the intense sensory contrasts between the two cities.[63] Richly detailed, her account is notable for the intensity of its scepticism. Deconstructing and interrogating censorship and propaganda in government policy and in newspapers and newsreels, the diary anticipates the work of later cultural historians and demonstrates how the idea of a People's War was questioned contemporaneously in Northern Ireland.

Although the Second World War clearly had a considerable impact on the future of Northern Ireland as a geographical and political entity over the second half of the twentieth century, literary or artistic reflection on this has been limited, and Tom Paulin's allusion in his poem 'The Caravans of Lüneberg Heath' to the war as a factor in the strengthening of the post-war British claim on Northern Ireland is strikingly rare in a

---

[62] Moya Woodside's diary (MO5462) is housed at the Mass Observation Archive, University of Sussex. The other Mass Observation diarists were Doreen Bates (MO5425), an English civil servant working in Belfast, and S.J.C. Harrison (MO5102), a student from Armagh cited above. The founder of Mass Observation Tom Harrisson visited Northern Ireland in 1944, and wrote of his (not entirely favourable) impressions in a two-part feature for the *Cornhill* magazine. See Harrisson, 'Ulster Outlooks', *Cornhill* 962 and 963 (October, November 1944), pp. 80–91 and pp. 210–223.

[63] Woodside, 16 September 1940, 1 February 1941.

literary context.[64] Compared with the vast quantities of cultural material of all kinds relating to the Second World War produced in Britain and the United States, contributions in Northern Ireland to this field appear to have been constrained and eclipsed by its post-war history of political violence. The province's experience of the war cannot easily be incorporated into a British or Irish narrative of the Second World War or 'Emergency', and, caught between the two, has often been omitted from both. The historian Derrick Gibson-Harries' conception of 'Ulster' as 'a huge unsinkable aircraft carrier and naval base' during the war is illustrative of its contested and uncertain role. The metaphorical potential in conceiving of the province as a giant ship and mobile participant in the war is swiftly undercut by the reference to a land-bound military installation and by the use of the word 'unsinkable', inevitably heavily freighted with irony in the context of ships and Northern Ireland.[65] The tension between movement and stasis in Gibson-Harries' metaphor echoes the contradiction between the perception that Northern Ireland was both literally and culturally isolated during the war, and the idea that at this time the province was invigorated by an influx of new ideas and external cultural personalities. The writings of the poet, critic, and arts administrator John Hewitt frequently reflect this contradiction, poised between pride in the separateness and specificity of Ulster writing and an anxiety that art and writing in Northern Ireland should be demonstrably relevant to developments in Britain and Europe.

The vagueness resulting from the inconsistent deployment of terminologies, and the Anglocentric perception that Northern Ireland was semi-detached from the war, are reflected in the opening scenes of *The Soldier's Art* (1966), the eighth novel in English writer Anthony Powell's sequence *A Dance to the Music of Time*. As noted by C.E.B. Brett, the opening scenes of the novel seem to take place against the backdrop of a Luftwaffe raid on Belfast in 1941, when Powell himself was stationed in the city as assistant Camp Commandant for Headquarters in the 53rd division of the British army's Welch Regiment.[66] Brief fragments describing the

[64] Tom Paulin, 'The Caravans of Lunëberg Heath', *Fivemiletown* (London: Faber and Faber, 1987), p. 65.

[65] Derrick Gibson-Harries, *Life-Line to Freedom: Ulster in the Second World War* (Lagan: Ulster Society Publications, 1990), p. 18. Gibson-Harries' conception is reminiscent of Operation or Project Habbakuk, a joint British–US plan during the Second World War promoted by Commodore Mountbatten. Plans were made to construct a vast, 2,000-foot-long aircraft carrier with a hull made from Pykrete—a mixture of ice and wood developed by the military engineer and inventor Geoffrey Pyke—which was designed to be so resilient as to render the vessel literally 'unsinkable'. See David Lampe, *Pyke: The Unknown Genius* (London: Evans Brothers, 1959), pp. 127–162.

[66] C.E.B. Brett, *Long Shadows Cast Before: Nine Lives in Ulster, 1625–1977* (Edinburgh and London: John Bartholomew & Son Ltd, 1978), p. 41.

physical environment of Powell's anonymous fictional analogue certainly suggest an attempt to evoke the surroundings of Belfast, named merely as a 'provincial city'.[67] These include the cityscape of 'docks and shipyards', the landscape around the fictional Divisional Headquarters, described as 'hedgeless fields partitioned one from another by tumbledown stone walls', the thud of guns 'shuddering waves from the surrounding hills', and the view from F Mess in which Nick Jenkins is billeted, where 'From its windows in daytime, beyond the suburbs, grey, stony hills could be seen, almost mountains; in another direction, that of the docks over which the blitz had been recently concentrating'.[68] The evocation of the anonymous city through such vague reference points recalls the censorship of radio and newspaper reports in Britain and Ireland during the war, when names of cities, towns, streets, and buildings were often omitted and locations cloaked in euphemism. It was wrongly thought by many that Belfast would be beyond the range of German bombers, and Northern Ireland also seems to have remained peripheral to the British wartime consciousness: as Trevor Allen has observed, battles taking place at sea to the north and west of Ireland received far less space and attention in the British press than those in the sky over southern England.[69]

The extent to which the war can be seen as a precondition of Northern Ireland's present is unclear. That the Second World War was an event of huge cultural, political, and social importance is accepted almost unquestioningly in Britain, where the war remains consistently popular as the subject of novels, films, and television series. If Éire's neutrality and consequent indirect role in the war complicate attempts to describe how the war affected cultural activities in the southern state, the awkwardness of Northern Ireland's position during the war and its traumatic post-war history of sectarian political violence have obscured or discouraged efforts to evaluate the impact of the war on culture north of the border. Louis MacNeice's sense of the war in general and personal terms as an 'interregnum' could also be applied to the place of his birth, and Winston Churchill's much quoted derogatory evocation of the 'dreary steeples of Fermanagh and Tyrone emerging once again' from the 'deluge' of the First World War, and complaint that 'The integrity of their quarrel is one of the few institutions that have been unaltered in the cataclysm which has swept the world', remain resonant in the context of the aftermath of the

---

[67] Anthony Powell, *The Soldier's Art* (London: Heinemann, 1966; repr. London: Arrow, 2005), p. 5.

[68] Powell, *Soldier's Art*, p. 5, p. 6, p. 7, p. 12, p. 19.

[69] Trevor Allen, *The Storm Passed By: Ireland and the Battle of the Atlantic 1940–41* (Blackrock, Dublin: Irish Academic Press, 1996), p. 27.

Second World War in the province.[70] IRA and republican activity during the war was limited by the severe restrictions imposed by the governments on both sides of the border, and some contentious rituals and traditions were suspended for the duration. Jonathan Bardon has claimed that 'the horrors of the Blitz, by throwing together people from both communities... reduced sectarian animosity in the city to its lowest level since the founding of Northern Ireland', but despite the fact that Orange Order Parades and Twelfth of July celebrations were cancelled for the duration of the war and replaced with religious services, the first post-war Twelfth in 1946 was reportedly one of the largest ever.[71] Victoria Stewart's account of how attempts by writers in Britain during the war to use earlier conflicts (in particular, the First World War and Spanish Civil War) as points of reference were 'problematized', when memories of the past were reconfigured by the experience of the present, is relevant here: in Northern Ireland the Second World War was significant enough to displace or modify local sectarian divisions and traditions.[72]

Strategically, the province provided an important base for Allied forces, during the Battle of the Atlantic and in the years leading up to D-Day. Over 300,000 service personnel passed through Northern Ireland during the war: in early 1944, 120,000 United States GIs alone were billeted in the province, which had become an 'essential holding area and training ground for troops awaiting space in England'.[73] A contributor to *The Bell* in summer 1942 claimed that Belfast was 'no longer a "provincial city"', and invited readers to 'Walk down Donegall Place [where] you will hear broken snatches of conversation in Czecho-Slovakian, in French, in Polish, in Dutch. You will hear the easy, pleasant drawl of the Middle West and the Deep South'.[74] The scale of the influx was perhaps more keenly felt in Derry, which had a much smaller population, and in rural areas. The crucial status of the naval base at Lisahally meant that a huge variety of outsiders passed through Derry during the war years: by April 1943, 149

[70] Louis MacNeice, *The Strings Are False* (London: Faber and Faber, 1965), p. 20, pp. 27–29; Winston Churchill, *The World Crisis: The Aftermath* (London: Thornton Butterworth, 1929), p. 319.

[71] Jonathan Bardon, *Belfast: An Illustrated History* (Belfast: Blackstaff Press, 1982), p. 245; Barton, *Northern Ireland in the Second World War*, p. 13; Bill Rolston, *Politics and Painting: Murals and Conflict in Northern Ireland* (Cranbury, New Jersey; London; Mississauga, Ontario: Associated University Press, 1991), p. 26.

[72] Stewart, *Narratives of Memory*, p. 57.

[73] Barton, *Northern Ireland in the Second World War*, p. 7; David Reynolds, *Rich Relations: The American Occupation of Britain 1942–1945* (London: Harper Collins, 1995), p. 109.

[74] John Dowling, 'In Defence of Belfast', *The Bell* 4, no. 5 (August 1942), pp. 329–331(pp. 330–331).

ships of the Royal Navy, Royal Canadian Navy, and US Navy were based there, whilst sailors from the French, Dutch, Norwegian, Australian, New Zealand, Indian, and Soviet navies could also be seen on the streets of the city. At one point in 1943 the number of service personnel based in the city almost doubled Derry's pre-war population of 48,000.[75] The temporary influx of troops and foreign refugees undoubtedly challenged the binary social structures of the province. Writers of both nationalist and unionist persuasions made concerted attempts to draw upon the events and terminology of the war to reinforce these structures, but the war years also enabled new, non-exclusive, and transgressive expressions of identity. As Gillian McIntosh has observed, 'war-time isolation encouraged the Northern Irish to rely increasingly on their own resources for entertainment. Moreover, the presence of so many outsiders in the state during the war had forced them to place a greater emphasis on, and gain a greater awareness of, their own identity'.[76] From Dublin, Ó Faoláin warned of the dangers to the north of 'hyper-internationalism', where 'it is not that there are no barriers—there is no sieve—everything comes flooding in on a people cut off from their roots and will as effectively smother them as our introversion will indubitably smother us if it continues', but the chaos of war posed a threat to authoritarian unionist hegemony and challenged sectarian norms: in Moore's fiction the Belfast of *The Emperor of Ice Cream*, located between the sectarian violence of the 1930s and the moribund austerity of the 1950s, is presented as a place of unprecedented positive cultural, economic, and social exchange.[77] In an article entitled 'Belfast Goes Back To 1939', published in the Dublin Catholic newspaper *The Standard* six months before the end of the war, a 'Special Correspondent' offers a gloomy prognosis of post-war life:

> Belfast's short day of wartime glamour is at an end. Every week now sees it return yet another stage nearer its pre-war way of life characterised by the ever-present problems of unemployment and religious bigotry. This inevitable but unwanted metamorphosis—with one foot in and one safely out, the Northern man-in-the-street enjoyed his position in relation to the war—is also taking place in every other city in Northern Ireland.

He goes on to predict the return of 'the cankerous misery of unemployment' and writes of a 'sense of values' gone 'haywire', concluding by asking provocatively: 'Would the way be easier if North and South marched together? From here the expert must take over!'[78]

---

[75] Richard Doherty, *Key to Victory*, p. 19.
[76] McIntosh, *Force of Culture*, pp. 93–94.   [77] 'Ulster', *The Bell* 2, no. 4, p. 9.
[78] 'Special Correspondent', 'Belfast Goes Back to 1939', *The Standard*, 12 January 1945.

In 2001 the *Belfast Telegraph* published an illustrated account of the Belfast Blitz which went so far as to claim that 'War was welcomed by most of the citizens of Northern Ireland': it is hard to conceive of an Irish, British, or European publication making a similar statement.[79] Through the upsurge in industrial production, the war was instrumental in alleviating the problem of unemployment in the province, at least in the middle years of the conflict, although to what extent is a matter of some dispute.[80] Jonathan Bardon has outlined the contradictory nature of the experience:

> The 1941 Blitz gave Belfast its first direct experience of total war and shattered the complacency of the authorities by laying bare the neglect of the two previous decades. If these years of war brought death and injury to many citizens and razed large areas of the city, they were also a time of positive change when suffering and later full employment blurred social and communal divisions, and decisive steps were taken to effect a permanent improvement in the condition of the people.[81]

The importance to the cultural life of the province of the post-war social changes in the fields of education and welfare that followed the election to Westminster of a Labour government in 1945 should not be underestimated, not least in terms of the schooling of generations of writers, politicians, and activists who reached adulthood in the 1950s and 1960s.

The war years seem to have opened a space where, like the diver Magennis in Tom Paulin's poem, one could exist 'inside history/and away far out of it'.[82] As Peter MacKay has observed, 'the war on many levels solidified notions of nationality [but] the mass movements of people during the war problematized international boundaries', and 'as such the war created

---

[79] *Bombs on Belfast* (Belfast: Belfast Telegraph, 2001), p. v. John Wilson Foster has written that 'almost everyone I know who lived through it in Belfast seems to have had a "good war" and remembered it with affection. In my childhood, adult relatives seemed to wear the Blitz (never the more serious-sounding "Blitzkrieg") as a badge of civic honour'. (John Wilson Foster, 'Was There Ulster Literary Life before Heaney?', in *Between Shadows: Modern Irish Writing and Culture* [Dublin; Portland, Oregon: Irish Academic Press, 2009], pp. 205–218 [p. 209]).

[80] Barton, Fisk, Litton, and Maguire are sceptical of the economic benefits of the war for Northern Ireland, whereas Doherty and Shea take a more positive view: Barton, *Northern Ireland in the Second World War*, pp. 13–15; Robert Fisk, *In Time of War: Ireland, Ulster and the Price of Neutrality* (London: Andre Deutsch; Dingle: Brandon, 1983), pp. 390–391; Helen Litton, *The World War II Years: The Irish Emergency: An Illustrated History* (Dublin: Wolfhound Press, 2001), p. 60; W.A. Maguire, *Belfast* (Keele, Staffordshire: Ryburn Publishing and Keele University Press, 1993), p. 155; Richard Doherty, *Key to Victory*, p. 48; Patrick Shea, *Voices and the Sound of Drums: An Irish Autobiography* (Belfast: Blackstaff Press, 1981), p. 154.

[81] Bardon, *Belfast: An Illustrated History*, p. 234.

[82] Tom Paulin, 'James "Mick" Magennis, VC', *London Review of Books* 22, no. 1 (6 January 2000), p. 6.

new patterns of intellectual and cultural commerce between nations and cultures (just as it was disallowing and troubling others)'.[83] The ways in which Irish men from both north and south of the border, and of both Catholic and Protestant backgrounds, were assimilated into the British armed forces are illuminating in this respect. Regardless of their origins, soldiers were referred to simply as 'Irish' and predominantly addressed as 'Paddy'—an imposition of identity that had curious repercussions for Northern Protestant service personnel.[84] Sam McAughtry explains in his memoir *McAughtry's War* (1985) how these labels could be positively reclaimed:

> I liked it. To be Irish is to be special and interesting. As far as I could see, other Northern Irish Protestants reacted in the same way. I was to see Antrim Protestants come out of themselves, begin to show a swash here and a buckle there within days of signing on, because the British expected it of them and because it offered a lovely release of the inhibitions, considering the times we were in.[85]

Later in a Lancashire pub he finds himself playing the stage Irishman, using phrases such as 'Sure and be Jasus' as he attempts to chat up girls.[86] McAughtry discovered an Irish identity away from Northern Ireland, but the impact of outsiders unaware of the nature of sectarian divisions as they arrived in the province should also be considered. The presence of American troops in the province during the war is generally described either as an external source of civic tension or as a glamorous, other-worldly influx, but their arrival also encouraged local self-examination, as McIntosh suggests. In a 1942 article entitled 'The Ireland that Never Was', the film-maker Richard Hayward attributed the failure of his film *The Luck of the Irish* in the United States to the discrepancy between romanticized American ideas of Ireland and the reality of life as it was lived, and expressed the hope that 'the American troops now in Ulster will take back with them a reasonably sane idea of Ireland as it is'.[87] The guide to

---

[83] Peter MacKay, 'Irish and Scottish Second World War Poetry', in *Modern Irish and Scottish Poetry*, edited by Peter MacKay, Edna Longley and Fran Brearton (Cambridge: Cambridge University Press, 2011), pp. 87–101 (p. 91).

[84] Exploring the use of 'Paddy' as an appellation for any Irish person serving in the British armed forces, Richard Doherty gives the example of the Dublin-born Battle of Britain fighter pilot Brendan Finucane, who served with distinction in the Royal Air Force until he was killed in action in 1942, and was known in the British press as 'Paddy' Finucane (Richard Doherty, *Irish Men and Women in the Second World War* (Dublin: Four Courts Press, 1999), p. 51).

[85] Sam McAughtry, *McAughtry's War* (Belfast: Blackstaff Press, 1985), p. 6.

[86] McAughtry, *McAughtry's War*, p. 8.

[87] Richard Hayward, 'An Ireland that Never Was', in *The P.E.N. In Ulster* (Belfast: Reid and Wright, 1942), pp. 8–9 (p. 9).

Northern Ireland for troops produced by the US Army sternly advised that 'Religion is a matter of public as well as private concern in Ulster and you'll be wise not to talk about it', but it seems that the presence of the soldiers encouraged greater freedom of expression.[88] In an unpublished essay entitled 'Life and Writing in North-East Ulster', written during the war, the poet Roy McFadden wrote that:

> Recent years…have witnessed a change. The Protestant middle-class is becoming more and more nationally conscious; the *ceilidhe* is no longer merely a Catholic rendezvous; the national language is growing. And, ironically enough, the Americans are telling the daughters of die-hard Orangemen what pretty colleens they are in troth and would they be able to say a word in Irish at all or maybe dance a jig or a reel. The first seeds of a new culture and a new literature are beginning to take shape in the 6 counties: a new literature which, while retaining an individual character, will fit in with the broad framework of the Irish pattern.[89]

Historians have tended to argue that Northern Ireland's involvement in the Second World War cemented partition and deepened the sense of separation from the southern state, but McFadden's essay suggests that, somewhat paradoxically, the arrival of the Americans in fact helped to push the province further into an Irish cultural sphere. A sense of tension between local and international pressures is once again palpable here, as events of global importance have unforeseen consequences at a local level. Of Gavin's experience of the Blitz in *The Emperor of Ice Cream* Brian Moore writes that 'Tonight, history had conferred the drama of war on this dull, dead town in which he had been born.'[90] Similarly, Emma Duffin, who volunteered with the St John Ambulance in Belfast during the Second World War, wrote in her diary the day after the Easter Tuesday Raid that 'I could not help feeling, perhaps unjustly, enjoying a certain amount of satisfaction from being included in the drama and tragedy', whilst the same day Moya Woodside wrote 'What awful scenes met me as I proceeded. It looked like photographs of Spain or China, or some town in the last war', immediately apprehending the devastation in its historical and international context.[91] Maeve Boyle, who served in the Royal Navy

---

[88] *A Pocket Guide to Northern Ireland* (Washington DC: United States Government Printing Office, 1942), p. 23.

[89] Roy McFadden, 'Life and Writing in North-East Ulster', McFadden Papers, Queen's University Belfast, MP5, p. 7. This is an undated essay apparently written for an English audience—it certainly presumes their ignorance of the local political and social context, and describes life in Northern Ireland at a time when J.M. Andrews was prime minister (November 1940–April 1943).

[90] Moore, *Emperor*, p. 202.

[91] Diary of Emma Duffin, 16 April 1941, Public Records Office of Northern Ireland (PRONI) D2109/18/19, p. 103; Woodside, 16 April 1941.

in Derry during the war, recalled: 'I enjoyed myself during the war. You could go to the pictures and sometimes I'd make two dates in one day. It was difficult not to use the wrong name at times. But the whole experience broadened your outlook. The city was very insular in those days.'[92] Given that the ways of speaking about Northern Ireland have so often been circumscribed by the topographies of partition and sectarianism, it is striking how the privileged and vexed status of the province resulting from its involvement in the Second World War seems to have briefly offered opportunities for reimagining it within broader European and global contexts. Recalling the war forty years on, Robert Greacen wrote:

> We lived, I suppose, in a private world, to some extent a make believe world. Out in the streets the army lorries hurtled on their secret errands of destruction, whilst we behind the blackout curtains dreamed our dreams of the Just Society—even in Belfast, even in Wartime. The world at war, after all, was only an immense enlargement of our own tense province where a sort of *apartheid* existed between the two communities. At what point could theory be translated into practice?[93]

Writers and artists often seem unsure of how to interpret the effects of the war on their work and the cultural life of the province. In 1943 Samuel Carr, a soldier stationed in Northern Ireland who described himself as a 'deracinated' Ulsterman, attributed 'the cause of this flowering of literary talent' to the fact that 'Ulster writers are now confined to Ulster, and are no longer exportable as journalists or business men or in any other form to England'. He continued to ask 'If this is partly an explanation of the revival, what will happen when peace comes. [*sic*] Is there a chance that Ulster will so have established itself by then in a cultural sense that the old temptation for writers and artists to migrate from it will no longer exist?'[94] Answers to these questions may be found in Roy McFadden's prose of the war and post-war years, in which a demonstrable shift from optimism to uncertainty and regret can be observed. 'Life and Writing in North-East Ulster' not only describes his impressions of how the conflict has upended and inverted traditional allegiances, but foresees a positive future for culture in Northern Ireland in the long term:

> This war has seen strange things. Enemies have become friends overnight; friends have become enemies; political colours have been turned and

---

[92] Quoted in Richard Doherty, *Irish Men and Women in the Second World War*, p. 268.

[93] Robert Greacen, contribution to 'The War Years in Ulster (1939–45): A Symposium', *The Honest Ulsterman 64* (1979–1980), pp. 11–62 (p. 20).

[94] Letter from Samuel Carr to John Boyd, 28 November 1943, John Boyd Collection, Linen Hall Library, Belfast.

re-turned, and dyed many colours . . . there is a growing feeling among intel-
ligent people in the 6 counties that the near future will see a new Ireland, with
Belfast once again 'the Athens of the North', a city of culture and progress.[95]

He goes on to outline with some enthusiasm the possibilities for writers arising from the 'vivid material' of urban life in Belfast, and hails a
generation of young poets (of which he is a member) at the heart of a
literary renaissance. McFadden's youthful optimism contrasts with his
later assessments of the effects of the war on Northern Ireland, which
encompass regret, nostalgia, and cynicism. By 1961 'the Athens of
the North has become the Ah-thens of our youth': in an article for
Threshold McFadden maintained that Belfast as a provincial town was
rich in material but blamed a poor cultural climate for the lack of writing, complaining of a suspicious, uninterested, or hostile community.[96]
He scorns the idea of 'Ulster Writing', arguing that one 'might as well
talk of Ulster toothpaste', and talks of regionalism as the 'failure of the
forties'.[97] For McFadden, the war years offered a brief period, seemingly
entirely circumscribed by the length of the conflict itself, in which culture was able to assert its importance within Northern Ireland.

The perception that the early promise of a literary generation swiftly
dissipated with the end of the war partly explains why literary criticism has
also been reluctant or slow to address Northern Ireland and the Second
World War. In an essay ironically entitled 'Was There Ulster Literary Life
before Heaney?', John Wilson Foster has noted that many students of Irish
literature seem unaware of any Northern writing before Seamus Heaney,
sensing a danger that the much-garlanded poet could become as synony-
mous with Northern Ireland as W.B. Yeats is with the southern state.[98] The
international fame and accomplishments of Heaney and his contemporaries, and the political violence against which much of their most examined
work was written, have fostered this limited appreciation of the literature of Northern Ireland, foreclosing the possibility of considering writers
whose work predates the Troubles. Discussion of 1940s literature in the
southern state meanwhile has tended to focus on the poetry of Patrick
Kavanagh or the work of Seán Ó Faoláin and others involved with *The
Bell*. As Foster observes, it may seem strange to future literary critics that
for over twenty years Heaney wrote about his Derry boyhood without

---

[95] McFadden, 'Life and Writing in North-East Ulster', p. 6.
[96] Roy McFadden, 'Reflections on Megarrity', *Threshold 5*, no. 1 (Spring/Summer 1961),
pp. 25–34 (p. 25).
[97] McFadden, 'Reflections on Megarrity', pp. 32–33.
[98] Wilson Foster, 'Was There Ulster Literary Life before Heaney?', *Between Shadows*,
p. 205.

reference to post-war modernity or to the Cold War.[99] More recently, however, Heaney and his contemporaries—a generation born around the time of the Second World War—have produced work addressing both the Northern Irish experience of that war and the long-term impact of the conflict on the province. Mindful of these delayed responses, I have chosen to concentrate on art and literature produced between 1939 and 1970, with the intention of uncovering the cultural impact of the war before this was obscured, overshadowed, or displaced by that of the Troubles.

The war has manifested itself as a more prominent and vivid presence in Northern Irish autobiography and memoir. Here writers who were children during the war have often presented the war years as a time of formative and positive or even frivolous experience: the poet John Montague, born in 1929, wrote in retrospect that 'I loved the war', and Robert Harbinson has described how his experiences as an evacuee in rural Fermanagh challenged his sectarian prejudices.[100] The war also made its mark on post-war generations. In *My Mother-City* (2007) Gerald Dawe is notably unequivocal when writing that 'the war was the centrepiece of our upbringing', and echoes Bardon's view that the war exposed deficiencies and encouraged progressive developments in the fields of education, health, and housing, though he is clear that 'the basic religious and political demographic fault-lines of the city' remained in place.[101] Dawe's lengthy appraisal of the life and work of Van Morrison, which hints at the impact of the arrival of American troops during the war on the musical life of the city, casts Morrison as emblematic of a new energy, and frames his birth in these terms: 'Born in 1945 in Belfast, as World War II ended and optimism and hope grew'.[102]

> If Protestantism was like the air one breathed, the ground one walked on was assumed to be British. Post-war Belfast was an emphatically British city. Belfast had a recent history in common with other British cities—from the war effort to the Blitz and the thousands of American GIs, to the Victory Parades and ration-books, while the city itself was marked with bomb sites and pre-fabricated houses.[103]

Robert Johnstone also registers the physical impact of the war on Belfast, writing that:

> Belfast had suffered like London in a just and victorious war, and evidence remained of that. I remember a small bomb-like object lay for years on our

[99] Wilson Foster, 'Was There Ulster Literary Life before Heaney?', *Between Shadows*, p. 206.
[100] John Montague, 'The War Years in Ulster', in *The Figure in the Cave and Other Essays* (Dublin: Lilliput Press, 1989), pp. 27–35 (p. 27).
[101] Gerald Dawe, *My Mother-City* (Belfast: Lagan Press, 2007), p. 29.
[102] Dawe, *Mother-City*, p. 30. [103] Dawe, *Mother-City*, p. 35.

kitchen window-sill. It may have been a souvenir collected elsewhere, but I liked to think it had been dropped by a German Stuka and accounted for the small crack at the bottom of the window pane. Swastikas were the signs of revolt my schoolfriends chalked up on the telegraph poles.[104]

The importance of the experience of urban destruction, held in common with cities in Britain, should not be underestimated in considering how the war strengthened bonds between Belfast and London and further detached Northern Ireland culturally and politically from its southern neighbour. Dawe argues that 'the shift towards a European self-consciousness that the Republic of Ireland managed during the 1970s and 80s, sits uneasily in Belfast precisely because of its historically intimate and highly-charged emotional ties with war-torn Britain of the 1940s and 50s'.[105] Such memories and observations echo Sonya O. Rose's argument that the 'internal frontiers' of individuals are threatened in parallel with the 'external frontiers' of nations:

> As the bombs rained down on British soil, destroying British houses, British monuments, factories and ports, citizens of Britain understood at some very deep level that their personal lives and wellbeing were at risk only because of their national belonging. They shared at least that much in common with everyone, and this recognition of common jeopardy contributed mightily to making national identity particularly meaningful for individuals.[106]

Bombs also rained down on Irish soil of course, north and south of the border, and if the references by Dawe and Johnstone to bomb sites, ration books, and pre-fabs draw Belfast into the cultural narrative of the British Home Front, they also invite consideration of whether Northern Ireland had its own specific wartime myths.

During the Troubles the presence of troops and explosive devices on Belfast's streets alienated the city from those across the Irish Sea, but during the Second World War scenes of wartime bomb damage in Belfast, whether in photographs or the officially commissioned and popular drawings of William Conor, served to align its scarred urban landscape with those of British cities. In visual and literary evocations of Belfast during the war, the City Hall may be seen to echo St Paul's Cathedral in London, in terms of the central location of both buildings, the similarity of their domes and towers, and the fact that both survived air attack at a time when surrounding streets were heavily hit. The poet Robert Greacen writes in his memoirs of a rumour in Belfast during the war of a bomb

---

[104] Robert Johnstone and Dennis Kirk, *Images of Belfast* (Belfast: Blackstaff Press, 1983), p. 9.
[105] Dawe, *Mother-City*, p. 98.   [106] Rose, p. 11.

so powerful that if dropped on the City Hall it would destroy the entire city, whilst Gavin, in *The Emperor of Ice Cream*, briefly exhilarated during the Blitz at the prospect of the collapse of so many of Belfast's industrial, political, and religious symbols, urges destruction on the building from the roof of his ARP post.[107] In *Poems from Ulster* (1942), selected and edited by Greacen, the City Hall appears in a woodcut frontispiece, in a central position at the base of the illustration, below a rising phoenix and between the flat roof of a factory and a church tower on the left, and a row of terraced houses and another commercial building opposite. Searchlights rise from the roofs, cutting through starry patches of night sky to form a cross behind the phoenix, above which a red hand of Ulster provides the only colour.[108] The focal phoenix can be seen to symbolize a new body of poets rising from the destruction of the Blitz, or the survival of the city itself, but the central presence of the City Hall amongst buildings symbolic of the industrial and religious life of Belfast is demonstrative of its visual resonance at this time.

Despite the evident visual echoes between bombed Belfast and British cities, there is little sense that, like the bombing of London, the Belfast Blitz could be converted into a mythical triumph. Wartime mythology in Northern Ireland is complicated not only by sectarian divisions within the province, but also by the ways in which so many of the anecdotes themselves arise from the border with the southern state: in addition to the abundance of stories, many of them comical, of cross-border smuggling of goods in both directions, perhaps the most enduring myth of wartime Belfast is the involvement of the Dublin Fire Brigade in the fire-fighting operation following the Easter Tuesday air raid. In the first chapter on memoir and autobiographical fiction I explore how the contestation of this myth in both fictional and historical writing exemplifies the contradictory nature of Northern Ireland's place in the People's War.

In addressing the cross-generic nature of wartime culture, I seek to map the literary history of wartime Northern Ireland against that of Britain, where appropriate. As I describe in the second chapter on poetry, it is hard to disentangle the concerns of young poets in Belfast during the war from those of their counterparts in literary London, mainly due to their complex and unresolved relationships with English poets of the 1930s. This reflects Edna Longley's view of the difficulty in drawing boundaries between the political climate of the 'pan-Irish, British, and Northern Irish

---

[107] Robert Greacen, *The Sash My Father Wore* (Edinburgh: Mainstream, 1997), p. 121; Moore, *Emperor*, p. 203.

[108] Robert Greacen, ed., *Poems from Ulster*, (Belfast: W. Erskine Mayne, 1942).

1930s'.[109] John Wilson Foster has detected echoes between the behaviour of writers in Belfast whose 'social heyday appears to have been the Second World War' and the activities of both the Auden group during the 1930s and writers in Fitzrovia during the 1940s and 50s, noting that all three literary communities were known for their frequenting of coffee houses, exploration of left-wing political ideas, and enjoyment of weekends in the country.[110] In this way, Robert Hewison's evocation in *Under Siege: Literary Life in London 1939–45* (1988) of a concentrated group of artists and writers in London during the war, who benefited practically and psychologically as a community from a sense of 'mutual solidarity', is echoed by the situation in Belfast at this time.[111]

Hewison's emphasis on the geographical smallness of the areas of Fitzrovia and Soho in which his cast of characters moved—a point impressed upon by his inclusion of a map of the district in the book—is echoed, and indeed exceeded, by the even greater concentration of the local cultural community in Belfast.[112] Rather than the several pubs and drinking clubs described by Hewison, in accounts of the period in Belfast, Campbell's coffee house is the only consistently present venue, though Davy McLeans' progressive bookshop in Howard Street also drew together left-leaning artists and writers. The concentrated nature of this artistic and literary world is reflected in this book by the recurrence of many of its characters across several chapters, emphasizing the extent of cross-pollination between literary genres, journalism, political writing, and visual artworks at this time. The war seems to have encouraged experimentation, as artists and writers attempted different roles: Colin Middleton was both poet and painter during the war years, and George MacCann, who served in the British army, experimented with both cubist and surrealist painting and also wrote short stories.[113] In his administrative role in the Belfast Museum and Art Gallery, John Hewitt was able to stimulate interest in contemporary visual art even as he developed his regionalist theories of culture in prose and produced his own poetry. Brian Moore evokes this atmosphere in *The Emperor of Ice Cream* by including quotations from poems by W.H. Auden, Louis MacNeice, Wallace Stevens,

[109] Edna Longley, 'Progressive Bookmen: Left Wing Politics and Ulster Protestant Writers', *Living Stream*, pp. 109–129 (p. 117).
[110] Wilson Foster, 'Was There Ulster Literary Life before Heaney?', *Between Shadows*, p. 209.
[111] Robert Hewison, *Under Siege: Literary Life in London 1939–45* (London: Weidenfeld and Nicolson, 1977; repr. London: Methuen, 1988), p. xv.
[112] Hewison, *Under Siege*, p. 65.
[113] Editorial footnote to a letter from Louis MacNeice to E.R. Dodds, 19 November 1939, *Letters of Louis MacNeice*, edited by Jonathan Allison (London: Faber and Faber, 2010), pp. 367–368.

and W.B. Yeats within the text itself, showing the crucial influence of modernist and 1930s poetry on the wartime cultural environment.

The path taken by Robert Greacen during the war, from Belfast to Dublin and then to London, traces an important link between three literary worlds. Indeed, his intermittently self-indulgent autobiographical writings on the war years sometimes read as attempts to write himself into the cast of characters described by Hewison, and later identified by Mark Rawlinson as comfortingly familiar. In an article published in 1976 entitled 'Writing Through the London Blitz', Greacen sketches a web of connections between writers, editors, and publishers: he recalls his encounter with Alex Comfort in 1942 after a lengthy correspondence, through whom he meets Wrey Gardiner, founder of the Grey Walls Press, and publisher of Comfort and Greacen's New Apocalyptic anthology *Lyra: An Anthology of New Lyric* (1942). Through Gardiner he comes to know John Bayliss and Derek Stanford. He also describes being put up in a condemned cottage by the writer and publisher Reginald Moore, and encountering Tambimuttu and others: 'There was the mandarin Cyril Connolly who asked me what the purpose of writing was and, when I hesitated, supplied the answer: "To write a masterpiece". I remember Stephen Spender in his Hampstead flat wearing a fireman's uniform, tall, kind, shy and with a Shelleyan intensity'. Despite the glamorous patina to such vignettes, he concludes his recollections by denying that he intended the war years to sound enjoyable, claiming that they were 'mostly dreary and occasionally dangerous'.[114]

One important way in which the artistic and literary environments in Belfast and London differed at this time was the lack of any meaningful aristocratic involvement in the arts in Northern Ireland. This study's cast of characters were predominantly middle and working class, most of whom knew a trade or worked at a day job away from writing or painting: Middleton had trained as a damask designer in the linen trade, Hewitt worked as a museum administrator, Gerard Dillon was a house painter and decorator, and Roy McFadden became a solicitor. Unlike London there was no body of artists or writers in Belfast at this time who could afford to do nothing else. From the tightness of these groups, long-lasting friendships and semi-professional networks were forged, as can be seen from the correspondence archives of John Boyd, Robert Greacen, and Roy McFadden, which suggest that later, on occasion, these writers felt a degree of nostalgia for the war years. This was a time when, despite the threats of aerial bombardment and invasion and the restrictions and privations of

---

[114] Robert Greacen, 'Writing Through the Irish Blitz', *Irish Times*, 4 June 1976.

the war, a considerable amount of fun seems to have been had. The English artist Nevill Johnson described life in Belfast after the Blitz of 1941:

> People talk of the swinging sixties as a breakaway to licence, as a nose-thumb to convention, but even in the forties, in sturdily provincial Belfast, the seeds of revolt were pushing through the fabric. On the surface a polite society sat enthralled at young Menuhin or spellbound before the tragic mien of Rachmaninov. We attended, respectful, the musical soirees of Mrs Warnock. We visited Mount Charles, inhaling the culture and the avuncular tobacco smoke of John Hewitt, notable poet with a sharp ear for the cuckoo. We paid homage to Gilbert Harding, sonorous polymath.
>
> But beneath this crust, in nests of anarchy and deviation, fanned and feathered by children of the manse, orgies took place and mayhem prevailed.[115]

The hints at sexual licentiousness in the cultural underworld sketched by Brian Moore in *The Emperor of Ice Cream* are the only other references to 'orgies' at this time that I have discovered, but Johnson's recollections do provide a welcome antidote to a sometimes anxious and excessively earnest tendency in some prose of the war years. If John Hewitt's writings on regionalism are sometimes dreary, or if some of the cultural and poetic debates conducted through the pages of *The Bell* or the Queen's University magazine the *Northman* seem repetitive and wearisome, it is worth being vigilant for the 'seeds of revolt' and 'nests of anarchy' lurking between the lines.

By considering pre-Troubles art and literature, this book urges a broader appreciation of Northern Irish culture. The presence of non-native artists and writers in the province during the war also surely complicates what is meant by 'Irish', 'Northern Irish', or 'Ulster' literature and culture. A letter from John Hewitt to the South African academic and historian Deborah Lavin in 1970, over the possible mounting of an exhibition of mid twentieth-century Ulster art, outlines the problems and inconsistencies faced by those who would define Northern Irish culture:

> Further, should all works have been executed within the period 1921–71? Should artists have been born within the Province, or lived here for an appreciable number of years? William Scott was born in Scotland, grew up in Enniskillen, went to the Belfast College of Art, but has not lived in Ireland since. I do not consider him Irish although his accent has persisted. And his style has no local reference and little if any influence. But what about Hans Iten whom you include on your list? He was Swiss but lived in Belfast from early manhood until his death, active with local art societies. And if Iten, why not Paul Nietsche? A German born in Russia, he had two long spells

of residence and died in Belfast. If residence is the determining factor, then Scott is out and these two are in.[116]

The war undoubtedly brought people to Northern Ireland who otherwise would not have been there, and who would not normally be thought of in that context. Prince Philip, then an officer in the Royal Navy, was seen in Derry during the war, and captured German soldier and future Manchester City goalkeeper Bert Trautmann apparently spent time in a prisoner-of-war camp in Northern Ireland.[117] Entertainers including Irving Berlin, George Formby, Bob Hope, Al Jolson, Glenn Miller, and Merle Oberon paid visits to the province to entertain the troops.[118] These incongruous injections of stardust caused considerable excitement at the time, and counter perceptions of mid-twentieth-century Northern Ireland as insular and culturally moribund. There were new sights, sounds, and spectacles to enjoy: the American troops brought jazz with them, demanded that cinemas open on Sundays, and baseball was played at Windsor Park.[119] Drama and importance were also 'conferred' (to borrow Brian Moore's expression) by the visits of Generals Eisenhower, Montgomery, and Patton, Commodore Mountbatten, and Eleanor Roosevelt, amongst others. The war also brought a significant number of writers to Northern Ireland, of course. Often stationed with the British army, these men spent extended periods of time in the province: here too it is worth considering the unusual coincidences between people, places, and cultural activities, instigated and encouraged by the war. The presence of English novelist Anthony Powell in Northern Ireland exemplifies these peculiarities, and the idea of books being read or written in incongruous or strange places during the war is notably present in *The Soldier's Art*, when a conversation between Nick and his divisional commander about the merits of Balzac and Trollope takes place during a training exercise.[120] Powell's time in the province seems to have left little imprint on his work, and he was less than enthusiastic about the places in which he was billeted—in his memoirs Portadown is described as 'politically reliable, if scenically unromantic', Newry as 'shabby though less architecturally unprepossessing than Portadown', and Belfast as a 'city not famed for its charm; perhaps even rather unjustly

[116] Letter from John Hewitt to Deborah Lavin, 31 December 1970, John Hewitt Papers, PRONI D/3838/5/1, ACC 17015.

[117] Richard Doherty, *Key to Victory*, p. 52; Barton, *Northern Ireland in the Second World War*, p. 139.

[118] Francis, Lacey and Mullen, *Atlantic Memorial*, p. 56; Romie Lambkin, *My Time in the War: An Irishwoman's Diary* (Dublin: Wolfhound Press, 1992), p. 93.

[119] Ronnie Hanna, *Pardon Me Boy: The Americans in Ulster 1942–45, a Pictorial Record* (Lurgan: Ulster Society [Publications] Limited, 1991), p. 77.

[120] Powell, *Soldier's Art*, pp. 45–48.

disparaged, some of the University quarter being not without all distinction'.[121] The very fact of his presence does enable connections to be drawn between very different literary worlds in wartime England and Ireland, however. These connections do seem to have been apprehended at the time: in his memoir *Even Without Irene* (1969), Robert Greacen describes how the presence of the English novelist and poet Rayner Heppenstall in Northern Ireland during the war provided a link to the world of George Orwell, Eric Gill, and John Middleton Murry.[122] The enlivening effect of the presence of outsiders should not be underestimated.

The role of the war in widening the Northern Irish canon is demonstrated by an untitled and unpublished anthology of poetry edited by Roy McFadden, seemingly assembled during the 1990s. It is an unusually broad selection, and although the vast majority of the poets represented were born and brought up in Northern Ireland or Ulster, it is significant that some non-native writers were included. Although no introduction to the anthology has yet surfaced (the contents pages do indicate that one had been planned), it seems likely that McFadden intended the work to gather together some of the poets that had largely been forgotten, or pushed to the critical margins: in 1995 he publicly expressed some irritation that he and his contemporaries had been effaced from the Irish cultural landscape, such was the critical attention lavished on the younger generation of Heaney, Longley, and Mahon.[123] In any case, it is striking to discover an anthology of Northern writing in which not one of the writers included were born after 1929, and where the oldest, John B. Yeats, was born in 1839. The latter alone among the writers is represented by prose, in the form of an unpublished letter to his son William, dated September 1918.[124] The diversity of the collection is also notable. The poetic generation of which McFadden was a leading member is well represented by John Boyd, Maurice James Craig, Robert Greacen, and the editor himself, the next oldest generation of poets is represented by John Hewitt and W.R. Rodgers, and poems by the painters John Luke and Colin Middleton are also included. Much space is given to writers born in the nineteenth century, such as Lynn Doyle, Alice Milligan, May Morton, Forrest Reid, Richard Rowley, and Helen Waddell. The anthology encompasses unofficial poetic forms, including a selection of Belfast street songs collected by Hugh Quinn, and poems in dialect by Moira O'Neill. Émigré writers

[121] Anthony Powell, *To Keep the Ball Rolling: The Memoirs of Anthony Powell*, vol. 3, 'Faces in My Time' (London: Heinemann, 1980), p. 102, p. 103, p. 108.
[122] Robert Greacen, *Even Without Irene* (Dublin: Dolmen Press, 1969), p. 83.
[123] Roy McFadden, 'Corrigibly Plural', *Fortnight 337*, (March 1995), pp. 41–42 (p. 41).
[124] Roy McFadden, unpublished and untitled anthology, Private Collection, pp. 247–248.

such as Padraic Colum, C.S. Lewis, and Louis MacNeice are represented, and there are also poems by English outsiders such as Norman Dugdale, Philip Larkin, Freda Laughton, Patric Stevenson, and Arthur Terry, and the Ukrainian painter Paul Nietsche. The Second World War had a decisive impact on the composition of the anthology: McFadden includes poems which address the war obliquely by George Buchanan and Patrick Maybin—local writers who had served in the Royal Air Force and the British army respectively—and more direct poetry by John Gallen, a contemporary of Greacen and McFadden at Queen's who served in the British army and was killed in the Far East after the war's end. Alex Glendinning, killed in Singapore in 1942 whilst serving in the RAF, is represented by two short poems, and the poems 'The Bombed House' and 'The Evacuees' by Freda Laughton address the Home Front experience.[125] Significantly, McFadden also includes poems by Drummond Allison, Sidney Keyes, Emanuel Litvinoff, and the Australian John Manifold, all of whom were stationed in Northern Ireland during the war. Keyes, who was killed in North Africa in April 1943, is represented by two poems, 'Ulster Soldier' and 'The True Heart', both signed with some poignancy, 'Omagh, 15th April 1942'.[126] In addition, a poem by Francis Stuart entitled 'Ireland' is signed 'Berlin 1944'.[127]

McFadden's anthology is notable for its inclusive approach to provenance and style, as it circumvents well-trodden debates over what constitutes 'Ulster' writing and enables the discovery of a web of historical, artistic, and personal connections through the reading of both the poems themselves and the brief biographical notes on the contributors at the end of the collection. Considering the impact of the wartime little magazine *Lagan* retrospectively in 1961, McFadden saw the inconsistencies and uncertainties of the writing of the time in negative terms:

> What *Lagan* did not do was to define what was meant by 'Ulster Writing.' Is Peadar O'Donnell an Ulster novelist? Is Patrick Kavanagh an Ulster poet?
> *Lagan* did a service by suggesting that whatever we were as writers we were not English. The use of the word 'Ulster' was, I think, equivalent to letting X represent the unknown quantity.[128]

Thirty years later McFadden's own anthology suggests that this 'unknown quantity' could be figured in more positive terms than merely 'not English'. Writers such as Keyes and Litvinoff may not have had a discernible or

---

[125] McFadden, unpublished and untitled anthology, pp. 119–120.
[126] McFadden, unpublished and untitled anthology, p. 114.
[127] McFadden, unpublished and untitled anthology, p. 223.
[128] McFadden, 'Reflections on Megarrity', *Threshold* 5, no. 1, p. 29.

long-lasting impact on writing in Northern Ireland, but their inclusion alongside local writers encourages the conception of an expanded Northern Irish cultural sphere and helps to move on discussion of the province's culture from tiring dissections of national, political, or religious identity.

This book cannot cover everything: it attempts to address an omission, but unfortunately in so doing necessarily makes its own omissions. Its gender imbalance is huge: apart from a few poems by Freda Laughton, Nesca Robb's autobiographical account of her time in England during the war, and some examples of popular short fiction and poetry, I have found no women's writing relating directly to Northern Ireland and the Second World War in the course of my research.[129] The socio-historical reasons for this must be addressed elsewhere. I have largely avoided examining the theatre, or contemporary broadcasting in detail. The theatre in Northern Ireland at this time seems to have been dominated by commercial productions in the major towns and cities, although there is evidence that the amateur scene and travelling productions in particular thrived at this time.[130] Of these productions, it is likely that many plays were staged simply to provide an escape from the war for their audience—Sam Hanna Bell recalls that the semi-amateur Ulster Group Theatre's popular production of St John Ervine's *Boyd's Shop* (1936), which ran on and off from September 1940 until the Luftwaffe raid of 14 April 1941, 'reminded men and women of homely virtues reported missing if not already dead in those sombre early days and black nights of the War'.[131] The popularity of theatrical performances at all levels at this time shows how the war stimulated interest in the arts and participation in cultural activities, but, possibly due to logistical and commercial considerations, the conflict seems to have had a relatively limited impact on the nature of the plays themselves. The playwright Thomas Carnduff felt that the war had not encouraged serious drama, and bemoaned the dominance of popular entertainment: 'You can put on any kind of show just now and be certain to make a profit. The people merely crowd into places of amusement, aimlessly, and without any choice.'[132] Bell found that 'documentary material on the origin

[129] Freda Laughton, *A Transitory House* (London: Jonathan Cape, 1945); Nesca Robb, *An Ulsterwoman in England* (Cambridge: Cambridge University Press, 1942).

[130] Michael Farrell, 'Drama in Ulster Now', *The Bell* 2, no. 4, 'Special Ulster Number and The Abbey Theatre', pp. 82–88 (p. 85, p. 87); Jack Loudan, 'Address given to Belfast Rotary Club in Grand Central Hotel on 19th March, 1945', unpublished and unpaginated typed manuscript, Jack Loudan Collection, Linen Hall Library.

[131] Sam Hanna Bell, *The Theatre in Ulster: A Survey of the Dramatic Movement in Ulster from 1902 until the Present Day* (Dublin: Gill and Macmillan, 1972), p. 70.

[132] Thomas Carnduff, *Life and Writings*, edited and introduced by John Gray (Belfast: Lagan Press/Fortnight Educational Trust, 1994), p. 52.

and development of the Ulster Group Theatre [was] of the scantiest', and relied for his account on the reminiscences of members recorded for a BBC documentary in 1965.[133] My own archival research in this regard has been similarly fruitless, and my account in any case concentrates on books, documents, and artefacts that the war has left behind. In this context, past theatrical performances are difficult to examine on similar terms, whilst home-grown radio and cinema in Northern Ireland at this time were severely limited and have already been comprehensively covered by existing cultural histories.[134]

As I have outlined, the fragmentary nature of some of the material under consideration, and the contingent or irregular ways in which works were published or appeared, means that there is considerable cross-pollination between the otherwise generically organized chapters of this book. The first chapter addresses autobiographical fiction and memoir, considering ways in which the stories of individuals have been integrated with known historical events. With reference to Brian Moore's *The Emperor of Ice Cream*, it engages with what Holger Klein described in *The Second World War in Fiction* (1984) as the 'embedding' of creative texts within supposedly factual accounts, focusing on the use of passages from the novel by social historians.[135] I also examine Benedict Kiely's *Land Without Stars* (1946), an autobiographical novel illustrative of how the war presented severe problems for nationalists in Northern Ireland. The second chapter describes the poetic climate in the province during the war, appraising the influence of Louis MacNeice and his English contemporaries on a much younger generation in Belfast gathered around Queen's University in the early 1940s, before considering the impact of the war on the work of two older poets, John Hewitt and W.R. Rodgers. The third chapter charts the effects of the war on visual art in Northern Ireland, and scrutinizes the war paintings of three Belfast artists, Colin Middleton, Gerard Dillon, and William Conor, tracing the impact of Continental styles on art in Belfast and exploring porous distinctions between official and unofficial war art at this time. The fourth and final chapter looks at politicized writing during and after the war, interrogating the various translations of the Second World War into existing local political conflicts, and describing the interpenetration of the Northern Irish literary and political spheres at this time.

---

[133] Bell, *Theatre in Ulster*, p. 61.

[134] Rex Cathcart, *The Most Contrary Region: the BBC in Northern Ireland, 1924–1984* (Belfast: Blackstaff Press, 1984); John Hill, *Cinema and Northern Ireland: Film, Culture and Politics* (London: British Film Institute, 2006).

[135] Holger Klein, 'Britain', in *The Second World War in Fiction*, edited by Holger Klein with John Flower and Eric Homburger (London: Macmillan, 1984), pp. 1–46 (p. 16).

Together the four chapters aim to recover the works of an eccentric collection of artists and writers during and after the war, and consider how the awkward position of the province in relation to the war is reflected in these works. My governing purpose is to address the effects of the Second World War on literature and culture in Northern Ireland by exploring publications and artefacts that have often remained submerged, sidelined, marginalized, or avoided, but I also hope that examining such material will allow new ways of approaching Northern Ireland's role in the war to emerge.

1

'His story was confirmed by others': Autobiographical Fiction and Memoir

The sheer scale of the Second World War undoubtedly presents significant challenges for writers of autobiography and memoir who wish to describe their experiences of the conflict. Autobiographical writing is overtly concerned with the development of the self and the individual, but war is, by its nature, a communal activity, which in the case of the Second World War consisted of a series of known episodes, experiences, and ordeals undergone by hundreds, thousands, and millions of people at once. This is the basis of Holger Klein's argument that fiction of the Second World War 'is embedded in other prose literature: histories, biographies and autobiographies detailing not what could be true, but what is true in the sense that it can be documented as fact or vouched for by specific persons'.[1] If the action in realist war fiction must be positioned within the action of the war, and in relation to factual accounts of the conflict, similar demands are also made on the autobiographer. Writing autobiographical fiction or memoir which addresses the Second World War may well require the marshalling of vast quantities and layers of contextual detail, at the same time as managing the expectations and prior knowledge of the intended reader, and Alan Munton's suggestion that war novelists have to 'clear a space within a period already heavily defined by other means, particularly by readers' knowledge of history' can also be applied to autobiographical writers.[2] The heavily documented context of the Second World War threatens to overwhelm stories of individual subjects, and given that narratives may have to be set against the greater historical reality of the war

---

[1] Klein, p. 16.
[2] Alan Munton, *English Fiction of the Second World War* (London: Faber and Faber, 1989), p. 28.

in order to be credible, writers are afforded less autonomy than might otherwise be the case. Munton argues:

> The reader, reading forwards, anticipates or finds satisfying the resolution offered by a known historical moment; he may feel even more confidently situated in present time because his knowledge of the past—of how it 'worked out'—confirms his present experience of the narrative. For the author, working backwards, history can be a constraint. Unless the work is a fantasy, fictional events must be related to or must confirm actual occurrences known to the readership.[3]

For readers of autobiography and memoir dealing with the Second World War, questions of how the subject's story relates to known and familiar episodes (or 'actual occurrences') are even more important: if an English writer should begin to describe their life in late August 1939, for example, they would inevitably encourage the expectation of an imminent description of their experience and memories of the beginning of the war. To avoid referring to this would appear to the reader to constitute a deliberate omission. I use the term 'known episode' to refer to those historical events that have been repeatedly identified and textualized, dated and described by a large number of sources, and that can easily be recruited into a variety of cultural forms, even if the details of their genesis and development are matters of historical debate. From a British perspective on the Second World War, chief amongst these would be the episodes prominent in the narrative of the 'People's War': the Dunkirk evacuation, the Blitz in London, the Battle of Britain, and VE Day.

The importance of relating personal experience to known episodes of the war can be observed in the structure of Stephen Gilbert's often overlooked *Bombardier* (1944), an autobiographical novel written and published during the war, which describes the author's experiences in France in the British Expeditionary Force, from the winter of 1939 until the evacuation of Dunkirk.[4] Gilbert's fictional analogue is Peter Rendell, who, like Gilbert, is from a middle-class Northern Irish Protestant background and is a Lance-Bombardier serving in the 3rd Ulster Searchlight Regiment. *Bombardier* is notable for its dissension from official depictions of British

---

[3] Munton, p. 21.

[4] Stephen Gilbert was born in Newcastle, County Down in 1912. He was schooled in England and Scotland, but returned to Northern Ireland to work on the *Northern Whig* between 1931 and 1934. He served in the 3rd Ulster Searchlight Regiment during the Second World War and was awarded the Military Medal following the Dunkirk evacuation of 1940. He produced five novels, all of them strange, including *The Landslide* (1943), which described the appearance of a jungle in the west of Ireland, and *Ratman's Notebooks* (1968), a horror story featuring an unnamed character who trains rats to attack his enemies. Gilbert died in 2010. See the Stephen Gilbert Collection, Queen's University Belfast, MS45.

army life and the Dunkirk evacuation in particular, and for its attention to the experiences of Irish and Northern Irish soldiers in the army at this time.

The main text of the novel is preceded by three organizing pages. There is a contents page which divides the book into nine sections, all but one of which is given the name of a French town, or area in north-eastern France, around which the action takes place. This culminates in the penultimate 'Dunkirk' and final section entitled 'England'.[5] The following page carries two headings: 'Scene', under which the locations 'Parts of Northern France', 'The English Channel', and 'The South of England' are listed, and 'Time', with corresponding seasons and years.[6] There is a 'List Of Principal Persons In Order Of Mention' on the next and final organizing page. The various components to this preamble constitute an overt acknowledgement on Gilbert's part that he is operating within a constrained context resulting from readers' expectations and their knowledge of recent history.[7] *Bombardier* was published in October 1944, when the ultimate outcome of the war in Europe was all but assured: in providing readers with the chapter titles 'Dunkirk' and 'England' before the main body of prose, Gilbert signals not only that the novel will engage with one of the pre-eminent known episodes of that ongoing war, but also hints that it is likely that its central character will emerge successfully from this. Some of Peter's thoughts on the possible progress of the war appear at an early stage of the novel:

> He wondered how long the war would last. If people asked him he always said ten years—and everyone laughed. They said there'd be starvation in Germany before that. The Germans couldn't win—yet obviously they had only gone into the war because they thought they *would* win, but how? The Maginot line was impregnable and the Belgians had a similar line.[8]

By 1944 the inefficacy of the Maginot line was legendary, and the dramatic irony in these lines is clear. *Bombardier*'s narrative is thus largely dependent on how Peter is personally affected by these known historical episodes, and how this personal experience diverges from familiar and much repeated official accounts.

How far to integrate the life of the subject with known historical events is a question for autobiographical writers of many epochs, of course, and, as Liam Harte has observed, is of particular relevance in Ireland, where nationalist autobiography has often identified progress of the self with

---

[5] Stephen Gilbert, *Bombardier* (London: Faber and Faber, 1944), p. 5.
[6] Gilbert, *Bombardier*, p. 6.   [7] Munton, p. 21.
[8] Gilbert, *Bombardier*, p. 23.

that of the nation. Of later twentieth and early-twenty-first-century auto-biographical writers such as Ciaran Carson and Michael Cronin, Harte claims that 'for all their hyper-vivid materiality and sensuously imagined specificity, these works also strive towards typicality in the way that they continually collapse personal biography into collective history'.[9] The com-bination of a politicized tradition and a strong sense of collective memory mean that Irish autobiography continues to be dominated by its relation-ship with history, but it is clear that the events of the mid-to-late twentieth century place the idea of a pan-Irish autobiographical tradition under con-siderable strain, since distinctions between the experiences of individuals north and south of the border must inevitably be drawn when considering the Second World War and the later eruption of the Troubles.

The works of autobiographical fiction and memoir addressed in this chapter provoke specific questions of identity at variance with Irish or British narratives of the war. Brian Moore's novel *The Emperor of Ice Cream* dissents both from Irish nationalist discourse and from the British People's War narrative of collective endeavour. Éire's neutrality, com-bined with deep-seated hostility to Britain, precluded or problematized Northern nationalist involvement in the British war effort, and Benedict Kiely's contortions in the novel *Land Without Stars* and in two further volumes of memoir illustrate the difficulties that the war and its legacy posed for nationalism. By contrast, writers from Protestant and union-ist backgrounds have been more likely to describe the war's formative effects in a positive light: as I noted in the introduction, the journalist Sam McAughtry, a navigator in the Royal Air Force during the war, shows in his memoirs the flexibility of Northern Protestant identity within the British armed forces. Notable for their topographical and spatial aware-ness, Robert Harbinson's boyhood memoirs *Song of Erne* and *Up Spake the Cabin Boy* describe how his wartime experiences, first as an evacuee in rural Fermanagh and then in industrial Belfast, challenged his nascent loyalist dogmatism and cured him of sectarian prejudice.

* * *

Patricia Craig states in her biography of Brian Moore that he himself always agreed that *The Emperor of Ice Cream* was 'the most directly autobiographi-cal' of his novels.[10] It describes the passage from boyhood to manhood of Gavin Burke, a seventeen-year-old from Catholic West Belfast, who to

---

[9] Liam Harte, 'Introduction: Autobiography and the Irish Cultural Moment', in *Modern Irish Autobiography: Self, Nation and Society*, edited by Liam Harte (Basingstoke: Palgrave Macmillan, 2007), pp. 1–13 (p. 11).

[10] Craig, *Brian Moore*, p. 74.

the horror and amusement of his family leaves school to join an Air Raid Precautions Unit: the novel opens with him pulling on his (tellingly) ill-fitting and uncomfortable British uniform for the first time. Gavin no longer believes in God or the Church, but remains 'unreasonably in dread of God's vengeance for the fact of this unbelief'—a dread seemingly manifested in a figurine of the Divine Infant of Prague which stands on the dresser in his bedroom, giving voice to his conscience by reminding him of his various sins of sloth, smoking, and masturbation.[11] In addition, he contends throughout the novel with the conflicting advice of a pair of personal guardian angels, the Black Angel and White Angel, the former subversive and anarchic, dedicated to self-satisfaction, the latter careful and conservative. During the 'phoney war' the freedom afforded by his new nocturnal job allows him to immerse himself in the excitingly alien worlds of bohemian socialist theatre and seedy Belfast night life, in so doing falling foul of his overbearing and dictatorial father. On the first night of the Belfast Blitz, Gavin is thrust into the midst of appalling human carnage when he works a long stretch at the temporary morgue in the city sorting through bodies—a mentally and physically exhausting and sickening experience which seems to shock him into manhood almost overnight. Following the air raid he is reunited with his father, who recants his Nazi sympathies in the bomb-damaged family home. The novel clearly draws on Moore's own experiences as a young man in Belfast (also in the ARP) during the early years of the war, and Patricia Craig and Denis Sampson's respective biographies include interviews with Moore in which he openly discusses the similarities between his younger self and Gavin Burke.[12] I do not intend to recapitulate these comparisons at length here, but read *The Emperor of Ice Cream* in terms of what it reveals about the complex relationships between autobiographical fiction and known historical moments, and consider its role in writing Northern Ireland into a more secure place in the history of the Second World War.

Perhaps due to the sensitive and traumatic nature of the Blitz material, until relatively recently critics have shied away from questioning the historical accuracy of the novel. Indeed, as we shall see, the novel has been deployed by historians in supposedly factual accounts. In an interview for Patrick Hicks' 1999 article 'History and Masculinity in Brian Moore', however, Moore himself agreed that he had conflated the first two air raids on Belfast for narrative effect: 'Yes, I think so. I was present of course at both raids and took part in them but it's funny I seem to remember the first raid as the really big one where all these people were killed and there were

---

[11] Moore, *Emperor*, p. 10.
[12] Craig, *Brian Moore*, pp. 74–86, Denis Sampson, *Brian Moore: The Chameleon Novelist* (Dublin: Marino, 1998), pp. 45–51.

firebombs and all sorts of things and that the second raid was less dangerous'.[13] This is verifiably not the case. The first raid on the city, on 7 April
1941, resulted in thirteen deaths, and the destruction was concentrated
mainly on the docks. The second raid, on 15 April, hit the residential
north of the city hard and, according to the Ministry of Public Security,
killed 745.[14] Denis Sampson has also remarked on Moore's tendency to
conflate moments in his own life in interviews, describing 'his frequent
ascribing of key experiences to the year in which he was eighteen, in particular his discovery of the works of James Joyce, the extensive bombing
of Belfast that destroyed the house on Clifton Street, and the death of his
father.'[15] Moore's conflations in *The Emperor of Ice Cream* exemplify what
Holger Klein describes as the 'embedding' of war fiction in other prose
literature, as distinctions between novel, autobiography, and eyewitness
collapse due to Moore's status, burnished by later historians, as intermediary for the authentic wartime experience.

   The Emperor of Ice Cream is written in the third person but incorporates
intense passages of free indirect discourse, the longer of which occur over
the opening pages, where the prose is also interrupted by quotations from
poetry that has dominated and shaped Gavin's imagination. Here, as he
struggles into his uniform and argues with his brother over his decisions,
he takes strength from the knowledge that he has the poets on his side:

The poets knew the jig was up; they knew the rich and famous would crum-
ble with the rest:

> You cannot be away, then, no
> Not though you pack to leave within an hour,
> Escaping, humming down arterial roads...

Or MacNeice, an Ulsterman:

> We shall go down like palaeolithic man
> Before some new Ice Age or Genghiz Khan.

Yeats said it too:

> Things fall apart; the centre cannot hold;
> Mere anarchy is loosed upon the world...

It was all prophetically clear. Hitler was Yeats' 'Second Coming.' He was the
rough beast, its hour come round at last, slouching towards Bethlehem to be
born. Yeats knew what nonsense it was, in this day and age, to talk of futures

[13] Patrick Hicks, 'History and Masculinity in Brian Moore's *The Emperor of Ice Cream*', *Canadian Journal of Irish Studies 25* (1999), pp. 400–413 (p. 408).
[14] Fisk, pp. 416–33. For a more detailed account of the air attacks on Belfast during 1941, see Barton, *The Blitz: Belfast in the War Years*.
[15] Sampson, p. 43.

and jobs. But how could you explain that to Owen, who had read nothing
for pleasure since his Boys' Own Weekly days? How could you tell him that,
for you, the war was an event which had produced in you a shameful secret
excitement, a vision of the grown-ups' world in ruins? It would not matter in
that ruined world if Gavin Burke had failed his Schools Leaving Certificate.
The records would be buried in the rubble. War was freedom, freedom from
futures. There was nothing in the world so imposing that a big bomb couldn't
blow it up.[16]

Gavin justifies the chaotic trajectories of his own life by identifying himself with literary imaginings of the imminent apocalypse: Moore thus
embeds the personal narrative within a greater political historical reality,
just as Gavin's academic records are buried in the rubble. The appearance
of W.H. Auden's 'Consider this and in our time' here certainly encourages
us to read Gavin's personal story in the context of the global conflict at
this early stage, since the poem counsels the need to develop a considered
view of current world events, and is alert to the possibility of air attack in
its mention of a 'helmetted airman' which points to the novel's traumatic
denouement. The poems quoted here and elsewhere in *The Emperor of
Ice Cream* were all included in *The Faber Book of Modern Verse* (1936)—a
largely modernist, anti-Georgian anthology containing several politicized
contributions by Auden and his contemporaries, and a volume that would
seem to offer to Gavin at this point a more secure belief system than the
Bible.[17] The passage also mocks Gavin's pretensions, as can be seen from
the contrast of Yeats' high art with the cliché (recalling perhaps his mother's
diction) 'in this day and age' and of 'ruined world' with the more prosaic
'Schools Leaving Certificate', but the overall tone is ominous. Chekhov's
gun here is the 'big bomb'. Knowing the devastation wrought on Belfast
by the Blitz, the narrative is predicated to an extent on how Gavin's story is
aligned with this known historical episode, and readers' anticipation and
dread must be managed, rather than created. The vision of ruins is crucial
to Gavin's progress: the 'freedom' he believes that destruction will bring is
later denied by the human cost of the damage. The fact that Gavin seems
to fit into the larger historical narrative with greater ease than he does
into his Catholic community in Belfast is also indicative of his progress.
Moore's sceptical and ironic vision and the awkwardness of Northern
Ireland's position in the Second World War preclude the possibility of

---

[16] Moore, *Emperor*, p. 11.
[17] Patricia Craig describes the Faber collection as 'a book which showed [Moore] a whole
new side to W.B. Yeats, and, even more importantly, brought him face to face with Eliot
and Auden, and thereby gave him a taste for poetry which stayed with him for the rest of his
life.' (Craig, *Brian Moore*, p. 76)

establishing any secure identification between Gavin and his nation or religion in the Irish nationalist autobiographical tradition. Gavin's pre-occupations circumvent the sectarian conflict, and though his ramblings here are naïve, and even juvenile, his concerns are worldly.

For Brian Moore the war was a time when his personal literary, cultural, and political horizons expanded. The socialist Freddy Hargreaves in *The Emperor of Ice Cream* was modelled on Teddy Millington—an itinerant who passed on the *Faber Book of Modern Verse* to Moore and encouraged him to read more modernist and non-provincial literature.[18] Millington also introduced him to socialist bookshops and drama groups, and in addition to working in the ARP Moore also socialized with Protestants for the first time during the war, often in Campbell's coffee house opposite the City Hall, frequented by many of the artists and writers with whose work this study is concerned. The subversive cultural underbelly described in the novel loosely corresponds to political trends in Britain during the war: Angus Calder has argued that public dissatisfaction in Britain with the running of the war between 1940 and 1941 fomented widespread revolutionary and socialist attitudes.[19] In the novel these are directed against Northern Ireland's entrenched binary political system, and its hegemonic and repressive unionist government. In this respect the fact that the deranged and brutal Post Officer Craig in charge of Post 106 shares a surname with the prime minister of the province from 1921 to 1940 is significant. In the post-war Belfast of Moore's earlier novels, any cultural invigoration resulting from the war seems to have dissipated, and in *The Lonely Passion of Judith Hearne* (1955) Mr Madden, the brother of Miss Hearne's landlady, returns from 'humming' New York to find a 'dull city where men made money the way charwomen wash floors, dully, alone, at a slow methodical pace', and 'clerkly men wrote small sums in long black ledgers'.[20] Eamon Maher writes of Gavin Burke's progress that 'This is the first time that a Moore character who is born and bred in Belfast manages to shed the shackles of religious oppression': significantly this takes place not merely against the background of the Second World War but as a direct result of Gavin's experience of the conflict.[21]

The Emperor of Ice Cream provides some striking illustrations of how Irish nationalism was briefly displaced and discredited by the war. Moore's initial portrayal of the Catholic nationalist community in the novel is of

---

[18] Craig, *Brian Moore*, p. 76.   [19] Calder, *People's War*, p. 17.
[20] Brian Moore, *The Lonely Passion of Judith Hearne* (London: Andre Deutsch, 1955), p. 41.
[21] Eamon Maher, 'Belfast: the Far From Sublime City in Brian Moore's Early Novels', *Studies 90*, no. 360 (2001), pp. 422–31 (p. 429).

a blinkered and bigoted group, for whom hatred of unionists, the British, and other perceived threats to their religion overrides all other considerations, even at this time of cataclysmic European upheaval. Gavin's father adheres to the strict doctrine that England's difficulty is Ireland's opportunity, gleefully welcoming British defeats in the early years of the war over the breakfast table each morning:

> ... his father read the newspaper as other men played cards, shuffling through a page of stories until he found one which would confirm him in his prejudice. A Jewish name discovered in an account of a financial transaction, a Franco victory over the godless Reds, a hint of British perfidy in international affairs, an Irish triumph on the sports field, an evidence of Protestant bigotry, a discovery of Ulster governmental corruption: these were his reading goals.[22]

Another character wishes to give practical assistance to the Luftwaffe. One of Gavin's colleagues at the ARP post, the nationalist Your Man Gallagher, along with his neighbours on the Falls Road, 'considered it a point of honour to leave a light shining in their upstairs windows at night in case any German bombers might come over the city'.[23] Having lost faith in the IRA, Gallagher supports the forces of Nazi Germany, pragmatically rather than ideologically, as more likely to succeed in defeating the British and uniting the thirty-two counties. Liam Gearon has noted the irony here of the colonized minority allying itself with one imperialist power in the hope of overthrowing another: a more emphatic critique is provided by the unsparing if contrived retribution visited upon Gallagher at the end of the novel, when he is seen standing with flashlight in hand, lamenting the loss of his wife and children in the bombing of the Falls. As Gearon has also observed, Moore's inclusion of the story of the Dublin Fire Brigade's night mission to Belfast, heard in hospital in the aftermath of the raid, helps to defuse the potential for reading the novel as any kind of loyalist critique of the nationalist minority.[24]

> An injured Heavy Rescue worker told them he had seen the engines of the Dublin Fire Brigade, pumping away in the York Street area, their peacetime headlamps blazing. His story was confirmed by others, and, soon, the hospital nuns, very pleased by this news, were telling patients how the Dublin Fire Brigade, God bless them, their peacetime headlamps blazing, had driven one hundred and thirteen miles, crossing the border from neutral Éire, to help with the conflagration.[25]

[22] Moore, *Emperor*, p. 36. Moore's own father was a surgeon, who worked throughout the Blitz tending the wounded and 'took immense pride in his son's behaviour at this appalling moment.' (Craig, *Brian Moore*, p. 81).

[23] Moore, *Emperor*, p. 61.

[24] Liam Gearon, *Landscapes of Encounter: The Portrayal of Catholicism in the Novels of Brian Moore* (Calgary: University of Calgary Press, 2002), p. 52.

[25] Moore, *Emperor*, p. 228.

The words 'His story was confirmed by others' are ironically resonant of the ways in which this episode has been contested in historical accounts of the Blitz, which themselves have drawn heavily on *The Emperor of Ice Cream*. Here Moore piles on the clauses to convey the excitement and urgency of the spreading rumours, and as the register slips swiftly from the demotic ('God bless them'), to the propagandist ('their peacetime head-lamps blazing') and to the historian's attention to detail ('one hundred and thirteen miles, crossing the border from neutral Éire'), he conveys in one sentence how the incident was rapidly appropriated and mytholo-gized. The fact that immediately a 'loyal pro-British patient' in the hospital responds to the news with the counterclaim that the 'English had loaded fire engines on ships in Liverpool and that those ships were already on their way across the Irish Sea' further dramatizes the way in which this most crucial of known episodes of the war in Northern Ireland was con-tested even as it happened.

Exactly how the involvement of the southern fire brigades came about is unclear: their arrival in Belfast provoked much comment at the time and has proved to be of enduring interest.[26] Historians offer differing accounts of whether the Minister of Public Security John MacDermott called Dublin directly to ask for help or if he first asked Northern Prime Minister Sir Basil Brooke for his consent to make this request, and the time in the early hours at which this happened is also unclear. At some point however, Eamon de Valera was woken, and having quickly agreed to provide assistance, fire engines from Éire arrived in Belfast at around 10 a.m.[27] Robert Fisk describes the unreliability of many accounts of this:

> The episode was to be turned into legend by the people of Belfast, many of whom still swear that the Irish firemen arrived in the city proudly flying Tricolours from their vehicles—which is untrue—and that the Irish crews spent their time bravely fighting fires for the Protestants in the Shankill Road, which is also untrue. But such stories were inevitable, for even today the facts of this extraordinary affair are still obscure.[28]

Fisk himself arguably contributes to the mythmaking with his own dra-matic account, as he describes MacDermott's call: 'there, crouched on the floor as his home vibrated to the explosions outside, MacDermott did

---

[26] Clair Wills, *That Neutral Island: A Cultural History of Ireland during the Second World War* (London: Faber and Faber, 2007), p. 215.

[27] For conflicting accounts of this episode, see Barton, *Blitz*, p. 129, and Fisk, pp. 421–422. A helpful source of information isSean Redmond's *Belfast is Burning 1941* (Dublin: IMPACT, Municipal Employees Division, 2002), which draws heavily on interviews with surviving Dublin Fire Brigade employees of the time.

[28] Fisk, p. 421.

something that no Northern Ireland Government Minister had done for his province before or would ever do again: he called Dublin and asked for help'.[29] Some newspaper reports at the time also sought to emphasize the momentous nature of the episode. The *Belfast Telegraph* hailed the 'magnificent spirit' of the southern fire brigades, and claimed that 'This is the good neighbour policy in action, worth months of speeches and assurances. Suffering can be the great leveller, cutting clean through all petty prejudices'. The *Irish Times* saw the episode in more elevated terms, proclaiming that 'Humanity knows no borders, no politics, no differences of religious belief. Yesterday, the people of Ireland were united', and asking 'Has it taken bursting bombs to remind the people in this little country that they have a common tradition, a common genius, and, above all, a common home?'[30] An article by Harry Craig published in the Dublin magazine *The Bell* over two years later contrasted continuing sectarian intimidation by forces under the direction of the Stormont government with anecdotal evidence that the experience of the Blitz, and the arrival of the southern fire brigades in particular, had challenged long-standing hostilities:

> The bombs that fell on Belfast made little distinction between the Catholic and his Protestant neighbour. Out of flaming homes a new comradeship was forged. Women who, a few weeks before, would have gleefully scorned each other cooked now on the same range. Suffering united the city. Dublin fire brigades, flying the Irish flag, met cheering people on the roadside.[31]

Craig's sentiments echo the levelling discourse of the British People's War, but instead of collapsing British social divisions, here we see the potentially transformative effects of the war on sectarianism and partition. Others have adopted the narrative with very different ends in mind: John Blake, commissioned by the Stormont government to write an official history of Northern Ireland and the Second World War, described a mass funeral of 150 people killed in the Easter Tuesday raid 'when Protestants and Roman Catholics joined in prayer', and wrote that people in Ulster will long remember the 'cheering sight' of the arrival of southern fire engines.[32] The novelist Sam Hanna Bell recalled in 1980 that in the aftermath of the Easter Tuesday raid that ' "Catholic" and "Protestant" sectors hastened to

---

[29] Fisk, p. 420.

[30] Quoted in Kevin Kearns, *The Bombing of Dublin's North Strand, 1941: The Untold Story* (Dublin: Gill and Macmillan, 2009), pp. 65–66.

[31] Harry Craig, 'A Protestant Visits Belfast', *The Bell* 7, no. 3 (December 1943), pp. 236–244(p. 241).

[32] John W. Blake, *Northern Ireland in the Second World War* (London: HMSO, 1956; repr. Belfast: Blackstaff Press, 2000, edited by Brian Barton), pp. 233–234.

each other's assistance. It was a remarkable time'.[33] More recently Juliet Gardiner has written:

> The 'blitz spirit' of unity and endurance had been strong during the raids as Protestants from the Shankill Road area crammed into the Clonard Monastery with Catholics. Women and children sheltered together in the crypt, and at one point, when it looked like the chapel would be hit, one of the priests, Father Tom Murphy, donned a tin hat and offered absolution to all present.[34]

It is possible that the Second World War may be increasingly explored as a way of establishing a semi-official shared history, cutting across sectarian boundaries by emphasizing the cross-community common experience of (crucially) externally inflicted devastation and highlighting the cross-border cooperation of the fire crews.[35] Moya Woodside wrote in her diary a few days after the Easter Tuesday raid that 'An action like this does more for Irish unity than any words from politicians', but noted too that the arrival of 'a large detachment of A.F.S. from Glasgow...makes us conscious of a comforting solidarity with Britain'.[36] As Richard Doherty has observed in his history of Derry and the Second World War, however, attempts to emphasize the common experience of war face considerable difficulties. Though Doherty is keen to assert that 'the contribution of Derry Catholics was as important as that of the city's Protestants and death was no respecter of religious affiliations', he also acknowledges that there is little interest locally in remembering the war, perhaps due to the fact that 'the nationalist majority population had no wish to remember being such a vital part in Britain's war effort and...survival.'[37]

Angus Calder has argued that *The Emperor of Ice Cream* itself constitutes an attempt to utilize the mythology of the Second World War to ameliorate sectarian divisions:

> Though this literally deals only with an individual's development and one father–son relationship, the novel pushes us to see this ending as prophetic

[33] Sam Hanna Bell, contribution to 'The War Years in Ulster: A Symposium', *Honest Ulsterman 64*, pp. 11–62 (p. 13). Hanna Bell's recollections are historically dubious, however, claiming of that same raid that it 'left two thousand dead or injured'.

[34] Gardiner, *Blitz*, p. 303.

[35] An exhibition mounted by Belfast City Council at the City Hall in 2011 to commemorate the 70th anniversary of the Blitz displayed one of the Dundalk-based fire engines used in the mission, and south of the border a documentary for RTÉ radio recorded eyewitness recollections to piece together the experiences of the fire crews themselves. See 'Blitz Fire Engine from Irish Republic in Belfast', BBC News website, 14 April 2011, <http://www.bbc.co.uk/news/uk-northern-ireland-13065528>; 'Documentary on One: Hidden Heroes of the Belfast Blitz', RTÉ Radio One, 16 April 2011, <http://www.rte.ie/radio1/doconone/radio-documentary-ww2-hidden-heroes-belfast-blitz-republic-firemen.html>.

[36] Woodside, 18 April 1941.   [37] Richard Doherty, *Key to Victory*, p. 81.

of the future of Ulster. Protestants and Catholics have been bombed indiscriminately.

The young IRA supporter who flashed a light deliberately to guide the bombers has been seen repenting bitterly. Moore has seized hope from the Irish Blitz experience and brought Belfast under the umbrella of the Myth. Just as in London, class differences were reportedly subdued, so in Belfast sectarian feeling is chastened.

Moore published his novel in 1965, when prospects for harmony in Ulster seemed good. By the end of the decade they would be in ruins. For all the quality of the writing, *The Emperor of Ice Cream* seems betrayed and diminished by Moore's attempt at a closure which would relate the Blitz to the sixties and beyond.[38]

Calder's disjointed efforts here to incorporate *The Emperor of Ice Cream* into British wartime mythology are contradicted by some important elements in the novel, including the satire implicit in the descriptions of the hierarchical idiocies of Gavin's ARP post, or the unsparing grimness of the graphic and distressing scenes in the temporary morgue following the Blitz. The disagreement between the patients in the hospital over the provenance of the fire engines is demonstrative of a sceptical approach to wartime mythology, and suggests that even in the midst of the devastation sectarian arguments continued, even if 'chastened'. The novel does of course show that Protestants and Catholics were bombed indiscriminately (as Gavin tells Gallagher, ' "They didn't hold back just because the Falls Road is Catholic" '), and the war is seen to give occasion to more interaction between the communities; but to equate the stratified English class system with sectarian divisions in Belfast risks effacing the unique position of Northern Ireland during the war. It may be interesting to consider whether *The Emperor of Ice Cream* might have developed differently had it been written ten or fifteen years later, as Belfast was being torn apart by bombs of a different kind, but it is hard to see how the traumatic climax of the novel might be translated into an optimistic prognosis for mid-1960s Northern Ireland. Nevertheless, Calder's assertions highlight the dangers of attempting to draw the province into British cultural historical narratives, and should encourage consideration of how the British People's War was adopted and refashioned in Northern Ireland, and how this process is reflected in Moore's novel.

Like many of its British counterparts, *The Emperor of Ice Cream* is a heavily social novel and is similarly driven, especially in scenes situated in and around the ARP post, by juxtapositions of disparate characters, thrown together by an accident of history and forced into communal existence

---

[38] Calder, *Myth of the Blitz*, p. 170.

as they face a common threat. Much of the novel is deliberately comic in its observation and dissection of character, and exploitation of situations peculiar to the war. Early in the novel Moore's evocation of the ARP post can be read as a mocking critique of the war effort in Belfast. In addition to Your Man Gallagher, Post 106 is staffed by a disparate collection of misfits:

'…This is Wee Tommy Bates.'

Wee, he was. Almost a dwarf, Gavin decided. He sat hunched over the fire, all prognathous jaw, monkey forehead and protruding teeth. 'And the big man here is Frank Price,' Soldier said. Frank Price nodded gently. He was sad and stout and ludicrous in battle-dress.

'And this here's Jimmy Lynan.' Who was bald and who hawked, spat in the fire, and offered his hand.

'And Hughie Shaw.' A clerkly little man, who was filling his pipe from a flat tin box filled with cigarette butts.[39]

Sketching these grotesques Moore lampoons a crucial archetype of the People's War, as the plucky, scruffy British Tommy, familiar from recruitment posters, Giles cartoons, and countless newspaper and magazine photographs, is here disfigured and ridiculed. In joining the ARP, Gavin himself is also presented as a figure of fun, ridiculed as 'Charlie Chaplin' by his sister Kathy when he first dresses in his ill-fitting uniform.[40] On the cover of the 1987 Paladin reprint of the novel, the artist Brian Sanders depicts Gavin peering over the frame of the design, his nose poking over the edge in a way that recalls Mister Chad, the cartoon graffiti character who appeared on walls throughout Britain during the Second World War asking 'Wot No Oranges?' or 'Wot No Petrol?', questioning rhetorically and indignantly whatever the current shortage was.[41] In the background, the semi-sophisticated patrons of a nightclub (presumably the Plaza Dance Hall), dressed in suits and evening wear, look on with mocking smiles. In *Post 381: The Memoirs of a Belfast Air Raid Warden* (1989), James Doherty expresses a degree of irritation that comic portrayals of the civil defence forces had persisted after the war, as 'the warden became a Keystone Cop type of character'.[42] Later in his account, Doherty acknowledges that comical situations did arise, and that the ARP counted among its ranks 'misfits' and 'characters', but insists that 'Contrary to the false image created, most wardens were a collection of dedicated men and women who were proud of the service'.[43] Although Moore's portrayal of the dissipated

---

[39] Moore, *Emperor*, p. 19.   [40] Moore, *Emperor*, p. 14.

[41] Paul Fussell, *Wartime: Understanding and Behaviour in the Second World War* (New York; Oxford: Oxford University Press, 1989), p. 262.

[42] James Doherty, *Post 381: The Memoirs of a Belfast Air Raid Warden* (Belfast: Friar's Bush, 1989), p. 6.

[43] James Doherty, *Post 381*, p. 6.

ARP workers could be seen to satirize official or idealized representations of civilian heroism, in the aftermath of the Blitz both Bates and Lynan are seen stretchering the dead into the morgue, and there is a sense of common purpose in the scenes following the climactic air raid that suggests that the Blitz has uncovered a will to cooperate in the face of a greater external threat.[44]

It is striking how the major historians of Northern Ireland and the Second World War have used *The Emperor of Ice Cream* in their accounts of the aftermath of the Belfast Blitz. Robert Fisk, in *In Time of War*, and Brian Barton, in *The Blitz: Belfast in the War Years*, both quote, word for word, the same passage from Moore's novel, describing the harrowing scenes in the temporary morgue at the Mater hospital:

> ...stink of human excrement, in the acrid smell of disinfectant, these dead were heaped, body on body, flung arm, twisted feet, open mouth, staring eyes, old men on top of young women, a child lying on a policeman's back, a soldier's hand resting on a woman's thigh, a carter, still wearing his coal sacks, on top of a pile of arms and legs, his own arm outstretched, finger pointing, as though he warned of some unseen horror. Forbidding and clumsy, the dead cluttered the morgue room from floor to ceiling...[45]

Given the uncompromising nature of its content, it is probably unsurprising that neither Barton nor Fisk attempt to interrogate this passage: it is allowed to stand, and the account moves on. That it is an extract from a work of fiction is barely acknowledged. Fisk introduces the passage by referring to Moore's 'semi-autobiographical novel', and Barton attributes the passage merely to 'Ulster author Brian Moore' (although in an earlier chapter he does refer to 'novelist Brian Moore' as he introduces another quotation from *The Emperor of Ice Cream*).[46] In another historical account, *Northern Ireland in the Second World War*, Barton refers to the novel as 'autobiographical'.[47] More recently, Juliet Gardiner has also used this passage in accounts of the Belfast Blitz in *Wartime: Britain 1939–1945* (2004) and *The Blitz: The British Under Attack* (2010). She also fails to make clear that the description is taken from a novel: in the former book it is attributed to 'the novelist Brian Moore, who was then an ARP officer attached to the Mater Hospital', and in the latter the quotation is credited to 'novelist-to-be Brian Moore'.[48] It is only in the footnotes and bibliography of Gardiner's books that the title of the novel appears, and even then its ostensibly fictional status is not acknowledged. In Sean

---

[44] Moore, *Emperor*, p. 210.   [45] Moore, *Emperor*, p. 233.
[46] Fisk, p. 425; Barton, *Blitz*, p. 146, p. 99.
[47] Barton, *Northern Ireland in the Second World War*, p. 122.
[48] Gardiner, *Wartime: Britain 1939–1945*, p. 456; Gardiner, *Blitz*, p. 300.

McMahon's *The Belfast Blitz: Luftwaffe Raids in Northern Ireland, 1941* (2010) the passage appears once more, preceded by McMahon's assertion that Moore's 'description of the shame, the pity and the meaninglessness of such slaughter remains the best summary of the Wednesday morning after the raid'.[49] The historians accord the passage the same unquestioned status as other supposedly factual eyewitness accounts.[50] Furthermore, in an earlier paragraph of *In Time Of War*, Fisk's description of the Luftwaffe's use of flares immediately prior to the Easter Tuesday raid of 15 April integrates Moore's description of this in the novel as 'beautiful, exploding with a faint pop in the sky above them, a magnesium flare floated up in the stillness, lighting the rooftops in a ghostly silver' with quotes from eyewitness interviewees including the journalist James Kelly (whose memory of the flares as 'like a giant candelabra spreading out across the city' is no less lyrical) and IRA volunteer Paddy Devlin.[51] *The Emperor of Ice Cream* has thus become a key text in factual accounts of the Belfast Blitz, and has itself become a source of known episodes, despite Moore's acknowledged tendency to conflate or truncate, or treat ironically some of these episodes for his own fictional devices.

The depiction of Gavin's initial excitement at the air raid also makes for uncomfortable reading, given the human misery that the reader knows is about to follow. Rather than feeling anxiety, sadness, or fear at the destruction, he is gripped by an 'extraordinary elation' and enjoys the bombing 'as though it were a military tattoo, put on for his benefit'.[52] From the flat roof of Post 106, Gavin and his older friend Freddie Hargreaves will destruction upon the landmarks and leaders of the city:

> 'Yes, and blow up St Michan's,' Gavin shouted, prancing in his war dance on the roof.
> 'Blow up City Hall.'
> 'And Queen's University.'
> 'And Harland and Wolff's.'
> 'Blow up the Orange Hall.'
> 'And the Cathedral and the dean.'[53]

[49] Sean McMahon, *The Belfast Blitz: Luftwaffe Raids in Northern Ireland, 1941* (Belfast: Brehon Press, 2010), p. 67.

[50] Not all have found the passage impressive, however. John Cronin wrote in 1971 that 'One would hope that, in those tremendously horrifying scenes during the air raids and in the morgue, even Brian Moore may have sweated off all his local resentments and may now be able to approach an Irish theme with truly effective authorial judgement'. (Cronin, 'Prose', in *Causeway: The Arts in Ulster*, edited by Michael Longley [Belfast: Arts Council of Northern Ireland, Gill and Macmillan, 1971], pp. 72–94 [p. 77]). Cronin's aside, suggesting that the Belfast Blitz is not a suitably 'Irish' subject for a novel, further illustrates the problematic place of the Second World War in Irish history.

[51] Fisk, p. 418.   [52] Moore, *Emperor*, p. 202.

[53] Moore, *Emperor*, p. 203.

The socialist and the teenager see the bombing as an exhilarating revolutionary force, exploding the oppressive physical and moral fabric of Belfast, as embodied by its political, academic, industrial, and ecclesiastical buildings. Their initial excitement is soon extinguished by practical considerations, however, as they descend to street level and are immediately returned to their ARP duties, helping an injured elderly woman to reach the hospital before volunteering to work sorting bodies at the morgue. This abrupt end to the episode parallels the shift in Calder's narrative of the People's War, where 'revolutionary attitudes' are put to one side as individuals resolve to work together to perform their allotted tasks. This shift is prefigured by the maverick socialist cleric Reverend McMurtry's earlier assertion that despite the iniquity of an 'imperialist war' it is 'marvellous news' that Churchill has taken over—here Moore evokes the contradictory nature of political discourse during the Second World War in Belfast.[54]

The 'war dance' of Gavin and Hargreaves reflects the much noted enlivening effect of the experience of air raids and their aftermath on writers and artists during the war, seemingly as keenly felt in Belfast as in Britain.[55] Robert Greacen's semi-fictional fragment 'Glory, Glory, Hallelujah!', published over the winter of 1941–42, also describes the Easter Tuesday air raid on the city:

> The first bomb was a bit of a surprise. We didn't believe it—you remember about the nice old lady and the giraffe? It couldn't happen here. Naples, Rotterdam, London, Potsdam, Coventry . . . yes, yes, of course, but it couldn't happen here! Soon the whole city was tingling with the fall of bombs—big bombs, small bombs, medium bombs, H.E. Bombs, fire-bombs, followed by aerial torpedoes, land mines and all the rest of the mixed bag of splendid Guy Fawkes flashes and fun and fervour unlimited. That was the night, Joxer, that was the night![56]

Whether ironic or not, the excitement of this passage, written by Greacen at the age of twenty-one, anticipates Gavin's conviction on the rooftop in Moore's novel that 'The world and the war had come to him at last'. Moore also shows how the war has invigorated Belfast in very much more than destructive terms: when he writes of Gavin that 'Tonight, history had conferred the drama of war on this dull, dead town in which he had been born' he suggests that the historical importance of the raid was apprehended

---

[54] Moore, *Emperor*, p. 97.

[55] See also Piette, pp. 39–44, and Rawlinson, *British Writing of the Second World War*, pp. 76–77.

[56] Robert Greacen 'Glory, Glory, Hallelujah!', *The Northman XI*, no. 1 (Winter 1941–1942), pp. 14–15 (pp. 14–15).

even as it happened.[57] More bluntly, Moore said in an interview in 1981 that 'Belfast finally became important when the Germans paid attention to it'.[58]

In binding together personal and historical narratives, *The Emperor of Ice Cream* has played a decisive role in connecting Northern Ireland's provincial history with the global history of the Second World War. Although Moore maintains an ironic distance from the British People's War, he emphasizes the culturally liberating effects of the war on the city and is unsparing in his condemnation of the moral bankruptcy of some Irish nationalist discourse, whilst the novel's shifting registers and varied cast of characters encourage consideration of the contradictory and often contested nature of Northern Ireland's place in that war.

* * *

The rural environment of Benedict Kiely's first novel *Land Without Stars* (1946) is far less affected by the Second World War. Here the partition of Ireland, rather than the distant war, is the insistent motor that drives the narrative. The town in which much of the action of the novel unfolds is strictly divided along religious lines, and there is no sense that the war can effect any change, positive or otherwise, on the nationalist community with which Kiely is concerned. In his cantankerous poem 'Yeats', Patrick Kavanagh refers somewhat dismissively to Kiely as a trader of 'literature on the margin', but as Thomas O'Grady has observed, Kiely's recourse to his home town of Omagh, County Tyrone, in early fiction and later in non-fiction, could well be read as adherence to the older writer's own famous preference, expressed in the 1952 essay 'The Parish and the Universe', for parochial rather than provincial literature.[59] In the sonnet 'Epic', written in 1951, Kavanagh confidently declares that 'I have lived in important places', and asserts the universal importance of rural life in Monaghan in 'the year of the Munich bother'.[60] *Land Without Stars* engages more uneasily with events of global consequence, and is illustrative of the awkward position of Irish nationalism in relation to the Second World War. Considering the novel alongside Kiely's later volumes of memoir *Drink to the Bird* (1991) and *The Waves Behind Us* (1999), and taking into account

---

[57] Moore, *Emperor*, p. 202.

[58] 'Six Irish Writers: Brian Moore', interview by John Cronin, BBC World Service (22 November 1981), cited in Fisk, p. 427.

[59] Patrick Kavanagh, 'Yeats', *Collected Poems* (London: Penguin Classics, 2005), p. 259; Thomas O'Grady, 'Provincial Life: The Early Novels of Benedict Kiely', *Irish University Review 38*, no. 1 (2008), pp. 20–37 (p. 28); Patrick Kavanagh, 'The Parish and the Universe', in *Collected Pruse* (London: MacGibbon & Kee, 1967), pp. 281–283.

[60] Kavanagh, 'Epic', *Collected Poems*, p. 184.

a preface written for the 1990 reprint of *Land Without Stars*, it can be seen that his writings remained intermittently troubled by defensiveness and guilt regarding the Second World War.

Published only a year after the war's end, the novel opens with two brothers, Peter and Davy Quinn, returning for Christmas 1939 to their family home in a small, unnamed town in Northern Ireland, the spires of which confirm it as a fictional double of Omagh. Peter comes from a seminary in Dublin. and Davy returns via Derry from Glasgow, where (his toolbox suggests) he is engaged in manual or industrial work of some kind. Despite this apparent involvement in the British war effort, Davy is a fiercely idealistic republican, given to strident and abrasive articulations of his political views. These eventually draw him into a risky involvement in a botched bank robbery with local outlaw Dick Slevin, after which he goes into hiding and is eventually shot dead by police as he attempts to evade capture. Peter Quinn steadfastly opposes his brother's idealism but also suffers from an unquiet mind, finding himself tempted by women and alienated from those around him. Losing the belief in his vocation, he soon leaves the seminary forever to return home, whereupon both brothers compete for the affections of the same girl, Rita Keenan. The novel is loosely autobiographical, in so far as Kiely was from Omagh and entered a seminary in County Laois in 1937, but following a lengthy convalescence after the flaring of an old spinal complaint from 1938 to 1939, decided that he was unsuited to religious life and left the institution.[61] Compared with *The Emperor of Ice Cream* and other autobiographical works referred to in this chapter, *Land Without Stars* is less consistent in approaching the locality in which it is ostensibly set: although Kiely maps out the landmarks and architectural features of Omagh in considerable detail, he is reluctant to give actual names to the streets or places described. The novel is structurally polyphonous: of the seven chapters, one each is related in the first person through Davy and Peter, and other chapters written in the third person slip frequently into free indirect discourse, most often to reveal the inner thoughts of Peter. The instability resulting from these textual shifts contributes to the considerable difficulty of situating Kiely's writings in relation to the Second World War.

The title of *Land Without Stars* is taken from lines by the Irish-language Munster poet Aodhagan Ó Rathaille, on whom, as he explains in *The Waves Behind Us*, Kiely was writing an essay over Christmas 1944. Translated, the lines read 'A land without produce or thing of worth of any kind/A land without dry weather, without a stream, without a star'.[62] Kiely recalled:

---

[61] Grace Eckley, *Benedict Kiely* (New York: Twayne Publishers Inc., 1972), p. 13, p. 17.
[62] Benedict Kiely, *The Waves Behind Us: Further Memoirs* (London: Methuen, 1999), p. 66.

I was trying to write about young brooding men in political trouble in the Six Counties that the Partition of Ireland by England (Government of Ireland Act, 1920) had so woefully established as a sort of limbo under the odd and not quite accurate title of Northern Ireland.[63]

The implicit claim that *Land Without Stars* should be read as a nationalist novel, bound through its title and thematic concerns to the sense of loss engendered by partition, is more complex than is immediately apparent. As it turns out, the young men in the novel are in 'political trouble' of a very loose description: they are pursued by the authorities after a misconceived bank robbery ends in a shooting, and Slevin, the leader of the mission, is openly scornful of Davy's republican beliefs.[64] Although Kiely mocks the 'odd and not quite accurate title' of Northern Ireland, with reference to the familiar quirk that one can look north from County Derry on the northern side of the border to Malin Head in the southern state, the observation is undercut by his inaccurate description of partition, and the Government of Ireland Act (1920) as an action taken by 'England', rather than the British Parliament, or Britain. As we shall see, such faux naivety, often amplified and problematized by the deployment of seemingly irrelevant pieces of detail and the deliberate unravelling of arguments through the use of non sequiturs, is characteristic of his writing of and about the war years. Such tendencies suggest that the Second World War presented the moderately nationalist Kiely with a problem, of how to reconcile his awareness of the pervasive effect of the war on his locality (and the colossal effect on the world at large) with his belief in a united Ireland. The uneasy co-existence of these ideas in Kiely's writings is indicative of a growing sense that events in Ireland have been overshadowed and overtaken by developments in mainland Europe and elsewhere in the world. The idea that Ireland can exist apart is debunked in the opening pages of the novel as Davy returns home:

> The darkness had followed him from Glasgow, the great clanging city, mother of ships, where thousands of people waited, tense, sullenly nervous, for the bursting of the storm. All over Europe the same darkness. A broken Poland. Great hordes of men moving east and west. The darkness spreading, west to Ireland, spreading through the streets of the little town, blackening the windows of his own home.[65]

---

[63] Kiely, *Waves*, p. 66.

[64] Benedict Kiely, *Land Without Stars* (London: Christopher Johnson, 1946; repr. Dublin: Moytura Press, 1990), p. 70. All subsequent references to 'Kiely, *Stars*' are to the Moytura reprint.

[65] Kiely, *Stars*, p. 2.

By contrast, the second chapter, written through Davy's voice, is a forceful articulation of the detachment felt by those nationalists who found they had become, through economic necessity, unwilling participants in the British war effort:

> God knows if it wasn't for the Gaelic classes, the light and the cheery company, a fellow would go mad in this town. We're in the war and we're not in it, neither fish nor flesh. We've got the blackout and rations. The streets are full of soldiers. No honest enthusiasm anywhere. The Orangemen want their jobs and their domination. I want my job. I have to live. I help to build huts to house British soldiers, the army of occupation. Then I go home, take off my dungarees, listen to the German radio and believe every word of it. God, what a life![66]

Kiely's use of the first person plural suggests that Davy views himself as representative of the nationalist community, who, as a result of partition and the consequent awkwardness of Northern Ireland's position in relation to the war, find themselves 'neither fish nor flesh'. Davy sees no 'honest enthusiasm' for the war effort into which, due to financial circumstances, he has been forced: as well as war work in Glasgow he has helped to build the huts in Tyrone that house British soldiers billeted in the province since the beginning of the war. At this stage, the war seems a mere inconvenience, as the blackout, the road blocks, and rationing are observed under sufferance. Later, the local shopkeeper Mr Keenan laments the conflict only to the extent that there is 'No money to be made, except at smuggling'.[67] Divisions between nationalists and unionists have continued regardless of the external threat, and there is no sign of the uneasy cross-community cooperation that characterizes Moore's ARP post. Keenan's terse 'hope to God' that Hitler will be denied victory is rooted in a fear that his cloth trade will be hit.[68] For Davy, events and developments outside the island of Ireland are seen in relation to the ideal of a thirty-two county Republic or dismissed altogether, and his German sympathies, such as they are, exist solely in relation to his hatred of Britain. Like Mr Burke in *The Emperor of Ice Cream*, Davy reads the papers avidly for news of British defeats and Axis triumphs, his face 'radiant' as Nazi troops enter Belgium and Holland.[69] Davy's primary hatred of the English or British is accompanied by a broader xenophobic distrust of foreign influence, which he views as a threat to indigenous Irish culture. Berating his brother for choosing to see a Hollywood film instead of attending Irish class, he asks 'if the clergy don't stand by the language, who will?' and argues that 'your native

---

[66] Kiely, *Stars*, p. 34.   [67] Kiely, *Stars*, p. 28.   [68] Kiely, *Stars*, p. 28.
[69] Kiely, *Stars*, p. 57.

language is a good in itself'.[70] This blinkered idealism is tempered by a grumbling pessimism. Searching for the footpath in the blackout he asks rhetorically 'under God what self respecting German, would bomb this place? He wouldn't have much to crow about back in the beer-garden'.[71] Davy's obsession with a united and independent Ireland is expressed negatively, dependent on a denial that the island exists in an international context, and a belief that aside from the potential removal of the British army from the Six Counties, the war can mean nothing for Ireland.

Kiely's short preface to the first 1946 edition of *Land Without Stars*, 'To The Reader', immediately sets the novel in this politicized context:

> No character in this book is based on or bears any resemblance to any real character or any real person living or dead. The incidents are entirely fictitious, nor can any actual locality or existing institution mentioned in the story—except in so far as there is an island called Ireland, divided by a political boundary into two fragments, the smaller of which is misnamed Ulster, the larger misnamed Éire. More natural boundaries divide the island into thirty-two counties in which counties live about four million people, none of them appearing in these pages.[72]

Like his 1999 explanation of the novel's title, this is wilfully disingenuous. As Kiely attempts to efface the novel's autobiographical roots and highly specific setting, the emphasis here on the partition of the 'island called Ireland' sidesteps the contextual background of the Second World War, which had its own implications for Ireland, and, arguably, for partition.[73] Perhaps tellingly, the preface was removed and replaced for the 1990 reprint of the novel—although as we shall see, this later 'Retrospect' itself presents a number of problems. Unlike *The Emperor of Ice Cream*, there is no point in *Land Without Stars* at which a known historical episode of the Second World War exerts a direct impact on the narrative, but there are several references to ongoing events in Europe, such as the invasion of the Low Countries and the Dunkirk evacuation, and descriptions of the increased numbers of British troops billeted in the locality, the blackout, and searchlights combing the sky at night. Even when the brothers travel to an Irish language summer school in the remote Rosses of Donegal, the war remains an intermittent presence in conversation and in Peter's thoughts, conveyed through the sounds of marching feet and of planes heard at night overheard.[74] These, we must assume, are British aircraft heading west on Atlantic patrol, but their intrusion is anomalous.

---

[70] Kiely, *Stars*, pp. 6–7.   [71] Kiely, *Stars*, p. 7.
[72] Benedict Kiely, unpaginated preface to *Land Without Stars* (London: Christopher Jackson, 1946).
[73] Kiely, *Waves*, p. 69.   [74] Kiely, *Stars*, p. 114.

Permission was not granted to the RAF for the use of the Donegal air corridor until January 1941, yet in the novel the planes fly over southern territory at some point around the time of the Dunkirk evacuation, which was completed by 3 June 1940.[75] The soldiers Peter hears through the shadowy dusk crossing the bridge are also mysterious. It must be assumed from the geographical location that they are members of the Irish army, but here they appear as symbols of the militarization of the entire planet:

> The sound of their feet went back through the centuries to the sea rovers working in unison to haul their boats zig-zagging upwards out of reach of the tide. The sound of their feet went out over the whole world, Germany, Britain, France, Poland, Italy, Finland, Russia, Japan, marching and singing songs to the sound of their own feet.[76]

The appearance of these soldiers dismantles Davy's idealized conception earlier in the novel of the Rosses as a place of 'Peace and freedom and no soldiers', although this itself is quickly contradicted by a troubling image: 'The war washes past under the rough ocean. Sometimes a piece of driftwood or a dead body, washed in to be buried in peace, comes up out of the sea.'[77] The Battle of the Atlantic resulted in the deaths of tens of thousands of sailors, many of whose bodies were washed up on beaches and rocks along the west coast of Ireland during the war. Lost in a nationalist reverie, Davy avoids the uncomfortable truth of how the driftwood and the corpses have come to be there, in a passage that echoes the closing lines of Louis MacNeice's 'Neutrality', written in December 1942:

> But then look eastward from your heart, there bulks

---

[75] Barton, *Northern Ireland in the Second World War*, p. 110. De Valera's concession of the air corridor did not emerge until after the war, although its existence was apparently known well before this. In his memoir of a wartime childhood, *Eleven Houses* (2007), the dramatist and director Christopher Fitz-Simon recalls his grandfather telling him after seeing Catalinas, Lancasters, and Sunderlands passing over Bundoran that the pact between de Valera and Churchill was common knowledge. (Christopher Fitz-Simon, *Eleven Houses: A Memoir of Childhood* [Dublin: Penguin Ireland, 2007], p. 92).

[76] Kiely, *Stars*, p. 104. Kiely appears to revisit this scene in *Drink to the Bird*:

> One day I watched and listened—to a platoon, or whatever, of them marching down the slope that led in from Enniskillen and Bundoran and the western ocean. They were singing that there would always be an England. Their singing was as awkward as their marching. They may have had sore feet. Anyway, a boozer is the place for singing. Not a cold, damp roadway in an alien town. They were young men torn away by war from home and on the road to God Knows Where!

(Kiely, *Drink to the Bird: A Memoir* [London: Methuen, 1991], p. 17) In this instance the young soldiers are clearly English, and clearly on the Northern side of the border. Again Kiely can be seen to reconfigure his impressions of the effects of the war on Ireland in retrospect.

[77] Kiely, *Stars*, p. 35.

A continent, close, dark, as archetypal sin,
While to the west off your own shores the mackerel
Are fat—on the flesh of your kin.[78]

Kiely avoids such explicit condemnation of the wilful ignorance of those who have chosen to look away, but the casual reference to 'driftwood or a dead body' as though their appearances on the strand were natural phenomena provides a grisly corrective to idealistic and isolationist nationalism. Davy sees the sojourn in Donegal as an opportunity to reclaim the physical reality of an Irish-speaking Ireland of 'Peace and freedom', but Peter is more withdrawn, and feels that the location of the Rosses on the geographical margins, 'neither in Europe nor in America', gives him 'a vantage point above the woes of Europe and the woes of men. It was escape'.[79] This 'escape' would seem to be illusory, however, when ghostly yet insistent reminders of the war intrude on land, from the sea and in the air.

Despite these intrusions, there is no sense in *Land Without Stars* that the war has effected any great changes on its rural setting or the lives of its characters: Davy would have been pursued and shot by the authorities regardless of the war in Europe, and Peter's loss of faith in his vocation results from an internal struggle that, if conscious of the war, is certainly not driven by it. The removal of a significant proportion of the novel's action to the Rosses may symbolize a wilful desire on the part of some nationalists to disassociate themselves from the war (or at least from the British-directed war effort), but Kiely clearly acknowledges that the possibility of such detachment has been threatened by global and technological advances in warfare.

Forty-four years after *Land Without Stars* first appeared, in a foreword to the 1990 reprint of the novel entitled 'Retrospect', Kiely addresses the perceived innocence of its characters:

> The young people in this novel seem to be so innocent. More innocent, even, than I was when I wrote the book. Was it, then, a more innocent world? Or has the world never been any better or any worse? The young I.R.A. men of that time read "Mein Kampf" because Hitler was against England. But their world was still innocent of the full implications and sideshows of the Hitler war, of the revelations of Belsen and Katyn Woods, of Hiroshima, of napalm in Viet-Nam, of the Abercorn Restaurant, and Derry's Bloody Sunday and

---

[78] MacNeice, 'Neutrality', *Collected Poems*, p. 224. MacNeice's poem was written in September 1942 following the death of his friend Graham Sheppard, who had drowned in the Atlantic after a German U-boat attack. For a detailed account of the discoveries of bodies on the beaches of the west of Ireland during the Second World War, see Wills, *That Neutral Island*, pp. 136–146.

[79] Kiely, *Stars*, p. 83.

Belfast's Bloody Friday, and the Chicago murders, nor of Charley Manson and the slaughter of Sharon Tate.

The moon was still a virgin, that orbèd maiden with white fire laden, and not an ash heap. Most Irish rivers ran clean. The streets were not constipated with motor cars. Nor did you breathe carbon monoxide on O'Connell Bridge. No, no, nothing worse than the homely body-odour of Anna Livia Plurabelle.[80]

This is a deeply troubling passage, but one to which Kiely himself would seem to adhere or attach some importance, as he recycles it in near identical form in his 1999 volume of memoirs, *The Waves Behind Us.*[81] Acknowledging the possibility that the greater historical perspective of a late-twentieth-century readership could adversely affect perceptions of the behaviour of Davy and others in *Land Without Stars*, he seeks here to exculpate the actions of young republicans during the Second World War by contrasting their naivety with a series of violent and traumatic episodes in post-war history. The historical conflation attempted in this diverse and perplexing litany, gathering together the 'Charley' Manson murders and the Vietnam War with events of the Troubles in Northern Ireland, and seemingly ascribing all of these to an unspecified post-war moral malaise, is clumsy and unconvincing, and the ambiguities resulting from Kiely's apparent ambivalence are compounded by the mélange of colloquial and literary imagery which follows the list of tragic and terrible events. The ironic appropriation of Shelley's description of the moon as an 'orbèd maiden' and the folksiness of the Joycean Liffey's 'homely body-odour' sit uneasily in immediate succession to references to the concentration camps, and Kiely's various laments relating to Ireland's decline in the second half of the century (these continue to encompass the length of girls' skirts and the disfigurement of Ballyshannon in Donegal by the construction of an electrical generator) seriously hinder the development of an argument.[82] Nevertheless, Kiely does seem to divide twentieth-century Ireland into pre- and post-war states of being, and thereby suggests that the Second World War created severe problems for traditional nationalism, by questioning the credibility or possibility of an idyllic and isolated rural, Irish-speaking Ireland in the face of these new global horrors. His unwillingness to argue this directly is symbolized by his tendency to refer to the Second World War as the 'Hitler war' or 'Second Big War' rather than by its American or British appellations or by the neutral Irish term

---

[80] Kiely, 'Retrospect', *Stars*, unpaginated preface.   [81] Kiely, *Waves*, p. 67.
[82] Percy Bysshe Shelley, 'The Cloud', *Shelley: Poetical Works*, edited by Thomas Hutchinson, new edition corrected by G.M. Matthews (London, New York, Toronto: Oxford University Press, 1970), pp. 600–602 (p. 601).

'The Emergency'.[83] Similarly evasive is the episode in *Land Without Stars* itself when Peter recalls a German priest who came to speak at the seminary—an 'exile' whose religious order were removed from their house in Austria 'by polite local officials who were never responsible but who acted under orders from other men who were exceedingly polite but still were not responsible', without Nazi religious persecution ever being referred to directly.[84]

The palpable awkwardness of Kiely's writing as he attempts to relate events elsewhere in the world to the Irish experience of the war years, may stem in part at least from an episode in his own career as a film critic in Dublin towards the end of the war, when in a review of the Noel Coward film *In Which We Serve*, published in the Catholic weekly newspaper *The Standard* in June 1945, he expressed reservations about newsreel footage of the concentration camps, then being shown in cinemas after the lifting of censorship restrictions. Clair Wills has accused Kiely of succumbing to a 'standing temptation to transform neutrality into a superior moral condition', in advising film-goers to 'Take (the newsreels) always, not with the proverbial pinch of salt, but with a detached comprehensive charity', and stating that 'neutrality does not mean cowardly shrinking from the truth, but a genuine compassion for all suffering'. Kiely's review concluded with the advice 'for heaven's sake, keep the children at home'.[85]

Irish neutrality does not emerge as a major concern of *Land Without Stars*, but an exchange between Rita and Peter, as they flee in a rowing boat over a lake from the house where Davy and Slevin have been hiding out, is significant:

'Peter, are you a coward?'

'I often wonder. Nowadays a man doesn't get a chance to find out. We're too civilized. We're too neutral.'

'We're not neutral here in the Six Counties.'

'In spirit we are. Except a few Orangemen. And in practice they're as neutral as Switzerland. They don't want any serious fighting. Anyway, war doesn't prove a man's courage. It's a mass hysteria. The bravest man I ever heard of was shot as a coward during the last war. Didn't like killing people. He died for his convictions.'[86]

[83] Kiely, *Bird*, p. 28; Kiely, 'Retrospect', *Stars*. Patrick Kavanagh also uses the term 'Hitler war' in 'The Parish and the Universe' (Kavanagh, *Pruse*, p. 281).

[84] Kiely, *Stars*, p. 46.

[85] Wills, *That Neutral Island*, p. 410; Benedict Kiely, 'To Tell of Horror', *The Standard*, 15 June 1945.

[86] Kiely, *Stars*, p. 149.

Coming as it does towards the end of the novel, these pronouncements have an air of finality about them, but as with much of Kiely's writings around the war the boldness is illusory. Neutrality 'in spirit' is indicative more of a vague aspiration than a practically enforced doctrine, and given the context it is unclear to which conflict 'the last war' refers. Again Kiely's equivocations frustrate attempts to fix the place of Ireland in relation to the global conflict.

Thomas O'Grady has read the novel as a 'prophetic parable of forces more powerful than sibling rivalry', in which Peter and Davy embody two branches of nationalism—the intellectual and cultural and the militant and political, which in the aftermath of partition competed 'to woo and win the elusive spirit of Ireland, conventionally feminized' in Rita Keenan.[87] O'Grady's allegorical analysis might, indeed, be extended to take in the desiccated, childless, and deformed old men Pete and Jacob, who offer shelter to Davy and Slevin, as emblems of an older nationalism that has failed.[88] This reading is compelling, but surely contains a further implication that the elusive yet disruptive impact of the Second World War on the narrative reflects the troubling repercussions of the war for Irish nationalism. The war does not affect the characters directly, and in a sense *Land Without Stars* is itself a neutral textual zone, critiquing nationalism against the background of the conflict. Perhaps contrary to Kiely's original intentions, many decades on the war could be seen to complicate and contribute to this critique, and the discernible backpedalling in the 1990 'Retrospect' suggests that he was aware that some elements of the novel had been reframed from without.

By 1991, in his memoir *Drink to the Bird*, Kiely seems far more willing to acknowledge the significance of the Second World War for his home town of Omagh, and references to the conflict abound in this rather rambling collection of memories and anecdotes about his childhood and young adulthood. Kiely describes Omagh as a 'garrison town' and as an integral part of the British Empire, where in the 1930s 'soldiers came and went between Omagh and Aldershot and India', but he does recognize the Irish identity of many of those soldiers.[89] He makes repeated reference to those from the town who fought in Europe and died at Dunkirk or in the D-Day landings, and writes of the barracks in Omagh that 'There were a lot

[87] O'Grady, p. 27.
[88] As Kiely notes in *The Waves Behind Us*, Peter and Jacob also appear in his short stories 'Homes on the Mountain' and 'A Journey to the Seven Streams'; Dick Slevin also appears in 'The Wild Boy' (*Waves*, p. 68).
[89] Kiely, *Drink*, p. 86.

of Irishmen in there, too, and later on, and on far foreign fields, and some of them old friends of mine. Nor were they compelled nor conscripted'.[90]

> Bugles from the military barracks divided the day as do bells in a monastery. The barracks stood like a medieval fortress on a high, walled place above the loops of the Strule. The original building still stands more or less on the same place, but Adolf Hitler provoked the extension of the barrack buildings across the river to cover a place once called Pumphill. On the Sunday before the digging machines broke the first sod on Pumphill a great meeting was held there to protest against the partition of Ireland by British tyranny. We were always hell for irony, had a special gift that way.[91]

References to the barracks' elevated location and the 'division' of the day by the bugles emphasize the army's often oppressive presence in the town and role in maintaining partition, but a joke is also made here at the expense of nationalists, who protest against British tyranny in the form of soldiers who are themselves preparing to engage in battle with the tyrannical Nazi regime. Kiely then notes that the first military action against the barracks was taken not by the Germans but by the Provisional IRA, who blew up the septic tank, whereby 'inevitably the action was described as Shitty-Shitty-Bang-Bang'.[92] These recollections contrast with the altogether more serious critique of young republicans in *Land Without Stars*, and the passage of time, along with the more informal style of the memoir, seem to have allowed Kiely to describe the impact of the war on the province with greater freedom.

* * *

Several writers from Northern Ireland have acknowledged the formative effect of the war on their boyhood. An essay by John Montague recalling his wartime childhood states in uncompromising fashion that 'I loved the war. It was a spectacular background to my small existence from the age of ten to sixteen', and similarly Dennis Kennedy has written that 'Despite the black-out, rationing and something called austerity, growing up in the war was not dull'.[93] The idea that the war had such an enlivening and positive impact on the growth of the male youth is pervasive, driving the narrative of works of memoir by Robert Harbinson and Will Morrison, amongst others. Montague recalls that his interest in and excitement about the progress of the war was unhindered by his republican origins:

> Like a commanding officer, I had a map, and moved pins to mark the progress of the German armies as they pushed through northern France and

---

[90] Kiely, *Drink*, p. 17.   [91] Kiely, *Drink*, p. 84.   [92] Kiely, *Drink*, p. 84.
[93] Montague, 'The War Years in Ulster', *Figure in the Cave*, p. 27; Dennis Kennedy, *Climbing Slemish* (Victoria, British Columbia: Trafford Publishing, 2006), p. 218.

on to Paris. My letters to my cousins in Longford were full of war plans, and signed in true army style, Captain or Lieutenant or General (later, Field Marshal) Montague. I was neither pro-British nor Republican, just a boy living on the edge of a giant historical drama.[94]

The experiences of children on the British Home Front, and their attested enjoyment of the disruption caused by the Second World War to the repetitive patterns of school and home life, have been widely explored in sources as diverse as Richmal Crompton's *William* series and John Boorman's autobiographical film *Hope and Glory* (1987). Such a tradition may also be discerned in Northern Ireland. The Belfast-born journalist and academic Dennis Kennedy, three years old at the outbreak of war, recalled in his memoir *Climbing Slemish* (2006) how he and his friends during the war had their own favourite Soviet Marshals, and were familiar with these personages from the newspapers which they eagerly devoured:

Mine had been Timoshenko, baldheaded and ruthless, but unfortunately he fell from favour and was not in the top three who were leading the charge. My brother had already picked Zhukov, so he was out. I preferred Rokossovsky to Koniev—much more Russian sounding—and almost daily we plotted on our maps the progress of their respective armies. In the end I came third, while my brother celebrated Zhukov's triumph. Still, we both knew it was Montgomery who had really won the war.[95]

John Montague's description of a damaged flying-boat as 'an enormous prehistoric creature, a pterodactyl with folded wings' shows how the new and exotic patterns and objects which appeared on the Home Front proved stimulating to young minds; he also evokes the ways in which far-away battles were assimilated into games and play, describing the Allied progress through Holland in terms of a Wild West cowboy chase.[96] Montague's essay closes with an adult reassessment of his original, seemingly uncompromising opening statement: 'I began by saying I loved the War, but that small boy has had to deal with its implications ever since. It is probably why, although I am a republican, I do not believe in physical force except as a form of resistance'.[97]

The first three books in Robert Harbinson's four-volume series of memoirs, *No Surrender* (1960), *Song of Erne* (1960), and *Up Spake the Cabin Boy* (1961), describe his growth from boyhood to adolescence during the 1930s and war years in very different terms.[98] These volumes of memoir

[94] Montague, 'The War Years in Ulster', *Figure in the Cave*, pp. 27–28.
[95] Kennedy, *Climbing Slemish*, p. 222.
[96] Montague, 'The War Years in Ulster', *Figure in the Cave*, p. 27.
[97] Montague, 'The War Years in Ulster', *Figure in the Cave*, p. 35.
[98] 'Robert Harbinson' was a pseudonym adopted by the Belfast-born writer Robin Bryans (1928–2005).

are less concerned with Harbinson's experience of known episodes of the Second World War in Northern Ireland than with the day-to-day texture of wartime life and its impact on his personal development.[99] He writes in *No Surrender* that the war initially meant little to him, but that inevitably it began to seep into his life 'like water on the sides of a damp cave', whilst in school 'Martyrs burning at the stake during history lessons, now had to make elbow-room for Nazism's victims. And religious instructions never passed without some cruelty of the Germans being placarded for our edification'.[100] Recalling that 'Hate for Germans puzzled me. Had they not produced Martin Luther who ranked next to King Billy? The hate loomed so disproportionately large in the adult world', Harbinson focuses on the immediate impact of the war on local concerns, conflicts, and assumptions—a recurring theme in the following volume *Song of Erne*.[101] He also emphasizes the beneficial economic repercussions of the war, writing that 'Belfast reacted swiftly to the coming of war, its streets vibrated with energy, everyone was working—even me', and recalls how the Harbinson home in East Belfast soon filled up with lodgers, as people poured into the city for war work: 'Besides bringing the breath of a wider world into our house, the lodgers also brought a higher standard of living. We could have sausages and fried potato bread for tea more often'.[102]

Harbinson's memoirs are most notable for the ways in which they describe the relations between urban and rural environments in wartime Northern Ireland. In his introduction to Harbinson's *Selected Stories* (1996), John Keyes claims that Belfast 'more than any city' has country connections, citing an influx at the end of the nineteenth century of country people who left behind relatives in rural areas. He also argues that 'With Harbinson, the country and the city are almost the same. So closely intermeshed are they that it is difficult to separate one from the other'.[103] In *No Surrender* and *Song of Erne* the navigation of divisions between town and country are shown to be vital to the growth and development of Robbie, as Harbinson refers to his younger self. In *No Surrender*, which

---

[99] Like Brian Moore, Harbinson does admit to exercising some chronological freedom: in an 'Author's Note' which follows a glossary of 'Local Terms' and precedes the main text of *Song of Erne*, he admits 'I have taken an author's privilege of telescoping time. Some things which, in fact, occurred up to 1946, have been regarded as happening during 1940–42'. (Robert Harbinson, *Song Of Erne* [London: Faber and Faber, 1960; repr. Belfast: Blackstaff Press, 1987], p. 11) All subsequent references to 'Harbinson, *Erne*' are to the Blackstaff edition.

[100] Robert Harbinson, *No Surrender* (London: Faber and Faber, 1960), p. 209.

[101] Harbinson, *No Surrender*, p. 207.

[102] Harbinson, *No Surrender*, p. 215, p. 214.

[103] John Keyes, 'Preface' to Robert Harbinson, *Selected Stories* (Belfast: Lagan Press, 1996), pp. 11–22 (p. 20, p. 21).

describes his early life in Belfast during the 1930s, he recalls being drawn by a 'clarion' to the country, making many trips to Lough Neagh. Town and country are presented as exactly coterminous (Harbinson writes that where the 'walls stopped, the fields began') but physically and spiritually antithetical.[104] Despite his fidelity to home and to his mother, in *No Surrender* Harbinson is lyrical in his loathing of the urban landscape of the city of his birth:

> Mill chimneys, caked under their black lichen of smoke, phallic obelisks pointing in mockery up at heaven; the streets where lived thousands of sweated labourers, ranged in fearful geometry, row upon wretched still-born row, and an outcrop of crude civic buildings, bloated into ugliness by the so-called city fathers of the last century; these were the core of Belfast. To decaying Protestantism, Belfast was a place of pilgrimage, a Mecca of Orangemen. Misery and darkness for the many; quick money for the few. Unloved children, old women rotting in dirt under their shawls, I knew as Keats and Hippolyte Taine knew. Since they wrote of the city's horrors times had changed little. Festering scab are words which described it well enough.[105]

His frequent pre-war trips to the countryside, either for the day or to camp overnight with his 'gang' are a form of escape, but it is his evacuation to rural County Fermanagh at the very end of this volume, the account of which takes up the entirety of the succeeding *Song of Erne*, that makes the greatest impression.

The train journey from Belfast into the west at the beginning of *Song of Erne* reveals a welter of insecurities and prejudices—some inculcated and some the product of wartime rumour:

> … someone told us we were about to cross the border. Of course, no one believed it. A train-load of us Protestant children being taken across the border into the Free State to be massacred? Things had not quite come to that, even if all the German spies that ever existed were hiding down in Dublin.
>
> My alarm over this was not so intense as in some children. I thought myself widely travelled. Had I not already been in four of Ulster's six counties?…
>
> Being so worldly-wise, I gave it as my considered opinion that despite authority's announcement we were not at the border. Where, I asked, were the battlemented walls, the moats and the vast palings with cruel iron spikes which separate the dirty Free State from our clean and righteous Ulster?[106]

In the ironic reference to 'four of Ulster's six counties' Harbinson vividly conveys the fidelity of his younger self to the post-partition province, in

---

[104] Harbinson, *No Surrender*, p. 166, p. 165.
[105] Harbinson, *No Surrender*, p. 165.   [106] Harbinson, *Erne*, p. 17.

which the sense of physical and moral separation from its southern neighbour has been accentuated by the advent of war. To begin with, Robbie does not take to his new surroundings, and makes a series of abortive attempts to escape, but much of *Song of Erne* describes the rapid dismantling of his insular and defensive attitudes:

> Seldom a day went by now without some new breaking free from the past. The young plant was shooting out new tendrils which gripped ever more firmly on other stems around it. Fears and superstitions that dogged in the city shadows dispersed as I found new horizons, new friends, new ambitions, and new longings to please people and be loved in return. I wanted desperately to belong, and be absorbed by the life I found in the west. Never for a moment now was the escape route back to Belfast contemplated.[107]

Harbinson's application of 'the west' in general terms to rural Fermanagh (a few pages earlier, indeed, the county is described as 'the far west') is perhaps significant, given the iconic importance of the west of Ireland to nationalist culture at this time as the most authentic, rugged, or wild part of the country, least affected by British rule. The rural west was much explored by writers and artists of the Celtic Revival during the late nineteenth and early twentieth centuries, and romanticized versions of the west remained important in the culture of the southern state during the 1940s and 1950s. Although Harbinson's 'west' is of course the west of Northern Ireland rather than the west of Ireland, in *Song of Erne* rural Fermanagh functions in similarly mythical terms, as a refuge from the oppressively industrial city of Belfast, and his usage serves to emphasize the extent of his remove in cultural and psychological as well as geographical terms.

The most striking change which Harbinson plots in his young self is in his sectarian assumptions, repeatedly challenged by his relocation: in Enniskillen he is amazed to discover the Catholic church and Protestant cathedral on either side of the same street.[108] Later he shares a room with a Catholic farmhand, Paddy, of whom he is initially wary: 'He was not . . . an Ulsterman but actually came from the Free State. Surely he must be a spy for de Valera, whom we burned in effigy once a year'.[109] Robbie's impressions change rapidly the following day, however, after witnessing the man's extreme physical strength, demonstrated by holding open the mouth of a horse while the farmer put his arm down its throat to administer medicine. Had Paddy relaxed his grip, the farmer would have lost an arm: 'What responsibility for the black-haired Paddy—and him a Fenian'.[110] Elizabeth Grubgeld has argued that Harbinson's autobiographical works

---

[107] Harbinson, *Erne*, p. 43.   [108] Harbinson, *Erne*, p. 47.
[109] Harbinson, *Erne*, p. 72.   [110] Harbinson, *Erne*, p. 74.

lack 'self-referentiality' being 'related in the simple past tense without overt distinctions between past self and present narrator or writer', and the use of sectarian terminology here is demonstrative of this.[111] Use of the term 'Fenian' and the patronizing tone of Harbinson's appraisal of Paddy's strength here dramatize and ridicule the retrogressive attitudes of his younger self, which are fully integrated into the text without separate retrospective comment from the point of view of the adult. Such a fluid and unstable literary form problematizes attempts to view the books as examples of war memoir: there is little sense in these volumes that Harbinson feels part of any greater historical drama, or even, like Dennis Kennedy or John Montague, that he existed on the margins of one, and the series focuses on the development of the subject often to the exclusion of the wider world at war.

In *Song of Erne* the pastoral setting of Fermanagh alienates Robbie from the war, as Harbinson describes his return to Belfast immediately after the Blitz, worried that his family have perished in the bombing:

> I had grown used to the open country with woods and rivers, and a sky never dull even when overcast with rain. But here the streets were like shut boxes, the air smelt dirty, and out of the windows were not apple trees but lamp-posts without children swinging on them as before the war.
>
> I saw clearly what I would have lost by running back to the city. Even during the unhappiest times in the country, escape was possible to the beauty of Fermanagh's meadows and hills. But from here there could be no escape. Even the first novelty of war held no more magic. I knew that I had returned to be cooped up, I would no longer have found interest in the silver barrage balloons swaying in the weak sunlight or waiting for nightfall to study the geometric pattern of searchlights combing the sky.[112]

The urban landscape here is made strange as a result of his immersion in the rural environment, but the paraphernalia of the war is thoroughly eclipsed by his newly acquired natural sensibility. A passage in *Up Spake the Cabin Boy* shows how Robbie's impression of his home city has been permanently altered by his time in Fermanagh, as he describes his first job as cabin boy on a reclaiming vessel moored on Belfast Lough:

> From the deck I could look out at the Lough to where, beyond it, the Cave Hill rose up. Terror and mystery these caves held for me as a child. I used to imagine their floors and the bones littering them—the pathetic remains of Protestant children kidnapped by the Fenians. Obviously enough, I had

---

[111] Elizabeth Grubgeld, 'Life Writing in the Twentieth Century', in *The Cambridge Companion to the Irish Novel*, edited by John Wilson Foster (Cambridge: Cambridge University Press, 2006), pp. 223–237 (p. 230).

[112] Harbinson, *Erne*, pp. 107–108.

never dared go near the caves. My two years, however, in Fermanagh had put all such nonsense from my head.[113]

The role of this ship, on which Catholics and Protestants work side by side, is heavily symbolic. Moored off the 'sloblands', and connected to these by a long pipe, its function 'was hardly romantic—it sucked up mud brought by the barges from the dredgers, and then pumped it through the long ant-eater snout to the shore, gradually building up the lost swamp land'.[114] The reclamation of this 'flat and deserted' landscape is a mechanical and industrial process, but echoes Robbie's own reconfiguration of the Belfast landscape in the light of his rural awakening. Indeed, the flocks of marsh birds that populate the mudflats prompt him to write 'I felt like being on this ship would be almost like living in Fermanagh again, with the added thrill of being at sea'.[115]

Robbie's behaviour when he first arrives in Fermanagh is unruly, and his tendency to get into trouble initially results in a peripatetic existence, moved on by a series of exasperated hosts after each infraction. It is made clear at the beginning of *Song of Erne* that his evacuation will be temporary and finite in duration, since it is planned that when he reaches the age of fourteen in just over a year he will return to Belfast to become a shipyard apprentice.[116] A love of learning developed at the various country schools he attends threatens to derail this plan, however:

> The greatest revolution in my life was that the bad old days of school in Belfast were over and done. I found that learning was not a war waged by heavily-armed teachers trying to find the slightest flaw in a child's make-up as an excuse to cane. Nor was it the biggest obstacle in parent's way—parents who were forever wanting to get the school-leaving age lowered, so that the few shillings of a message-boy's packet might be added to the family wage.[117]

Robbie is encouraged to sit a scholarship exam for Portora Royal School in Enniskillen (alma mater of Samuel Beckett and Oscar Wilde), but on returning to Belfast to obtain the necessary signature from his mother to allow him to sit the exam, Harbinson recalls that 'The scholarship papers were put in the fire—such nonsense, I did not belong to those kind of people'.[118] Country and city are thus established as polar sites of learning and labour, of intellectual ambition and philistinism, and, in the context of the Blitz, of growth and destruction.

---

[113] Robert Harbinson, *Up Spake the Cabin Boy* (London: Faber and Faber, 1961), p. 59.
[114] Harbinson, *Up Spake*, p. 45, p. 46.   [115] Harbinson, *Up Spake*, p. 46.
[116] Harbinson, *Erne*, p. 15.   [117] Harbinson, *Erne*, pp. 103–104.
[118] Harbinson, *Erne*, p. 107.

Robbie's formal educational ambitions seem to peter out after this set-back, but his growing literary awakening makes a clear impact on the text. *Song of Erne*'s prose is intermittently interrupted by fragments of verse, and the changing nature of these interruptions is illustrative of his own personal development. The first three such quotations are of loyalist origin. Early on in the memoir, as the train threatens to take the proudly loyal children over the border into 'Free State' territory, the infants respond to the perceived threat by singing the anti-papist song 'Dolly's Brae', a verse of which is quoted on the page. Later, as he prepares to leave Enniskillen, a verse of the loyalist song 'The Enniskillen Dragoons' appears at the end of the chapter. Then in a description of a raucous fireside sing-song, around a third of the way into the volume, a verse of the Orange favourite 'The Protestant Boys' interrupts the prose. During his longest and most successful billet with smallholding siblings Maggie and Christy, and as Robbie's interest in literature grows, the text is irregularly broken up by quotations of a much greater variety of provenance and form. Fragments of Shakespeare, John Donne, the 121st Psalm, traditional country songs, mumming songs, and a charm all appear, as do pieces of Harbinson's own juvenilia, and the volume closes with his own poem 'Song of Erne'.

Discovering the poetry of Louis MacNeice is particularly important to Robbie's imaginative development. Towards the end of the volume Harbinson describes happening upon a soldier, Tom Williams, who is stationed nearby, lying in a field reading Louis MacNeice's *Selected Poems*. Williams lends the boy the volume, which has a profound effect on him:

> ... unlike others Louis MacNeice was not only not dead, but had been born in Belfast—my own town! At first this seemed impossible, but the truth of the matter slowly dawned on me. Poems were something for *now*. I listened agog as Tom read:
>
> *I was born in Belfast between the mountains and the gantries*
> *To the hooting of lost sirens and the clang of trams.*[119]

The poem 'Carrickfergus', which transfixes Robbie, describes MacNeice's early childhood and memories of the First World War in Ulster: read and invoked in the context of the Second, many of the references to sugar rationing, camouflaged steamers, and huge army camps are instantly familiar. The poem also serves to restate Harbinson's own urban origins, reminding him of his birth on the dockside 'facing the blue mountains of Antrim' and signals that his time in Fermanagh is finite.[120] Harbinson's evacuation inverts one of the tropes of nineteenth-century nationalist autobiography identified by Sean Ryder, in which:

---

[119] Harbinson, *Erne*, p. 208.   [120] Harbinson, *Erne*, p. 208.

the journey is often one from the country to the city, or an educational journey from the province to the metropolis and back, or sometimes a journey
through the country itself by which the hero is forced to transcend his or her
own class or regional limitations and become truly national in perspective.[121]

By contrast, *Song of Erne* describes a journey from the city to the country and back again—moves that enable Harbinson to overcome inculcated sectarian prejudices and to broaden his literary horizons. Similarly,
Robbie's trips across the border by bicycle allow him to become 'truly
national', without becoming nationalist, in perspective:

> The first time we went over, I was surprised to find it no different from
> our own Protestant side. Grass and trees were just as green, the river just
> as cool. Even the people looked like people, and no dirtier than our own.
> None of them tried to kidnap us, not even when we went apprehensively
> into Catholic churches to blow out votive lamps in our excess of Protestant
> missionary zeal.[122]

Once Robbie has returned to Belfast he is unable to revisit his formative rural experiences. Bored by shipboard life in *Up Spake the Cabin
Boy*, he describes returning to the country, slipping away from the boat,
and retracing his initial train journey to Fermanagh. Having successfully
threaded his way through the shipyard in Belfast without being apprehended, and having avoided being questioned by police in Fermanagh, his
joyful reunion with Maggie and Christy is swiftly threatened by a simple
administrative obstacle: his lack of a ration book:

> This unforeseen snag upset the careful concealment of my escape. I too had
> overlooked the ration book problem. Even here in the depths of the country,
> far from the belching war chimneys of Belfast, body and soul could not be
> held together without red-tape.[123]

After a month he returns home to face the wrath of his mother, at which
point wartime Fermanagh attains an almost Edenic resonance. In *Song of
Erne* the country occupies an interstitial place in space and time, where
Christy 'could exist with no difficulty in the ancient inherited world of a
half-magical Ireland as well as in the modern one', but here it is shown to
be subject to contemporary rules and regulations, and is, as such, at war.[124]

---

[121] Sean Ryder, ' "With a Heroic Life and a Governing Mind": Nineteenth-Century Irish
Nationalist Autobiography', in Harte (ed.), *Modern Irish Autobiography*, pp. 14–31 (p. 27).
[122] Harbinson, *Erne*, p. 112–113.   [123] Harbinson, *Up Spake*, p. 85.
[124] Harbinson, *Erne*, p. 179.

2

'An angry wind strumming the wires': Poetry

Seamus Heaney, Michael Longley, and Derek Mahon—three poets who have tended to dominate accounts of cultural life in late twentieth-century Northern Ireland—have all produced significant poems addressing the Second World War. The three were all born just before or during the war: Heaney in April 1939, Longley in July 1939, and Mahon in November 1941.[1] Many of Heaney's Second World War poems describe childhood memories, and reflect on the impact that the war had on the rural landscape around his home. These are mostly found in his later work (several appear in the 2006 collection *District and Circle*), although some references to the war can be found in earlier collections: prose poems 'England's Difficulty' and 'Visitant' were published as early as 1975 in *Stations*. The Second World War poems of Longley and Mahon are often more international in scope. Longley's two-line poem 'Terezin' from *Gorse Fires* (1991) describes a photograph of a room of hanging violins, confiscated from Jews at the concentration camp of the same name and collected to be distributed to children of Nazi parents.[2] In Mahon's 'The Home Front', in the opening section of the long poem 'Autobiographies', he describes the 'frozen armies' gathering at the gates of Leningrad at the time of his birth, setting his own early years in wartime Belfast against contemporaneous events elsewhere in Europe.[3]

---

[1] Fran Brearton, 'Poetry of the 1960s: The Northern Ireland Renaissance', in *The Cambridge Companion to Contemporary Irish Poetry*, edited by Matthew J.B. Campbell (Cambridge: Cambridge University Press, 2003), pp. 94–112 (p. 94). Robert Greacen recalls being taunted with the term 'Ulster Renaissance' by the writer F.L. Green, in Campbell's coffee house in Belfast during the Second World War (Greacen, *Sash*, p. 131). The term was later used by Heather Clark for her study of Heaney and his contemporaries, *The Ulster Renaissance: Poetry in Belfast 1962–1972* (Oxford: Oxford University Press, 2006).

[2] Michael Longley, 'Terezin', *Gorse Fires* (London: Secker and Warburg, 1991), p. 39.

[3] Derek Mahon, 'Autobiographies', *New Collected Poems* (Oldcastle, Co. Meath: Gallery Press, 2011), pp. 83–86 (p. 83).

The Second World War features more prominently in works by the next generation of Northern poets, as can be seen from Ciaran Carson's *The Irish for No* (1987), Frank Ormsby's *A Northern Spring* (1986), and Tom Paulin's *Fivemiletown* (1987) and *The Invasion Handbook* (2002). Poems by this later generation have more confidently inked Northern Ireland onto the map of a European and global war, and show how the experience of the Second World War allows connections to be drawn between the province, so often figured as isolated and its problems as intractable, and the wider world. In 'The Caravans of Lunëberg Heath', the long poem which closes *Fivemiletown*, Paulin describes how the buildings of the poet's school were literally constructed from wreckage left over from the war, and writes of 'provincial world history' where 'one tight thread/ links Lüneberg *Heidel* to the Clogher Valley'.[4] In Carson's 'Dresden' from *The Irish for No*, a veteran of RAF Bomber Command who had flown missions over the eponymous city during the Second World War keeps the shattered remains of a china shepherdess with his war medals in a biscuit tin and is troubled by the imagined memory of china ornaments collapsing and shattering in 'a thousand tinkling echoes—/All across the map of Dresden'.[5] Ormsby's 'A Northern Spring', a sequence of thirty-six poems, offers a polyphonous and fragmentary account of the experiences of American soldiers and airmen stationed in County Fermanagh during the build-up to the invasion of Normandy, and during the invasion itself. Robert Greacen's recollection in 1979 that 'The world at war, after all, was only an immense enlargement of our own tense province where a sort of *apartheid* existed between the two communities' seems to anticipate this poetic discourse, and indeed one aim of this chapter is to show how some of the concerns and debates which preoccupied later generations of northern poets and critics were foreshadowed in works by Greacen and his contemporaries during the war itself.[6]

Many of the works I have referred to thus far were published forty years or more after the end of the Second World War. The belatedness of these engagements may be partly attributed to the impact of the Troubles on Northern Irish poetry, but it is also possible that the various commemorations of the fortieth, fiftieth, and sixtieth anniversaries of the D-Day landings and VE and VJ Days during the mid-1980s, 1990s, and 2000s, all extensively covered by the media, awakened an interest in the war, or

---

[4]   Paulin, 'The Caravans of Lunëberg Heath', *Fivemiletown*, p. 66.
[5]   Ciaran Carson, 'Dresden', *Collected Poems* (Oldcastle, Co. Meath: Gallery Press, 2008), pp. 77–81 (p. 80).
[6]   R Greacen, contribution to 'The War Years in Ulster (1939–45): A Symposium', *Honest Ulsterman 64*, p. 20.

indeed that the passage of time allowed interest to build. In the introduction to his anthology *Earth Voices Whispering: An Anthology of Irish
War Poetry 1914–1945* (2008), dedicated, significantly, to the memory
of Robert Greacen, Gerald Dawe notes that although the Troubles have
'occupied considerable political, cultural and poetic space, public and private reaction to the wars of the first half of the twentieth century have not
been as widely considered, even though the cost in human and political
terms was much greater'. For poets born in the 1930s and 1940s, Dawe
observes that 'war is tangential, something overheard or witnessed from
afar, etched in the lives and words of family members and neighbours, and
found in the childhood landscapes of their poems'.[7] An enduring sense of a
postponement, or of keeping the war at a distance, is alluded to by Heaney
in an interview published in 2008, when he talks of the recurrence of the
Second World War in his later poetry as 'a matter of coming to terms with
reality' and, more obliquely, as 'A matter of things once taken for granted
being granted too casually their sombre significance'.[8] I have discussed in
the previous chapter how writers of Catholic and nationalist backgrounds
have sometimes betrayed unease over the Second World War, and Seamus
Heaney's war poems in *District and Circle* perhaps reflect such unease, as
he questions the extent of the impact of the war on Mossbawn, despite
the unavoidable and incongruous presence of the American military and
its machines in the area. In 'The Aerodrome' he writes that 'Wherever the
world was, we were somewhere else,/Had been and would be', echoing
the first section of his autobiographical essay 'Mossbawn' (written almost
thirty years earlier) when he describes how 'The American bombers groan
towards the aerodrome at Toomebridge, the American troops manoeuvre
in the fields along the road, but all of that great historical action does
not disturb the rhythms of the yard'.[9] Heaney seems to remain uncon-
vinced that the war had any lasting impact on Mossbawn or on his rural
upbringing. The Northern Irish countryside was physically altered by
the construction of airfields and military bases, by the influx of evacuees and refugees, and by the blackout, but rural areas were not targeted
in air attacks and suffered far less as a result. Heaney's 1975 prose poem

[7] Gerald Dawe, 'Introduction', in *Earth Voices Whispering: An Anthology of Irish War
Poetry 1914–1945* (Belfast: Blackstaff Press, 2008), pp. xvii–xx (p. xvii, pp. xviii–xix).
[8] Dennis O'Driscoll, *Stepping Stones: Interviews with Seamus Heaney* (London: Faber and
Faber, 2008), p. 358.
[9] Seamus Heaney, 'The Aerodrome', *District and Circle* (London: Faber and Faber,
2006), pp. 11–12 (p. 11); Heaney, 'Mossbawn', in *Preoccupations: Selected Prose 1968–
1978* (London: Faber and Faber, 1980), pp. 17–27 (p. 17). The first section of 'Mossbawn',
entited 'Omphalos', was broadcast on BBC Radio 4 in 1978 (*Preoccupations*, pp. 17–21
[p. 21]).

'England's Difficulty' describes being brought outdoors at night on an adult's shoulders to see the sky over Belfast glowing during the Blitz.[10]

This chapter reconsiders the importance of an earlier generation of northern poets who lived through the war as young adults and were unable to keep it at a distance from their work. Robert Greacen described the impact of the war on his own development as a poet:

> The formative period in my creative writing life was the 1940s, the first half of which saw the most terrible war in human history with its disruption of life, its mass carnage and organized brutality, its movement of populations— against all of which we poets beat our wings in vain.[11]

This earlier generation has been marginalized in discussions of Northern Irish poetry, as is evident from the testy reaction of Greacen's friend and fellow poet Roy McFadden to Jon Stallworthy's 1995 biography of Louis MacNeice. Reviewing this book, McFadden took particular exception to Stallworthy's claim that MacNeice's reputation had been re-established by the 'next generation' of Northern Irish poets:

> ...whom he names, indiscriminately, as Mahon, Muldoon, Paulin, McDonald, Heaney and Longley. He expresses gratitude to 'ten friends who read the typescript and improved it with their comments and corrections'. Mr and Mrs Longley and Tom Paulin are among the advisers named. Did they omit to point out that the 'next generation of Northern Irish poets' to that of MacNeice in fact consists of Craig, Greacen, McFadden, Fiacc and Montague? Mr Stallworthy should note for the paperback to restore the legitimate 'next generation' to its proper place in the succession.[12]

The international success of post-war generations of Northern poets—war babies and baby boomers—in the final third of the twentieth century has certainly eclipsed those writers who were present and active in the province during the Second World War. Until recently, critical appraisal of this period has been scarce, with the exception of Terence Brown's *Northern Voices* (1975). Richard Kirkland's contribution to *The Oxford Handbook of Modern Irish Poetry* (2012) provides an important corrective to this, describing the wartime revival as a 'more troubled, if equally vigorous, affair' than the emergence of talent during the 1960s, but concluding that 'it is in their ultimate failure to refashion [local] antinomies that their interest now resides'.[13]

---

[10] Seamus Heaney, 'England's Difficulty', *Opened Ground: Poems 1966–1996* (London: Faber and Faber, 1998), p. 85.

[11] Greacen, *Sash*, p. 169.

[12] McFadden, 'Corrigibly Plural', *Fortnight 337*, p. 41.

[13] Richard Kirkland, 'The Poetics of Partition: Poetry and Northern Ireland in the 1940s', in *The Oxford Handbook of Modern Irish Poetry*, edited by Fran Brearton and Alan Gillis (Oxford: Oxford University Press, 2012), pp. 210–224 (p. 211, p. 224).

Gerald Dawe's recent anthology is striking in the broadness of its selection, but anthologies have also tended to avoid the poets examined in this chapter. Of four significant anthologies of Irish poetry, Brendan Kennelly's *Penguin Book of Irish Verse* (1970), John Montague's *Faber Book of Irish Verse* (1974), Paul Muldoon's *Faber Book of Contemporary Irish Poetry* (1984), and Thomas Kinsella's *New Oxford Book of Irish Verse* (1986, rev. edn. 2001), none contains any poetry by Robert Greacen, one (Kennelly) contains a sole poem from McFadden, and only the Kennelly and Montague anthologies contain any poetry by John Hewitt or W.R. Rodgers.[14] Frank Ormsby's *Poets from the North of Ireland* (1979, rev. edn. 1990) features poems by Greacen, McFadden and Rodgers, but as with the other anthologies, none of the poems selected refer directly to the Second World War. As Kirkland's assessment indicates, some avoidance of this period is understandable: undergraduate poetry by Greacen and McFadden is sometimes clumsy in its evident desire to respond to events of immense historical magnitude, and time has not been kind to much of Rodgers' apocalyptic verse. Here I am less concerned with quality than with describing some of the cultural and historical pressures at work on poets in the province at the time.

Michael Longley has described the Belfast Group of poets to which he belonged as having given 'an air of seriousness and electricity to the notion of writing'.[15] Quoting Longley, Fran Brearton observes that this was 'something which had been lacking in Belfast, despite the best efforts of the earlier generation of McFadden, Hewitt and Rodgers to promote a Northern cultural energy in the 1940s'.[16] McFadden himself pre-empted Brearton's assessment in 1961. Looking back at the literary activity of the war years with regret, he wrote that although fifteen years previously it had seemed that a group of writers in Northern Ireland 'was emerging to form the basis of a local contemporary literature', this had ultimately failed. He lamented that 'today the group has disintegrated, the wild geese have flown away or been changed into domestic fowl. We have no coherent body of writing'.[17] McFadden reaffirmed his belief in the special atmosphere of the

---

[14] It should be noted that McFadden voluntarily withdrew his work from John Montague's anthology, citing an unspecified 'nasty experience' (Letter from Roy McFadden to Robert Greacen, 7 July 1968, Robert Greacen Collection, Linen Hall Library Belfast, Box 4, File 5).

[15] Michael Longley, 'The Longley Tapes', interview with Robert Johnstone, *Honest Ulsterman 78* (Summer 1985), pp. 13–31 (p. 22).

[16] Brearton, 'Poetry of the 1960s: The Northern Ireland Renaissance', *Cambridge Companion to Contemporary Irish Poetry*, p. 101.

[17] McFadden, 'Reflections on Megarrity', *Threshold 5*, no. 1, p. 25.

war years in an essay published thirty-three years later, but modified his pessimistic assessment of post-war developments in the province:

> Literary decades are invented by critics for their own convenience. However, up to a point, the Forties commanded a particular unity, in that the war occupied much of the decade, with a common climate of carnage, boredom and, ironically, the exhilaration and heightened sense of being that responds to danger.[18]

He goes on to describe how poetic activity was stimulated during the war by 'the blackout and by a moving trainbound population of troops and workers' and centred around the literary magazines and small-scale, independent publications such as *The Northman, Lagan*, and *Northern Harvest*.[19] McFadden notes with some sadness the fact that few poets chose to remain in Northern Ireland, claiming that by the end of the war he and John Hewitt were the only poets still living in Belfast. He also expresses perceptible resentment at subsequent generations of northern poets when he claims that after the closure of the magazine *Rann* in 1953 'the North fell largely silent again—for a decade and a half—until affluence beckoned with an open hand and the Muse became the kept woman of the universities'.[20]

McFadden was and remained a committed pacifist, but a degree of nostalgia for the war years is discernible in these retrospective analyses and in private correspondence between Greacen and McFadden from the early 1960s, when they briefly contemplated collaborating on an anthology of 1940s northern poetry. In these writings McFadden seems regretful that an opportunity to make a greater impression on both the locality and the world of letters was missed by the group of which he felt himself to be a member.[21] This chapter examines poems by Greacen and McFadden which directly respond to the war, before exploring the poetry of two older poets: John Hewitt and W.R. Rodgers. Hewitt aside, on an empirical basis the war had a clear impact on these poets. Of the forty-two poems in Greacen's first collection *One Recent Evening* (1944), eighteen refer directly to the

---

[18] Roy McFadden, 'The Belfast Forties', *Force 10* (Autumn 1994), pp. 68–73 (p. 68).

[19] McFadden, 'The Belfast Forties', *Force 10*, p. 68. The Queen's University Belfast student magazine *The Northman* was briefly known as the *New Northman* during the 1930s and early 1940s, but reverted to the title of *The Northman* for the Winter 1941–1942 edition. Despite this change in names, both *The Northman* and the *New Northman* should be considered as the same publication, and the change in name had no impact on the numbering of editions. It is possible that the change of name may have been inspired by the popularity at this time of the left-leaning London magazine the *New Statesman and Nation*.

[20] McFadden, 'The Belfast Forties', *Force 10*, p. 72.

[21] Letters from McFadden to Greacen, 12 November 1962, 4 December 1962, Greacen Collection, Box 4, File 3.

war, of McFadden's first, *Swords and Ploughshares* (1943), seven from
nineteen, and Rodgers' first collection, *Awake! and Other Poems* (1941),
is dominated by references to the patterns and paraphernalia of modern
warfare.

A genuine belief in some kind of 'energy' was certainly palpable in critical prose writing of the war years: in an essay published in February 1943
Greacen wrote that a 'literary resurgence has come to fruition in a time of
darkened streets, or reorientation of life in a thousand details, at a period
when huge masses of armed men and machinery tumble through our
countryside'. His tone was overwhelmingly optimistic:

> Undoubtedly the presence of so many foreign troops on the streets is having
> the effect of drawing on the imagination of local people and of blowing a
> wholesome spirit through a closed-in and soured atmosphere. Young Ulster
> is on the march—energetic, enthusiastic, idealistic.[22]

In a discussion with Geoffrey Taylor published in *The Bell* in July 1943,
Roy McFadden argued that 'There is no mist on our bogs, but there
have been bombs on our cities; and I think it natural that we should be
more concerned with a society that produces and tolerates such enormities than with the silk of the kine'.[23] A. Trevor Tolley has observed
the contradiction between McFadden's vehement denunciation of
rural subject matter in the exchange and the nature of much of his
early poetry, such as the collection *Flowers for a Lady* (1945), which
is 'increasingly permeated by his feeling for Ulster life and the Ulster
landscape'.[24] Both Greacen and McFadden published bold pronouncements on poetry during the war years that were at odds with the poetry
they themselves were actually writing: contradiction might indeed be
said to be a feature of their work. In poetry and prose, both poets often
attempted to define themselves against the southern state, here implied
in McFadden's crude contrast of 'bombs' with 'bogs'. Similarly, the 'silk
of the kine'—a traditional (and significantly rural) characterization of
Ireland as the finest of cattle—is contrasted with the 'enormities' of war,

---

[22] Robert Greacen, 'When Peace Breaks in Ulster', *The Bell* 5, no. 5 (February 1943),
pp. 397–399(pp. 397–398, p. 399). 'Young Ulster' may refer to the society of the same
name founded by the playwright Thomas Carnduff in 1936. Many of the writers with
whom this study is concerned, including John Hewitt, Denis Ireland, and Roy McFadden,
attended and spoke at Young Ulster gatherings in Belfast during the Second World War.
The 1943–47 minute book of the society is held in the Thomas Carnduff Archive, Queen's
University Belfast, MS21/13.
[23] Roy McFadden and Geoffrey Taylor, 'Poetry in Ireland: A Discussion', *The Bell* 6, no.
4 (July 1943), pp. 338–346(p. 343).
[24] A. Trevor Tolley, *The Poetry of the Forties* (Manchester: Manchester University Press,
1985), p. 165.

produced by an implicitly more powerful 'society' of greater contemporary consequence.[25]

Greacen and McFadden used Belfast's experience of the war to assert the relevance and importance of their work, and the Second World War arguably aided their resistance of dominant southern poetic forms. The war gave the young northern poets a more secure platform from which to write, as Northern Ireland's direct and sustained experience of the conflict and the hardening of the border as a physical reality deepened the sense of separation from the southern state. In a later part of the dialogue not quoted by Tolley, McFadden articulates an anxiety he shared with his contemporaries:

> Culturally, I know, we are bastards, and perhaps it is not such a bad thing for the thoroughbred is liable to strange ailments. We are faced with the problem of creating a literary tradition in the north; but, though it must inevitably be strongly influenced by contemporary happenings in English poetry, there is no reason why we should not absorb that influence and build it into something of our own. Sometimes I think we are the least English part of Ireland.[26]

Edna Longley does not dwell on work by Greacen, McFadden, or Rodgers in any of the essays that make up *The Living Stream: Literature and Revisionism in Ireland* (1994), but an exploration of the concerns and influences evident in their war poetry gives further credence to her conception in this volume of Northern Ireland as a 'frontier-region, a cultural corridor, a zone where Ireland and Britain permeate one another' and to her identification of an important 'intersection between the British 1930s and the flawed political entities in Ireland'. She argues that 'This intersection, which cuts two ways and may have implications for culture and poetry in the other island too, was itself subject to change during the years 1939–1945'.[27] In 1942 Robert Greacen anticipated this analysis with clarity:

> The conclusion from the political and geographic facts is surely this—that the Six Counties, so far, despite all its reputed hard-headedness, has not had the cunning (if altruism is left out of the count) to act as the bridgehead between Ireland and Great Britain and to suck the best out of the English,

---

[25] The expression 'silk of the kine' is found in James Joyce, *Ulysses*, edited by Hans Walter Gabler (New York: Random House, 1986), p. 12: 403. According to Declan Kiberd, the expression, in Irish 'síoda na mbó', is an image of Ireland taken from the famous lyric 'Droimeann Donn Dílis' (Kiberd, *The Irish Writer and the World* [Cambridge: Cambridge University Press, 2005], p. 61).

[26] McFadden and Taylor, 'Poetry in Ireland: A Discussion', *The Bell* 6, no. 4, pp. 343–344.

[27] Edna Longley, 'From Cathleen to Anorexia' and 'Progressive Bookmen', *Living Stream*, p. 195 and p. 121.

the Gaelic and the Anglo-Irish cultures. Until very recently, the Northern Irish writer looked for a lead either to the Southern capital or to London: today he is beginning to realize, with pardonable arrogance, that he is in a position to inform both capitals about each other and, more important, to tell them about Ulster.[28]

One such 'intersection' or 'bridgehead' can be discerned in the trouble-some impact of English poetry of the previous decade on poets in Belfast during the war. As noted in the previous chapter, 1930s poetry is hugely important to Brian Moore's heavily autobiographical novel of Belfast at war, *The Emperor of Ice Cream*, in which the imaginative life of the pro-tagonist, seventeen-year-old Gavin Burke, is dominated by the poems that appear in *The Faber Book of Modern Verse* (1936). Quotations from some of these, including the Wallace Stevens poem from which the novel takes its title, W.H. Auden's 'Consider', Louis MacNeice's 'An Eclogue for Christmas', and W.B. Yeats' 'The Second Coming', appear within the text of the novel itself.[29] Later it is mentioned that Freddie Hargreaves—Gavin's older friend and guide through Belfast's enclaves of socialism and hedonism—is reading *The Waste Land* and Auden and MacNeice's *Letters from Iceland* at the ARP post.[30] The importance of the 'End of Days' poems by Auden, MacNeice, and Yeats to Gavin's apocalyptic view of the world would tend to support Patricia Craig's claim that the discovery of the Faber collection was crucial to Moore's own artistic development, and their presence in the novel also suggests that these poets loomed large in the imaginative consciousness of Moore and other aspiring Belfast-born writers of his generation: he and McFadden were born in 1921, Greacen in 1920.[31] Moore recalled in 1974 that at the outbreak of war he was 'very left wing… it was an era when anyone who read was very left wing, we were all under the influence of Auden and Spender and these people'.[32]

---

[28] Robert Greacen, 'A Survey of Ulster Writing', *The Northman XI*, no. 2 (Winter 1942–1943), pp. 10–14 (p. 10).

[29] Moore, *Emperor*, pp. 11–12.   [30] Moore, *Emperor*, p. 69, p. 76.

[31] Craig, *Brian Moore*, p. 76. One of Robert Greacen's later collections of poetry is enti-tled *The Only Emperor*, and includes at least one poem which directly recalls the Second World War. 'Drummond Allison, 1921–43' subtitled 'Killed in action on the Garigliano, Italy, 2 December 1943' describes an evening spent with the eponymous English sol-dier poet, a friend of Greacen, in wartime Belfast, and laments Allison's premature death (Greacen, 'Drummond Allison, 1921–43', *The Only Emperor* [Belfast: Lapwing, 1994], p. 9). The title poem which opens the volume describes a bomb scare in Troubles-era Belfast, in which Greacen walks on 'intent on Wallace Stevens as a bomb explodes (p. 7).

[32] 'An Answer from Limbo', BBC Radio Ulster, 11 May 1975, BBC Northern Ireland Archive, Ulster Folk and Transport Museum, Cultra, Co Down, # BBC (BBE 19/UT619). The programme's recording date is listed in the archive as 4 May 1975, but the announcer at the beginning of the broadcast reports that Moore's contribution was recorded at a seminar on contemporary Irish writing in Toronto the previous year.

During the early years of the war at least, the poetry of Auden and his contemporaries greatly preoccupied Greacen and his friends. In his autobiography *The Sash My Father Wore* (1997), Robert Greacen wrote that following his discovery of literature and socialist politics at school, reading these English poets encouraged his adolescent socialist convictions towards the end of that decade. Instead of working on homework, Greacen would listen to Marxist lectures, watch Soviet films by Eisenstein and Pudovkin, plays by Clifford Odets, or would sit in his bedroom reading Auden, C. Day Lewis, or Stephen Spender. Older friends at Queen's described Russia to him in glowing terms, and assured him that reports of the existence of 'concentration camps' and reports of the extermination of minorities were 'capitalist lies'.[33] His immersion in socialist culture led to a temporary infatuation with the Soviet Union, briefly and colourfully sketched:

> I could indeed hear the 'opening of a new theme'. Bliss was it in that Red Dawn to be alive, but to be young was a veritable Soviet heaven!
>
> Within a year or two, I was to be sadly disillusioned by it all. The dream crumbled before the iron realities like the Soviet–German pact and the disclosures of savage Stalinist repression of the kind that came to be openly admitted by Soviet leaders. The god had failed. For the time being there was blinding new light in eastern Europe, and it was spreading a crimson glow over the sleeping west. Awake! Awake! Even in faction-ridden, obscurantist Belfast, if one peered closely into the heavens, it was possible to discern the proud Red Star. It could shine for us, too, and the Lagan could flow crimson.[34]

Underlying Greacen's prose, characteristically exaggerated for comic effect, is a perceptible regret that the apparent hope that a socialist revolution might present a solution to 'faction-ridden' Belfast's sectarian divisions proved illusory.

For much of the latter half of the 1930s the *New Northman* published what might be expected of a student magazine, carrying reports on sport and music in the university, features on foreign travels, political commentary, and book reviews. Some mid-1930s issues do respond to international political developments: the Winter 1935–1936 edition, for example, carries a report on a meeting of the Belfast Peace League, noting its disquiet with the activities of 'the armament manufacturers and the war profiteers'.[35] Poetry was published without fanfare, with a few poems dotted around the magazine. The first poem by Robert Greacen to appear was in the first wartime issue of the *New Northman*, in Autumn 1939. 'From My

---

[33] Greacen, *Sash*, p. 61.   [34] Greacen, *Sash*, p. 62.
[35] 'The Peace League', *New Northman IV*, no. 1 (Winter 1935–1936), p. 16.

Window (Pre-War)' was attributed only to 'R.G.', but the bracketed reference to war demonstrates the eighteen-year-old Greacen's desire to write as
a poet of contemporary significance: many subsequent poems published
during the war are also given titles or subtitles which anchor the works to
the date of their composition and proclaim their relevance to matters of
current and pressing importance.[36] Then in the following issue an article
by T. Cusack on William Morris (prompted by the fact that on 24 March
1940 Morris would have been 106) focused on Morris's poetry and revolutionary socialist credentials, and concluded by pronouncing him 'founder
of a tradition of Socialist poets, to-day carried on by Auden, Spender,
MacNeice, Cecil Day Lewis, and others'—a quartet whose names would
repeatedly surface in the magazine over the next few years.[37]

   Such material anticipated the new direction that the magazine would
take from its Winter 1940–1941 issue, which carried an editorial on its
first page entitled 'A New Order in The "New Northman"?', written by
one of the new editors, Robert Greacen—the other was his friend and fellow poet John Gallen. Promising that the magazine would henceforth be
free from discussion of university affairs, Greacen deplores the 'isolation'
of Queen's from the surrounding community, arguing that this is 'clearly
illustrated by the continued failure of the *New Northman* to occupy the
long-vacant niche that exists in Northern Ireland for an indigenous literary magazine, and its persistent elbowing into the already congested ranks
of politically vociferous native journals'.[38] Self-conscious, perhaps, of the
magazine's provincial origins, the article contrasts the perceived lack of success of the *New Northman* with Oxford and Cambridge university magazines that had found specialized readerships all over Britain, and notes
that Trinity College Dublin manages to produce eight issues of its own
magazine for each edition of the *New Northman*. Greacen proposes that
the magazine's new incarnation should be rooted in Queen's, but invites
contributions from 'a larger body of Northmen', including local young
writers who find it difficult to publish their work, and older writers who
turn at present to English publishers, or to outlets in Dublin. His call for
'a new character, a less obfuscated style, clearer prose, sweeter verse, more
consideration for common standards of taste' is followed on the same page
by Roy McFadden's poem 'Song'.[39]

---

[36] R.G., 'From My Window (Pre-War)', *New Northman VII*, no. 3 (Autumn 1939),
p. 87.
   [37] T. Cusack, 'William Morris', *New Northman VIII*, no. 1 (Spring 1940), pp. 13–15
(p. 15).
   [38] 'A New Order in The "New Northman"?', *New Northman VIII*, no. 3 (Winter 1940–
1941), pp. 45–46 (p. 45). The editorial was unsigned.
   [39] 'A New Order in The "New Northman"?', *New Northman VIII*, no. 3, p. 46.

Having seemingly already discarded his socialist convictions, Greacen confesses in this editorial to a 'personal aversion to politics as a human activity. As was Jeremy Bentham, so am I disposed to look on politics as a necessary evil and, as such, preferably left, like vivisection or prostitution, to those with a flair for it'.[40] Writing that political dialectics 'verge on the anachronistic', he argues that after Churchill's comment that any issue other than winning the war is irrelevant, matters such as the treaty ports controversy 'have reached the inoperable stage... War aims, post-war organization and the like ideological preoccupations are like the pious resolves of the stricken toper to lead a better life if he is spared'.[41] Announcing that the magazine intends to avoid domestic politics entirely, Greacen comments sarcastically that pronouncements by the *New Northman* on the Irish situation 'cannot be welcomed either by the contending parties, who want no blurring scholasticisms introduced among their beautifully clear cut issues, or by the University, which is disadvantageously situated to be an outpost for political franc tireurs'.[42]

The magazine had undergone radical surgery. The same edition featured short stories and poems, including an impenetrable piece of surrealist fiction entitled 'Provided "X" is Real' and published under the initial 'G'. In a short essay entitled 'Words and Emotions in Contemporary Literature', Jack Boyd argued for a return to high modernist principles, claiming that the debilitating effect of modern mass culture on audiences had presented the modern artist with considerable problems, and advising serious writers to avoid using certain words 'which were once pregnant with meaning and rich in suggestive overtones', such as 'patriotism', 'blood', 'mother', or 'home'. Citing Joyce and Eliot as true revolutionaries, Boyd continued:

> The younger writers have adopted different ideologies and creeds. There are Marxists, surrealists, and the rest. But the war came and upset everything. W. H. Auden and C. Isherwood, after writing a book, *Journey to a War*, now fled from a war; MacNeice has cleared the last ditch; Huxley is interested in yogi and Eastern Philosophy. All are safe in America.[43]

The tone of disapproval here at the flight from Europe of Auden, Isherwood, and MacNeice is echoed in many of the writings of the young Belfast poets during the war. Communist sympathies had been discredited by the Molotov–Ribbentrop pact of August 1939—a circumstance which may

---

[40] 'A New Order in The "New Northman"?', *New Northman VIII*, no. 3, p. 45.
[41] 'A New Order in The "New Northman"?', *New Northman VIII*, no. 3, p. 45.
[42] 'A New Order in The "New Northman"?', *New Northman VIII*, no. 3, p. 45.
[43] Jack Boyd, 'Words and Emotions in Contemporary Literature', *New Northman VIII*, no. 3, p. 54. This was John Boyd, later editor of the little magazine *Lagan* and a friend of both Greacen and McFadden.

explain the reluctance of this younger body of creative writers in Queen's to adhere to existing political groupings.[44] From the content of the magazine it is clear that the poetry of Auden and his contemporaries remained much on the minds of Greacen and *his* contemporaries, however.[45] Towards the back of that same Winter 1940–1941 issue Greacen reports on the first meeting of 'A New Group The Verse and Drama Reading Society' [*sic*], at which the Englishman Harold F. Brooks—an assistant lecturer attached to the English department during the war—spoke on the influence of Wilfred Owen on poets of the 1930s. The article concludes thus:

> After dealing with Messrs. Auden, Spender and MacNeice, Dr Brooks brought the talk to a fitting conclusion by having a passage read from Mr T.S. Eliot's recently published 'East Coker'.
>
> The next meeting will take place in the English Seminar on January 16, 1941, when we shall read Messrs. Auden and Isherwood's 'The Ascent of F6'.[46]

The following issue reported that 'First this term we ascended Auden and Isherwood's *F.6*. Whether it was exhaustion of the mountain air that turned our heads, I cannot say, but at our next meeting we read A.A. Milne's *Mr Pim Passes By*'.[47] The interest in these writers is hardly unusual, but the references to Auden and his contemporaries do encourage the idea that taking control of the *New Northman* was part of a project to draw together a new group, defining itself (in part) against poets of the previous decade.[48]

---

[44] In the province itself, the hegemonic nature of unionist rule also undoubtedly depressed many younger writers of the time and discouraged them from any involvement with existing political parties and institutions at a local level.

[45] Auden's poetry was also popular with non-academic readers in Belfast at the time. Moya Woodside reports that at a meeting of ten friends in October 1940 to discuss forming a winter reading group, one contributor recalled having just read 'September 1940' and 'Refugee Blues' one night just before the air-raid siren sounded (Woodside, 26 October 1940).

[46] Robert Greacen, 'A New Group The Verse and Drama Reading Society', *New Northman VIII*, no. 3, p. 65.

[47] 'Pro Bono Suo', 'Verse and Drama Reading Society', *New Northman IX*, no. 1 (Spring 1941), p. 15.

[48] Roy McFadden seems later to have had reservations about the idea of poetic groupings, writing in 'The Poet's Audience' that:

> From time to time in the history of literature, poets become aware of the need for an audience. We saw it most recently in the Thirties with Auden, Spender and C. Day Lewis. The desire to belong to a group is, of course, a natural one; but when it reaches the point of a poet attempting in his poetry to express a group feeling then it becomes a real danger: for any group feeling or consciousness exists at a very low level: most patriotism, desire for national vengeance; adoration of some national idol. A poet is not a television set. He is an individual concerned with his own experiences and its translation into something significant in terms of the past and present.

(McFadden Papers, MP5, unpublished, single sheet handwritten).

Writing after the death of Robert Greacen, Patricia Craig described the emergence of a 'coterie of talented and nonconformist writers' in Belfast during the war:

> As well as Greacen and McFadden, it included authors and BBC men such as John Boyd and Sam Hanna Bell, novelists, poets, critics and dramatists. It was, in some sense, presided over by writers of a slightly older vintage, like the poet John Hewitt—and it bridged the gap between Louis MacNeice/W.R. Rodgers and the 1960s generation of Heaney–Longley–Mahon.[49]

It is important not to overstate the importance of such a 'coterie': it is arguable that the emergence of such a group was inevitable in a city with few outlets for publication and a muted tradition of creative writing, and that resident writers assembled and interacted simply because they wrote at all, rather than because they adhered to any distinct literary or political ideology. It could even be argued that in Belfast at this time the practice of writing itself constituted nonconformity. In such a way, and as Craig implies, there was considerable overlap between older and younger generations of writers in the city: the little magazine *Lagan*, for example, carried poems by McFadden alongside contributions by older writers such as Sam Hanna Bell, Joseph Tomelty, Hewitt, and Rodgers. In the introduction to the collection *Lyra* (1942), its editors Alex Comfort and Greacen are certainly keen to foster the impression of a group of young writers in Northern Ireland (with Greacen himself at its head), as they write that 'The Irish-Ulster group, who are more like a school than any of the others, includes Greacen, McFadden, Gallen, and Brooks (who is English). They are evolving something which again is new—a form of poetic realism'.[50] This frustratingly nebulous proclamation of 'poetic realism' is swiftly followed by an attack on Stephen Spender: here and elsewhere Greacen is forthright in condemning what he is against, but less effective in articulating a positive alternative. Given their youth and given the vast and confusing context against which they wrote, these shortcomings are understandable, but the vehemence of Greacen's and McFadden's attacks on Auden and his contemporaries—in particular, McFadden's dismissals

[49] Patricia Craig, 'Robert Greacen: Ulster Poet of Considerable Gifts', *Independent*, 22 May 2008.

[50] Alex Comfort and Robert Greacen, 'A Word from the Editors', in *Lyra: An Anthology of New Lyric*, edited by Alex Comfort and Robert Greacen (Billericay, Essex: The Grey Walls Press, 1942), pp. 12–14(p. 13). In the same introduction, Comfort and Greacen also claimed that 'Any attempt to represent it as a school is perversity pure and simple. Its sole object is to collect and present in a permanent binding poems which the editors felt deserving of a wider public' (p. 12), and that 'The fact that the book becomes, of itself, a contribution to a new romanticism, is again a reflection of our taste' (p. 13).

of Louis MacNeice—should not go unchallenged, nor should Greacen's apparent adherence to the New Apocalypse—a so-called movement which in retrospect can be seen to have faltered in the face of such upheaval.[51]

There seems little 'realism' of any kind in the poems Greacen himself contributed to *Lyra*, none of which address the war directly. The editorial is implicitly critical of Spender for asking why younger poets offered no imaginative analysis of 'the struggle in which we are engaged' (Comfort and Greacen suggest that younger poets see the war instead as a 'cosmic calamity like the rain or the big winds'), so the mention of a father 'Soldiering his introspection to the daily struggle' in Greacen's own 'Lines for Friends expecting a Baby at Christmas 1941' is indicative of the problematic inconsistencies between his prose and his poetry.[52] It is hard to identify a coherent approach or adherence to a particular set of views or beliefs in the writings of Greacen and McFadden: Terence Brown has described how the young poets' attempts to follow the New Apocalypse during the war were largely unsuccessful, and by 1976 (the year after Brown's *Northern Voices* was published) Greacen himself admitted that McFadden and he had merely 'fellow-travelled' with the movement.[53] Contradictions can be found in abundance between the poetry and prose of both writers during the war. Greacen may have attempted to turn the *New Northman* into an organ of the New Apocalypse movement, publishing contributions from such luminaries as Henry Treece and Greacen's later collaborator Alex Comfort, but, as Brown observes, the influences on his early poetry can also be traced to the 'Pylon' school. Roy McFadden was similarly inconsistent. Claiming boldly in *The Bell* in 1943 that 'The past, as we have realised in the north, has no virtue except in so far as it may point a moral for the present', in the poem 'The Pattern', published in the collection *Swords and Ploughshares* that same year, he wrote that

---

[51] The 'New Apocalypse' is an imprecise term. It has been described as:

> A group of writers who flourished briefly as a group in the 1940s, united by a reaction against what they saw as the 'classicism' of W.H. Auden. It was characterized by wild, turbulent, and at times surreal imagery. They described themselves as 'anti-cerebral', claiming a 'large, accepting attitude to life', invoked the name of D.H. Lawrence, and approved of Dylan Thomas. George Barker, Vernon Watkins and Henry Treece were associated with the movement.

('New Apocalypse', *The Oxford Companion to English Literature*, edited by Dinah Birch [Oxford: Oxford University Press, 2011], <http://www.oxfordreference.com/view/10.1093/oi/authority.20110810105459520>)

[52] Comfort and Greacen, 'A Word from the Editors', *Lyra*, p. 13; Greacen, 'Lines for Friends expecting a Baby at Christmas 1941', *Lyra*, pp. 36–37 (p. 36).

[53] Terence Brown, 'Robert Greacen and Roy McFadden: Apocalypse and Survival' in *Northern Voices: Some Poets from Ulster* (Dublin: Gill and Macmillan, 1975), pp. 128–139 (p. 129); Greacen, 'Writing Through the Irish Blitz', *Irish Times*, 4 June 1976.

'out of the frail/Flotsam of the shipwrecked centuries,/I speak, builded with their bone and anger'.[54]

I do not believe that the crooked and disputed faultlines of the New Apocalypse, New Realism, Surrealism, Personalism, or Neo-Romanticism are of much use in a Northern Irish context: unlike London, the poetic community in the province was too small, and, as McFadden implies in the *Force 10* article, too bound by the timeframe of the war, to sustain similar fractures or the ensuing competition between such groups. Robin Skelton has suggested that the New Apocalypse 'all boiled down to...a general discontent with the social-objective way of writing which prevailed in the thirties, plus some rather vague ideas about the importance of "mythical" imagery'.[55] It is enough to say that Greacen, McFadden, Gallen, and Gillespie were young men with vaguely leftist convictions, though often anti-political, collaborators for a time, poets who attempted a rejection of Ireland's historic divisions and preoccupations and were of a reasonably romantic sensibility. As Greacen's friend Derek Stanford observed in his memoir of the 1940s: 'Literary movements, especially in Britain, can subsist on a bare minimum of theory. Far more indispensable to them are willing or sympathetic editors and publishers'[56] Any sense of a movement in Belfast at this time is clearly dependent on the contextual background of the Second World War, which encouraged creative endeavour and enabled the dissemination of the results of such endeavour, undoubtedly granting these young poets far higher profiles than they could have expected in peacetime. The young northern poets inspired some curious boosterism on the part of the Belfast newspaper the *Northern Whig*, for example, which published an article in late 1941 with the headline 'Art Soars in North, Declines in South', citing the current number of the *New Northman* and the poetry of Greacen and McFadden.[57] The following January the newspaper hailed the fact that 'More and more undergraduates and members of staff are taking to the writing of poems and short stories', posed the oblique question 'Queen's and the Arts: A New Literary

[54] McFadden and Taylor, 'Poetry in Ireland: A Discussion', *The Bell* 6, no. 4, p. 343; Roy McFadden, 'The Pattern', *Collected Poems 1943–1995* (Belfast: Lagan Press, 1996), pp. 317–318(p. 317).

[55] Robin Skelton, 'Introduction' to *Poetry of the Forties*, (Harmondsworth: Penguin, 1968), pp. 15–31 (p. 25).

[56] Derek Stanford, *Inside the Forties: Literary Memoirs 1937–1957* (London: Sidgwick and Jackson, 1977), p. 85.

[57] I have been unable to locate an exact reference for this article. A cutting is included in Roy McFadden's cuttings scrapbook (McFadden Papers, CN2) dated 4 November 1941, but the article does not appear in that day's edition of the newspaper nor in any editions of the *Northern Whig* from that week. It seems likely that the date was wrongly recorded by McFadden himself.

Movement?', and claimed that 'They Will Tell The South'.[58] The *Whig* clearly had its own cross-border agenda, but such headlines show how the advent of war impelled northern poetry to define itself against southern modes of expression.

The new direction taken by the *New Northman* under Greacen and Gallen was not favoured by all. In the following issue (Spring 1941) the Hibernophobic, Belfast-born, English-based playwright St John Ervine was stinging in his criticisms, in an essay spread over three pages entitled 'What's Wrong with the "New Northman"'. Describing the Oxbridge literary magazines which Greacen wished to emulate as 'sludge', Ervine attacks the *New Northman* on the grounds that it lacks value for money for the outsider, being filled with trivia about clubs of relevance only to Queen's students. The public, he says, is not interested in amateurs or experiments, and he deplores the publication of:

> ...feeble imitations of sour and disgruntled 'modern' poems, derived stuff whose most startling novelty is an abstention from initial capital letters, whose deepest defect is a tendency to confuse dull prose with duller verse, and stories which seem to have been written by persons who were begotten and born in underground urinals.[59]

Ervine also criticized the intentional editorial avoidance of political matters, urging the magazine to address economic disparities between Northern Ireland and the southern state, and warning of the threat posed by the prospect of a united Ireland to Belfast's status as a leading industrial city.[60] Letters to the magazine also took issue with Greacen's pronouncements: the poet and playwright Thomas Carnduff wrote 'as a worker' that 'Queen's University, or anything emanating from that institution, means very little to me', and R.P. Maybin called for more discussion of war aims.[61] At Queen's, fellow students also quickly made their dislike of the changes known, and the *New Northman* reverted to the title of *The Northman* for the Winter 1941–1942 issue. A year after that, in a magazine half its previous size and under a redesigned masthead, new editors wrote that in its previous incarnation the 'almost exclusively literary journal...was singularly deficient in interest for the ordinary Queen's student,

---

[58] Rachel B. Field, 'Queen's and the Arts: A New Literary Movement?', *Northern Whig and Belfast Post*, 5 January 1942.

[59] St John Ervine, 'What's Wrong with the "New Northman"', *New Northman IX*, no. 1, pp. 5–7 (p. 5).

[60] Ervine, 'What's Wrong with the "New Northman"', *New Northman IX*, no. 1, p. 7. I discuss Ervine's political views further in the fourth chapter on political writing.

[61] *New Northman IX*, no. 1, p. 11. Patrick Maybin was a close friend of John Hewitt— the men in fact met at a meeting of the poetry circle at Queen's. I refer to their wartime correspondence in the following chapter.

not excluding the Arts faculty', and reassured readers that they aimed to appeal to broader tastes and focus more on university matters.[62] Greacen's contributions, both poetic and critical, were still published in this issue, but in 1943 he left Belfast for Dublin. The attempt to make Queen's the centre of a new poetic movement had failed, and it was not until twenty years later that this ambition came to fruition.[63]

Greacen's Poundian roles as collaborator, convenor, and organizer of poetry and poets during the 1940s, in Belfast and then in Dublin and London, were arguably as important as his own poetic career. Over the decade, in addition to editing the *New Northman* and publishing his own collections *One Recent Evening* (1944) and *The Undying Day* (1948) Greacen also edited *Poems from Ulster* (1942); *Lyra* (1942) with Alex Comfort; *On the Barricades* (1944) with Bruce Williamson and Valentin Iremonger; *Northern Harvest* (1944) and its successor *Irish Harvest* (1946); and *Contemporary Irish Poetry* (1949), again with Iremonger. Listing most of these in a letter to Greacen in 1963, McFadden joked that during the forties his friend had been 'anthologising the unedited conscience of his race...with a zeal and persistence that haven't been repeated since'.[64] Before Greacen was twenty-one his work had been published in *Horizon* and *The Bell*, the pre-eminent literary journals in London and Dublin.[65] Greacen admitted in his memoirs that his academic career at Queen's was fatally damaged by his involvement in literary ventures, and having abandoned his degree he left for Dublin in 1943, to pursue a diploma in Social Studies at Trinity College.[66] His various professed adventures in England during the war (he claimed in his memoirs to have obtained assistance in breaching the travel restrictions with the help of an RUC sergeant who was a friend of an aunt) open up connections with the literary life of wartime London, as he worked with Alex Comfort and encountered, amongst others, Cyril Connolly, Reginald Moore, Tambimuttu, and Stephen Spender himself.[67]

In the early years of the war Greacen's professed antipathy towards the 1930s poets was sustained, however. The slim volume *Poems From Ulster* collected poems by himself, Brooks, Comfort, Gallen, and McFadden, as well as Leslie Gillespie and Nicholas Moore. Greacen's introduction

[62] W.N. Howe and A.B. Morrison, 'Editorial Notes', *The Northman XI*, no. 2 (Summer 1941), pp. 1–3 (p. 1).
[63] Heaney, 'Belfast' in *Preoccupations*, pp. 28–37 (p. 29).
[64] Letter from McFadden to Greacen, 27 April 1963, Greacen Collection, Box 4, File 5.
[65] Robert Greacen, 'Preface', in *Collected Poems 1944–1994* (Belfast: Lagan Press, 1995), pp. 13–15 (p. 14).
[66] Greacen, *Sash*, p. 126.
[67] Greacen, 'Writing Through the Irish Blitz', *Irish Times*, 4 June 1976.

deliberately contrasted the approach of these younger poets with the older generation of Auden and his contemporaries:

> One of the most significant facts for the potential poets of the Forties was the disintegration of the group that had attracted so much attention during the previous decade. Some of them had gone to the USA; New Verse was discontinued, New Writing became less frequent and less dynamic, and a sea of silence swamped the vociferous literati who had told us so often of their devotion to the extreme left . . . There has been a marked turning away from the frequently tinsel-like objectivity of the Thirties, and a new sincerity, simplicity and ardour have replaced the work of the effete hangers-on of the Auden–Spender–MacNeice–Lewis movement, of which only the quadruple alliance remains.[68]

The phrase 'vociferous literati' had already appeared in Greacen's third *New Northman* editorial in Summer 1941 (the recycling of material under different titles would continue for the rest of his writing career) in which he went on to take issue with '*Objective Reporters*, as some of them were called, [who] took to alcohol or writing scenarios for Hollywood, *in* Hollywood, having left too hurriedly even to pack their pylons into their suitcases'.[69] These attacks seem designed to disassociate Greacen's own work from that of these antecedents, since unfavourable comparisons were clearly being made at the time: that same edition of the *New Northman* carried a letter from Charles Monteith, later a commissioning editor and subsequently chairman of Faber and Faber, but at that time serving in the Royal Inniskilling Fusiliers and based in Northern Ireland. Monteith argued that in the province 'all our writers are caught in a lethal dilemma, from which they must escape or die—London or Dublin, which?' and criticized the muddled attempts of young writers to adhere to left-wing ideas, claiming that their chronic inability to choose whether to follow routes suggested by the work of Auden and Spender or to subscribe to an Irish nationalist agenda had weakened Ulster literature:

> You will see what I mean if you examine the work of Mr. Greacen, the most ambitious and promising of your poets. He evidently considers himself bound to write dutiful imitations of Auden and work himself into synthetical social rages. But after dreary passages of disjointed statements and confused imagery, he suddenly writes genuine poetry about Ireland and its curious spirituality which 'haunts life'.[70]

---

[68] Robert Greacen, 'Introduction', in Greacen (ed.), *Poems from Ulster*, pp. 3–5 (p. 4).
[69] R.G., 'New "New" Writing', *New Northman IX*, no. 2 (Summer 1941), pp. 17–18 (p. 17).
[70] Charles M. Monteith, 'Letter to the Editor', *New Northman IX*, no. 2, p. 31.

It is to Greacen's credit that he was willing as editor to publish such penetrating and uncomplimentary assessments of his own work, which in this case identifies poetic debts that he had publicly disavowed.

The idea that writers in the province had felt compelled since partition to choose between the literature of England and that of the newly independent southern state came under considerable scrutiny during the war. John Hewitt's explorations of regionalist ideas clearly attempted to resolve this dilemma, but of Greacen and McFadden it is the latter whose writings consistently display a closer affiliation with their birthplace. Written during the early years of the war, the unpublished essay 'Life and Writing in North-East Ulster' outlines some untapped subject matter for the Protestant writer in Belfast:

> It is by the Protestant writer that the problem awaits solution: the problem of seizing the sprawling city of Belfast with its furtive, cobbled side-streets and their slogans (*No Pope Here; Remember 1690; Up the I.R.A.*): the ugly city circled with tumbling hills and straggling fields, whose workers are only a few generations removed from the soil: Queen's Bridge thronged with the 'Island men' returning from the shipyard: the Falls road with the cage-cars on petrol: of taking this great blustering, tragi-comical mass and shaking a coherent literature out of it. Nowhere else in the world is there so much vivid material crying out to be used.
>
> The choice before the Ulster Protestant writer has long been one of taking the boat to England or the train to Dublin. Ruled by a political party whose knowledge of history begins and ends with 1690, he has had little opportunity of discovering that his province had a rich culture and civilization of its own.[71]

Evocative descriptions of Belfast scenes seem to provide the basis for McFadden's tangible optimism at this time that the province can develop its own modern tradition of writing, informed by political strife and realist industrial imagery.

The outbreak of the Second World War seems to have presented younger poets in Northern Ireland with an opportunity to escape the historic choice outlined by McFadden and Monteith. In a letter to the *Irish Times*, published on 11 July 1941, Greacen provoked outrage with talk of 'poetical impotence and sterility' in Ireland, and a denunciation of the 'inlooking' nationalism of preceding generations. Most of the letter was reprinted as part of a longer editorial entitled 'Modern Irish Poetry' in the *New Northman* later that year:

> Clique writing about Cathleen ni Houlihan and Brian Boru, like the private allusions of the minor members of the English 'Pylon' School of the

---

[71] McFadden, 'Life and Writing in North-East Ulster', McFadden Papers, MP5, p. 7.

Thirties, will leave little or no impression on the wider world of letters, when there is the urgent necessity for the reaffirmation and the reassessment of the elemental human values that have come into brutal contact with bomb and bayonet.

Greacen proposes that Irish poetry should be a 'spearhead of progressive thought' and 'should show an awareness of modern trends without being slavishly imitative either of the later Yeats or of T.S. Eliot or of the MacNeice–Auden–Spender–Lewis School?'[72] Greacen's references to pylons at this time are important. The term ' "Pylon" School' derived from Spender's poem 'The Pylons' and referred to those poets of the 1930s who had frequently dealt in industrial imagery, but 1941 also saw the publication of Louis MacNeice's critical study *The Poetry of W. B. Yeats*, the introduction of which describes hearing of the declaration of war whilst in Galway and contemplating the writing of the book itself:

> As soon as I heard on the wireless of the outbreak of war, Galway became unreal. And Yeats and his poetry became unreal also . . . My friends had been writing for years about the 'facts' of psychology, politics, science, economics, but the fact of war made their writing seem as remote as the pleasure dome of Xanadu. For war spares neither the poetry of Xanadu nor the poetry of pylons.[73]

In the face of a politically fractious and increasingly technologically sophisticated world, demonstrably capable of annihilating culture of any kind, MacNeice felt that the poetry of his contemporaries had swiftly been rendered irrelevant. His perception that Galway too 'became unreal' is also telling, implying that the outbreak of war had similarly swiftly effected a disconnection between Ireland and the pressing reality of war.

Echoes of MacNeice's introduction are clearly discernible in Robert Greacen's own less nuanced dismissals of Irish 'clique writing' and English poetry of the 1930s as outmoded and anachronistic in the face of the war. Greacen's editorial manifestos are strident when condemning the kind of poetry he dislikes, but vague when attempting to articulate what he is in favour of. In his first editorial for the *New Northman* in 1940 he writes of the need for a 'new character' and 'sweeter verse, more consideration for common standards of taste', argues in the 1941 'Modern Irish Poetry' essay that 'Simplicity, sensuousness and passion, as Milton holds, together with artistic and intellectual courage and honesty, are the only paths that lead

---

[72] 'Modern Irish Poetry', *New Northman X*, no. 3 (Autumn 1941), pp. 33–34 (p. 33).
[73] Louis MacNeice, *The Poetry of W. B. Yeats* (London: Oxford University Press, 1941), pp. 17–18.

to the truly intense poetic focus', and in *The Bell* two years later claims that 'It took the explosion of 1939 to release pent-up, genuine feeling and energy, and to quicken the sense of contemporary reality'.[74] None of this means very much at all, but it is possible to identify three main forces against which Greacen positions himself during the Second World War: the sectarian culture and politics of Northern Ireland, the neutrality of the southern state, and the poetry of W.H. Auden and his contemporaries published over the previous decade. Much of the poetry written and published by Greacen and his friends over the war years reacts against these pressures and influences. Linda Shires has argued that young British poets of the Second World War 'could no longer accept the tone, idiom and interests of the Auden generation' but that 'the poets who made their reputations in the forties were responding to their literary forefathers—in mimicry and in defiance—as well as to their own historical time'.[75] Both mimicry and defiance can be read in the poetry and prose of both Greacen and McFadden at this time, and it is worth considering in particular the impact of the poetry of Louis MacNeice on their work. The older poet's weary and vituperative attitude to the place of his birth, his fierce condemnation of neutrality, and his own status as a member of a larger group of poets are all factors which help to establish MacNeice as an important forerunner to the younger generation, but it is in the poetry itself that his influence can be most clearly felt.

* * *

In *The Auden Generation: Literature and Politics in England in the 1930s* (1976) Samuel Hynes notes the symbolic importance of journeys, especially by rail, and of border and frontier imagery to poems by W.H. Auden and his contemporaries, mindful in this observation, perhaps, of Auden's 'Night Mail' and Spender's 'The Express' and 'View from a Train'. Trains, like pylons, symbolized modernity, and similarly cut across natural landscapes, but with a speed and rhythm which could be more effectively incorporated into the poetry. Hynes claims that the crossing of borders had both personal and political implications: if a young man had to cross a metaphorical border into the unknown to become a man of action, Continental Europe's fragile and falling borders had also entered the poetic consciousness as urgent symbols of the divisions between war and peace, tyranny and freedom.[76]

---

[74] 'A New Order in The "New Northman"?', *New Northman VIII*, no. 3, p. 46; 'Modern Irish Poetry', *New Northman X*, no. 3, p. 33; Greacen, 'When Peace Breaks in Ulster', *The Bell* 5, no. 5, p. 397.

[75] Linda Shires, *British Poetry of the Second World War* (London and Basingstoke: Macmillan, 1985), pp. 5–6.

[76] Samuel Hynes, *The Auden Generation: Literature and Politics in England in the 1930s* (London: Bodley Head, 1976), p. 73.

For writers in Belfast during the Second World War, the cross-border journeys between that city and Dublin, and the wartime cultural, sensual, and social differences between the two cities, were particularly fruitful. These differences caused considerable anxiety, sometimes manifested in the poetry as defiance towards the southern state, often involving a degree of moral indignation over Irish neutrality, but tempered by an underlying self-consciousness regarding the apparent inferiority of Belfast's cultural and literary status in comparison with its southern neighbour. Dublin's exoticism and Belfast's recalcitrance are thus loaded with ambiguity in the poetry of Greacen and McFadden, where the wartime differences are explored with the sense that the distance of 87 miles between the two is subject to considerable elasticity.

Train journeys feature prominently in the journalism of the Protestant nationalist writer Denis Ireland—a frequent contributor to the *New Northman, Lagan,* and *The Bell* during the war. The essay 'Leaves from a Journal' describes travelling by train from Belfast to Dublin in the early years of the war to contribute to a radio broadcast, and focuses on a house on the border, the sight of which has preoccupied Ireland over the thirty-five years he has been taking this journey:

> ...if a kind of psychic participation in the life of a house conveys anything of ownership, then the house is practically mine already. It stands to one side of the black boggy tableland over which the railway runs, on the lower slopes of a heavily wooded mountain: a square, honest-looking house of the kind you find dotted about the Irish countryside: the kind of house in which if there is a gun-room there is probably also a library, a square, friendly room filled with the musty smell of books that no one has read, or possibly even disturbed, for half a century.

Denis Ireland imagines inhabiting this house, at once archetypal and specific, whose rooms would be decorated with busts or pictures of Henry Grattan and John Philpot Curran:

> I could then lay down my *Irish Press* or *Belfast News-Letter*, as the case may be, my situation being both geographically and culturally a sort of half-way house between them, and instead of being disturbed by the inanities of the present, I could lean back in my library chair and be not entertained but instructed by my pictorial patriots...[77]

Denis Ireland's reverie, in its creation of a literal and symbolic half-way house, demonstrates a desire to escape or resolve a perceived oppositional cultural stand-off between Belfast and Dublin, and his recourse to

---

[77] Denis Ireland, 'Leaves from a Journal', *New Northman VIII*, no. 3, pp. 53–54 (pp. 53–54).

nineteenth-century liberal Protestant statesmen suggests a complementary frustration with twentieth-century Irish politics and 'the inanities of the present'. Roy McFadden's poem 'Train at Midnight' from his first published collection *Swords and Ploughshares* (1943) also suggests a train journey as a means of traversing and transcending political conflicts linked to the land itself:

> Train, hurrying over hungry lean
> Insurgent fields flaunting their green
> Tatters of flags, pause to aver
> Your anger and compassion for
> This unreal country, always out of time.[78]

The 'insurgent fields' rendered as 'green/Tatters of flags' symbolize an exhausted, scarred, yet still active and defiant ('flaunting') Irish nationalism, cut across by the speed and strength of the train, which is urged to pause, and voice its 'anger and compassion'. This 'anger', along with the description of an 'unreal country, always out of time' suggests some exasperation at the southern state's wilful avoidance of the contemporary European political turmoil, as the word 'unreal' echoes MacNeice's recollection of Galway as 'unreal' at the outbreak of war. Flags aside, the journey in 'Train at Midnight' is almost totally decontextualized, and is clearly less important than the train itself, an agent of moral reawakening for the nation, sending out an 'arcade of smoke/A salutation that will wake/ Dreamers across the countryside'.

Other wartime poems by Greacen and McFadden explore these realities and unrealities more explicitly, often in terms of a perceived polarity between Belfast and Dublin, and succeed in reinforcing the oppositional relationship which Denis Ireland sought to escape. Crudely speaking, this established Belfast as industrially productive but culturally barren and afflicted by sectarian conflict, and Dublin as culturally vibrant but morally suspect. Such a perception of Belfast, though complicated by the Second World War, certainly survived the 1940s and arguably endured throughout the second half of the twentieth century—a point forcefully made by Edna Longley in 'A Barbarous Nook: The Writer and Belfast'.[79] Greacen recalled that cultural activity in Belfast during the 1930s and 1940s was discredited and marginalized by powerful and intolerant political and religious forces, and appreciated only by a select band of dedicated

---

[78] McFadden, 'Train at Midnight', *Collected Poems 1943–1995*, p. 310.
[79] Longley observes that 'As regards "Literature in Belfast", Belfast's image, through most of its history, has combined Philistia with its other possible aspects as "Bigots-borough" (James Douglas's coinage) or Cokestown-across-the-water.' (Edna Longley, 'A Barbarous Nook: The Writer and Belfast', *Living Stream*, pp. 86–105 [p. 86]).

practitioners. In a chapter in his 1997 memoir *The Sash My Father Wore* entitled 'Going South' he wrote 'I can sum up my reasons for going south to Dublin in a word—escape. I was dissatisfied with my personal life in Belfast. I felt oppressed by the general narrowness and philistinism. I wanted new doors to open, new opportunities'.[80] Greacen's poem 'Cycling to Dublin', published in his first collection *One Recent Evening* in 1944 and dedicated to Leslie Gillespie, a fellow undergraduate poet at Queen's, similarly describes these prevailing attitudes:

> We were the Northmen, hard with hoarded words on tongue,
> Driven down by home disgust to the broad lands and rich talk,
> To the country of poets and pubs and cow-dung
> Spouting and shouting from every stalk...[81]

The 'hoarded words' imply that the cycling friends feel unable to express themselves fully as poets within the identity of a 'Northman' (the allusion to the magazine is salient) and have been driven south by a desire to vent their emotions away from the disapproval of others. The word 'hoarded' is evocative of hidden and accumulated treasure, and, like McFadden's essay 'Life and Writing in North East Ulster', suggests that a rich seam of northern experience can be mined by young writers under the right conditions. It is also worth remembering that Dublin provided Greacen and some of his friends with the first professional outlet for their works in the form of the Gayfield Press, founded by Blánaid Salkeld and her son Cecil Ffrench in 1937, which produced limited editions of single poems with woodcut illustrations by local artists.[82] These included Greacen's 'The Bird', Maurice James Craig's 'Black Swans', and Roy McFadden's 'Russian Summer'.[83] 'Cycling to Dublin' does not present crossing the border as any kind of panacea, since the southern state is rendered in terms which conform to the chaotic, rural, and over-emotional stereotype of the Celtic other, 'spouting and shouting'. The promiscuous implications of 'spouting' and 'stalk' are reinforced by the attractions of 'Dublin's fair city' as they appear in the clichéd and italicized refrain, the 'colleens, fair colleens', who are 'ever so pretty'. The journey south offers an escape from a repressive environment for the northmen, and the southern state crucially is credited as a country of 'poets', but a degree of moral disapproval may be read in Greacen's brief evocation of drunken chaos, unravelling in an ellipsis.

---

[80] Greacen, *Sash*, p. 133.
[81] Greacen, 'Cycling to Dublin', *Collected Poems 1944–1994*, pp. 34–35 (pp. 34–35).
[82] 'Salkeld, Blánaid', in *The Cambridge Guide to Women's Writing*, edited by Lorna Sage (Cambridge: Cambridge University Press, 1999), p. 552.
[83] McFadden, 'The Belfast Forties', *Force 10*, p. 68.

The poem which follows 'Cycling to Dublin' in *One Recent Evening*, 'Memories of Dublin' (subtitled 'November, 1940'), illustrates more fully Greacen's relationship with the city:

> Clashing coloured life and gaiety,
> Dirt and yells, and the shrill suspense
> Of empty alley-ways; Blackpool lights; cooking smells.
>
> All this in past or future tense.
> The façades of the eighteenth century –
> Burke and Goldsmith frozen for posterity,
> Who whistle and spit near culture's sanctuary,
> And drawl opinions on an isolated war.
> . . .
> The city is so much scenery from the Abbey:
> The people are waxen marionettes.
> For them, the rush for drinks and shabby
> Buses; then nausea, dull, bottled joy in heart.[84]

Here the city is again the location for drinking and shouting, twinned here with Blackpool, the British cultural capital of licentiousness. During the war, Dublin offered sensory pleasures forbidden in the north: it was, as Greacen recalled in 1976, a *'ville lumière*, offering steak and nylons to ill-fed Northerners'.[85] Here the southern capital's 'lights' distinguish it from Belfast, where the blackout remained in force, whilst 'cooking smells' hint at the widespread availability in Éire of foodstuffs subject to rationing north of the border. The poem is jealous of the 'colours of all spectrums' and displays an adolescent fascination with 'Shannon's virility'. Comparison with another English city might establish Dublin here as an alternative Soho (the post-war destination for a number of Irish writers) for northmen starved in wartime of sex, whiskey, bacon, and eggs.

If the poem's disapproval of those who 'drawl opinions on an isolated war' is evident, the force of this is tempered by the confusing reference to the statues of Burke and Goldsmith which appear either side of the entrance to Trinity College ('culture's sanctuary', apparently). Matters are clarified by a later poem whose title echoes this line. 'On the Sense of Isolation in War-Time Ireland' from *The Undying Day* (1948) again invokes Burke, and also recapitulates derogatory national stereotypes. The poem begins by describing 'We' Irish as 'that vainly violent, lawless crew/ Whose generous verve leaves all to chance/But seldom halts the irregular advance', continuing to list a series of Anglo-Irish writers of the past, the 'unfettered great' who 'gave no inch to fate' and who 'shall make the

---

[84] Greacen, 'Memories of Dublin', *Collected Poems 1944–1994*, p. 35.
[85] Robert Greacen, 'Writing in Emergency Dublin', *Irish Times*, 6 April 1976.

Anglo-Irishry endure': Burke, Swift, Sheridan, Congreve, Goldsmith, Moore, and Yeats, the last of whose 'shadow falls across the Liffey still/ Pressing its callous spell on Irish will'. Greacen's attitude towards these forebears is ambivalent, but he calls upon them as a means of disparaging the present crop of Dublin writers, cast as 'yes-men glimmer[ing] in pretence,/Secure in their own dribbling competence', in contrast with their antecedents who 'the world for subject took/And wed the fearless thesis to their book'. The poem ends with the sarcastic lines 'So now in days of fevered fret and stress/Let Europe measure out our Irishness!', addressing the cultural implications of Irish neutrality and indicting Dublin and its writers with myopic introversion for concentrating on local concerns and freezing out 'those who speak with honest passion' at a time of international crisis.[86]

The supposedly carefree atmosphere of wartime Dublin is much dwelt upon by the young northern poets. Belfast-born Maurice J. Craig's poem 'Kilcarty to Dublin', dated 1943, describes how:

> ... life goes on in the last lit city
> Just in the way it always has done
> And pity is lost on the tongues of the witty
> And the wolf at the door is a figure of fun.[87]

Similarly, Greacen in his 'Poem to K.D.' sends 'greetings' to a friend in London:

> From this careless Augustan city of grace and slums,
> Where in Merrion Square the whispers of death
> Gauze over the rhododendrons and the parched grass.
> I greet you from a neutral country in a neutral hour
> When the blood pace slows and nothing stirs
> But the leaves in the parks, so gently:
> So gently that not even the newspaper headlines
> Can fluster the plumes of swans, gliding, gliding,
> As on a lake of fire, fringed by pink water.[88]

Dublin's parks were a common reference point for both Greacen and Roy McFadden. In 'St Stephen's Green, Dublin', published in *Flowers for a Lady* (1945), McFadden also sends a 'greeting' from neutral Dublin, emphasising the extent to which he feels detached from home in these opening lines:

---

[86] Greacen, 'On the Sense of Isolation in War-Time Ireland', *Collected Poems 1944–1994*, pp. 69–70.

[87] Maurice J. Craig, 'Kilcarty to Dublin', in Dawe (ed.), *Earth Voices Whispering*, p. 242.

[88] Greacen, 'Poem to K.D.', *Collected Poems 1944–1994*, p. 46.

> The north lies backward in a fold of time.
> I send you greeting from the singing south
> Where there is sun and unselfconscious laughter.[89]

Descriptions of Dublin's untroubled wartime gaiety are familiar, but the idea of Northern Ireland lying 'backward in a fold of time' is unusual, since it inverts the perception that due to its belligerent status it is Belfast, rather than Dublin, that is of greater contemporary consequence. This view underpins much of the poetry examined in this chapter, and was asserted with force by Seán Ó Faoláin, who wrote in *The Bell* in July 1942 that 'the strength of the North is that she does live and act in the Now. Belfast has an immediacy. Ulster has a contemporaneity'.[90] With the first line of 'St Stephen's Green, Dublin', repeated at the beginning of its penultimate stanza, McFadden suggests that south of the border Belfast's experiences may be forgotten, ignored, or consigned to history, before outlining in similarly oblique terms, over the following eight stanzas, the folly of so doing.

In this poem McFadden casts himself as an outsider in the southern state, 'A foreign flower in your bleak midwinter garden', who has been psychologically scarred by unspecified traumatic experiences, and who carries death 'Curled like a worm in the brain, twisting the eye,/Sharpening the casual word with bitterness'.[91] As a roving intermediary, he charges himself with the responsibility of warning carefree Dublin of its potential downfall:

> Old city, with a young girl's face,
> Your mask is foreign to my broken streets.
> Your easy laughter mocks the living dead.
> Take heed of history, for I have seen
> Such as you broken and swept away
> As the sea smooths the footprints from the sand.
> With all your wisdom, still remember this.[92]

Here the mask of a 'young girl's face' is contrasted with 'broken streets': the bomb-damaged urban landscape, we might assume, of Belfast, a reading encouraged by the portentous lines 'I have seen/Such as you broken and swept away', and by the later reference to 'bombs in the North'. McFadden's use of the imagery of 'broken streets' draws together the violent histories of the two cities—for residents of Belfast scenes of urban

---

[89] McFadden, 'St Stephen's Green, Dublin', *Collected Poems 1943–1995*, pp. 271–3 (p. 271).

[90] 'An Ulster Issue', *The Bell* 4, no. 4, pp. 229–231 (p. 231).

[91] McFadden, 'St Stephen's Green, Dublin', *Collected Poems 1943–1995*, pp. 271–272.

[92] McFadden, 'St Stephen's Green, Dublin', *Collected Poems 1943–1995*, p. 272.

destruction were of urgent contemporary resonance, but for Dubliners the words might evoke memories of the devastation of the centre of their city during the Easter Rising a quarter of a century previously. Such relatively recent history is hinted at in McFadden's appeals to Dublin itself, presently at peace and 'Proud with the arrogance of history', to recall the fragility of 'cultures, loves and histories', which can 'Drop with gulls into the quiet rivers/To float, face down into anonymous seas'. McFadden's entreaty to consider the seemingly inevitable mutability of all civilizations then widens to encompass the whole island, and is made within earshot of the Belfast Blitz:

> You who remember history, recollect
> That history moves like rivers into seas,
> Accepting no horizons: that its strands
> Of generous sun and dancing limbs are drowned
> Or spattered with white shipwreck, whiter bones.
> This is an island out of step with time.
> Listen to the other city sounds at night:
> Bombs in the north, the stampede to the hills.[93]

Although the poem overtly addresses the whole 'island', these lines must surely be read as a warning for the southern state to heed the air attack experienced by the inhabitants of Belfast, which forced them from their homes in a 'stampede to the hills'. The use of 'island' here echoes Louis MacNeice's twice repeated use of the phrase 'neutral island' in the poem 'Neutrality', even when addressing the southern state's neutrality. It is likely that the imaginative resonance of an 'island' in this context overrode the matter of the border. The influence of MacNeice's poem may also be discerned in the reference to a strand scarred by 'whiter bones': 'Neutrality' ends with the gruesome spectacle of mackerel of the west of Ireland growing 'fat—on the flesh of your kin'—a reference to the many sailors and merchant seamen who perished in the Battle of the Atlantic, and whose bodies later washed up on beaches along the west coast of Ireland.[94]

Having addressed Dublin for the bulk of 'St Stephen's Green, Dublin', McFadden returns at the poem's close to his 'greeting' to the North, culminating in these lines:

> Where I walk neutral streets with calls to peace.
> I send you greeting in a time of war,
> When only those who love can dare to live,
> When only those who love will never die.[95]

---

[93] McFadden, 'St Stephen's Green, Dublin', *Collected Poems 1943–1995*, p. 272.
[94] MacNeice, 'Neutrality', *Collected Poems*, p. 224.
[95] McFadden, 'St Stephen's Green, Dublin', *Collected Poems 1943–1995*, p. 273.

Unlike MacNeice, the avowedly pacifist McFadden is unable to attack Irish neutrality with serious venom, and here he states his belief in love as a counter to the prevalent destruction. In 'Dublin to Belfast: Wartime', a much shorter poem also published in *Flowers for a Lady*, McFadden describes the return journey between the cities as 'tunnel[ling] back to war'. Here Dublin seems immune to the effects of the conflict and unworried by the prospect of war, with 'uncensored lights/Careless of retribution from the skies,/ Unreprimanded and insouciant streets'. Belfast, by contrast, is described as a 'braced and vulnerable town', and the poem's closing lines further suggest that the city remains under threat. In 'St Stephen's Green, Dublin', gulls are symbolic of the mutability of civilizations and cities, plunging into 'quiet rivers' to float 'face down' towards the sea, and here again the birds appear as harbingers of potential disaster: 'The brazen gantries and the querulous gulls/Harsh from the islands occupied by storm'.[96]

The 'gantries' that appear here are as resonant of Belfast in poetry of the 1930s and 1940s as Spender's pylons or Auden's gasworks were of England at the time. The English poets found strange beauty in their industrial landscapes, but the shipyard gantries of Belfast tend to appear in poems as forbidding emblems of cruelty, or of religious and political conservatism. Gantries are of particular importance to Louis MacNeice's renderings of the city during the 1930s. In 'Belfast', industrial and religious oppression are fused in one symbol as 'Against the lurid over the stained water/ Where hammers clang murderously on the girders/Like crucifixes the gantries stand'; famously in 'Carrickfergus' he describes his birthplace lying 'between the mountain and the gantries'; while in 'War Heroes' he foresees soldiers returning to Belfast after a ten-year-long war to see 'dead men hanging in the gantries' and 'a lame bird limping on the quay'—the source, perhaps, of the ominous gantries and gulls in McFadden's poem.[97] Gantries are similarly imposing presences in Robert Greacen's poem 'Ulster':

> Standing under the wing of gantries,
> The phallic sentinels of Belfast's lough,
> He ponders beneath pride's vacant sneer,
> Hating and loving futile majesty.[98]

Like MacNeice's 'Belfast', the one-word title invites this poem to be read as an attempt to define the characteristics of the province, and as such it follows familiar lines, describing it as 'firm and gaunt and black', 'coarse

---

[96] McFadden, 'Dublin to Belfast: Wartime', *Collected Poems 1943–1995*, p. 279.
[97] MacNeice, 'Belfast', 'Carrickfergus', and 'War Heroes', *Collected Poems*, p. 25, pp. 55–6 (p. 55), pp. 42–43 (p. 42).
[98] Greacen, 'Ulster', *Collected Poems 1944–1994*, p. 36.

and ungrateful', and asking whether it is 'the mother-symbol/Of stolid, stupid sordidness?', before hailing its soul 'tense with beauty' and bursting in 'fierce reticence', at once 'Old and grim like basalt,/Yet fresh in day's caress'.[99] Greacen's winged and 'phallic' gantries are reconstituted in animal and sexual terms, but retain as 'sentinels' the sense of foreboding (and, importantly, stasis) evoked by those in MacNeice's poems.[100] 'Ulster' was first published in the *New Northman* in Winter 1940–1941—the same issue in which Greacen as editor set out his non-political and literary vision for the magazine. The poem was printed facing Jack Boyd's article which, as I have outlined, castigated MacNeice and his contemporaries for fleeing to America: the juxtaposition is demonstrative of MacNeice's proximity to the poetry and prose of the younger generation, even as they disavowed him.

Edna Longley has written that 'It is interesting that MacNeice, for whom Belfast was the first city, should have been in the vanguard of absorbing the city into English poetry generally', but his impact on poetry in Northern Ireland during the war has yet to be fully traced.[101] As we have seen, many of Greacen and McFadden's poems of wartime Belfast and Dublin betray the influence of MacNeice's own pre-war and wartime poetic engagements with Ireland, the most quoted and most direct example of which was 'Neutrality', written in September 1942 following the death of his friend Graham Sheppard, who had drowned in the Atlantic following a German U-boat attack.[102] The poem has been discussed at length by Clair Wills, amongst others, but what concerns me here is how MacNeice's severely critical attitude to Ireland north and south during the 1930s and war years resounded through the work of the younger poets.

In the sixteenth section of the lengthy autobiographical poem *Autumn Journal*, published in May 1939, MacNeice uses the image of a medieval Irish round tower to figure the southern state's isolation in the face of impending war, as exclamation marks convey the poet's sarcastic and desperate rage: 'Ourselves alone! Let the round tower stand aloof/In a world of bursting mortar!'[103] Robert Greacen and Valentin Iremonger's draft introduction to their Faber anthology *Contemporary Irish Poetry* (1949)

---

[99] Greacen, 'Ulster', *Collected Poems 1944–1994*, p. 36.

[100] Winged gantries make another appearance in Greacen's 'The Man Who Weeps', subtitled 'December 1940', a pre-Belfast Blitz poem in which he writes 'I only know of bombing from the English papers...' in contrast with Ulster where 'swirl the saffron Irish vapours,/Across her hills wingèd gantries ride' (Greacen, *Collected Poems 1944–1994*, pp. 22–23 [p. 23]).

[101] Edna Longley, 'A Barbarous Nook', *Living Stream*, p. 105.

[102] Clair Wills, 'The Aesthetics of Irish Neutrality During World War Two', *boundary 2* 31, no. 1 (Spring 2004), pp. 119–145, doi:10.1215/01903659-31-1-119.

[103] MacNeice, *Autumn Journal, Collected Poems*, pp. 99–164 (p. 139).

included a strikingly similar attack on Irish neutrality in prose, which also utilized the image of a round tower. Greacen claimed that the contentious passage was cut by T.S. Eliot, a director of Faber and Faber at the time, and reprinted the unpublished sentences in his memoir *The Sash My Father Wore*:

> Few people really believed that Ireland would succeed in preserving her neu-
> trality: consequently as the problems to be solved in Ireland were similar
> to those in any country, it was obvious that it was no use burying one's
> head under the wool-blanket of Celtic twilight. Ivory Round Towers, even
> if complete with the green-whiskered wolfhounds of Banba, Deirdre of the
> Sorrows, the harp that once [*sic*] and the dying fall of the mellifluous and
> kingly Gaelic, would hardly provide cover against the assault of tommy-
> gunned, jack-booted airborne divisions.[104]

Greacen and Iremonger's deliberate juxtaposition of Celtic mythology with modern weaponry, and their exaggerated sarcasm and polemical tone, are heavily reminiscent of MacNeice's attack on the independent south-ern state in *Autumn Journal* ten years previously. MacNeice was similarly scornful of the mythology, declaring: 'Kathaleen ni Houlihan! Why/Must a country, like a ship or car, be always female,/Mother or sweetheart?' and savagely dismissive of the Irish language: 'Let the school-children fumble their sums/In a half-dead language'.[105] These lines were directly echoed by St John Ervine in his excoriation of the remodelled *New Northman* in Spring 1941, which mocked Eamon de Valera's insistence on the impor-tance of the Irish language, suggesting mischievously that for a married man with children in the southern state contemplating the severe disparity between the provision of unemployment assistance north and south of the border 'The right to have his infants taught arithmetic in Gaelic might not seem to him sufficient compensation'.[106] Allusions to MacNeice's writings permeate the pages of the magazine even when he is not mentioned by name.

MacNeice's series of poems 'The Coming of War', published in Dublin by the Cuala Press in *The Last Ditch* in 1940 and later revised as 'The Closing Album' for *Plant and Phantom* in 1941, seem to have had the greatest impact on Greacen and McFadden's poetry. Traces of 'Dublin', the opening poem in 'The Coming of War', may be found in Greacen's poetic evocations of the same city, especially 'Memories of Dublin'. The 'gentle veils of rain' of the former find their echo in the 'soft rain' of the lat-ter, whilst MacNeice's 'catcalls and the pain,/The glamour of her squalor'

---

[104] Greacen, *Sash*, p. 137.
[105] MacNeice, *Autumn Journal, Collected Poems*, p. 138, p. 139.
[106] Ervine, 'What's Wrong with the "New Northman"', *New Northman IX*, no. 1, p. 7.

are reflected in Greacen's 'Clashing coloured life...Dirt and yells'.[107] The poets share a concern for Dublin's Georgian architecture, its squares and statues: MacNeice's portrayal of the 'squalor' of an 'Augustan capital' is discernible in Greacen's 'careless Augustan city of grace and slums' in 'Poem to K.D.', and 'the bare bones of a fanlight/Over a hungry door' in MacNeice's 'Dublin' can be read as the antecedent of 'the ragged fanlight' in Greacen's fiercely anti-colonial 'Georgian Twilight'.[108] Although MacNeice refers to Belfast in 'Valediction' as his 'mother-city', it is rendered in this poem and in 'Belfast' in the same collection in decidedly masculine terms, dominated by the sounds of hammering from the shipyards and the drums of Orange parades.[109] Greacen's phallic gantries follow this tendency to represent Belfast as often oppressively male in character. And as MacNeice's Dublin is feminized—he writes of 'her seedy elegance' and states that 'she will not/Have me alive or dead'—McFadden's 'St Stephen's Green, Dublin' similarly feminizes the city, describing an 'Old city, with a young girl's face'.[110]

Terence Brown has noted the emphasis on domesticity in 'Cushendun', the second section of 'The Closing Album', in which MacNeice describes in heavily sensuous terms time spent in a cottage in the eponymous Antrim village over the summer of 1939.[111] Here it initially seems possible to withdraw from the escalating political tension, as is suggested by the first word of the third stanza: 'Forgetfulness: brass lamps and copper jugs/And home-made bread and the smell of turf or flax'. By the fourth and final stanza the prospect of conflict intrudes, however, via the medium of the wireless:

> Only in the dark green room beside the fire
> With the curtains drawn against the winds and waves
> There is a little box with a well-bred voice:
>   What a place to talk of War.[112]

This domestic scene also stands for Ireland itself of course, both in the inevitable symbolism of the colour of the room and in the way that

[107] Greacen, 'Memories of Dublin', *Collected Poems 1944–1994*, p. 35; MacNeice, 'The Coming of War', *Collected Poems*, pp. 680–686 (p. 680). *The Last Ditch* was published in the summer of 1940 (the *Times Literary Supplement* published a review of the collection on 8 June 1940) and Greacen's 'Memories of Dublin' is subtitled 'November, 1940'.
[108] Greacen, 'Poem to K.D.', 'Georgian Twilight', *Collected Poems 1944–1994*, p. 46, p. 68.
[109] MacNeice, 'Valediction', 'Belfast', *Collected Poems*, pp. 7–10 (p. 8), p. 25.
[110] MacNeice, 'The Coming of War', *Collected Poems*, p. 680; McFadden, 'St Stephen's Green, Dublin', *Collected Poems 1943–1995*, p. 272.
[111] Terence Brown, 'Louis MacNeice: An Anglo–Irish Quest', in *Northern Voices*, pp. 98–113 (p. 101).
[112] MacNeice, 'The Coming of War', *Collected Poems*, p. 682.

the 'winds and waves' outside evoke Ireland's literal status as an island and its isolated geographical and political position in relation to the coming war. McFadden's 'In Ireland Now' similarly enacts an attempted withdrawal to a domestic lair, before acknowledging the war outside in oblique terms:

> In Ireland now, at autumn, by frugal fires,
> We hurry to lock the present out with the closed door
> And night-slammed windows; huddling into a past
> Where life at times could turn a nonchalant head,
> We watch the heads of flame swirl in the draught,
> The demon dancers on reflecting walls,
> Backed by an angry wind strumming the wires.[113]

The poem invokes Plato's allegory of the cave, but here the subjects of the poem attempt in vain to hide from a reality it seems they would rather not contemplate.[114] As in 'Cushendun', it seems that it is no longer an option to 'turn a nonchalant head', and here the wind 'strumming the wires' suggests that news transmitted by telephone or telegraph can penetrate the domestic scene, just as MacNeice's cottage is troubled by the wireless news. The second stanza casts Ireland 'on the edge of a crumbling continent', and contrasts 'local hills goodnaturedly at play' and pampered 'girlish fields' with 'the passionless slaughter of millions, all faceless, unknown'. Collective guilt is implied, as McFadden finds that 'the mass resolves' into 'a singular/Soul pulsing in your wrist, the killer's pulse', thrusting responsibility for these atrocities onto the reader. There is a helplessness about this poem, a sense that 'In Ireland Now' no action can be taken to address the horrors going on elsewhere (the bombing of Belfast is not alluded to in the poem, apart perhaps from in the final line, which warns that 'winter's onslaught gathers overhead'). McFadden's predicament, which sometimes dampens the moral force of the poetry, lies in the fact that the pacifism to which he adhered was ultimately unable to satisfy his moral disquiet at atrocities being committed elsewhere.

It seems that for all the editorial bluster against Auden and his contemporaries, and apparent interest in the fashions of the New Apocalypse, a

---

[113] McFadden, 'In Ireland Now', *Collected Poems 1943–1995*, p. 309. The poem was first published in the *Northman XI*, no. 1, p. 13.

[114] F.S.L. Lyons described Irish culture during the war with reference to the allegory, writing that 'It was as if an entire people had been condemned to live in Plato's cave, with their backs to the fire of life and deriving their only knowledge of what went on outside from the flickering shadows thrown on the wall before their eyes by the men and women who passed to and fro behind them' (Lyons, *Ireland Since the Famine* [London: Collins/Fontana, 1971], pp. 557–558).

more important antecedent for Greacen and McFadden's war poetry may be found closer to home in MacNeice, whose distress at Ireland's introversion, isolation, and stasis in the face of colossal historical upheaval they clearly share. Despite the discernible debts of influence, McFadden in particular maintained an exclusionist policy towards the older poet.[115] In the 1943 dialogue with Geoffrey Taylor he dismissed MacNeice when he spoke of the lack of progress made in trying to create a literary tradition in the north:

> So far the results have been disappointing. MacNeice was never Irish, and it is mere sentiment to imagine him so. If he had continued to live in Belfast we might well have some foundation for a new architecture in Irish poetry. As it is, he is merely one of an ever-growing catalogue of names irretrievably lost to this country.[116]

Attempts such as these to exclude MacNeice from the Irish poetic canon anticipate a debate that would resurface amongst Irish poets and academics during the 1980s and 1990s, but it is striking how McFadden's forceful condemnations of the older poet in prose contradict the traces of MacNeice's influence discernible in his poetry.[117] In the essay 'Life and Writing in North-East Ulster', he writes that MacNeice 'must be surrendered to the English for he has forgotten (if he ever knew) the native idiom', before praising the 'swaggering rhythms and great blasts of contempt' which characterize the poetry of W.R. Rodgers, by contrast hailed as a 'great Ulster realist'.[118] McFadden then hails the promise of his friends and contemporaries, citing Maurice James Craig and Greacen as poets who have achieved recognition outside their own country, even if 'the latter... has unfortunately fallen in with the MacNeice–Heysham-boat tradition'.[119] This illustrates the awkwardness of McFadden's position. Having dismissed the idea that MacNeice could be considered an Irish or Ulster poet with reference to the older poet's departure for England, he then judges the success of his contemporaries on the basis of how their work has been received outside Ireland, which in the cases of Craig and

---

[115] McFadden did admit in 1988 that his first introduction to contemporary poetry had been through reading MacNeice's *Selected Poems* in 1940, which he had bought from Davy McLean's Progressive Bookshop (see McFadden, 'Louis MacNeice: Late of this Parish', McFadden Papers, MP27, p. 1—this is the typed text of a talk given at the Ulster Arts Club in June 1988).

[116] McFadden and Taylor, 'Poetry in Ireland: A Discussion', *The Bell* 6, no. 4, p. 343.

[117] Anthony Roche explores Denis Donoghue's contentious 1987 review of Alan Heuser's *Selected Literary Criticism of Louis MacNeice* and the ensuing debate in the *London Review of Books* in 'A Reading of Autumn Journal: The Question of Louis MacNeice's Irishness', *Text and Context* (Autumn 1988), pp. 71–90 (pp. 74–77).

[118] McFadden, 'Life and Writing in North-East Ulster', McFadden Papers, MP5, p. 8.

[119] McFadden, 'Life and Writing in North-East Ulster', McFadden Papers, MP5, p. 8.

Greacen can only mean publication in England. This in turn contradicts McFadden's criticism of Greacen in the following clause of the sentence for having 'fallen in' with an apparently outdated MacNeician tradition of crossing the Irish Sea. It is surely possible to read this confusion as anxiety on McFadden's part regarding the influence of MacNeice on his own work, particularly when he concludes the essay by stating that 'the immediate problem facing Belfast writers is the problem of extending the idiom to include the factory chimneys, without forgetting the hills forming their background', thereby proposing a literary landscape reminiscent of the sonorous opening line of MacNeice's poem 'Carrickfergus'.[120]

If Greacen's and McFadden's poems on Ireland and the war seem rooted in experience and, despite their protestations, guided by the example of Louis MacNeice, their poems which try to address wider international questions are more problematic. McFadden's 'In Ireland Now' was first published in the Winter 1941–1942 edition of *The Northman*, which also carried a further and typically stinging attack by St John Ervine on the younger generation of poets. The Greacen-edited collection *Poems from Ulster* was the subject of a particularly exasperated diatribe. Citing the poem 'Elegy on a Hill', Ervine asked:

> What *is* the object of this wilful obscurity? Chaucer has been dead for over 500 years, and the English he used is now archaic, but I can grasp his meaning, even when I have to use a glossary; but the glossary has not yet been compiled which will enable me to understand the meaning of some of the poems in this book. Partly, I think, it is because none of you knows how to punctuate. You are worse, in this respect, than women novelists, and God knows, they're pretty awful.[121]

He also attacked Greacen's assertions in the preface of *Poems from Ulster* that poetry was the natural medium for young men, writing:

> The cruellest and most credulous soldiers in Hitler's army are the young men. It is the youth of Italy which cheers when Mussolini calls liberty a fetish . . . That guff about old men bequeathing horrible legacies to young men is well enough in the mouth of an Auden, but in the mouths of Ulstermen—come, come!
>
> I notice that Mr McFadden is terribly upset about Belgium's starving children. Why Belgium's particularly? Was he upset enough to get out of his leather chair?[122]

---

[120] McFadden, 'Life and Writing in North-East Ulster', McFadden Papers, MP5, p. 8; MacNeice, 'Carrickfergus', *Collected Poems*, p. 55.

[121] St John Ervine, 'St John Ervine on *Poems from Ulster*: A Letter to Robert Greacen', *The Northman XI*, no. 1, p. 2.

[122] Ervine, 'St John Ervine on *Poems from Ulster*', *The Northman XI*, no. 1, p. 2.

Ervine's irritation levels an important charge against poems by Greacen and McFadden that address the international situation. Notwithstanding their experience of the Belfast Blitz (McFadden noted the irony that as a pacifist his house was destroyed in the bombing), as non-combatants who spent the war in Ireland they were reliant on second-hand accounts of events elsewhere, and in this important respect such poetic engagements lack authenticity and credibility.[123] Terence Brown has suggested that attempts 'to interpret international events in war-torn Europe in terms of the New Apocalypse...lacked real roots in imaginative experience, so declin[ed] into a wan, if professionally competent, verse-making'.[124] In the case of some poems Brown's assessment might be considered over-generous. The piece of writing at which Ervine directs particular opprobrium is McFadden's 'Poem', which opens with these lines:

> Sitting futile in a room,
> While Belgium's starving children,
> Pouch-eyed, brow-puckered, humourless,
> Shrivel into premature age,
> My head is heavy with my sins and the sins of my brothers.[125]

Here McFadden assumes some guilt for the fate of the children, attributing this (it would seem) to a general corruption on the part of the human race. In the concluding stanza he claims to love the world and grieve for it as he sits 'pinioned between fat arms of a leather chair,/Vainly sending my soul into those countries/That have felt the bad blood from the broken vein of the past', feeling haunted by the suffering of others:

> Seeing between the lines of irrelevant reading
> And in the personal images moving among the ashes,
> The flabby bellies and sadly accusing eyes
> Of hungry children, and hearing their silence.[126]

This might well be described as a case of irrelevant writing, and given his inertia, McFadden's guilt and distress, as Ervine suggests, are certainly lacking in credibility. Tellingly, 'Poem' was not included in McFadden's *Collected Poems*, published in 1995.

---

[123] In unpublished recollections McFadden wrote: 'After the 1941 Blitz, Robert Greacen had to search for me, for, true to form, I, the pacifist, got blitzed, while the enthusiastic prosecutors of the war sheltered under the blessing of bishops of country houses too far away to merit a bomb' (McFadden Papers, MP35 [ix]).

[124] Brown, 'Robert Greacen and Roy McFadden: Apocalypse and Survival' in *Northern Voices*, p. 131.

[125] Roy McFadden, 'Poem', in Greacen (ed.) *Poems from Ulster*, p. 19.

[126] McFadden, 'Poem', in Greacen (ed.) *Poems from Ulster*, p. 19.

Similarly lacking roots in imaginative experience, Robert Greacen's 'Lament for France' addressed the German invasion of 1940. This thoroughly unsuccessful poem is alternately grandiose and demotic, as the lament itself ('All the frontiers are twisted back, all the faces/Have become one face, the gigantic face of terror') is interrupted by three imagined interjections by German soldiers, each of which mocks a part of the French national motto:

> ('Nothing will stop us now,' say the feet,
> 'Down are the barriers. Nothing stands in the way!
> What do they say—do they say 'Liberty'?
> My truncheon, Hans, that's the answer to freedom!')[127]

The poem then attempts to address the Holocaust, as other German voices are heard to say 'Death to the Jews!' and laugh that 'They say that men are brothers! They'll be brothers all right./Brothers at the abattoir!' Despite the fact that the Nazi soldiers will take 'everything/That can be assessed, all that will be taken down', the poem ends with an optimistic affirmation of faith in the French Republic:

> In the heart, the Republic lives beyond her death,
> Till grave-faced men shall bring the phoenix-birth.
> Where brothers shall be equal, proudly free,
> They will remember France, salute her memory.[128]

This well-meaning poem is fatally damaged by the inept and crassly imagined conversations of the Nazi soldiers, and Greacen's apparent romanticized belief in French Republican ideals sits uneasily beside more cynical and critical attitudes towards Ireland and Britain that surface in other poems and in prose. The poem that precedes 'Lament for France' in *The Undying Day*, 'The Glorious Twelfth', subtitled '*12 July, 1943*', refers to the suspension of Orange Order parades for the duration of the Second World War:

> Four years since fire has run swift rivers into Europe
> From Dunkirk to Briansk, from Naples to Novgorod,
> From Caucasus to Clyde, from Warsaw to Belfast.
> And now, in Derry and Downpatrick, no Ulstermen are marching
> To the rustle of their banners and the flogging of their drums.
> Our red-brick cities have their blackened skeletons,
> Our people carry the public and the personal wound.[129]

[127] Greacen, 'Lament for France', *Collected Poems 1944–1994* (pp. 65–66), p. 65.
[128] Greacen, 'Lament for France', *Collected Poems 1944–1994*, p. 66.
[129] Greacen, 'The Glorious Twelfth', *Collected Poems 1944–1994*, pp. 64–65 (p. 64).

Contrasting war-torn Europe with a concomitant kind of demilitarization in Northern Ireland, Greacen exploits a striking irony, although the cynicism of the observation is swiftly undercut by a chilling acknowledgement of local wounds.[130] This poem can be read as a forerunner to Tom Paulin's idea of 'provincial world history', and Greacen's conception here of a web of causes and consequences spreading across Europe is notably more effective as a means of connecting events at home with atrocities abroad than McFadden's expressions of guilt and paralysis in 'Poem'.

In 'The Poet Answers' from *One Recent Evening*, Greacen does attempt to make sense of the poet's role in wartime. He begins by asking readers to 'take a warning from the violent times', as bombers fly home across a landscape that recalls Blitz-ravaged Belfast—'over the smoking chimneys from blazing docks/With wings singed by hatred or delivered duty'—before confronting those from whom he feels under a different kind of attack. These are the 'sterile critic' and the 'common man', with their shared contempt for the poet's 'personal vision', as well as 'the propagandist sliding rulers of metric value', all of whom demand poems of the 'political struggle' and have no interest in the poet's 'faint and copulative heart'. The answer to such demands, writes Greacen, is 'plain, the answer shouts itself':

> I am I, I am the poet, the maker, the breaker,
> I am the prophet, the madman, the dreamer, the healer,
> I am the killer, the universal panacea
> For the broken, the inarticulate, the oppressed, the tortured.
> I make—therefore I am! I make![131]

This is followed by the bombastic assertion that 'My world is all the world, all worlds,/My agony is the agony at Calvary and Dachau'. The poem provides another stark illustration of the gap between Greacen's ambition to address such weighty matters and his ability to do so in poetry.

Greacen and McFadden remained civilians, but John Gallen, Greacen's friend and co-editor, served in the British army in the Far East during the war, and was killed after its end, in a climbing accident in India in January 1947. Published in *The Northman* that summer, Greacen's obituary of his

---

[130] Twelfth of July celebrations were reportedly cancelled during the war, due to a fear that parades involving military drums and banners by marchers who did not face conscription and might otherwise have been marching to a real war would have drawn a caustic response from the British army and government (James Kelly, *Bonfires on the Hillside: An Eyewitness Account of Political Upheaval in Northern Ireland* [Belfast: Fountain Publishing, 1995], p. 119). John Hewitt wrote of the Twelfth in 1941 that 'All is quiet here. We rippled over the Twelfth almost imperceptibly. Half a dozen flags and 2 orange lilies and a photo of old men in sashes in the "Whig!"' (Letter from John Hewitt to Patrick Maybin, 22 July 1941, Hewitt Papers, PRONI, D/3838/3/12).

[131] Greacen, 'The Poet Answers', *Collected Poems 1944–1994*, pp. 38–39 (p. 39).

friend emphasized the comradeship of their time on the magazine, praising Gallen as a 'true and resourceful ally' in combating the 'hostility' and 'apathy' shown towards them at Queen's. Greacen is keen to forestall 'cant later about his dying for Democracy', however, and as a 'corrective' to any such perception concludes his article with an extract from Gallen's final editorial for the magazine, a creative piece which describes a young writer in wartime facing considerable pressure from others to stop producing 'bilge' and enlist in the army. The young man eventually cracks and agrees to join up, but admits he doesn't have 'the faintest idea' what he is going to fight for and concedes that the motives for his decision are low ones: 'the herd instinct, social advantages, and escape from boredom'. Once in the army, his experience is miserable, since 'Everyone was so disgusted with the poor boy that he was hardly ever spoken to in the army, and he was run over and killed by a red bus on his very first leave. And the moral of that is: Truth is the opinion of the majority; never tell a lie'.[132] Such a savagely cynical parable in miniature questions the ability of the individual to act meaningfully in war. Without questioning the sincerity of Greacen's grief, it is difficult not to view his decision to reprint this particular extract in the context of his own decision not to enlist, which, in Northern Ireland, he was free to make.

Gallen's poem 'For R.A.' is one of three reprinted in the same issue of *The Northman*. In it the poet begs forgiveness from the dedicatee (seemingly a lover) for having 'unmade the world', and as in poems by his contemporaries Greacen and McFadden attempts to bear responsibility for atrocities in which he was not directly involved:

> My spell raised Hitler, and my guilty hands
> Made Belsen. Now by myself impeached, I dare not
> Presume to penance till you, by time unreached
> Fear not to speak to me my own forgiveness.[133]

The similarity of these lines to those already quoted from Greacen's 'The Poet Answers' and McFadden's 'Poem' is notable. Contemporary readers may be discomfited by the way that both 'The Poet Answers' and 'For R.A.' bring named concentration camps into their admissions of guilt, but these poems do raise questions of how poems by combatants and non-combatants should be read together, and show how such questions are further problematized in the context of Northern Ireland, where conscription was not imposed. If Greacen and McFadden's clumsier poems may be dismissed as the work of adolescent bystanders, Gallen is less easily sidelined. Due to the

---

[132] Robert Greacen, 'John Gallen: An Appreciation', *The Northman* XV, no. 3 (Summer 1947), pp. 14–15 (p. 15).
[133] John Gallen, 'For R.A.', *The Northman* XV, no. 3, p. 16.

rapidly changing nature of warfare at this time, combatant poets cannot be considered uniquely authentic voices, and one of the most powerful poems in response to the Belfast Blitz, Padraic Fiacc's 'Der Bomben Poet', was written by someone who did not experience it at all. The seventeen-year-old Fiacc was in the United States when he wrote 'My home town/Has just bin/ Blown up' and articulated conflicting feelings of detachment and engagement in the lines 'I have nothing to write/Poems about'.[134]

* * *

John Hewitt also considered his position as a Home Front poet. In 'Minor Poet's Dilemma, 1940', he looks for guidance from poetic antecedents:

> Caught in my prime in pitiful disaster,
> my world's walls gape atilt, about to fall:
> where must I turn for comfortable master
> to fill the hush of terror's interval?

There are two poets to whom Hewitt contemplates turning: Edward Thomas, who 'when earth was breaking,/brooding on vole and hawthorn, deathward went', and Roman Landor, who at eighty still made 'immortal quatrains of pure sentiment'.[135] The reference to Thomas, who was killed on the Western Front in 1917, returns us to the problematic relationship between combatant and non-combatant poets. Thomas's own status as a 'war poet' certainly highlights this troubled area: though best known for his involvement in the First World War (he joined the British army before conscription was introduced), the bulk of his work in prose and poetry examined England, its countryside, environment, and rural culture (hence Hewitt's reference to 'vole and hawthorn'), whilst some of his poems that relate directly to the war were written before he had reached the Western Front.[136] As Robert Greacen recalled in 1976, the strength of identification between conflict and poetry encouraged by memories of Rupert Brooke and other soldier poets of the First World War fuelled an expectation in the early years of the Second for heavily circumscribed poetry about the war which had not been fulfilled.[137] At a time when, in Britain at least, demands were being made of poets to produce work which

---

[134] Padraic Fiacc, 'Der Bomben Poet', *Ruined Pages: Selected Poems*, edited by Gerald Dawe and Aodán Mac Póilin (Belfast: Blackstaff Press, 1994), p. 19.

[135] John Hewitt, 'Minor Poet's Dilemma, 1940', *The Collected Poems of John Hewitt*, edited by Frank Ormsby (Belfast: Blackstaff Press, 1991), p. 151.

[136] E. Longley, 'Thomas, (Philip) Edward (1878–1917)', *Oxford Dictionary of National Biography (DNB)* (Oxford: Oxford University Press, 2004; online edn. 2009), <http:// www.oxforddnb.com/view/article/36480>.

[137] Greacen, 'Writing through the Irish Blitz', *Irish Times*, 4 June 1976.

addressed the war, the invocation of Thomas suggests that Hewitt was aware of these calls.[138]

In the end, Hewitt did not produce many war poems at all, and at this time instead tended to explore the landscape and cultural history of his immediate locality in poetry and prose. One poem which does refer to the war is 'The Volunteer', written in 1951, which recounts the story of a ship's engineer who retires to a small cabin 'among the whins' near an Ulster village. Despite his age, on the outbreak of war the man volunteers to serve at sea, but is repeatedly mocked by inhabitants of the village, when he hears nothing in response to his offer from 'Head Office'. Eventually, 'one black week, when all the bulletins/were bomber raids, retreats and fallen towns', a letter arrives at his shack, to tell him that his name has been added to a list pending vacancy: 'John bore the letter in a trembling fist,/and read it twice at every neighbour's fire'.[139] The poem is clearly and sincerely sympathetic towards the seaman, but does not comment substantially on the war: instead Hewitt explores the isolation of the volunteer from the community in the context of the Second World War. There is no overt moral condemnation here, but as in MacNeice's 'The Coming of War' series, rural Ulster again appears 'unreal' in this context, its inhabitants remaining detached from the international situation. It is possible that the poem also refers to Hewitt's own attempts to volunteer for service with the British armed forces during the war: variously turned down and ignored by recruiting officers due to his reserved occupation in local government, he nevertheless admitted to feeling 'a recurring sense of guilt' at his inability to become directly involved.[140] In his unpublished memoir *A North Light*, Hewitt expressed regret at not having served in the forces:

> And so, though I tried, admittedly not hard enough to hurt, I was not able to take any part in what I realised must have been the greatest imaginative experience of my generation; and may be in that loss I have suffered a serious deprivation which has left me perhaps less adult than my years require.[141]

[138] See, for example, 'To the Poets of 1940', *Times Literary Supplement*, 30 December 1939.

[139] Hewitt, 'The Volunteer', *Collected Poems of John Hewitt*, pp. 119–120 (p. 120). Another poem with the same name describes the death of his uncle in France during the First World War (Hewitt, *Collected Poems*, p. 267).

[140] John Hewitt, *A North Light: Twenty-Five Years in a Municipal Art Gallery* (unpublished autobiography, John Hewitt Collection, University of Ulster, Coleraine), pp. 99–100, p. 102; Frank Ormsby, 'Biographical Chronology', in Ormsby (ed.), *Collected Poems of John Hewitt*, pp. xxix–xl, pp. xxxiv–xxxv. Edited by Frank Ferguson and Kathryn White, *A North Light* was published by Four Courts Press, Dublin, in 2013.

[141] Hewitt, *North Light*, p. 99.

Instead he joined the Civil Defence Forces, and also lectured widely on art and literature in British army camps around Northern Ireland during the war. Hewitt recalled satirically that 'when Hitler attacked the Soviet Union, and talks on our new, approved ally were in demand' he was employed for his left-wing, but importantly non-communist, credentials: 'And so the Marxist Dialectic was wafted from Ballymoney to Newry'.[142]

A journey to or from one of these meetings seems to have inspired the poem 'Ulster Winter (1942)', originally entitled 'Winter in Armagh'.[143] It opens with an army lorry speeding along a winter road 'Between black hedges under a grey sky', and the first four of six stanzas describe a wet, sometimes boggy landscape, intermittently enlivened by flocks of starlings and flashes of colour from decaying leaves. Hewitt then turns his attention to his companion in the cab of the lorry, and concludes the poem with these two stanzas:

> I glanced at the young soldier by my side,
> Gripping the wheel with a grubby-knuckled hand,
> A cockney by his tongue, and wondered if
> I spoke my thoughts he'd even understand.

> For I am native, though my fathers came
> From fatter acres over the grey sea:
> The clay that hugs the rows of exile bones
> Has shaped my phantom nationality.[144]

These lines suggest that the presence of troops in the province during the war fed into Hewitt's regionalist conception of the British Isles, whereby he sought to reconfigure Britain and Ireland on a federal basis as a group of culturally and politically distinct regions.[145] So distinct, indeed, that the soldier is described as 'cockney', and the poet's sense of alienation from the young man is such that he wonders if communication between them is possible. This poem also shows how Hewitt sought rootedness for his own identity as an Ulsterman in the soil, the 'clay', which has received and moulded the 'exile bones' of Hewitt's planter forebears. Gerald Dawe sees in Hewitt's poetry 'the struggle against art's enticement, the lure of the imagination, distant horizons, the unknown—and the need to resist this in both poetic and political terms'.[146] In 'Ulster Winter (1942)', as in

---

[142] Hewitt, *North Light*, p. 99.

[143] Hewitt, 'Ulster Winter (1942)', *Collected Poems of John Hewitt*, p. 485, note p. 656.

[144] Hewitt, 'Ulster Winter (1942)', *Collected Poems of John Hewitt*, p. 485.

[145] John Hewitt, 'Regionalism: The Last Chance' in *Ancestral Voices: The Selected Prose of John Hewitt*, edited by Tom Clyde (Belfast: Blackstaff Press, 1987), pp. 122–125.

[146] Gerald Dawe, 'Against piety: a reading of John Hewitt's poetry', in *The Poet's Place: Ulster Literature and Society Essays in honour of John Hewitt, 1907–87*, edited by Gerald Dawe and John Wilson Foster (Belfast: Institute of Irish Studies, 1991), pp. 209–224 (p. 218).

Hewitt's long poem 'Conacre' written the following year, it is the land that acts almost mystically as an anchor for such resistance, at a time when the interconnectedness of previously disparate parts of the world was becoming dangerously apparent and 'distant horizons' drew ever closer.

As well as giving lectures and working at the Belfast Museum and Art Gallery, Hewitt's role as a convenor of writers and artists was also hugely important to the cultural life of Belfast at this time. With his wife Roberta, he welcomed artists and writers of many nationalities to their house at 18 Mount Charles during the war, including writers stationed in Northern Ireland with the British armed forces such as Hamish Henderson, Rayner Heppenstall, Emanuel Litvinoff, and John Manifold. He also offered encouragement to the younger generation of Belfast poets, even if they subsequently disavowed his ideas. Roy McFadden's personal recollections of encounters with Hewitt are warm, but he did not share the older poet's localized vision.[147] The poets with whom the earlier part of this chapter is concerned showed little interest in Hewitt's regionalist ideas, as McFadden recalled in 1961:

> Inoffensive shoemakers, clergymen, mechanics who had happened to toss off the odd poem in their youth, were exhumed from their century-old graves and held up as our literary ancestors. But we shook our heads. They remained shoemakers, clergymen and mechanics. Ulster horseshoes have an extra nail hole. We remained uninspired.[148]

McFadden's relationship with Hewitt's poetry was more complex, as can be seen in two wartime essays which offer conflicting appraisals of the older poet's 'realism'. In 'Life and Writing in North-East Ulster' McFadden defends Hewitt's work from critics who characterize it as 'Georgian', and praises 'the essential realism of his work which speaks for an agricultural community still more afraid of the sidhe-mounds than H.E. Bombs', but in 'The Position in Ulster' he criticizes Hewitt's 'lapse into photographic realism'.[149] In both essays McFadden contrasts Hewitt's poetry with the 'complementary' work of his contemporary W.R. Rodgers, and, further complicating the vexed matter of 'realism', argues that Rodgers was the 'first great Ulster realist' whose 'arrogant, swaggering rhythms and great blasts of contempt are as much a part of the 6 counties as the Cave Hill or the Mournes'.[150] Robert Greacen was also keen to praise Rodgers, writing

---

[147] Roy McFadden, 'No Dusty Pioneer: A Personal Recollection of John Hewitt', in Dawe and Wilson Foster (eds.), *The Poet's Place*, pp. 169–180, (pp. 171–172).
[148] McFadden, 'Reflections on Megarrity', *Threshold 5*, no. 1, p. 32.
[149] McFadden, 'Life and Writing in North-East Ulster', McFadden Papers, MP5, p. 8; McFadden, 'The Position in Ulster', McFadden Papers, MP5, pp. 4–5.
[150] McFadden, 'Life and Writing in North-East Ulster', McFadden Papers, MP5, p. 8.

in 1942 that even if the older man's poems recalled Auden and Gerard Manley Hopkins, they still rang 'true and vital. His imagery is always courageous, with just a hint of foolhardiness: in fact Rodgers rarely fails to excite and stun'. Conceding that Rodgers is guilty of 'tiresome revelling in alliteration', Greacen nevertheless lauds his 'all round sheer excellence' and concludes by voicing a fear for his future development as a poet since 'one feels that he has said everything that he has to say and that he could hardly better his technique'.[151]

Since then, Terence Brown has described Rodgers as 'a romanticist of words, delighted in their instability and in word games, verbal associations for their own sake', and reads his early poems as the work of a personality at war with itself, attempting to reconcile Calvinist duty with the Romantic desire for rich and diverse experiences.[152] Rodgers' reputation has arguably suffered since his death in 1969: Derek Mahon wrote in 1993 that 'Now he is remembered as an idiosyncratic period rhymester who started late and stopped early and produced at most five or six lyric poems of continuing interest', but hailed him as 'unique—a renegade Presbyterian minister with an all-Ireland perspective'.[153] Such appraisals have emphasized the singular stylistic approach and powerful rhythms of Rodgers' verse, and focused on his vocation as a minister, but his war poetry raises important questions regarding the place of Northern Ireland in relation to the Second World War, and also betrays the influence of Louis MacNeice on his work. John Wilson Foster has written that 'Many of the pieces are explicitly war poems, written by a non-combatant innocent of bloodshed, whose knowledge is filtered through newspapers and newsreels', and in which the war persists as 'an unavoidable, if distant fact'.[154] In such a way, 'Stormy Day', from his first published collection *Awake! and Other Poems* (1941), describes a blustery day in a city park, where cherry and beech trees cavort and dip in the wind and boats on a lake are 'roped and ready for hire'. The scene is troubled, however, by the intrusion of some static news boards:

> There! Do you see, crucified on palings,
> Motionless news-posters announcing
> That now the frozen armies melt and meet
> And smash? Go home now, for, try as you may,

[151] Greacen, 'A Survey of Ulster Writing' *The Northman XI*, no. 2, p. 13.

[152] Terence Brown, 'W.R. Rodgers: Romantic Calvinist', in *Northern Voices*, pp. 114–127 (p. 114, p. 119).

[153] Derek Mahon, 'Sudden, Wild Profusion', *Irish Times*, 15 January 1993.

[154] John Wilson Foster, ' "The Dissidence of Dissent": John Hewitt and W.R. Rodgers', in Dawe and Longley (eds.), *Across A Roaring Hill*, pp. 139–160 (p. 151).

> You will not shake off that fact to-day.
> Behind you limps that dog with tarry paw,
> As behind him, perfectly timed, follows
> The dumb shadow that mimes him all the way.[155]

In 'Sing, Brothers, Sing!' Rodgers counsels against the transformation of warfare by wireless into constantly babbling aural entertainment, and, echoing Andrew Marvell's 'To His Coy Mistress', cautions that 'At our back door we failed to hear/War's dust-bin chariot drawing near', whilst in 'Music in War-Time' the war is seen to overwhelm the individual imagination, as 'All things, even our thoughts' shapes, subscribe/To these importunate times'.[156] Here an orchestra is reconfigured as an arsenal, where a trumpet 'Juts and jets jumpily like a gun', and 'lean violins dive and flow/ In close formation...Whirling and wheeling and whorling/Like aerial convoy'.[157] The music itself echoes the patterns of submarine warfare, as an 'alien phrase up-pokes and breaks/Tentatively like a periscope', a drum 'drops its depth charge', and counterpoint below combs 'the thoughtless unknown depths/A clear and harmonious lane-way/For following and conducted ears'.[158]

As with Robert Greacen, connections may be drawn through Rodgers' friendships and publication history between the relatively isolated literary environment in Northern Ireland and other wartime poetic circles, in England and south of the border. Prior to the publication of his first collection *Awake! and Other Poems* in 1941, he successfully submitted poems to the London magazines *Horizon*, *The Listener*, and the *New Statesman and Nation*; in 1940 Rodgers received a letter from John Lehmann asking if he planned to write more, since the Hogarth Press was keen to continue its tradition of publishing work by the most striking new poets.[159] In 1945 there were, it seems, plans for Rodgers to collaborate with Graham Sutherland on an illustrated poem for a new magazine, but frustratingly

---

[155] W.R. Rodgers, 'Stormy Day', *Awake! and Other Poems* (London: Secker and Warburg, 1941), p. 44. Many of the poems in this volume were reprinted in *Poems*, edited by Michael Longley (Oldcastle, Co. Meath: Gallery Press, 1993).
[156] Rodgers, 'Sing, Brothers, Sing', *Awake!*, pp. 20–21 (p. 21); Rodgers, 'Music in War-Time', *Awake!*, pp. 54–55 (p. 54).
[157] Rodgers, 'Music in War-Time', *Awake!*, p. 54.
[158] Rodgers, 'Music in War-Time', *Awake!*, p. 54, p. 55.
[159] Letter from John Lehmann to W.R. Rodgers, 4 November 1940, W.R. Rodgers Papers, PRONI, D2833/C/2/2/10. *Awake! and Other Poems* was later published by Secker and Warburg. In 1940 Cyril Connolly, editor of *Horizon*, wrote to Rodgers encouraging him to continue submitting poems but rejecting 'End of a World' on the grounds that it was too similar in metre to the poems by Rodgers that *Horizon* had already published. Connolly compared Rodgers' poetry to a honeycomb without much honey and suggested that he send it instead to the Trotskyite publication *Partisan Review* (Letter from Cyril Connolly to W.R. Rodgers, 23 December 1940, Rodgers Papers, D2833/C/2/2/6).

these seem to have come to nothing.[160] The forging of these links encourages the perception that Rodgers was keen to escape Ulster's political and
religious strictures. Unlike John Hewitt, Rodgers appears to have felt profoundly disconnected from his immediate environment. Nowhere is this
more apparent than in a short article entitled 'Black North', published in
the *New Statesman* in November 1943. Written during a year's leave spent
in Oxford, the piece attempted to describe the social and political composition of Northern Ireland for the benefit of the magazine's English readers, but caused outrage in Rodgers' parish of Loughall in County Armagh
by posing the inflammatory question 'Have we in Ulster a "fascist" government?', and claiming that the 'pitfall' of the Ulster Protestant character
was its 'hypocrisy'.[161] Rodgers' biographer suggests that the writing of this
article amounts to a conscious effort on the minister's part to distance himself from the community of which he had inevitably become an important
part.[162] Although Rodgers managed to repair some of the damage, and
was even elected to the local Unionist Council, his departure for London
in 1946 to take up a role at the BBC offered by Louis MacNeice does
encourage the idea that Rodgers felt at odds with and exhausted by the
political and religious life of the province. Like the younger poets Greacen
and McFadden, Rodgers appears to have felt some release from this during
a visit to Dublin in the summer of 1941, when he stayed with Geoffrey
Taylor, poetry editor of *The Bell*, and greatly enjoyed evenings spent in the
company of writers including John Betjeman, Austin Clarke, and Frank
O'Connor, before returning reluctantly to Armagh.[163]

The poems in *Awake! and Other Poems* were written between 1938
and 1940, and the collection is dominated by the advent of the Second
World War, contextually anchored by the physical paraphernalia of guns,
planes, telegraph wires, and ships. Significantly, for the 1942 American
edition, the title was amended to *Awake! and Other Wartime Poems*.[164]
The publication of the book was itself affected by the war, when the first
printing was destroyed entirely in the bombing of Plymouth in 1940,
and the prospect of air attack is addressed in several poems.[165] 'The

---

[160] The magazine was to have been entitled *Flair*, and would have been published by
Percy Lund Humphries Ltd—it was planned that Sutherland would illustrate Rodgers'
poem 'Lent' (Rodgers Papers, D2833/C/3/3).

[161] W.R. Rodgers, 'Black North', *New Statesman and Nation*, 20 November 1943.

[162] Darcy O'Brien, *W. R. Rodgers* (Cranbury, NJ: Associated University Presses, 1970),
p. 55.

[163] O'Brien, *W. R. Rodgers*, pp. 42–43.

[164] Wilson Foster, 'The Dissidence of Dissent', in Dawe and Longley (eds.), *Across a
Roaring Hill*, p. 150.

[165] This was explained to readers in a note opposite the contents page of the original
1941 edition.

Raider' describes the isolated figure of the 'lone airman', a pilot 'Frocked and fanged by fire, by nagging fingers/Of guns jagged and jogged, with shell-bursts tasselled', and wonders if the man's eyes ever 'alight and loiter' on the country below, or if his gaze 'easily dissolve(s)/Upon the moving surfaces'.[166] In 'The Far-Off Hills' Rodgers again uses the aerial perspective of the aviator to address the dehumanizing and distancing effects of modern warfare, lamenting the fact 'that distance puts/Ten-league boots on brutality', as bombs drop from the aircraft:

> Miles below, in a spidery splash,
> On the pin-point town,
> Gumming grimacing faces to the pavement,
> While the alert executor, lark-light,
> Tiny climber in titanic chasm,
> Rinses the pin-prick pity in the burst
> And cloudy roundabout of pride.[167]

The mapping of war is also evident in 'Escape', where Rodgers figures the coming of war as a threatening, growing web of connections:

> The roads of Europe are running away from the war,
> Running fast over the mined bridges and past the men
> Waiting there, with watch, ready to maim and arrest them,
> And strong overhead the long snorings of the planes' tracks
> Are stretching like rafters from end to end of their power.
> Turn back, you who want to escape or want to forget
> The ruin of all your regards. You will be more free
> At the thoughtless centre of slaughter than you would be
> Standing chained to the telephone-end while the world cracks.[168]

With its emphasis on connections the poem echoes Robert Greacen's 'The Glorious Twelfth', which conjures a network of fire, running 'swift rivers into Europe'. In this web, made up of roads, plane contrails, and telephone lines, Rodgers signals the importance of technology to the war, and emphasizes how progress in this field has drawn the entire continent into the conflict, where danger now presents itself along a road, from the sky, or at the end of a cable. The words 'running away from the war' also appear in the fifth section of Louis MacNeice's sequence 'The Coming of War', where they describe the drive west to Sligo in the summer of 1939, escaping the 'Black/North—the winch and the windlass,/The drum and the Union Jack'.[169] Given Rodgers' use of 'Black North' as the title for his *New*

---

[166] Rodgers, 'The Raider', *Awake!*, p. 39.
[167] Rodgers, 'The Far-Off Hills', *Awake!*, pp. 17–19 (p. 17).
[168] Rodgers, 'Escape', *Awake!*, p. 45.
[169] MacNeice, 'The Coming of War', *Collected Poems*, p. 683.

Statesman article it is clear that 'The Coming of War' should be regarded as an antecedent here. MacNeice also denied the possibility of escape: although he manages to leave the oppressive paraphernalia of Ulster behind him, the west of Ireland ultimately proves no haven from the international conflict, and in the seventh section the war repeatedly 'comes down' on him in Galway, as though he felt a physical weight descending.[170] Rodgers' seemingly paradoxical assertion that those at the centre of the conflict will be 'more free' perhaps suggests that the war will offer an opportunity for Rodgers himself to escape from the bounded and conservative climate of his parish and of Northern Ireland itself. In one important and much-quoted phrase from the notes for *Awake! and Other Poems*, Rodgers wrote that he felt he had been 'schooled in a backwater of literature out of sight of the running stream of contemporary verse': the quickening excitement of these poems suggests that the war offered a means of escape from the backwater.[171]

The war's defining presence in this first collection certainly suggests that it acted as a creative release. Cathartic purgation is loudly proclaimed by 'Action Stations', in which Rodgers describes how evil was once something inside him, leaving his heart 'locked and rotted with/Inaction', but that now 'private avenues of feeling' are no longer 'contained and occluded'. The catalyst for this is clear:

> War shot its spark, and our shut chimneys
> Shed and vehemently vomited
> Their woolly volumes. From our hearts' hearths,
> Past the dampers, checks, and private chokes
> And sooted flues of feeling, issued
> In ashy sheets the shy repressions.[172]

Excitement at the unleashing of creative possibilities is tempered by the constant presence of 'Evil', now outside the body, and 'overt and aloof' in the skies and the seas. The war becomes a fixation to which other

---

[170] MacNeice, 'The Coming of War', *Collected Poems*, pp. 684–685.
[171] Quoted by Michael Longley, 'Introduction', *W.R. Rodgers: Poems*, edited by Michael Longley (Oldcastle, Co. Meath: Gallery Press, 1993), pp. 11–22 (p. 15). Roy McFadden denied Rodgers his backwater, however, recalling that:

> …'the running stream of contemporary verse' was evident in the great wash of books in the manse at Loughall. And we all dipped into it at Davy McClean's, where more books were read than bought; and where indeed Wesley Sutton displayed in the window his handwritten copies of the reviews of *Awake!*, like bulletins outside a palace of royal births and deaths. We all splashed in the stream of poetry, for it was totally accessible; and unlike today, its current was not narrowly culverted in one direction.

(McFadden, 'The Dogged Hare', McFadden Papers, MP35 [vii].)
[172] Rodgers, 'Action Stations', *Awake!*, p. 42.

considerations are subordinate, as the reader must 'Look how/All the lines of our lives converge on/The gun's focus and the bullets' fan'.[173] This image of a fan can also be traced back to 'The Coming of War', where 'fan-shafts of sun' as MacNeice drives through the countryside to Sligo echo the 'bare bones of a fanlight/Over a hungry door' in Dublin in the opening section. Along with the 'tumbledown walls' going 'leap-frog/Over the moors' in Mayo, and the water 'combed out/Over the weir' on the Corrib, MacNeice deploys fans in 'The Closing Album' to animate the poems with rippling movement, showing how the muted effects of the outbreak of war were felt in Ireland as they radiated from a European centre.[174] In keeping with the explosive tone of 'Action Stations', Rodgers' 'fan' of bullets is clearly a far more violent image, but it may be seen to reflect the map sketched in 'Escape', where 'roads' and 'tracks' likened to 'rafters' stretch from the 'thoughtless centre'.

In 1990 Edna Longley outlined a positive conception of a 'female, feminist, connective' web in Northern Ireland of multiple affiliations, local, national, and international, giving writers and others 'the ability to inhabit a range of relations rather than a single allegiance. The great advantage of living in Northern Ireland is that you can be in three places at once'.[175] The larger-scale wartime webs of cause and effect outlined by Greacen and Rodgers are threatening by comparison, and draw Northern Ireland into traumatic contemporary European histories, but they similarly serve to question entrenched local positions and enable the province's own history to be contextualized anew. The multiple meanings of the word 'chained' in 'Escape' must be heeded, but such imagery is complemented by Rodgers' associative use of language, whereby disparate words are yoked together as a result of their sound and appearance rather than any etymological correspondence, resulting in linguistic eddies, swirls, and eruptions that articulate the tumultuous and sometimes chaotic patterns of conflict.[176]

* * *

---

[173] Rodgers, 'Action Stations', *Awake!*, p. 42.
[174] MacNeice, 'The Coming of War', *Collected Poems*, p. 680, p. 683, p. 684.
[175] Edna Longley, 'From Cathleen to Anorexia', *Living Stream*, p. 195.
[176] It is perhaps telling that Roy McFadden uses distinctive wartime imagery to describe a page of Rodgers' manuscripts:

> ... every word in the page has a barrage balloon above it, like the balloons that come out of people's mouths in the children's comics. Each balloon has a word in it. And every balloon has another alternative balloon above it, all rising and soaring to the seventh heaven of unachievement.
>
> I remember seeing one of his manuscripts. It looked like an inverted sow feeding an enormous airborne farrow.

(McFadden Papers, 'The Dogged Hare', MP35 [vii].)

During the eruptions of violence in Northern Ireland in the late 1960s and early 1970s, both Robert Greacen and Roy McFadden drew comparisons between the febrile atmosphere in the province and their experience of the war years. In a letter to Greacen in August 1969, McFadden wrote of the fires and petrol bombs that 'It's almost like wartime again. One measures food and remembers that rationed but keyed-up existence'.[177] This sense of recognition drove McFadden back to reconsider the poetry of the forties: in the following week's letter he describes rereading poems by Valentin Iremonger with pleasure, and observes that it was a pity that Iremonger was never taken on by a major publishing house, 'Especially now when, according to JHH, our generation has been completely forgotten'.[178] The war continued to prey on McFadden's mind, and that September he wrote that he had never liked Belfast 'where the shawlies in Cromac Street matched shawled official minds; but I will never leave it. When I was growing up, it was an ignorant, prejudiced place. Now Belfast is sophisticated. It suffered education during the war'.[179] After two years, McFadden's gloom seems to have intensified, as he describes life in Belfast to his friend (Greacen was by then living in England). McFadden writes of army searches, of bomb scares real and imagined, of boarded up windows, and, with a blackly Orwellian acronymic misplacement, of the prospect of central Belfast being demolished by the 'ARP'. He concludes that 'It's worse than the war, because the thing is happening from inside'.[180]

Robert Greacen also drew parallels between Northern Ireland's experiences of the Second World War and of the Troubles. In a letter to the *Irish Times* in 1974 he mused on the swift growth in stature of the 'Northern Renaissance' group of younger poets:

> There seems to be a literary ferment in Belfast comparable with the upsurge in creative writing that characterised the period of the Second World War. Does violence stimulate creativity? Perhaps it does in the sense that when life and limb are in danger we tend to concentrate more on permanent than temporary values. Or, more prosaically, is it that when people must perforce stay at home a number of them take to poetry to while away the long evenings.[181]

---

[177] Letter from McFadden to Greacen, 17 August 1969, Greacen Collection, Box 4 File 3.
[178] Letter from McFadden to Greacen, 25 August 1969, Greacen Collection, Box 4 File 3. 'JHH' refers to John Hewitt.
[179] Letter from McFadden to Greacen, 27 September 1969, Greacen Collection, Box 4 File 3.
[180] Letter from McFadden to Greacen, 20 November 1971, Greacen Collection, Box 4 File 3.
[181] Robert Greacen, 'Northern Poets', *Irish Times*, 18 June 1974.

This is a tentative analysis, and Greacen's contentious idea that violence stimulates creativity is qualified by the more practical suggestion that remaining undercover during long evenings (confinement that those who lived through the Blitz would remember) may equally well encourage the writing of poetry. Indeed, as Hewitt in particular repeatedly claimed, it is probable that the territorial confinement of the war years, when government restrictions on the movement of civilians made travel to Britain difficult and to Europe impossible, was a hugely important stimulant to creative endeavour in Northern Ireland. On occasion, the urge to write poetry or prose may simply be an instinctive reaction to something strange: Greacen recalled that, having expected to be overtaken by 'mass hysteria' during the war, 'the only answer was that if I kept on writing I might be able to remain detached and sane. Writing seemed to be a necessary therapy which, if frustrated, would lead to mental numbness and inner death'.[182] Like Greacen, I would hesitate to draw a direct link between the violence of these historical periods and any resulting artistic production, but poetry produced in Northern Ireland during the war is clearly animated by anxiety at a map redrawn. As the province was opened up to new cultural influences, the work of its poets belies a profound sense of fear that Northern Ireland, having edged onto the international stage, was now prey to new and threatening forces. Such a sense of uncertainty over the province's place in the world is exemplified by the fourth stanza of Maurice James Craig's post-Belfast Blitz poem 'Easter Tuesday, 1941', published in *The Northman* towards the end of 1941:

> Steel and concrete, floating
> On the estuary bog
> Rest on nothing sounder
> Than a drifting log.
> No burrow can protect you
> From the power of the dog.[183]

---

[182] Greacen, *Sash*, pp. 121–122.
[183] Maurice James Craig, 'Easter Tuesday 1941', *The Northman*, XI.7 (Winter 1941–1942), p. 7.

3

'Strange Openings': Visual Art

Somewhat perversely, the Second World War created conditions in which visual artists in Northern Ireland could flourish. The unprecedented influx of foreign troops and refugees brought many new cultural modes and traditions to the province, and the conflict's attendant anxieties, uncertainties, and visual stimulants that resulted seem to have encouraged artists to experiment with form and composition to a greater degree than had previously been possible.[1] The visual arts also received new and important official backing in the form of the Council for the Encouragement of Music and the Arts in Northern Ireland (CEMA [NI]), established in 1943 to encourage public interest in the arts through programmes of travelling exhibitions and lectures across the province.[2] Some commercial demand for art also seems to have survived the privations of war: in December 1940 the Mass Observation diarist Moya Woodside reports that on ordering a picture frame she had been ready to commiserate with the art dealer on what she had presumed was a spell of bad trade, but instead the man told her that 'he hadn't been so busy for the last 7 years', serving not regular customers but 'quite unfamiliar people who came in and paid cash' and who were buying all they could afford. The dealer confides that when the Swedish and Continental stock that was presently so popular ran out he feared he would not be able to replace it.[3]

---

[1] One such refugee was Alice Berger Hammerschlag, an abstract painter, who fled mainland Europe in the late 1930s. She met her husband Heinz, also a refugee, in Belfast during the Second World War, and they married in 1947. Hammerschlag was closely associated with the Lyric Theatre, where she managed the New Gallery and designed stage sets, and her work was widely exhibited during her life and is held in the collections of the Arts Council of Northern Ireland, the Ulster Museum, and the Hugh Lane Gallery in Dublin. At the opening of her memorial exhibition it was said that she was of 'inestimable value to the progress of art in Northern Ireland' (Diarmuid Kennedy, 'The Legend Who Lived in Lost Belfast', *Belfast Telegraph*, 5 April 2007).

[2] *CEMA (Northern Ireland) First Annual Report Covering the period 1st February, 1943 to 31st March, 1944*, Arts Council of Northern Ireland Archive, PRONI, AC 2/1/1; Gillian McIntosh, 'CEMA and the National Anthem: The Arts and the State in Postwar Northern Ireland', *New Hibernia Review 5*, no. 3 (2001), pp. 22–31 (p. 22).

[3] Woodside, 9 December 1940.

As we shall see, more pessimistic voices do contradict the idea that the war years were of great profit to artists in Northern Ireland, but a new-found sense of community between artists and writers in Belfast is certainly palpable in the little magazines and occasional publications such as John Boyd's *Lagan* and Robert Greacen's *Northern Harvest* that appeared over the war years, and the pressures and restrictions of life on the Home Front seem to have encouraged an unofficial and mutually supportive group of artists and writers to gather in the city, aiding the circulation of radical ideas.[4] This was also the first time a significant group of artists from Northern Ireland began to achieve renown outside their immediate locality without emigrating, and it is notable that the third annual Irish Exhibition of Living Art held in Dublin in 1945 was dominated by a group of artists from the province.

The pre-war cultural atmosphere in Northern Ireland appears to have offered little encouragement to aspiring painters. Prevalent attitudes towards artists were memorably summed up by the Protestant nationalist journalist and critic Denis Ireland in an introduction to the catalogue for a 1968 touring exhibition dedicated to the memory of William Conor:

> A man sketching in France is still a French citizen, as much within the law as anybody else. A man sketching in Victorian and Edwardian Belfast was outside, if not the law, at any rate, the *mores*; he wasn't doing anything useful, wasn't helping to propel that tide of red brick up the lower slopes of the Black Mountain.[5]

Artists seem to have been viewed in their own communities with suspicion and hostility, to the extent that as a young man Conor sketched on the streets of Belfast shielded by a newspaper, in an attempt to fool passers-by into thinking that he was studying racing form.[6] John Hewitt recalled that as a boy of seven or eight, and aware that artists were unlike other people, he once followed Conor along a street, curious to know where he was going:

> He was William Conor, the artist. His brightly coloured shirt, his big tie, his flat black hat, all marked him out as different. A man who lived to paint pictures; who didn't teach in a school, or drive a bread-cart, or wear an apron

---

[4] Edna Longley, 'A Barbarous Nook', *The Living Stream*, p. 104.

[5] Denis Ireland, 'Introduction. William Conor: The man who stayed at home', in *William Conor 1881–1968*, (Belfast: Arts Council of Northern Ireland, 1968), pp. 5–7 (p. 6).

[6] Judith C. Wilson, *Conor 1881–1968: The Life and Work of an Ulster Artist* (Dundonald: Blackstaff Press, 1981), p. 7.

behind a counter. A strange and wholly alluring person. He forged on with that slow urgent characteristic stride of his.[7]

Hostility endured. Gerard Dillon initially became a decorator after it was made clear to him that painting was not an acceptable profession where he grew up in West Belfast, and he eventually moved away to London.[8] An unsigned essay in the Socialist Party newsletter *Northern Star* in June 1940 entitled 'The Sahara of the Arts' acknowledged that although Ulster was 'far from poor' in the world of letters, in terms of visual art 'Local paint-ers, *good* local painters, are neglected and, in exhibitions, scorned'.[9] Such scorn was a matter of abiding interest to John Hewitt, who refined his explanations for the enduring distrust of and resistance to creative expres-sion in the province in a number of writings over his career, beginning with a flurry of essays and reviews published during the war. In 'Painting in Ulster', an essay which appeared in the one-off anthology *Northern Harvest* (1944), Hewitt wrote despairingly of the 'culturally conservative climate of the province', adding that 'One of the gravest obstacles has been and to some measure still is that our Ulster buying public has been unwilling to give adequate support to local effort'.[10] Suggesting that mete-orological and geographical forces were ranged against the aspiring artist, he claimed that landscape painting in Ulster had long been hampered by the province's damp climate.[11] In a radio talk in 1945 Hewitt argued that a lack of aristocratic and ecclesiastical patronage was partly responsible for the shortfall:

> No King established his court among us. No Church has been rich enough, and the aristocracy, apart from the brief Georgian flourish at the end of that Century, has had little cultural influence. Our merchant-class came to power too late. And there were no cities crammed with craftsmen to draw upon for the traditional skills.[12]

In the essay 'The Bitter Gourd: Some Problems of the Ulster Writer,' pub-lished in *Lagan* in 1945, Hewitt lamented the lack of artistic and liter-ary heritage in Ulster, attributing this deficit to the absence of a single

---

[7] John Hewitt, 'Pictures', radio broadcast on BBC Northern Ireland Home Service, 1 March 1948, Coleraine Hewitt Collection, Box 12, 4/5, p. 1.
[8] James White, *Gerard Dillon: An Illustrated Biography* (Dublin: Wolfhound Press, 1994), p. 23.
[9] 'The Sahara of the Arts', *Northern Star 1*, no. 4 (June 1940), p. 9.
[10] John Hewitt, 'Painting in Ulster', in *Northern Harvest: Anthology of Ulster Writing* (Belfast: Derrick MacCord, 1944), pp. 140–147 (p. 141, p. 142).
[11] Hewitt, 'Painting in Ulster', *Northern Harvest*, p. 144.
[12] John Hewitt, 'Art in Ulster', radio broadcast on BBC NIHS, Sunday 11 November 1945, Coleraine Hewitt Collection, Box 12, 4/1, p. 3.

common and regional ancient language, and blaming in part the ethnic composition of the province:

> Scotsmen, Englishmen and Irishmen have here in Ulster become clotted in an uneven and lumpy mixture. The juxtaposition of these rubbing, striking, colliding elements has frequently produced brilliant results in organisation and material enterprise: our best men are the Lawrences, Kelvin, Hart, Bryce; extroverted men of tremendous energy, skill and integrity, but deficient in creative genius.[13]

The argument continues somewhat vaguely: detecting an inherent 'inarticulateness' in the 'Protestant block', Hewitt claims that the best articulators of Ulster's separateness have tended not to be native Ulstermen, citing Carson, F.E. Smith, and Randolph Churchill in support of this. More solid is his argument that the rapid industrialization of Belfast during the nineteenth century was uncongenial to creative expression, that the 'absurdly vaunted material values' of the province, the pride in having 'the largest shipyard, the largest ropeworks... did really make the artist's position extremely difficult'.[14]

Fellow socialists in Belfast at this time were also keen to blame nineteenth-century industrialization for the cultural and political conservatism of the province. Two years earlier, in 1943, Robert Greacen had expressed dismay at the deleterious effect of 'a stale industrialism, all guts and no heart' on the political culture of Ulster, and the 1944 edition of *Lagan* carried an essay by Denis Ireland entitled 'Smoke Clouds in the Lagan Valley', which similarly attributed the stifling of radical Protestantism during the nineteenth century to the burgeoning industrialization of the city.[15] Ireland did not believe that creative expression had been entirely suppressed, however, and wrote of Conor's folded newspaper that it 'acted both as shelter and release; hence the instantaneous quality of his street sketches, their uninterrupted flowing rhythm'.[16] The cultural conservatism of industrial metropolitan Belfast and its establishment during the nineteenth and early twentieth centuries did not encourage artistic experimentation with avant-garde forms and styles, and even Conor's more impressionistic street scenes, cited by Ireland, are undeniably stylistically conservative. Reporting in May 1944 on a groundbreaking meeting

---

[13] John Hewitt, 'The Bitter Gourd: Some Problems of the Ulster Writer', *Lagan* 3, (1945), pp. 93–105(pp. 93–94).

[14] Hewitt, 'The Bitter Gourd', *Lagan* 3, p. 98. Ironically, during the First and Second World Wars, William Conor and others produced a number of officially commissioned paintings of shipyard scenes in Belfast.

[15] Greacen, 'When Peace Breaks in Ulster', *The Bell* 5, no. 5, p. 397; Denis Ireland, 'Smoke Clouds in the Lagan Valley', *Lagan* 2, (1944), pp. 25–36.

[16] Denis Ireland, 'Introduction', in *William Conor 1881–1968*, p. 6.

to discuss a community arts theatre in Belfast, attended by the Church of Ireland's Dean Kerr, Presbyterian Dr Frazer-Hurst, and the leading Catholic priest Dr Ryan, the 'Northern Notebook' of the Communist newsletter *Unity* commented sarcastically on the prospects for 'a revival in the cultural life of the province':

> There is no shortage of painting talent amongst the workers of Belfast, as the gable walls of the city amply demonstrate. But this talent is rather hampered by a tradition which seems to say that only one theme is worthy of treatment: that of a river-crossing by a certain Dutch gentleman one day in July, 1690.[17]

Admitting that communists and socialists could often seem uninterested or even hostile to artistic expression themselves, over the following months *Unity* made a clear and conscious effort to devote more energy to cultural matters, with a regular column by 'P.W.G.' on literary matters as well as previews of live and radio classical music concerts. In February 1945, 'Overheard at an Exhibition', a satirical piece by the artist George Campbell, lampooned the resistance of the Belfast public to more avant-garde modes by imagining an inane stream of commentary by one exhibition visitor to another:

> Do you paint or draw, darling? You should because mother said everyone should have something to fall back on—not literally speaking of course—something to have as a sideline just in case there is a slump or something. You know how these politics are . . . oh, look at that picture! Isn't it horrible? It must be upside down. Let's go to the other room.[18]

Facing such dismissive attitudes, aspiring artists in Belfast also suffered from a lack of stimuli, in terms of works of art that could be appreciated first hand. At the outbreak of the Second World War a single dedicated art gallery in Stranmillis in South Belfast served the whole province. The city was not untouched by the Victorian zeal for museums, but the city fathers initially favoured science rather than art. Noel Nesbitt's *A Museum in Belfast* (1979) describes how the Belfast Museum opened in 1831 with the intention of satisfying the 'fast growing desire' for scientific knowledge of the citizens of Belfast, displaying artefacts relating to natural history, archaeology, and ethnography.[19] The Belfast Free Public Library which opened in 1888, funded by grants from the Government Committee of the Belfast Corporation, provided a space for temporary art exhibitions on the top floor, but the city did not obtain a permanent home for paintings until the Belfast Museum and Art Gallery (later the

[17] 'Red Hand', 'Northern Notebook', *Unity*, 4 May 1944.
[18] George Campbell, 'Overheard at an Exhibition', *Unity*, 22 February 1944.
[19] Noel Nesbitt, *A Museum in Belfast* (Belfast: Ulster Museum, 1979), p. 7, p. 11.

Ulster Museum) finally opened after a series of delays in 1929. Hewitt, who joined the museum as an art assistant in 1930 and would remain an employee until 1957, was highly critical of the incomplete building in *A North Light*, describing it as:

> ...a monument to civic indecision and lethargy; its original cost ninety thousand pounds, just the cost of a wartime bomber. During the war, every-time I heard on the radio of a bomber being lost, I thought 'There goes the other bit of the Museum and Art Gallery.'[20]

The new building relegated the visual arts to the uppermost floor, and the museum's conservative acquisitions policy, dating from 1910, consisted of plans to buy watercolours, topographical drawings and maps of Belfast, and examples of modern British and French art.[21] The largest of five rooms on the upper floor contained oils by Turner, Orpen, and Lavery, and the other four displayed watercolours, portraits of various civic dignitaries, more works by Lavery. and the Robert Lloyd Patterson Collection. The controversial assembly between 1929 and 1933 of the Lloyd Patterson Collection, made possible by a bequest from the eponymous local con-noisseur, did suggest that some attempts were being made to display more contemporary styles.[22] The London Group was strongly represented in the collection, which introduced the public to works by Duncan Grant, Paul Nash, Walter Sickert, and Stanley Spencer, but the gallery remained resistant to European modernism in the pre-war years, and an exhibition of sculptures by Rodin held between December 1932 and March 1933 was exceptional.[23]

Against this background the Second World War had a galvanizing effect on the Belfast Museum and Art Gallery. Though the upper floor and per-manent collection were evacuated on the outbreak of war, numerous and varied temporary exhibitions were held over the war years. An exhibition on the post-war future of Belfast, in which ten architects outlined their visions for a remodelled city, was particularly successful, and attracted 11,000 visitors to the gallery over a twelve-day period before it was moved to the centre of Belfast.[24] In addition to exhibitions organized by CEMA

---

[20] Hewitt, *North Light*, p. 11.   [21] Nesbitt, p. 31.

[22] The bequest itself consisted of a collection of minor works by Victorian artists, but after a damning independent report commissioned from the visiting art critic Frank Rutter it was decided to sell the majority of these and use the proceeds to purchase modern British art, through the Contemporary Art Society in London. For a detailed account of this epi-sode, see Brian Kennedy, *Ulster Museum, A Catalogue of the Permanent Collection: 1, British Art 1900–1937 Robert Lloyd Patterson Collection* (Belfast: Friends of the Ulster Museum, 1982), pp. 3–5.

[23] Nesbitt, p. 37.

[24] Gerald Morrow, 'Northern Chronicle', *The Bell* 6, no. 2 (May 1943), pp. 151–155(p. 153).

(NI) of works by Irish and British artists, and other shows of paintings and drawings depicting the Home Front, for the first time the gallery began to display many works by overseas artists, as the British Council developed cultural links with the exiled governments of German-occupied European countries. Exhibitions held between 1942 and 1945 showing the art and life of Allied nations included works by artists from Belgium, Czechoslovakia, the Netherlands, and Yugoslavia.[25] Reflecting on his time at the gallery, Hewitt was keen to emphasize the international scope of the exhibitions held during the 1940s and 1950s:

> Our people had, over the years, a chance to see not only Scottish and Welsh painting and work from the North West of England, but Turkish, Dutch, Australian—Drysdale, Dobell, Nolan; Italian—Chirico, Severini, Carra, Morandi, Campigli—and in sculpture one expansive show took in Moore, McWilliam, Chadwick, as well as the best of the Irish, north and south.[26]

In pre-war Belfast, by contrast, the dearth of contemporary paintings was such that European travel, although expensive and unfeasible for most people, was probably the best way of broadening one's artistic horizons, and two of the figures who dominate this chapter, John Hewitt and Colin Middleton, were able to pursue this course. The influences on Middleton's early work can arguably be traced to those artists whose work he had seen on occasional trips to Britain and Europe, such as van Gogh (Middleton visited an exhibition in Leicester in 1928) or Ensor and other Flemish masters, whose work he explored during a visit to Belgium with his father in 1931.[27] Hewitt also benefited from trips to the Continent with his father during the late 1920s, visiting galleries in Bruges and Brussels in 1927 and Paris in 1929.[28] The painter John Luke also travelled to Paris with the English artist Nevill Johnson, who had settled in Belfast in 1935 and begun to paint under Luke's tutelage. Johnson recalled their experience of cubist and surrealist art as 'exploring and tasting rare fruits . . . Life-enhancing stuff it was', contrasting this glamorous world with cultural life back home on the margins, where 'In spite of (or resulting from) the gritty masochism of its inhabitants Belfast harboured also a gaggle of rebels, mavericks, odd-balls, poets and sensible men'.[29] The war precluded European travel, and, as Catherine Marshall describes, painters including Daniel O'Neill were in large part dependent on the kindness of a Belfast librarian for the privilege of examining reproductions of contemporary art:

---

[25] Nesbitt, p. 37.   [26] Hewitt, *North Light*, p. 124.
[27] Dickon Hall, *Colin Middleton: A Study* (Belfast: Joga Press, 2001), p. 5.
[28] Hewitt, *North Light*, pp. 13–14.
[29] Johnson, *The Other Side of Six*, p. 39, p. 41.

The isolation and displacement of the Second World War had, inadvertently, allowed European ideas of Modernism to be examined and assimilated—the source being the City Reference library, in Belfast. Here, the Chief Librarian, Mr Jenkinson, would, contrary to library rules, allow O'Neill and his fellow painters to borrow illustrated texts for the weekend, thereby enabling them to study colour reproductions of the European Moderns. Travel to see the originals would have been impossible, even if they had the means, due to the restrictions of the War.[30]

The paradoxical possibility that in being cut off from the Continent Northern Ireland became more open to modern European artistic influences was explored at length by John Hewitt.

In 'The Bitter Gourd' he suggested that artists in Northern Ireland were forced into commercial exploitations of their talents which frustrated more fruitful artistic projects:

A man may spend a lifetime copying the features of company directors or prelates. Another man will link his name with a known area, to a bundle of mountains or a stretch of coast and continually repeat his own convention for rendering these in terms of pigment. Never in our history have we had a painter who lived in a country place and made not merely the scenery of it, but the whole tangled bird's nest of its life, its people, their business and behaviour, their garments, gestures and architecture, the stuff and substance of his work. The cosmopolitan school of Paris has wiped such an ideal from our minds.[31]

In Hewitt's assessment, painting in the province was caught in an invidious position between a conservative industrial and religious establishment which was reluctant to support artistic endeavour beyond portraiture or landscape painting, and a Parisian School of painting whose lure he feared would discourage artists from exploring their native land. This dilemma had been articulated in more strident terms by Seán Ó Faoláin in a 'Special Ulster Number' of *The Bell* in July 1941, when he wrote that:

Up there, on the other hand, a ruthless industrialism, and an equally devastating hyper-internationalism, are at the same time preventing life from being cultivated with humanity. There it is not that there are no barriers—there is

---

[30] Catherine Marshall, 'Daniel O'Neill', in *The Hunter Gatherer, the Collection of George and Maura McClelland at the Irish Museum of Modern Art*, edited by Catherine Marshall (Dublin: Irish Museum of Modern Art, 2004), pp. 37–46 (p. 39).

[31] Hewitt, 'The Bitter Gourd', *Lagan 3*, p. 99. In *A North Light*, Hewitt writes of his father's brother, who had attempted to make a career from painting in late nineteenth-century Belfast, recalling that 'Art as a means of living did not rate high in our estimate of careers. A younger brother of my father, Sandy, had, late in the last century, been an art student, but the hazards of his craft drove him over to the commercial side, and even there his struggle had been hard' (Hewitt, *North Light*, p. 2).

no sieve—everything comes flooding in on a people cut off from their roots and will as effectively smother them as our introversion will indubitably smother us if it continues.[32]

Ó Faoláin's apocalyptic pessimism is driven by an ever-present anti-partitionism and by his concern for the widening gap between north and south, but Hewitt's arguments are more difficult to disentangle. His feelings about the potential influence of European art on painting in Ulster changed noticeably over the war years, seemingly in tandem with the development of his theory of regionalism. The fears expressed in 'The Bitter Gourd' in 1945 of the effect of 'the cosmopolitan school of Paris' signal a shift from views expressed by Hewitt in an essay published in the anthology *Now in Ulster* the previous year. In 'Under Forty: Some Ulster Artists', he praised the more experimental activities of contemporary artists in Northern Ireland, and detected a movement over the five years since the outbreak of war from a preoccupation with cubism and impressionism to a new awareness of 'problems which still have validity in Great Britain and on the Continent'.[33] Use of the word 'validity' here is indicative of Hewitt's long-standing anxiety about the relationship between Irish and Continental art.

In a guide to the Belfast Art Gallery published soon after the end of the war, Hewitt outlines an historical assessment of why Ireland 'in the last thousand years has had no indigenous tradition of the Fine Arts'.[34] Blaming the shattering effects of 'gusts of foreign invasion and...civil war' he claims that 'the colonial economic structure...left no room for the growth of any aesthetic tradition', and again cites a lack of ecclesiastical, political, or royal centres of power large or rich enough to encourage and support artistic communities or schools of painting as the main reason why talented individuals tended to travel abroad to further their careers in the visual arts.[35] Hewitt was optimistic that the combination of technological innovation and provincial institutional initiative had at last given rise to a situation where post-war artists no longer felt the need to emigrate in order to succeed, but was apprehensive about the potential impact of British and European artistic developments on local production:

... the time lag in the rate at which aesthetic developments inaugurated on the Continent became effective in this westernmost edge of Europe has, until

---

[32] 'Ulster', *The Bell* 2, no. 4, p. 6.
[33] John Hewitt, 'Under Forty: Some Ulster Artists', in *Now in Ulster*, ed. by Arthur and George Campbell (Belfast: Campbell Bros. and WG Baird, 1944), pp. 13–35 (p. 13).
[34] John Hewitt, *Belfast Art Gallery* (Museum Guide, date unknown, reprinted from *The Studio*, January 1947), p. 15.
[35] Hewitt, *Belfast Art Gallery*, pp. 15–16.

recent years, left the mode in which our resident artists express themselves outside the contemporary flow. Now, with the accelerated speed of communications, with the general rise in the cultural level, with the unflagging campaign of loan exhibitions carried out by the Belfast Gallery and, latterly, by C.E.M.A. (N.I.) there is evidence of the gap being narrowed. But it would be wrong for us to attempt completely to close it, in order to make aesthetics in Ulster merely a reverberation of the gossip of the London and Parisian studios, or our pictures weak imitations of the international manners, for the best art is always a rooted art.[36]

The idea of a 'time lag' and 'gap' between Ireland and the European metropolitan artistic capitals recurs in Hewitt's writings on this subject. In *A North Light* he describes the modelling master at the Belfast art school he attended during his final year of secondary education:

In the first decade of the century he had gone to France and come back a convert to Impressionism. This fairly demonstrates the existence of the time-lag between Continental usage and its being taken up in our westernmost island. That forty years evident at the century's start became progressively shortened, decade by decade, with the increase in travel and in the availability of the mass media of communication, so that now the delay in adopting the latest mode of executing or assembling a work of art, has, for the quickest of talents, narrowed to a bare twelve months.[37]

Despite Hewitt's fears, and repeatedly and earnestly expressed beliefs in the value of a regionalist approach to cultural production, there remains in his writings a nagging sense that art in Northern Ireland should be judged by, or even live up to, British or European standards: the guarantors, it might be inferred, of 'validity'. Eamonn Hughes writes of *A North Light* that, following the 'surprise of foreignness' of his first visit to the Continent in the 1930s, Hewitt's concern was 'to judge local work by European standards in an attempt to diminish the gap he perceives between Northern Ireland and elsewhere', and indeed, in such writings, Hewitt often appears to be irreconcilably caught between contrary impulses: lamenting the historical insularity of the province, expressing a desire to open it up to contemporary influences, but also keen to preserve distinctive regional modes of expression.[38]

The shift in Hewitt's thinking is even more pronounced when his post-war wariness is compared with his involvement with the Ulster Unit during the 1930s. Exhibiting for the first and only time in December

[36] Hewitt, *Belfast Art Gallery*, p. 18.   [37] Hewitt, *North Light*, p. 13.
[38] Eamonn Hughes, 'Sent to Coventry: Emigrations and Autobiography', in *Returning to Ourselves: Second Volume of Papers from the John Hewitt International Summer School*, edited by Eve Patten (Belfast: Lagan Press, 1995), pp. 261–275 (p. 273).

1934, this group emulated the similarly short-lived Unit One collective in England—a disparate collection of painters, sculptors, and architects who tried to define an international modernist aesthetic.[39] Unit One, whose members included Ben Nicholson, Barbara Hepworth, and Henry Moore, collapsed after two years in 1935, having been unable to unify its intentions in a single manifesto.[40] Hewitt helped to organize an exhibition by members of Unit One at the Belfast Museum and Art Gallery, which included sculptures by Henry Moore and Barbara Hepworth and paintings by Edward Burra, Paul Nash, Ben Nicholson, and Edward Wadsworth.[41] He wrote in *A North Light* that 'Of the earlier exhibitions I handled none was more influential on my thinking than that of the now forgotten Unit One . . . For the more progressive it demonstrated more clearly than ever before how far out of step with the time's drift elsewhere was the work venerated and practised by their exhibiting contemporaries'.[42] The Ulster Unit, formed in 1934, was a collective of mainly young, London-educated artists, invigorated by their time in England and keen to improve awareness of modern art in Northern Ireland.[43] Members included John Luke, George MacCann, Colin Middleton, and Romeo Toogood, and like its English predecessor the group dissolved soon after the first exhibition held in December 1934, which had similarly revealed a lack of common purpose.[44]

In a preface to the exhibition catalogue, the secretary to the collective John Hewitt wrote enthusiastically about the prospect of growing closeness between Ulster artists and their European counterparts:

> In this Unit, Ulster has for the first time a body of artists alert to continental influence while that influence is still real and vital. It is no vain hope that with a consistent group bound by more ties than those of mere geographical proximity, working on experimental lines and no longer in an archaic dialectic, Belfast will move step by step not only with Great Britain but with France and Scandinavia.[45]

The contrast between his optimism here and his deep reservations over 'weak imitations', expressed a decade later in both 'The Bitter Gourd' and

[39] Hall, p. 7.

[40] Bryan Appleyard, *The Pleasures of Peace: Art and Imagination in Post War Britain*, (London: Faber and Faber, 1989), p. 59.

[41] John Hewitt, *Colin Middleton* (Belfast: Arts Council of Northern Ireland, 1976), p. 9.

[42] Hewitt, *North Light*, p. 60.

[43] Ríann Coulter, 'Nationalism, Regionalism and Internationalism: Cultural Identity in Irish Art, 1943–1960' (unpublished doctoral thesis, Courtauld Institute of Art, University of London, 2006), p. 95.

[44] S.B. Kennedy, *Irish Art and Modernism*, p. 77.

[45] John Hewitt, 'Preface', *Ulster Unit*, (unpaginated exhibition catalogue, Belfast: 1934).

the museum guide, may suggest a recoil from a Europe ravaged by war and fascism but more properly illustrates the development of his theory of regionalism, itself encouraged by the pressures of the war. This was formulated with aims not only of bridging sectarian divisions in the province, but also of defining a strong regional identity for the province in the face of creeping Anglo-American cultural homogenization, accelerated by the presence of so many British and US troops in Northern Ireland during the war.

An outline of his theory, initially inspired by reading Lewis Mumford's *The Culture of Cities* (1938), appears in an article entitled 'Regionalism: The Last Chance' published in 1947, in which he advocates breaking up national government organizations into smaller regional bodies to tackle specific problems—citing US President Roosevelt's Tennessee Valley Authority, established in 1933, as an 'outstanding example' of this—and describes a devolutionary process beginning with the stimulation of local culture and leading to economic and social revival.[46] Arguing that strongly held and defended regional identities need not preclude the membership of a larger cultural and political association, he suggests that for Ulster this could take the form of participation in a federal Ireland or federated British Isles—a radical notion in the socio-political context in which he was writing.[47]

The Second World War exerted a formative influence on Hewitt's theories. Tom Clyde writes that 'Ulster regionalism did not spring fully-formed from the brow of John Hewitt, but was rather the result of a slow process of growth which was given a new and radical boost by a particular set of circumstances'.[48] As Clyde elaborates, prominent among such 'circumstances' was, of course, the Second World War, and Hewitt himself clearly acknowledges the importance of the war years to his life and work in the numerous references to these in writings throughout the rest of his life. His optimism in 'Regionalism: The Last Chance' about the chances for the success of regionalist policies in Northern Ireland undoubtedly sprang from the cultural activities that he had witnessed and instigated during the war, as he approvingly cites little magazines and literary journals, the activities of CEMA (NI), and the works of Sam Hanna Bell, John Boyd, and Joseph Tomelty.[49] Most of these activities took place on the margins, often involving the unofficial voices and frequenters of Campbell's coffee

---

[46] Hewitt, 'Regionalism: The Last Chance' in Clyde (ed.), *Ancestral Voices*, p. 123.

[47] Hewitt, 'Regionalism: The Last Chance' in Clyde (ed.), *Ancestral Voices*, p. 125.

[48] Tom Clyde, 'A Stirring in the Dry Bones: John Hewitt's Regionalism', in Dawe and Wilson Foster (eds.), *The Poet's Place*, pp. 249–258 (p. 250).

[49] Hewitt, 'Regionalism: The Last Chance', in Clyde (ed.), *Ancestral Voices*, p. 124.

house, and Hewitt expresses dissatisfaction with the attitudes to, and contributions of, the various branches of the official apparatus of the northern state to cultural production in the region, singling out the Stormont government, BBC Northern Ireland, and Queen's University for criticism. Hewitt's frustrations with administrative powers in Belfast over his twenty-seven-year involvement with the Belfast Museum and Art Gallery are well documented in *A North Light*, and he clearly felt that the potential for regional revival lay for the most part outside Northern Ireland's conservative institutional framework.

Like others, in retrospect Hewitt took a positive view of Northern Ireland's enforced wartime isolation, and in the 1972 essay 'No Rootless Colonist' wrote nostalgically of the opportunities it had afforded:

> ... with the Second World War, we were cut off from the larger island to the east and from the Europe which, by travel, we had grown to enjoy and accept as also part of our inheritance. Consequently, we were forced to take our holidays in Donegal or elsewhere in the province of Ulster. It was then that our long acquaintance with the middle Glens of Antrim began. Even dutiful exercises like lecturing in army camps broadened my experience of the six partitioned counties of the North. And walking in the Rosses I felt myself no stranger.[50]

Such emphasis on isolation should not obscure the fact that many British, European, and American soldiers and European refugees arrived in the province during the Second World War. Clyde suggests that 'the presence of so many outsiders must have forced upon people an awareness of their identity, as distinct from these others, and of what it is that makes them different', and the exhibitions staged in the Belfast Museum and Art Gallery were perhaps the most visually arresting illustrations of the impact that these visitors had on the cultural life of the province.[51] Letters from Hewitt to his friend Patrick Maybin in 1942 mention exhibitions of Polish War Art in August and Czech paintings in December of that year, and emphasize the effect these had on his own understanding of Irish political history. Following a talk by a Lieutenant in the Czech army, Hewitt realizes 'that to solve the Irish problem we must know more than Ireland . . . I shall have to study the patterns of Nationalism in light of Slovenia and Moravia and SubCarpathian Russia not in the twilight of Cromwell and King Billy', and compares the division between rural Catholic Slovenia and industrialized Protestant Bohemia with the partition of Ireland.[52]

---

[50] Hewitt, 'No Rootless Colonist', in Clyde (ed.), *Ancestral Voices*, pp. 146–157 (p. 152).
[51] Clyde, 'A Stirring in the Dry Bones', in Dawe and Wilson Foster (eds.), *The Poet's Place*, p. 251.
[52] Letters from John Hewitt to Patrick Maybin, 24 August 1942 (p. 2) and 9 December 1942 (pp. 3–4), Hewitt Papers, PRONI, D/3838/3/12.

Hewitt's practical role of encouraging and publicizing art in the province was seemingly vital to the success of cultural ventures in Northern Ireland during the war.[53] In 1943 he was promoted to the position of chief assistant at the Belfast Museum and Art Gallery, organized Middleton's first solo exhibition, and helped to found CEMA (NI).[54] It was a year on which he later placed particular importance:

> This year 1943 is notable for the evidence which emerged strongly that Belfast was entering an unusually vigorous phase in the creative arts. Small exhibitions in dingy rooms down-town, in a frame-maker's shop, gave the first evidence of new talents, such as those of Gerard Dillon, Daniel O'Neill, and the Campbell brothers, George and Arthur. In the literary field the appearance of the first of the annual issues of *Lagan*, edited by John Boyd and his associates, is our best record, demonstrating that a new generation of writers was coming forward, and the establishment of the Ulster Group Theatre showed advance on another front. While the basic causes for this wide striving are not readily teased out, the war-time isolation of Northern Ireland was certainly a factor, compelling us to till our own gardens.[55]

Despite his role in its foundation, it is notable that once again the developments celebrated by Hewitt were led not by the embryonic state-funded organization CEMA, but resulted from the activities of the members of an unofficial community operating on the margins and gathering in the 'dingy rooms down-town', or at John and Roberta Hewitt's Mount Charles flat. Although Hewitt cites *Lagan* here, *Now in Ulster*, which appeared the following year, provides a more comprehensive group portrait of the artists and writers gathered in Belfast at the time. This one-off anthology, edited by Arthur and George Campbell, carried short stories by James D. Gildea, Sam Hanna Bell, and Gerry Morrow, essays by Hewitt, Hubert R. Wilmot, and Denis Ireland, verse by Hewitt and Roy McFadden, and, in a move that distinguishes *Now in Ulster* from other contemporary publications, monochrome reproductions of paintings by the Campbell brothers, Gerard Dillon, John Luke, and Colin Middleton,

---

[53] The extent of Hewitt's fame and influence in wartime Belfast may be gauged from an incident involving the painter Markey Robinson, recalled by James MacIntyre in his memoir *Making My Mark*. Robinson had been sketching an army barracks on the Antrim Road when he was spotted by a passing military police patrol, and was dragged into the barracks for questioning. His sketchbook was confiscated, and it took four hours of interrogation before police were satisfied that Robinson was not a German spy. He was eventually released, 'having given the name of John Hewitt, the Keeper of Art at the Ulster Museum, as guarantor' [James MacIntyre, *Making My Mark: an artist's early life* (Belfast: Blackstaff Press, 2001], p. 94).

[54] Ormsby, 'Biographical Chronology', in Ormsby (ed.), *Collected Poems of John Hewitt*, p. xxxv.

[55] Hewitt, *Colin Middleton*, p. 18.

amongst others.[56] Hewitt's essay 'Under Forty: Some Ulster Artists' offers a personal overview of the state of the provincial arts scene, in which he divides the artists whose works appear in the anthology into broad categories. One group, of George Campbell, Gerard Dillon, and Dan O'Neill, is characterized by the 'direct, unequivocal notation' of painters described as:

> ... strongly emotional. Their subject matter is drawn largely from the life of men in towns, the life at hand, seeking no escape into the psychological world of Middleton or the ideal world of Luke. [These artists respond] More often to the pity. The pity for the shabby, the hopeless, sometimes shocked into the violence of the street accident or the air raid. It is therefore no mere chance that both Dillon and Campbell are here represented by pictures of the Blitz, surely the event of our time with the harshest impact—at any rate, for those of us who have not fought.[57]

With the benefit of hindsight, Hewitt's distinction here appears reductive. Although Middleton's surrealist work during the war can be read as psychological explorations of the world of the unconscious, some of his paintings do engage directly with the destruction of the built environment during the Belfast Blitz of 1941. As Hewitt observes, two of the sixteen paintings reproduced in *Now in Ulster*, George Campbell's *Dead Street* (1941) and Gerard Dillon's *Bombed Street* (1941), depict the effects of the Blitz, the traumatic impact of which is registered variously. *Dead Street* uses menacing, almost abstract smudges, whereas in Dillon's impressionistic *Bombed Street* barely discernible groups of stunted figures huddle together in a ruined street. The placing of these reproductions in the little magazine beside Colin Middleton's *The Dark Tower* (1941), which also depicts a damaged building, suggests that Middleton's painting can be read as a more oblique engagement with the effects of the bombing, and I shall return to this work later in this chapter. Contrary to the impression promoted by Hewitt's observations, Middleton's discontinuous and heterogeneous wartime output also includes a number of neo-impressionistic paintings of Belfast street scenes that display a deep fidelity to the communities and streets of working-class Belfast, or indeed 'the life at hand'. In addition, Hewitt's claim that Gerard Dillon, in concert with Campbell and O'Neill, is an artist given to 'direct, unequivocal notation' oversimplifies the deep ambiguities in works produced by Dillon over the war

---

[56] The Campbell brothers had published *Ulster in Black and White* (Belfast: WG Baird, 1943) the previous year, containing reproductions of works by themselves and the artists Patricia Webb and Maurice Wilks. According to John Hewitt, John Luke stopped painting altogether between 1939 and 1943 (John Hewitt, *John Luke 1906–1975* [Dublin and Belfast: Arts Councils of Ireland, 1978], p. 47).

[57] Hewitt, 'Under Forty: Some Ulster Artists', *Now in Ulster*, p. 33.

years, and fails to acknowledge the complexity of his relationship with the landscape and iconography of the west of Ireland. Hewitt's attempt to group these artists into such categories may be attributed to an eagerness to foster the notion of a body of Ulster artists broad enough to encompass different schools.

Theoretical questions aside, practical difficulties had perhaps the greatest impact on artists during the Second World War. In Britain and Ireland travel restrictions, shortage or unavailability of materials, and (in Britain only) conscription clearly impeded the activities of painters and sculptors. These privations had some unexpected and exciting results, exemplified by the activities of Henry Moore, who, faced with a shortage of sculptural materials, worked on paper in his capacity as an official war artist, and produced a hugely popular series of drawings of sleepers sheltering in the London Underground during bombing raids.[58] Shortages arguably heightened the material significance of some works of art: in Northern Ireland the shortage of paper forced William Conor to sketch on the reverse of Red Cross advertising material, whilst Gerard Dillon framed some of his paintings of the Belfast Blitz using wood gathered from bomb sites; conversely John Hewitt recalled Colin Middleton using old canvases to make sandbags for Air Raid Precautions.[59]

Intermittently imposed travel restrictions between Britain and Northern Ireland stimulated local involvement in artistic activity in the province, as Gillian McIntosh describes:

> Wartime travel restrictions meant that few artists from Britain were able to visit the state. This forced CEMA to rely almost entirely on local talent. The late 1940s saw the development of a regionalist ethos by CEMA; its reports are littered with references to local artists and performers, it used the resources of local art collectors, and it purchased work by local artists. This was reflected in the development of an interest in the arts by local groups.[60]

In one crucial respect artists in Northern Ireland were undoubtedly freer than their British counterparts, as the lack of conscription allowed the generation of Dillon and Middleton to pursue creative activities rather than being drafted into the forces.

---

[58] Appleyard, p. 70; Peter Stansky and William Abrahams, *London's Burning: Life, Death and Art in the Second World War* (London: Constable, 1994), pp. 5–70.

[59] Catherine Marshall, 'William Conor', in Marshall (ed.), *The Hunter Gatherer*, pp. 19–24 (p. 22); MacIntyre, *Making My Mark*, p. 102; Nicola Armstrong, Form III, Friends' School Lisburn, 'An interview with Dr John Hewitt, Senior Ulster Poet, on the Belfast Blitz 1941', unpublished and undated interview, Coleraine Hewitt Collection, Box 18.

[60] McIntosh, 'CEMA and the National Anthem', *New Hibernia Review 5*, no. 3 (2001) pp. 23–24.

The wide range of official and unofficial cultural responses to the *blitz-krieg* on cities in Britain and Northern Ireland shows how the patterns, sensations, and incongruous juxtapositions resulting from these unprecedented and specifically urban scenes of destruction proved both inspirational and troubling for artists and writers at the time. In an illustrated article for *Picture Post* magazine in May 1941 Louis MacNeice describes damage caused by bombing in London as 'a spectacle', compares the patterns of smoke and water he saw with those of an Impressionist painting, and writes that: 'When the All Clear went I began a tour of London, half appalled and half enlivened by this fantasy of destruction. For it was—if I am to be candid—enlivening'.[61] In an essay published a few months later MacNeice contrasts the experience of seeing the rich West End the morning after a bombing, which he describes as 'almost exhilarating', with his impressions of the destruction of a poor area the same night, which he calls 'heart breaking'.[62] As discussed in the first chapter of this book, the enlivening sensual effect of such symbolic destruction on the spectator and the conflicting emotions that result from this are described in Brian Moore's *The Emperor of Ice Cream*, where the protagonist's feelings of exhilaration when bombs begin to fall on City Hall, Queen's University, and Harland and Wolff's shipyard—clear symbols of patriarchal and political authority in the city—evaporate when the awful human cost of the raid is revealed the following morning.[63] Artists and writers had to be mindful of treading a difficult line between excitement and pity, as the visual spectacle of the Blitz was accompanied by an inescapably brutal loss of civilian lives. In an interview in 1971 Graham Sutherland recalled this dilemma in relation to his *Devastation* series of paintings of bomb damage in Swansea and London, executed throughout 1940 and 1941:

> The City was more exciting than anywhere else mainly because the buildings were bigger, and the variety of ways in which they fell more interesting. But very soon the raids began in the East End—in the dock areas—and immediately the atmosphere became much more tragic. In the City one didn't think of the destruction of life. All the destroyed buildings were office buildings and people weren't in them at night. But in the East End one did think of the hurt to people and there was every evidence of it.[64]

---

[61] Louis MacNeice, 'The Morning After The Blitz', *Picture Post*, 3 May 1941, reprinted in *Selected Prose of Louis MacNeice,* edited by Alan Heuser (Oxford: Oxford University Press, 1990), pp. 117–122 (p. 118).
[62] MacNeice, 'London Letter 5', *Common Sense 10*, no. 7 (July 1941), pp. 206–207, reprinted in Heuser (ed.), *Selected Prose*, pp. 131–136 (p. 131, p. 132).
[63] Moore, *Emperor*, p. 203.
[64] Graham Sutherland 'Images Wrought From Destruction', *The Sunday Telegraph Magazine*, 10 September 1971, reprinted in Martin Hammer, *Graham Sutherland: Landscapes,*

Citing works such as Frank Dobson's *Bristol, November 24th, 1940* (1940), which depicts the destruction of a Georgian terrace, Stuart Sillars has argued that much representational art of Blitz destruction during the war directly echoes Burkean Romantic ideas of the Sublime as exemplified by the Gothic ruin, supporting this with reference to reports of 'intense excitement' felt by those who experienced the bombing recorded in official mental health analyses of the time:

> For both those used to suffering mental illness and those generally catego-
> rised as 'normal', the experience of bombing is one related to a heightened
> state of awareness: the new sights and sounds of the blitz, the suspension
> of the usual order, the sheer risk and closeness of death or injury, gave the
> experience of living a fresh intensity. This intensity is in no small measure
> founded on fear, this fear derived in part from the visually spectacular.[65]

London-based artists and writers were particularly stimulated by such sensations, and Elizabeth Bowen, T.S. Eliot, Henry Moore, and Dylan Thomas are among others who responded to the Blitz in their works. The bombing of Belfast also inspired creative responses. James MacIntyre recalls being allowed by his parents to travel into the city centre to sketch the destruction, two months after the Belfast Blitz, when he was fifteen years old:

> At Lower Donegall Street I saw that though St Anne's cathedral had escaped
> the bombing, its neighbours had been razed. As I stood at the bottom of
> North Street I looked in silence at what remained of Waring Street, Bridge
> Street and High Street. Windowless husks of buildings and lone towering
> gable-ends stood eerily tranquil among the mounds of rubble, stacked high,
> waiting for removal. Huge fawn and white Clydesdale horses, coats shin-
> ing with sweat, hauled cartloads of wooden crates towards the cargo boats
> anchored at Queen's Quay. People quietly crisscrossed the streets, intent on
> their own affairs. And, clattering past, all unknowing of the trauma, were
> the trams.[66]

MacIntyre's line drawings of the destruction are included in his autobiography. Many such representational drawings and paintings of
bomb-damaged cities were produced during the Second World War (in
Belfast, William Conor's drawings are the most notable artistic record),
but resemblances between the chaotic shapes and scenes thrown up by
the aerial bombing of urban areas and the stylistic modes of other artistic

War Scenes, Portraits 1924–1950 (London: Scala and Dulwich Picture Gallery, 2005), pp. 102–105 (p. 102).

[65] Stuart Sillars, *British Romantic Art and the Second World War* (Basingstoke: Macmillan, 1991), p. 97.

[66] MacIntyre, *Making My Mark*, p. 57.

movements have also been noted, and have encouraged some to make bold assertions.[67] Writing prior to the Belfast Blitz in the Winter 1940–1941 edition of the *New Northman*, Jack Boyd claimed that surrealists 'must be having the time of their lives: for the war must be better than any surrealist could have hoped for'.[68] In 1961 the British writer and artist Adrian Stokes claimed that the patterns of cubism had anticipated the scenes of destruction caused by the heavy bombing of urban areas:

> A collapsed room displays many more facets than a room intact: after a bombing in the last war, we were able to look at elongated, piled-up displays of what had been exterior, mingled with what had been interior, materializations of the serene Analytic Cubism that Picasso and Braque invented before the first war; and usually, as in some of these paintings, we saw the poignant key provided by some untouched, undamaged object that had miraculously escaped.[69]

Bryan Appleyard's contentions that futurism and vorticism were defeated by the First World War when it revealed the terminal logic behind their 'machine fantasies' and that subsequently the Second World War 'appeared as a cruel, dreamlike validation of much that was modern' are similarly sweeping.[70]

Surrealist imagery might also be discerned in the juxtapositions, shapes, and situations thrown up by the destruction of the Blitz. There is clear surrealistic potential in many of the widely circulated photographs taken in the aftermath of air attacks on London, such as Fred Morley's confected scene of a milkman carrying a crate of bottles down a street reduced to rubble, or the photograph showing a postman collecting mail from a pillar box itself partly buried by debris.[71] Angus Calder, whose *The Myth of the Blitz* uses Morley's milkman on its cover, detects the influence of inter-war surrealist photography in Bert Hardy's work for *Picture Post* during the Second World War, citing Bill Brandt, whose own officially commissioned wartime documentary photography also displays surrealist elements.[72] The surrealistic and even strangely comic potential of bomb sites was also

---

[67] Conor's popular *Air Raid Memories* (1941) series of sketches of Blitz damage were commissioned by the War Artists Advisory Committee and exhibited at Robinson and Cleaver's department store, Donegall Square, in August of the same year (Wilson, *Conor 1881–1968*, p. 68).

[68] Boyd, 'Words and Emotions in Contemporary Literature', *New Northman VIII*, no. 3, p. 54.

[69] Adrian Stokes, 'The Painting of Our Time, Part One: The Luxury and Necessity of Painting', in *The Critical Writings of Adrian Stokes* (London: Thames and Hudson, 1978), pp. 145–160(p. 155). In this collection the essay is dated 1961.

[70] Appleyard, p. 61.

[71] Morley's photograph of the milkman was apparently posed using an assistant (Christopher Howse, 'Never Mind the Milkman, the Ruins are Real', *Daily Telegraph*, 7 September 2010).

[72] Calder, *Myth of the Blitz*, p. 142.

realized in Belfast during the war, through the work of a pair of performance artists recalled by Robert Harbinson:

> ... a site just off Castle Junction had been conveniently cleared by the
> Germans. The space left by their bombs provided two men with an arena in
> which to perform wonders with their bodies. Clad only in a sort of bright
> bathing costume one of them reclined gracefully on a bed of nails, with an
> apparent minimum of discomfort. Meanwhile, the other balanced a ladder
> surrealistically on top of his head. At the end of the ladder, up in the air, a
> chair was balanced, its height to be measured only against the bomb-scarred,
> stranded fireplaces of the next building.[73]

The influence of surrealism is also discernible in paintings which depict
or respond to the destruction of buildings on the Home Front, and tracing the relationship between form and historical incident through a series
of wartime paintings by Colin Middleton provides a new line of enquiry
into the work of a notoriously problematic artist. In this respect, Dickon
Hall's assessment that Middleton's 'Numerous drawings of bombed buildings and terraces show another aspect of the artist at work, the swift, acute
and detached line of a draughtsman struck by the strange shapes of this
new cityscape' is illuminating.[74] If surrealist art seemed in danger of being
eclipsed by scenes of real destruction, or by representational paintings or
photographs, some of Middleton's works incorporated the physical destruction visited on Belfast into the psychological world of surrealism. In this he
may have followed the path taken by 1930s surrealists in their responses
to the Spanish Civil War, when artists who had previously displayed little
overt interest in politics were rapidly impelled by the fascist threat to reflect
the intricacies of the increasingly violent political situation.[75] Middleton's
own oeuvre is so varied as to frustrate claims of congruence between his
wartime paintings and a distinct radical political viewpoint, but considering his works in their historical context does enable a sharper appreciation
of some of the forces that impacted upon artists in Northern Ireland at
this time. Ríann Coulter's analysis of Middleton's wartime paintings has
centred on his search for Jungian symbols and use of the female archetype,
but I want to concentrate instead on material evidence within the pictures,
and believe that an examination of some of the war paintings disproves
Catherine Marshall's assessment that time 'had little place in Middleton's
philosophy. In his search for the essential and enduring, he ruthlessly elimi-
nated contemporary references'.[76]

[73] Harbinson, *Up Spake*, p. 92.   [74] Hall, p. 9.
[75] Robin Adèle Greeley, *Surrealism and the Spanish Civil War* (New Haven, CN; London:
Yale University Press, 2006), pp. 1–12.
[76] Coulter, 'Nationalism, Regionalism and Internationalism'; Coulter, ' "An Amazing
Anthology of Modern Art": Place, Archetype and Identity in the Art of Colin Middleton',

The detection of resemblances between figures and tropes of artistic styles and actual wartime scenes may seem an anachronistic pursuit, but similarities were clearly noted at the time. Patrick Maybin, a close friend of John Hewitt from Belfast, was a doctor who joined the Royal Army Medical Corps on the outbreak of war. Stationed initially in Northern Ireland and then in Britain, and subsequently posted to North Africa and Italy, he wrote numerous detailed letters to his friend during the war, discussing works of art, literature, and philosophy. It is worth quoting at length from one startling letter written in late 1943:

> Tunisia is a much richer and more friendly country than Algeria. The battle-fields have been nearly all cleared up. Some of the towns have been bombed and bombarded till hardly a house is habitable. Here and there one comes on a huge salvage dump of several acres—burnt out trucks and tanks and cars, and demolished guns. At places—a level crossing, or a road junction—in the shade of a group of cactus plants, a small group of white wooden crosses. One scene stays in my mind: a flat coastal plain, brown in the lit sunlight; a road along the margin of a wide beach, sweeping around to the edge of a small port, so much bombed that not a living person was to be seen; at the sea's edge a crashed bomber, one huge wing with its black Nazi cross angled across the sky. Behind it the pier, with the cranes twisted and tilted across the dock; a wide expanse of purple blue sky, and a low bar of cloud across the horizon. The scene was familiar, not in detail but in mood; I remembered why—it is the mood of Colin Middleton, 1940.[77]

Maybin's vivid description is so detailed as to constitute an ekphrastic composition in itself. It includes many elements familiar from Middleton's wartime surrealist paintings, such as the sense of traumatic aftermath, the apprehension of conflict, and the juxtaposition of recognizable material objects in an alien landscape devoid of human presence. The letter also demonstrates the psychological power of the complex interplay between artistic style and wartime reality and shows how this was felt contemporaneously. Middleton had never travelled to Tunisia and never experienced desert warfare, but here, 1,500 miles from Belfast, Maybin is struck by the resemblance between the scene before him and a Middleton painting, and feels the need to record this in a letter.

* * *

Visual Culture in Britain 9, no. 1 (Summer 2008), pp. 1–26; Catherine Marshall, 'Colin Middleton', in Marshall (ed.), *The Hunter Gatherer*, pp. 47–59 (p. 50). Marshall arguably contradicts her own conclusion with earlier and well-founded claims in the same essay that *Strange Openings, Magpie Delivery*, and *Siren Over Belfast* were inspired by the wartime blackout (p. 48).

[77] Letter from Patrick Maybin to John Hewitt, 6 November 1943, Hewitt Papers, PRONI, D3838/3/10.

Born in 1910, Colin Middleton grew up in the middle-class Belfast sub-
urb of Cavehill and was educated at the nearby Royal Academy grammar school. His father worked in the linen industry as a damask designer
and had studied painting at the Manchester School of Art, and unlike
many of his contemporaries Middleton grew up surrounded by artists,
painters, and designers. After leaving school he entered the family firm
as an apprentice and attended the Belfast College of Art as a part-time
student, where contemporaries included Tom Carr, John Hunter, William
Scott, and Romeo Toogood.[78] Middleton depended on occasional trips
to London and Europe to satisfy his interest in art during the 1930s, and
it was at this time that he discovered Salvador Dali and British surrealists
such as Tristram Hillier and Edward Wadsworth. Surrealism proved to be
a liberating discovery for Middleton, and was to have a profound impact
on much of his work for the rest of his life.[79] When his father died in 1935
he took over the family business, preventing him from leaving Belfast and
pursuing an artistic career in London or Paris.[80] An emotional man, of
whom John Hewitt wrote to Maybin in 1944 that 'he's an odd creature—
Genius maybe—but God help anyone who gets too close to his flame', the
war began for Middleton with deep personal sadness when his first wife
Mae, herself a painter, died in 1939. He married his second wife Kathleen
(Kate) towards the end of the war.[81] Over a career which spanned more
than fifty years until his death in 1983, he produced an astonishingly varied body of work, ranging from the surrealist works to post-impressionist
landscapes, expressionist pieces, and abstract homages to Kandinsky. In
addition, as Dickon Hall observes, he was a particularly skilled draughtsman—John Hewitt attributed this talent for precision, so evident in the
surrealist pieces, to his original trade as a damask designer.[82] Catherine
Marshall writes that his 'chameleon-like changes of style' could well be
described as 'an art historian's nightmare', and of the sheer variousness of
Middleton's first one-man show 1943, Hewitt recalls that 'an immediate
reaction...was that the artist was hypersensitive to influence'.[83] Another

---

[78] Hall, p. 4.   [79] Hall, p. 7.   [80] Hewitt, *North Light*, p. 62.
[81] Letter from John Hewitt to Patrick Maybin, 6 November 1944, Hewitt Papers,
PRONI, D/3838/3/12. This letter also contains an account of the beginning of Middleton's
relationship with Kate.
[82] Hewitt, *North Light*, p. 63.
[83] Marshall, 'Colin Middleton', in Marshall (ed.), *The Hunter Gatherer*, p. 47; Hewitt,
North Light, p. 100. One artist with whom Middleton might be compared is the Norwegian
painter Arne Ekeland (1908–1994). Ekeland's paintings are also hugely varied in style and
execution, and his oeuvre similarly includes abstract, expressionist, figurative, and surrealist pieces. See *Arne Ekeland, Paintings: 1937–85*, exhibition catalogue introduced by Ole
Henrik Moe (Newcastle upon Tyne: Polytechnic Gallery, 1986).

critic was less guarded, and opened his review of the exhibition with a volley of questions:

> What in thunder is this man Middleton driving at? Is he driving at anything? Or is he just a deliberate deviser of meaningless arrangements of incongruous objects, in the hope of attaining a cheap notoriety? Is he pretending to mean something important and profound, whilst, in reality, he means nothing at all? In plain language: is he a charlatan? Is he a fraud?[84]

Middleton's predilection for experimentation has remained a source of critical confusion and speculation, and despite his evident technical versatility the lack of a single recognizable Middleton style arguably prevented him from achieving wider renown. Hall suggested that 'Middleton's work seems to have been created more for himself than for the public, and this would in part explain his disregard for the usual conventions of stylistic consistency'.[85] For his friend Hewitt he epitomized 'the puzzle and the problem of the artist now', and was the victim of a fragmented age: in *A North Light* he wrote that 'Too honest, too open-minded, [Middleton] has refused to drive or goad his genius along a single avenue'.[86] In 1947 Middleton wrote to Hewitt to ask about the prospect of regular picture sales in Belfast, expressing his dislike of the metropolitan bias of the art world even as travel between Northern Ireland and Europe became quicker and easier:

> I somehow feel that the whole idea of Bond Street and the centralisation of major picture dealing is all wrong. Painters, poets and the like are not born into darkest Belfast to paint or sing to a galaxy of epicureans congregated round a shrine. Mark you: I'm not preaching against the *circulation* of songs and pictures—I should hate to think that I should never see a Van Gogh in the flesh again—nonetheless...[87]

The sentence tails off with an ellipsis, suggesting that, as it was for Hewitt, the tension between the metropolitan and the provincial was a conundrum that Middleton, who remained in Belfast for the duration of the war, found hard to resolve. Assailed by manifold artistic styles, in a new age of photography and cheap commercial reproduction where no single school of painting could dominate, it may be that Middleton simply felt unable to limit himself to a single mode, or that his deployment of a multiplicity of styles was a considered strategy of self-expression. Hall has argued that

---

[84] Edwyn Watkins, 'Colin Middleton: A Personal Estimate of the Significance of his Work', (dated 27 August 1943), Biographical File, Colin Middleton Archive, Ulster Folk and Transport Museum, Cultra, Co. Down.

[85] Hall, p. 15.   [86] Hewitt, *North Light*, p. 101.

[87] Letter from Colin Middleton to John Hewitt, 6 October 1947, Hewitt Papers, PRONI, D/3838/7/23/21.

in creating an anthological body of work Middleton was trying to address the problem of the provincial painter by being genuinely contemporary, and certainly the artist's (perhaps ironic) self-proclamation as 'the only surrealist painter working in Ireland' conveys a keen desire to differentiate himself from his peers and from his national and cultural background.[88]

Middleton's own pronouncements on his works are relatively rare and decidedly enigmatic, but are consistent in their seriousness. In a note written for his first one-man exhibition dated 29 August 1943, which he describes as 'the outcome of requests for elucidation regarding the nature of my work', Middleton writes that his paintings arose from a 'process of personal integration' and suggests that his work is driven by current events when he states that 'Today, as never more urgently in the known past, humanity is faced with the problem of survival'. Describing survival as both physical and spiritual, he goes on to question 'whether the Artist is to be considered as a superior intellect manufacturing luxury articles for a select circle of tradesmen and patrons, or—is the craftsman to be a vital link in the social chain', and asks rhetorically if the craftsman is to aspire to be 'entertainer or visionary? profiteer or prophet?' If these questions imply that Middleton felt that he had some public role as part of this 'social chain', this is problematized by his claim to be dedicated to individual expression and to have 'no concern' with schools of painting, as it is indeed by his ambiguous conception of the metaphorical 'chain':

> These ... paintings are the outcome of an unconscious will to perfect 'the link' as a necessary stage in the perfecting of 'the chain'.
>
> Since we are dealing throughout with symbols, 'the chain' may be regarded in a purely utilitarian sense as a shackle, or, as a symbol of co-operative strength: a linking of hands, hearts, minds: of purpose: of perfection, having neither beginning nor ending, and therefore transcending survival.[89]

Middleton's own emphasis on the symbolic content of his paintings may have driven subsequent critical appraisals of his work, but this should not be allowed to obscure the impact of the historical context on his wartime compositions. An untitled autobiographical poem written in October 1941 reveals a profound emotional restlessness in Middleton at this time:

> The youth who left his father's grave, a man
> possessed of new possessions to possess,
> an endless quest for equilibrium ...
> ...

[88] Hall, p. 13, p. 18.
[89] Colin Middleton, 'Note on One Man Exhibition' (dated 29 August 1943), Biographical File, Middleton Archive.

the child that first beholds its own bright blood
and trembles still and still retains the taste;
the child that cherishes the first bad word
incomprehensible, a power to wield.[90]

October 1941 marked six months since the Easter Tuesday air raid on
Belfast. The Blitz seems to have had a severe effect on Middleton, though
accounts of this differ: according to Kenneth Jamison the artist found himself unable to paint at all for these six months following the raid, although
in a letter written in July of that year Hewitt tells Maybin of a period of
concerted activity: 'He's painting green luminous phosphorescent moth-
ers and children with intense decay and death screaming out of them. His
work seems deeper in content and less sympathetic. He threatens to go on
to crucifixions and agonies!'[91] The idea of a 'quest for equilibrium' is interesting in the context of the Second World War. The loss of his father in
1935 was clearly deeply painful, but Middleton's sense of his subsequent
life as a search for balance in the face of opposing forces also describes the
unsteady position of the artist in relation to the war. Stepping back and
addressing himself in the third person, in this consciously poetic solilo-
quy he questions the value of artistic pursuits at this time, and another
Middleton ellipsis indicates an awareness of the uncertain place and role
of the artist in wartime, stretched like his London counterparts between
excitement and pity.

The Dark Tower (1941) is a surrealist scene played out on the type of anonymous, undulating plain familiar from the works of Salvador Dali.[92] Two spin-
dly towers dominate the middle distance of the painting—asymmetrical and

[90] The poem is reprinted in Hewitt, *Colin Middleton*, p. 14.
[91] Kenneth Jamison, *The Art of Colin Middleton* (unpaginated exhibition catalogue,
Belfast: Arts Council of Northern Ireland, 1965); Letter from John Hewitt to Patrick
Maybin, 22 July 1941, Hewitt Papers, PRONI, D/3838/3/12.
[92] This landscape might also be compared with the desert which forms the setting for
the conclusion of Louis MacNeice's 1946 BBC radio play, also entitled *The Dark Tower*, a
reworking of Robert Browning's 'Childe Harold to the Dark Tower Came' through which
the echoes of the Second World War clearly reverberate. MacNeice's desert shifts in form,
described by the central character Roland first as 'Flat—no shape—no colour—only here
and there/A mirage of the past' then as having 'no end/Nor even any contour, the blank
horizon/Retreats and yet retreats; without either rise or fall' before mountains begin to close
in as 'A circle of ugly cliffs—a lobster-pot of rock!'; finally, as the play ends, the Dark Tower
itself rises 'Like a wart coming out of the ground!' (MacNeice, *The Dark Tower*, in *Selected
Plays of Louis MacNeice*, edited by Alan Heuser and Peter McDonald [Oxford: Oxford
University Press, 1993], pp. 111–148 [p. 142, p. 144, p. 146, p. 147]). Citing this radio
play, Peter McDonald has argued that deserts figure in MacNeice's work as one of the central images for the individual in wartime (Peter McDonald, *Mistaken Identities: Poetry and
Northern Ireland* [Oxford: Oxford University Press, 1997], p. 106). I have not been able
to trace any direct connection between MacNeice and Middleton, but the coincidence is
striking.

eccentric structures whose resemblance to recognizable buildings is vexed by their irregular dimensions and planes. Recalling Maybin's letter the previous year perhaps, John Hewitt went so far as to claim one tower as 'now a monstrous air-machine plunged in the sand, and now a great blind fish or eel-creature'.[93] The towers are echoed by two similar constructions on the horizon. In the foreground the heavily stylized figure of a woman in a dress dances beneath a stylized human eye situated on a two-dimensional quadrilateral, which looks away to the right. The towers seem to be missing pieces gouged from their sides, as though damaged by bomb blasts, and bricks litter the ground on which the woman dances. Notwithstanding Hewitt's lyrical view of the painting, and putting the overtly surrealist imagery of the woman and the eye to one side, these towers can be seen in the context of British romantic depictions of urban bomb damage such as John Piper's series of paintings of bombed churches in Bristol (1940) or Sutherland's *Devastation* series, but are also reminiscent, and particularly given the monochromatic reproduction used in *Now in Ulster*, of contemporary photographs. A clear parallel can be drawn between Middleton's towers and James Doherty's photograph of Belfast's Trinity Street Church on 12 July 1941, after it had been decapitated and lost its spire in the Easter Tuesday raid.[94] We might also compare the towers with John Armstrong's War Artists' Advisory Committee commission *Coggeshall Church, Essex* (1940)—a painting which similarly depicts a church tower ripped open by a bomb blast and which shows how easily surrealist techniques could be recruited for official war art.[95] It is worth remembering that surrealism was also co-opted, albeit indirectly, into an important advertising campaign for the British Government at this time. One of Abram Games' extraordinary *Your Britain. Fight For It Now* (1942) series shows a bright and clean two-dimensional image of the planned Finsbury Health Centre (to be constructed post-war) forming a wall which half covers a dark, filthy, and ruined structure—a bomb-damaged building in which a bandy legged boy with rickets stands, joylessly trailing a small pink toy boat through a puddle. A tombstone looms against the rear wall of the ruin, and the words 'neglect' and 'disease' are daubed on the cracked and stained walls. Darracott and Loftus point out in their survey of wartime posters that the symbolic deployment of colour and the fusion of modern architecture with dilapidated ruin in a single

---

[93] Hewitt, 'Under Forty: Some Ulster Artists', *Now in Ulster*, p. 15.

[94] James Doherty, *Post 381*, p. 48.

[95] John Armstrong (1893–1973) was an English painter whose work became increasingly surrealist in character following the Spanish Civil War, and became increasingly dominated by visions of the destruction of buildings (see *Invocation* [1938]). Unsurprisingly, his war art produced under the auspices of the WAAC included a number of similar depictions of bomb damage. (Mark Glazebrook, 'Introduction' to *John Armstrong 1893–1973* [exhibition catalogue, London: Arts Council of Great Britain, 1975]).

image 'show Games' familiarity with surrealist work by artists such as Dali and de Chirico', and the poster shows how during the Second World War the grammar of surrealism, the use of incongruous juxtaposition and realist technique, could be recruited with relative ease to art forms intended for a mass audience, and for political ends.[96] Middleton himself seems to have associated surrealism with the apprehension of war and violence: in an interview in 1973 he said that the flaring of sectarian violence in Northern Ireland in the early 1970s had encouraged the use of 'strong, bright colours' in his work.

> That's another thing that has been motivated by the tension up in the North. People expect you to turn up to painting the troubles in the same way as a newsman goes out with a camera and takes photos of it. I had enough of that during the blitz in '41.
> Somewhat of the same thing happened then that's happening now. The tension, the repressed anxiety... all the things that build up and push in on the emotional side... I find that it builds up, it's re-activated the old surrealist bug, and it's coming up.[97]

If, as Kenneth Jamison claims, Middleton was unable to paint for six months following the Blitz, it is possible that *The Dark Tower* itself was painted before the bombing of Belfast.[98] Even if this was the case, Middleton would surely have been aware of the scenes of destruction that followed earlier raids on cities and towns in Britain, from photographic reports in magazines and newspapers, or from newsreel reports. The landscape of the composition, the neutral undulation on which the towers stand, and the consciously enigmatic symbolism of the woman and the eye would all seem to be products of the psychological world (or the result of Middleton's encounters with earlier surrealist artworks), but the damaged towers themselves and the debris in the foreground root this work in the year and place of its composition. The inclusion by the editors of *Now in Ulster* of a reproduction of this work alongside two other more conventional representations of the Belfast Blitz by George Campbell and Gerard Dillon in the illustrated section of the little magazine bears out this contextual reading. The similarities in size and design between such little magazines and the *War Pictures by British Artists* series produced by the WAAC during the war, which also printed monochrome reproductions of recent paintings, further demonstrate the ways in

[96] Joseph Darracott and Belinda Loftus, *Second World War Posters* (London: Imperial War Museum, 1972), p. 31.

[97] Harriet Cooke, 'Colin Middleton', *Irish Times*, 1 January 1973.

[98] Jamison, *The Art of Colin Middleton*.

which boundaries between official and unofficial art were collapsing at this time.[99]

The meaning of the woman and giant eye which appear in *The Dark Tower* is unclear: cynical readings of Middleton's surrealist works have seen the use of such imagery as little more than mischief-making, poses, and knowing attempts to shock and confuse the Belfast public. Addressing another of Middleton's surrealist paintings from 1941, *The Fortune Teller*, Hall detects 'a sense of showing off' and accuses Middleton of employing 'impenetrable imagery' in so doing.[100] *The Fortune Teller* is free from overt references to the Blitz or the ongoing conflict. Here another mysterious woman (a topless flamenco dancer, perhaps) appears in an anonymous and barren landscape, surrounded by seemingly random objects and birds, comprising a faceless grandfather clock, a ladder, two cockatiels, and another, smaller yellow bird housed in an open-fronted cabinet on the ground. In the background a church on a hill appears to have a vast door opening from its tower. The discordance of the scene is amplified by the sheets of paper or fabric blowing across the landscape: one larger sheet is loosely caught on the woman's head, and one sheet above the cabinet, although completely blank, immediately calls to mind an open newspaper, its shape suggesting that it is being held by an invisible reader. The sheets do not offer an explanation for this particular assembly of objects, nor their juxtaposition with the dancer and the birds, but they do form an unexpected link between *The Fortune Teller* and another of Middleton's wartime paintings.

The title of *The Holy Lands* (1945) would seem to refer to the eponymous area of inner-city South Belfast to the east of Queen's University. Rendered in a semi-vorticist style, rows of terraced houses similar to those found in this part of the city fan out across the middle and far distance, and the hillside in the foreground seems to have been introduced to aid the composition. The figures that populate the scene make this a positive portrayal of urban Belfast at play, seemingly illustrative of the intermittently warm feelings towards his home city experienced by Middleton during the war. Amongst the figures on the hillside are a courting couple, an elderly man sitting alone with his walking stick, and a bowler-hatted man reading a newspaper, while in the foreground some boys play football. The threat of war would appear to be absent (and indeed, by 1945 the threat of air attack had all but disappeared for the residents of the

[99] *War Pictures by British Artists No. 2: Blitz*, introduced by J.B. Morton, (London: Oxford University Press, 1942), reproduced paintings of bomb damage by Edward Ardizzone, Henry Moore, John Piper, and Graham Sutherland, amongst others.

[100] Hall, p. 8.

city), and like Middleton's 1941 Annadale paintings, the scene seems to endorse a conventional and reassuring view of civilian life. A peculiar note of discord is sounded, however, by the blank sheets of newspaper that blow across the scene, similar to those which drift across the desert in *The Fortune Teller* and threaten to envelop the woman in the flamenco skirt. In *The Holy Lands* the sheets are more tidily organized: spines aligned in the same direction towards the horizon, they flutter from the hillside across the skyline from right to left, echoing a flock of birds in the resulting shape. Against the vorticist backdrop of the terraces the airborne papers are eerie, even ghostly, and none of the figures on the hillside seems to have noticed them. The sheets also appear in a post-war painting, *Elijah* (1948), where seven fly in a circle around a woman and two Blakeian images of the eponymous prophet, the larger of which crouches on a pile of books, while the smaller figure squats on one of the airborne loose sheets. Without entering at length into the allegorical and symbolic implications of this later work, it is worth remembering in the context of the Blitz that the biblical prophet Elijah calls down fire from the sky as he conducts his test to ascertain the relative powers of the false god Baal and Yahweh the God of Israel.[101] If *The Holy Lands* is considered alongside its surrealist counterparts, the loose sheets can be seen to hint at undisclosed chaos and implied destruction, and connect the recognizable and named world of urban Belfast to the troubled world of the unconscious that Middleton calls up in the earlier and later works.

More straightforwardly concerned with contemporaneous Belfast are Middleton's neo-impressionistic paintings from the latter half of 1941. These include a series of Belfast street scenes, the composition of which Kenneth Jamison claims held a therapeutic value for the artist, in the face of personal tragedy and the strain of life lived in the shadow of war: 'As though to dispel the dark memories these paintings of this period are an affirmation of the normality of life in city streets where children play and people go about their tasks'.[102] Both *Lagan: Annadale, October 1941* (1941)—the first Middleton painting purchased by the Belfast Museum and Art Gallery after his debut exhibition—and *Allotments on Annadale Embankment* (1941) recall André Derain, or even, in the studied naivety of their technique, L.S. Lowry. If *The Dark Tower* and *The Fortune Teller* were exercises in alienation and defamiliarization, the Annadale paintings, also produced in 1941, are precisely the opposite, as Middleton recovers what had been threatened by the Belfast Blitz that same year by evoking

---

[101] 1 Kings, 18:38.
[102] Kenneth Jamison, 'Painting and Sculpture', in Michael Longley (ed.), *Causeway: The Arts in Ulster*, pp. 43–70 (p. 50).

scenes of peace and contentment in named and recognizable areas of his home town.[103] These works may sit uneasily beside the surrealist paintings of that same year, but this is exactly where they could be found in the Hewitt-organized exhibition of 1943. As Coulter observes, the decision of the Museum to purchase *Lagan: Annadale, October 1941* was significant:

> The first Middleton to enter a public collection, this was a conservative choice within the context of the exhibition and yet the loose brush strokes, glimpses of exposed canvas and simplified figures produced a conscious naivety that positioned *Lagan, Annadale,* among the more radical works in the Gallery's collection. Significantly, as a representational image of everyday life set in a familiar area of Belfast, *Lagan, Annadale* could be clearly identified as a local picture. While Middleton's surrealist and symbolist canvases displayed the 'continental influence' that Hewitt celebrated, his impressionistic images of civilian life struck a chord in wartime Belfast.[104]

There is a sense of community in these wartime representational scenes of Belfast: though generally without faces, the figures that populate the paintings are recognizable and humble as they go about their business or recreation. In her study of William Conor—an unlikely antecedent whom Middleton nonetheless held in high regard—Judith C. Wilson emphasizes Middleton's fidelity to the topography of Belfast, as he depicted in detail the 'little red-brick rows', often identified by name 'as in *Nelson Street, Mary Street, Glenard*—a detail Conor never supplied'.[105] The 1939 painting *Fish and Chips* is demonstrative of how Middleton was able to use distinctly surrealist techniques to represent a quintessential Belfast street scene. Here the eponymous fish and chip shop and a pawnbroker's take the foreground, between which a terrace of houses can be seen, and a red brick factory with smoking chimney and a church or chapel with a cross on its roof are also visible in the background. The shapes of the buildings have been simplified and stylized: they are rendered in flat planes of colour, lack any texture, and cast heavy shadows. The technique is reminiscent of de Chirico, but the effect is much less menacing. No persons or animals intrude on the scene, but the mood is leavened by the restrained use of primary colours and the deployment of a few semi-comic details. The pawnbroker's is identifiable by the traditional three yellow balls on its sign, but the chip shop displays a small blue fish on the wall of the building and

---

[103] Other works in this vein include *If I Were a Blackbird* (1941) and *Shop Street Corner* (1942).

[104] Coulter, 'Nationalism, Regionalism and Internationalism', p. 106.

[105] Wilson, *Conor 1881–1968*, p. 120.

a sign in the shop window reading 'FISH AND CHIPS' in white capitals on a red background.[106]

Whilst the influences on Middleton's diverse wartime oeuvre were both local and international, many of these paintings reveal an abiding concern with the city of Belfast and its built environment. Middleton also produced some demonstrably abstract works at this time, such as *The Child's Brain: Opus 1 No. 16 group II* (1940) and *The Dark Lady* (1941), from which any overt local concerns seem to be absent, but in a later expressionist painting entitled *The Refugee* (1941), which initially appears to respond in general terms to the pain of the dispossessed across Europe, a group of buildings and most significantly a factory chimney can be seen on the left of the composition. Although his paintings are clearly often heavily symbolic, his preoccupation with the built environment shows that Middleton was also capable of responding more directly to historical traumas, and allows connections to be drawn with British and Continental contemporaries and forebears.

Siren over Belfast (1944, Fig. 3.1) is one such simultaneously symbolic and literal response to the Belfast Blitz and the pain of its aftermath. This apocalyptic painting depicts a scattering of buildings dwarfed by a huge, red-lipped, vaguely sphinx-like demon or monster with a mane of flames, which fills the sky above. Apart from three factory chimneys and a church tower (characteristic references to the industrial and religious Belfast cityscape) the buildings are rough, windowless, single storey, and humble, and the eye is drawn to the bright flames emanating from the creature's head. The punning title links the siren used to warn of an imminent air raid with the mythological female siren, and the combination of the open screaming mouth of the monster with the bright red lips and flames cause the painting to emit a palpable sense of very loud noise. In addition, some kind of guitar-like instrument is being played in the foreground; whether by the siren itself or by a pair of disembodied hands is unclear. The sound hole of the guitar echoes the cyclonic pattern that must be taken as the eye of the siren, and the guitar's neck recalls the barrel of a gun. Creativity, destruction, and violence are fused in the heavily symbolic image of the siren, but the human and animal elements of the composition—the small figures of a girl in a green dress with a red ribbon in her hair in the middle distance, seemingly carried off her feet by the blast, and a red animal (a fox or a dog, perhaps) running beside her—are reminders of the human and personal cost of the destruction, and leaven the symbolic import of

---

[106] Middleton's uninhibited use of text here recalls the frequent appearance of words and advertisements in the works of the contemporaneous Dublin artist Harry Kernoff, but the deployment of surrealist technique is far more radical.

Fig. 3.1 Colin Middleton, *Siren over Belfast* (oil on canvas, 1944)
By kind permission of the Estate of Colin Middleton, © Estate of Colin Middleton, IVARO, 2014.

the work. In this work the paint has been applied in thicker layers: in contrast with the smooth planes and undulations of *The Dark Tower* and *The Fortune Teller* we see a more expressionist surrealism closer to Max Ernst during the 1930s than to Dali. Indeed, Ernst's *The Angel of the Hearth* series (1937) is arguably an important antecedent for *Siren over Belfast*. Produced following the defeat of the Republican forces in Spain, Ernst's paintings show a monstrous, many-limbed bird-like demon, dancing and raging over an anonymous, flat landscape. In 1938 Ernst briefly gave the work the title *The Triumph of Surrealism*—a despairing comment on the failure of communism and surrealism to resist fascism successfully which he explained as 'an ironic title for a kind of juggernaut which crushes and destroys all that comes in its path. That was my impression of what would happen in the world, and I was probably right'.[107] In a 1980 newspaper interview Middleton himself responded to a 'charge of eclecticism' with

---

[107] Quoted in Uwe M. Schneede, *The Essential Max Ernst*, translated by R.W. Last (London: Thames and Hudson, 1972), p. 154.

Fig. 3.2 Colin Middleton, *Strange Openings* (oil on canvas, *c.*1942, Irish Museum of Modern Art)

By kind permission of the Estate of Colin Middleton, © Estate of Colin Middleton, IVARO, 2014.

reference to Ernst. The journalist reported that Middleton felt that he had 'been accused of imitating every big name in Europe. The only one omitted is Max Ernst, whose work really stimulates him'. In the same interview Middleton claimed to feel an affinity with Catalonia and praises Dali's work of the 1930s and 1940s, after which period he suggested that religion began to dominate Dali's paintings to the detriment of their quality.[108] Seen in the context of these European antecedents, *Siren over Belfast* shows again how Middleton brought a set of artistic styles previously alien to Ireland to bear on local subject matter.

Strange Openings (*c.*1942, Fig. 3.2) is a far more clinical and detached representation of the Belfast urban landscape following the Blitz. Stylistically it is a close companion to *Fish and Chips*, but lacks the warm colours and semi-comic touches of the earlier work and is very much a post-Blitz painting. The title refers to holes that appeared in the side of

---

[108] Pat Murphy, 'Ireland's Greatest Surrealist', *Irish Times*, 31 December 1980.

buildings as a result of bomb blasts, and the painting depicts doorless and windowless rows of terraced houses, and, looming larger, presumably industrial buildings with large, similarly perfectly rectangular openings in their sides. The style adopted by Middleton here again recalls de Chirico's arcades and piazzas of his *pittura metafisica* period, in the theatrical intensity of the flat, stylized surfaces and the depth of the shadows. In this way, *Strange Openings* makes no reference to the chaotic effects of the Blitz, the irregular patterns of destruction, disruption, and fragmentation that proved so stimulating to many artists and writers. It is a far remove from the sound and fury of *Siren over Belfast*, and the haunting title of *Strange Openings* echoes its eeriness of tone: no human or animal intrudes on this deserted urban landscape, and no sheets of newspaper blow through the scene. The composition is entirely made up of straight lines, and the holes in the sides of the buildings appear as part of their design rather than damage occasioned by bomb blasts, in contrast with the chunks bitten out of the sides of the towers in *The Dark Tower*. Where *Siren over Belfast* emits noise and pain, this composition is a deserted stage set, dominated by a portentous silence. Yet despite Middleton's nod to de Chirico, *Strange Openings* ultimately remains faithful to the closely packed terraced backstreets, the outside lavatories and brick walled back yards, as once again the recognizable and knowable in Belfast is rendered in a distinctly foreign style.

For Middleton, it seems, the importance of place was heightened by its destruction. In an interview with Michael Longley in 1967 he articulated a kind of mystical identification with places using a near mantra: 'Place is everything. Place is terribly important. Places, places, places. I just can't go out for a day's sketching—that's meaningless, utterly horrible, terrifying'.[109] Hewitt's observation about Northern Ireland's wartime isolation forcing artists and writers to till their own gardens, thereby resulting in an 'an unusually vigorous phase in the creative arts', is illuminating in this respect, and is certainly applicable to Middleton: the works I have discussed show him stating emphatically in paint his fidelity to place by turning to his home town as subject matter, even as he continued to explore a variety of Continental styles.[110] Though Middleton engages with differing effects of air raids in these works, a concern for the built environment is common to his non-abstract pieces: his war paintings show that the impact of the Blitz on art in the province went beyond representational depictions of the damage. These works show how the blitzed cityscape was the site of a complex dialogue between representational and non-representational

---

[109] Michael Longley, 'Talking to Colin Middleton', *Irish Times*, 7 April 1967.
[110] Hewitt, *Colin Middleton*, p. 18.

artistic modes, initiated by the unprecedented, cataclysmic, and hugely traumatic collision between international and local histories.

* * *

Gerard Dillon was on holiday in Connemara at the outbreak of war in September 1939. He was twenty-three. Refused permission to cross the Irish Sea as he had no intention of enlisting in the British army, he returned initially to his family home in the Falls Road area of Belfast, where he had been born and brought up. Having lived in London during the 1930s, where he had worked as a decorator and moved in artistic and cultural circles entirely alien to his strictly Catholic background in Belfast, he soon found the atmosphere in the poverty-stricken and strongly nationalist area stifling. Belonging to a group by turns hostile to the British war effort and supportive of Irish neutrality, Dillon was greatly affected by the febrile political atmosphere, as his biographer James White explains: 'It became impossible to ignore the conditions imposed by the war and to adopt the previous attitudes of ignoring as far as possible all signs of political authority'.[111] Matters were made worse by the fissure in his own family: although his mother was stridently and vocally nationalist, his father had served in the British army during the Boer war and two of his brothers enlisted to fight in the Second World War—causes of incessant domestic strife between his parents.[112] When travel restrictions allowed, Dillon divided his time between Belfast and Dublin during the war years, spending much of his time in Belfast in the family house in Lower Clonard Street, with curious consequences, as his biographer James White describes:

> He seemed to be charged with an energy for painting and he painted all the walls of the house white like the Connemara cottages, and on the walls of the kitchen and staircase he painted a series of double heads influenced by the stonecarvings he had seen in the west. He even painted the blinds on the kitchen window, and the children would stand outside in the dark evenings when the blinds were pulled down and pretend they were at the picture house. Even these images on the blinds have a monastic feeling, as if he wanted to reflect the concept of the stained glass windows in churches when seen from the outside.[113]

Dillon's attempts to turn a corner of urban wartime Belfast into a Connemara cottage register his eccentric preoccupation with the west of Ireland and its importance to his wartime oeuvre. His creation of this defensive lair also shows that he had a close affinity with material things, as is borne out by his use of found objects. Ríann Coulter's exploration of Dillon's engagement

[111] White, *Gerard Dillon*, pp. 34–35.　　[112] White, *Gerard Dillon*, p. 20.
[113] White, *Gerard Dillon*, p. 49.

with the west during the 1940s and 1950s focuses on his homosexuality, which, she argues, he felt to be at odds with his Catholic and nationalist identity. She suggests that paintings such as *Potato Pickers* (1944) or *Grey Beach* (*c.*1950) draw on imagery from an officially approved myth of the west in various attempts to mask their homoerotic content.[114] Here I reappraise his west of Ireland paintings in the context of the Second World War, which arguably also posed a challenge to his nationalist identity.

Many of Dillon's works do address the war directly: an exhibition which opened in Dublin in February 1942 included several paintings of Belfast after the Blitz, as well as *Shades,* a study of an army sentry outside his box. At this time Dillon also socialized with American soldiers, often in the company of the Campbell brothers in Dubarry's pub, where the artists would execute quick sketches of the soldiers for little more than the price of a drink.[115] James MacIntyre recalls a meeting with Dillon:

> Our conversation turned to the Blitz and Gerard told me that he had framed his paintings of the carnage with scarred timber taken from bombed sites.
> 'People bought them and they imagined I was so hard up I couldn't afford to buy frames,' he chuckled.
> I thought this was inspirational.[116]

His use of found materials in this way—later he would experiment with collage as a form and incorporate old gloves, string, and pictures torn from magazines and newspapers into his works—enables the material destruction of the Blitz to be incorporated into his own work in a strikingly literal way.[117] On the opening of the 1942 exhibition, Mainie Jellett, something of a mentor to Dillon during the war, said that it took courage for a young man to embark 'on a painting career at a time like this, with the forces of destruction rampant, whilst the forces of construction were struggling for life'.[118]

Away from these works, it was during the war that Dillon's more substantial paintings began to reflect in earnest the landscape and people of Connemara and the Aran Islands, which he first visited in 1943. The bird's-eye perspective and vibrant colours of *The Little Green Fields* (1945, Fig. 3.3) perhaps recall the influence of Marc Chagall, but Dillon also draws on an important element of compositional design from medieval Irish stonemasonry. The painting depicts a patchwork of small fields enclosed by dry stone walls such as those found on

---

[114] Coulter, 'Nationalism, Regionalism and Internationalism', p. 19.
[115] White, *Gerard Dillon*, pp. 41–42.
[116] MacIntyre, *Making My Mark*, p. 102.
[117] Catherine Marshall, 'Gerard Dillon', in Marshall (ed.), *The Hunter Gatherer*, pp. 29–35 (p. 29).
[118] White, *Gerard Dillon*, p. 39.

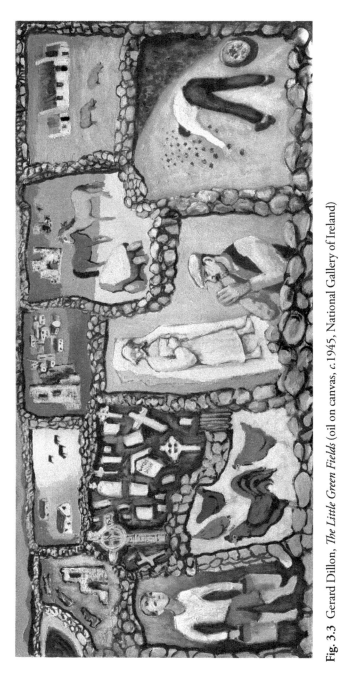

Fig. 3.3 Gerard Dillon, *The Little Green Fields* (oil on canvas, *c*.1945, National Gallery of Ireland)

By kind permission of the Estate of Gerard Dillon and the National Gallery of Ireland.

the islands and in the west of Ireland. Dillon uses these walls to divide ten different scenes within the same landscape. These include a graveyard (in which one of the headstones carries Dillon's own name), a boy carrying a pail in each hand, a man digging potatoes, some hens, a small village with a church, a pair of horses near a Neolithic stone table, a ruined tower, and a man praying to the carved statue of a saint. John Hewitt noted in 1949 that the panelled form of *The Little Green Fields* can be traced back to the carved decorations on medieval Irish High Crosses; Coulter writes that Dillon depicts 'an unspoilt rural idyll, untainted by both modernity and British rule'.[119]

Notwithstanding these observations, the composition also bears fruitful comparison with a pair of works from English painter Stanley Spencer's *Shipbuilding on the Clyde* series of wartime paintings, painted under the direction of the War Artist's Advisory Committee.[120] The elongated rectangles that make up the wings of Spencer's vast triptychs *Burners* (1940) and *Welders* (1941) are echoed in the shape of Dillon's painting, but a more fundamental similarity is the decision to compartmentalize the canvas. Workers in Spencer's triptychs are separated from their companions by geometrical divisions made by the different sections of metal on which they are working: there is no clue to the shape of the ship on which they are working as a whole, and we are, as Timothy Hyman observes, 'in the belly of the whale'.[121] Of *Welders*, Margaret Garlake writes that 'the treatment of their bodies, bent and distorted in order to perform their work, vividly illustrates the extent to which war had diminished personal liberty, particularly for working class men'.[122] In light of this, Dillon's *The Little Green Fields* might be reassessed: rather than inhabiting a 'rural idyll', the figures in the painting can be seen to be constrained by centuries old restrictions, and as locked into their manual occupations as the Clydeside shipbuilders. It is notable that none of the hands of the three human figures in Dillon's painting are free: on the left the boy's hands are both taken up with the buckets; in the centre the man's hands are clasped in prayer; and on the right another man is bent over a field hard at work. Such figures

---

[119] Hewitt is quoted in S.B. Kennedy, *Irish Art and Modernism*, p. 361; Coulter, 'Nationalism, Regionalism and Internationalism', p. 176. Both Hewitt and Coulter refer to this painting as *West of Ireland Landscape*, but the National Gallery of Ireland lists the work as *The Little Green Fields*, and since the painting belongs to that collection I use the latter title. The possible nationalist undertones arising from the title *The Little Green Fields* should not go unacknowledged.

[120] For a full history of this series of commissions, see Andrew Patrizio and Frank Little, *Canvassing the Clyde: Stanley Spencer and the Shipyards* (Glasgow: Glasgow Museums, 1994).

[121] Timothy Hyman, 'Stanley Spencer: Angels and Dirt' in *Stanley Spencer*, edited by Timothy Hyman and Patrick Wright (London: Tate Publishing, 2001), pp. 10–41 (p. 35).

[122] Margaret Garlake, *New Art, New World: British Art in Postwar Society* (New Haven and London: Yale University Press, 1998), p. 98.

may indeed embody the rugged masculinity of 'devout, Gaelic-speaking, "manly" men', endorsed by de Valera's government and the Catholic Church, and which Coulter believes Dillon drew on for such works, but given his feelings of confinement during the war and his potentially vexed sense of national identity, this work may be reread in terms of restriction and frustration.[123] Like Spencer's shipbuilders, the men are disconnected, facing away from each other and engaged in different pursuits. Further examples of Dillon's paintings in which the canvas has been divided up are *High Cross Panel* (1949), *The Spectator* (1950), and *The Irish at Play* (1953), all of which recall the medieval Celtic design. In *Forgive us our Trespasses* (1942) a confession box occupies roughly the upper left quartile of the composition, which depicts the interior of a church. Figures of worshippers queuing for confession do not overlap the confessional at all, which itself is described simply by linear divisions creating three small boxes in which the priest (half obscured by a curtain) and two kneeling worshippers can be seen. In this painting Dillon divides the composition more overtly to evoke the restrictions imposed by religion: indeed, the church has arguably taken care of the symbolism of the scene already.

Another work, *Demolition* (1950), has a more complex history. In the early spring of 1945 Dillon returned to London, taking on work as a 'ganger' leading groups of other Irish workers doing emergency repairs of bombed houses.[124] *Demolition* gives us a view of a house whose front wall has been removed, as though by a bomb blast: the composition is compartmentalized by the different rooms and workmen can be seen in each room, as James White observes 'from the standpoint of a doll's house open for a child to play'.[125] The workers are not disconnected from each other in *Demolition* as they are in *The Little Green Fields* (two pairs are evidently in conversation), but the ability to reflect both medieval Celtic design and twentieth-century bomb damage in broadly similar designs is striking.

Such compartmentalization of the canvas can be seen in a diverse range of compositions around this time, examination of which allows a reconsideration of Dillon's oeuvre within a broader international context than the focus on his debt to medieval Celtic design has thus far permitted. The Mexican artist Diego Rivera's mural *The Making of a Fresco Showing the Building of a City* (1931), for example, is divided into six main sections

---

[123] Coulter, 'Nationalism, Regionalism and Internationalism', p. 175.
[124] White, *Gerard Dillon*, p. 50.
[125] White, *Gerard Dillon*, p. 53. Citing Louis MacNeice and George Orwell, Mark Rawlinson has argued that during the Second World War it became 'literary convention' to describe bombed-out houses with reference to doll's houses as part of a ubiquitous discourse of 'the figurative and conceptual containment of war's destructiveness' (Rawlinson, *British Writing of the Second World War*, p. 96).

by a trompe l'oeil wooden scaffold, within which artists and labourers can be seen at work. As the title suggests, this is a mural which itself depicts the painting of a mural, echoing the Renaissance tradition. Like Dillon in *Island People* (1950) and Spencer in *Burners* and *Welders*, Rivera has included himself as the artist within the composition. While Rivera's work seems on first inspection to celebrate the nobility of the ordinary worker, the colossal symbolic figure of whom dominates the central panels of the mural, *The Making of a Fresco* is a complex work, and, like Spencer's Clyde triptychs, its metacritical vision complicates the respective places of individual workers, artists, and patrons in relation to collaborative projects.

The separation of figures by divisions within a composition has also been used in representations of military scenes. In 1943 the US artist Benton Spruance produced *Fathers and Sons*—a lithograph divided into organic shapes, echoing the lines of a dead tree which stretches across from the left of the composition. These shapes may represent the kind of foxholes dug by troops engaged in combat in open country, and within these cramped spaces an American and a German soldier confront each other: helmeted, masked, and holding weapons. The sky above is pockmarked by explosions and streaked with aircraft contrails, and in the cutaway ground beneath the soldiers their forms are echoed by the similarly contorted figures of two skeletons from the previous war. One of these still wears a helmet of American or British design, whilst a coal-scuttle helmet of similar design as that used by the German army during the First World War lies beside the skull of the other. The lithograph illustrates unambiguously the human cost and physical pain of combat conditions, but, as in other works I have referred to, symbolic potency here derives from the compartmentalization of the composition. There is no evidence of a direct link between Spruance and Dillon, but *Fathers and Sons* does bear direct comparison with a later work by the Belfast artist: in *The Brothers* (1966) three skeletons can be seen incarcerated in coffins underground, as though the ground had been cut away. Dillon, Spencer, Rivera, and Spruance were geographically disparate artists, but their use of division and compartmentalization allows us to draw connections between these works, which describe in various ways the economic, historical, political, and religious pressures exerted on the individual during the 1930s and 1940s.

Dillon's *The Little Green Fields* and Spencer's Glasgow paintings are interesting foils to many examples of officially commissioned wartime art, which attempted to encourage support for the British war effort through the careful presentation of scenes of collective endeavour, in rural, agricultural, or industrial contexts. Spencer's triptychs are paradoxical: although they were officially commissioned, and illustrate the complex combination of diverse technical skills that go into the building of a ship, the compositions themselves communicate a profound disconnection between the workers. No direct connection between Stanley Spencer and Northern Ireland can be discerned until the early 1950s, when he visited his brother, a musician who lived in Belfast, on four occasions. He produced at least four portraits of his niece and one panoramic cityscape, *Merville Garden Village near Belfast* (1951), which contrasts the new post-war housing development with the older garden it enclosed.[126] According to John Hewitt, at this time Spencer struck up a friendship with influential Hungarian-born local collector Zoltan Frankl, who bought three of his works including the shipbuilding painting *Caulkers*. Hewitt and Spencer also grew close, and after conducting lengthy taped conversations with the artist for a radio interview, Hewitt identified Spencer's Clydeside paintings with industrial Belfast:

> And in Belfast where we know the ways of shipyard folk, we enjoyed his remembering being in Port Glasgow as a war artist, and liking the working people that he lodged with, and when he drew a number of their portraits and presented them, these became by far the best framed works of his he ever saw; the best of craftsmanship and the best of material going into their making.[127]

This idea of the craftsman is important: Spencer's inclusion of himself as the figure of the artist in both *Burners* and *Welders* may have constituted an attempt to demonstrate that the war artist, far from being a detached observer, was an integral part of the war effort.

William Conor also saw himself as a craftsman and as a user of materials. In a speech to the Royal Ulster Society in 1958 he declared:

> In this topsy turvy age, when everyone is shouting 'forward', and no one is expected to ask 'where' it would seem as if nothing matters or rather, it matters nothing what the artist paints or sculpts, and the artists themselves are so fiercely individualistic that they don't know what each other is getting at. Sometimes I think the artist, as an honest and skilled craftsman, is quickly disappearing and it would seem that the very deficiencies in work today are seized upon as something very novel and original.
> Art exists only where things are made to last forever.[128]

Many of the works Conor produced during the Second World War evoke orthodox ideas of collective endeavour, in which his view of craftsmanship as integral to Belfast's industrial prowess is evident. Of a much older generation than Dillon and Middleton, Conor was fifty-eight by 1939, and had already been an official war artist in the First World War, visiting

---

[126] Hyman and Wright (eds.), *Stanley Spencer*, p. 224.
[127] Hewitt, *North Light*, p. 175.   [128] Wilson, *Conor 1881–1968*, p. 87.

munitions works and army camps such as Ballykinlar to make sketches of the everyday life of the Ulster Division.[129] These sketches had been exhibited at the Belfast City Hall over Christmas 1916 alongside portraits of Carson and Craig, and Conor was later commissioned to paint the opening of the first Northern Ireland Parliament in 1921—a painting which hangs in Stormont today.[130] In April 1940 he received a letter from the Ministry of Information in London on behalf of the War Artist's Advisory Committee, offering him £50 for between six and eight drawings, and £1 a day in expenses, should he be away from home to study things first hand.[131] All drawings were to be submitted to the Ministry for censorship, and artists were barred from showing family or friends any of the works before submission. Duly recruited, Conor reluctantly assumed a relatively high public profile in the Northern Ireland war effort: a special exhibition consisting of work commissioned by him was a feature of Belfast's War Weapons Week and opened in December 1940.[132] Conor was the only artist permitted to draw the arrival of the US army in the province: *Landing of the First American Troops in Northern Ireland* (26 January 1942) shows Major-General Russell P. Hartle, in command of US troops in the province, the Duke of Abercorn, then Governor of Northern Ireland, Sir Archibald Sinclair, the British Air Minister, and Private Milburn Henke, the first American soldier officially to step onto United Kingdom soil, leaving the gangplank at Dufferin Quay in Belfast as the band of the Royal Ulster Rifles plays in the background.[133]

Despite Conor's elevated status, according to his friend William Carter he had little enthusiasm for the work:

> The work he did then was not, I think, of any great significance in his life as an artist. I think he hated the war and he hated everything to do with it. Of course economically it was a difficult time, the wartime interfered with normal work and normal activities and the fact that he couldn't travel easily outside the Province. I think it was a bad period of his life that he didn't like to remember or talk about.[134]

It cannot be said that the war had any discernible lasting impact on his career as a painter, aside from the officially commissioned pieces: after

[129] Wilson, *Conor 1881–1968*, p. 13.
[130] Eileen Black, 'Scenes of Ulster Life: The Paintings and Drawings of William Conor', *Irish Arts Review Yearbook 18*, (2002), pp. 146–152 (p. 148).
[131] The activities of the WAAC under the direction of Kenneth Clark have been related in detail elsewhere, in Meirion and Susie Harries, *The War Artists* (London: Michael Joseph in association with the Imperial War Museum and the Tate Gallery, 1983), pp. 159–163, and in Stansky and Abrahams, *London's Burning*, pp. 16–28.
[132] Wilson, *Conor 1881–1968*, p. 65.   [133] Wilson, *Conor 1881–1968*, p. 70.
[134] Wilson, *Conor 1881–1968*, p. 71.

1945 Conor reverted to his familiar territory of portraits and local scenes, touched little by the outside world or overt political considerations. It is notable, however, that many of the titles of Conor's wartime works refer to named streets and locations in Belfast, in contrast to works produced before and after the war which, portraits aside, frequently deal in archetypes, and have generalized titles. This is partly due to the nature of the work, but also suggests that, like Middleton, Conor recovered a sense of fidelity to his home city in his wartime pictures.

Conor's drawings for the WAAC during the Second World War are also vital to an understanding of the officially approved views of the province at war that the British and Northern Irish governments wished to promote. Although Conor completed *The Launch* in 1923, long before the Second World War, its imagery prefigures many of his wartime paintings, and significantly it was included in *The Irish Scene,* a large book of colour reproductions of his paintings published in 1944. The composition shows three men watching the bow of a ship as it is launched down a slipway, a union flag just visible flying from the bow.[135] A review of Conor's 1923 one-man exhibition describes the emphasis on collaborative endeavour in his industrial works:

> The reaction of the life-struggle in a manufacturing community upon the individual is nearly always the basis on which his art is founded. This idea pervades that fine painting 'The Launch', one of his most recent achievements. Here the interest does not centre on the spectacle of the great ship sliding magnificently down the slips, but on the figures of the three shipyard workers who watch intently the seal of final success set upon their labours.[136]

The wartime shipyard commission *Riveting* (1940, Fig. 3.4), a watercolour on paper, also features a trio of workers. In sharp contrast to Spencer's Glasgow series, here the side of the ship is drawn as a vast, monolithic curved wall, and the focus of the composition is on the three men working together in the bottom half of the painting. Conor's concern was with the collaborative and human face of heavy industry. This contrasts with another Belfast shipyard painting produced under the auspices of the WAAC: Edward Mansfield's *The View across the Musgrave Yard, Belfast: with the Centre Plate of a ship in the foreground and Ship No 1154 ready to leave the slips* (1942).[137] Here the pattern of booms and scaffolds that surround the ship on the slipway is used to break the composition up into an almost cubist collection of geometrical shapes, though the potential

---

[135] William Conor, *The Irish Scene* (Belfast: Derrick MacCord, 1944).
[136] *Colour 19*, nos. 4–5 (November/December 1923), pp. 10–12: repr. in Wilson, *Conor 1881–1968*, p. 25.
[137] This painting is in the collection of the Imperial War Museum, London.

ambiguity of these lines and blocks of colour is reined in by the inescapable resonance of the white ensign of the Royal Navy, which appears just below the evening sun in the top left corner.

Conor's officially commissioned war pieces are far more unambiguous, and are in some cases almost nakedly propagandist. *Men of the Home Front* (1940), like many of the works drawn with crayon on paper, shows

Fig. 3.4 William Conor, *Riveting* (crayon on paper, 1940, Ulster Museum)
By kind permission of the Estate of William Conor and the Ulster Museum.

shipyard workers crossing Queen's Bridge, Belfast, probably on the way home after a shift. The body language of the men seems relaxed, and they talk in groups of four or fewer as they walk. One man removes his hat to scratch his head. This is not a depiction of a well-drilled and disciplined civilian army, and the emphasis is on the informality and ordinariness of the workers and their camaraderie. Conor also drew the women of the home front. *F.A.N.Y.'s Crossing Donegall Place, Belfast* (1940) depicts three uniformed nurses (of the First Aid Nursing Yeomanry) with confident and smiling faces, their legs marching purposefully in unison, whilst in *Collecting Scrap Metal* (1940) four women drag a mangle across a terraced street. They also seem sprightly despite the effort clearly being expended, as two older women look on from across the street. *Evacuation of Children, Great Northern Railway Station, Belfast* (*c.*1940) is a bustling, chaotic scene showing women of all ages escorting children onto a train. The atmosphere is affectionate and cheery, and rather than expressing fear or sorrow the women and children are smiling. In sharp contrast to the compartmentalization of Spencer's shipbuilding paintings (and, indeed, Dillon's wartime compositions), Conor's drawings frequently promote the idea of civilian and industrial life as a collaborative group endeavour. In so doing, and without reference to innumerable contradictions, social conditions, and historical antagonisms, such works offer a wholly positive view of the urban geography of Belfast at this time, where sites of industrial production were located next to and between residential areas, with the former, to a considerable extent, defining the latter.

* * *

It is clear that the pressures acting on the production of visual art in Northern Ireland during the war years were many, various, and often acute. Given the lack of material evidence, it seems unlikely that the Second World War had any long-term impact on artists working in the province. It is tempting to refer once more to Louis MacNeice's sense of the war years as an 'interregnum', and concede that as the war ended and the unique presences and pressures resulting from the conflict dispersed and receded, artists in Northern Ireland returned to localized pre-war concerns.[138] Having described the wartime blossoming of Hewitt's regionalism, Tom Clyde concludes:

> It is obvious that any protest eventually fades: people die, move away, get seduced by other ideas and, if no obvious progress is being made, simply fade away. Related to this process is the fact of the end of the War. The troops

---

[138] MacNeice, *Strings Are False*, pp. 20, 27–29.

in Northern Ireland left, taking their money with them; artists were able to travel again [and] recalling Winston Churchill's infamous phrase, the old quarrels re-emerged undiminished.[139]

Despite this, Clyde admits that regionalist ideas formulated by Hewitt during the war were taken on by the cultural institutions of the province, the BBC, CEMA (NI), Queen's University, and the Ulster Museum, and states that, as a result, 'no Ulster poet since that time has found his or her self so confused, isolated and burdened by cultural cringe as Hewitt and his predecessors did'.[140] The difficulty of defining the extent of the long-term impact of the war on culture in Northern Ireland echoes one of the central concerns of this book: the seemingly contradictory proposition that art in the province became increasingly open to outside influences during the war, even as it turned in on itself and reflected specifically regional concerns. This paradox is certainly present in much of the material discussed in this chapter, especially in Hewitt's critical prose and Middleton's paintings. Hewitt, whose writings frequently suggest that the war years had an enlivening and rejuvenating effect on culture in the province, himself undermined this view when late on in *A North Light* he admitted that his ideas of progress may have been illusory. He describes the period 1939–1949 as:

... a starved decade, largely concerned with the problems of art in my own province and country, a period in which, because of the flaring-up of activity in a war-isolated community, we were probably disposed to exaggerate its value without the constant check of European standards...[141]

This would seem to contradict his wartime assertion that 'we now have artists working on problems which still have validity in Great Britain and on the Continent', and Hewitt himself remained unable to resolve this issue.[142] Asked in conversation with Brian McAvera what elements most influenced the production of art in the post-war years in Northern Ireland, S.B. Kennedy's answer also reflects this ambiguity:

I'm sure the most important was the aftermath of WW2 in the period 1945–1955. We had survived! And that was no mean thing. It was suddenly possible to do things: the Brave New World. I'm sure that lots of artists felt that they were striking out, yet looking back, the period between 1945 and 1960

[139] Clyde, 'A Stirring in the Dry Bones', in Dawe and Wilson Foster (eds.), *The Poet's Place*, p. 256.
[140] Clyde, 'A Stirring in the Dry Bones', in Dawe and Wilson Foster (eds.), *The Poet's Place*, p. 258.
[141] Hewitt, *North Light*, p. 153.
[142] John Hewitt, 'Under Forty: Some Ulster Artists', *Now in Ulster*, p. 13.

was really a continuation of issues and subjects that had been dealt with in the decades before the war.[143]

What is clear is that the war instigated an unprecedented influx of overseas soldiers and refugees; that this influx resulted in the deeply symbolic opening up of the bomb-damaged Belfast Museum and Art Gallery to exhibitions of works by foreign artists; that the war brought together in Belfast a mutually supportive group of artists and writers, represented in print by a number of small-scale publications; that the global scale of the conflict forced its way into the visual art of the province at this time, encouraging the assimilation and development of Continental styles and helping to displace and modify what had been a parochial tradition; that the bombing of Belfast had a profound impact on artists from the city, manifested in a distinctive engagement with the built environment and in representations of named streets and areas of the city; and that although the Home Front work of the most prominent official war artist in the province at the time conforms, in the main, to official projections of the British war effort, there is evidence elsewhere of cross-pollination between official and unofficial art in the province.

The artists I have discussed lack a common style, and indeed one thing that can be said to characterize visual art in the province during the war years is its singularity and eccentricity. Setting paintings by Colin Middleton and Gerard Dillon against works by British and European antecedents and counterparts, it is clear that the idiosyncratic approaches of these two artists make it very difficult to subordinate their work to other, externally established stylistic modes and traditions. The Second World War forced artists to confront new problems and scenes, either because they were paid to do so or because they felt impelled to do so. If the vibrancy of the wartime community of artists and writers in Belfast faded after the war, that sense of eccentricity remains.

[143] 'Brian McAvera in conversation with S.B. Kennedy', in *Post War Pre Troubles: Collective Histories of Northern Irish Art*, edited by Brian McAvera (Belfast: Golden Thread Gallery, 2005), pp. 11–39 (p. 38).

4

Ulster Quislings and Drapery Romances: Political Writing

In 1942 the Socialist Party in Belfast published a poetry pamphlet entitled *15 Poems*, to be sold to raise money for the Russian Red Cross. It featured poems by nine writers, including Maurice James Craig, John Hewitt, Colin Middleton, and W.R. Rodgers. The typeface used on the cover of the pamphlet betrays the influence of Soviet design, but it is an opaque collection, few of whose poems appear to respond directly to the war or reflect the concerns of the party under whose auspices it appeared. In a letter to W.R. Rodgers, encouraging him to contribute to the anthology, John Hewitt wrote that 'The verses will not be propagandist or left or Soviet salutes—just typical poems as good as we can get'.[1] Rodgers' offering 'Neither Here Nor There' evokes a land where 'all's lackadaisical', 'flat, indifferent', conceding only in the final line that 'at night there is the smell of morning'.[2] John Hewitt's contributions are also pessimistic.[3] His first, 'The Little Lough', describes a 'small narrow lake' but is perhaps best read as a fearful love poem on the eve of war, in the lines 'Tho' many things I love should disappear/in the black night ahead of us'.[4] 'Sonnet in Autumn' similarly laments the disappearance of cherished things in the face of an overwhelming threat, as 'The heedless rose has blown/unmarked, unheeded in the hooting throng', suggesting that even nature reflects the new anxiety, as 'the hard bright berries of the haw/report an older, an austerer law,/a season older, suddenly afraid'.[5]

---

[1] Letter from John Hewitt to W.R. Rodgers, 28 October 1941, Rodgers Papers, D2833/C/1/8/1.

[2] W.R. Rodgers, 'Neither Here Nor There', *15 Poems* (Belfast: Socialist Party, 1942), p. 3.

[3] These might be contrasted with earlier poems by Hewitt which offered unconditional praise for the Soviet Union, such as 'A Chant for the Workers of the World on the 13th Anniversary of the Revolution' (1930, cited in Edna Longley, 'Progressive Bookmen', *Living Stream*, p. 120).

[4] John Hewitt, 'The Little Lough', *15 Poems*, p. 4.

[5] Hewitt, 'Sonnet in Autumn', *15 Poems*, p. 5.

Small as it was, *15 Poems* is demonstrative of the interpenetration of political, poetic, and artistic spheres in Belfast at this time. John Wilson Foster has described the Northern Ireland Labour Party (NILP) during the 1940s as an 'enormously important asylum to the artistic or merely arty', but the tendency of radical political and artistic groupings in Belfast to overlap and inform each other during the war was probably most apparent in gatherings at Campbell's coffee house opposite the City Hall, an unofficial debating chamber characterized by fiery conversation.[6] Robert Greacen sketches a typical wartime morning there in his memoir *The Sash My Father Wore*, where characters including Denis Ireland, William Conor, Richard Rowley, Joseph Tomelty, Sam Hanna Bell, and F.L. Green drop in to the café, described as 'an island of tolerance in our bitterly divided community. Dissent is permissible and nobody will drench you with coffee for not saying "the right thing" '.[7] A 1961 BBC radio documentary which featured the memories of former patrons emphasized the importance of Campbell's as a forum for political, literary, and artistic debate during the 1930s and 1940s. The poet John Irvine recalled that the café was untroubled by any presiding chairman figure, allowing all comers to contribute freely to discussions; in a similar vein the artist Padraic Woods compared it to Doctor Johnson's coffee house, with the important difference that instead of patrons gathering round a great man, everyone there considered themselves a Doctor Johnson.[8] The café brought disparate individuals together: there, it was claimed, the landscape painter James Humbert Craig could sit down with left-wing expressionist artists and speak a 'common language'.[9] Campbell's also attracted political and religious figures. In his autobiography *Bonfires on the Hillside* (1995) the journalist James Kelly recalled the future Independent Unionist MP Norman Porter engaged in 'conspiratorial plotting and planning' with Ian Paisley at a table near the stairs, and Elizabeth McCullough, a schoolgirl in the early years of the war, describes in her memoir *A Square Peg: An Ulster Childhood* (1997) the rattling of coffee cups as Paisley held court among the students of the Presbyterian Training College on the first floor, together with Jewish international bridge players, junior architects, and members of the Belfast Arts Theatre.[10]

---

[6] Wilson Foster, 'Was There Ulster Literary Life before Heaney?', *Between Shadows*, p. 213.

[7] Greacen, *Sash*, p. 130.

[8] 'The Table in the Window', BBC Radio Ulster (9 November 1961), BBC Northern Ireland Archive, #Museum 7612.

[9] 'The Table in the Window', BBC Radio Ulster (9 November 1961).

[10] Kelly, *Bonfires on the Hillside*, p. 149; Elizabeth McCullough, *A Square Peg: An Ulster Childhood* (Dublin: Marino Books, 1997), p. 115.

As this chapter will describe, the supposedly collegiate and tolerant atmosphere of Campbell's is hardly representative of the established political culture in Northern Ireland at this time, but such gatherings as occurred at the coffee house illustrate the close co-existence of unofficial and marginal artistic, literary, and political communities in Belfast during the war. Magazines such as *Lagan, Northern Harvest,* and (in Dublin) *The Bell* are notable for the diversity of their contributors, and are illustrative of the cross-pollination between creative, journalistic, and political writing at this time. Left-wing publications in Belfast also took an interest in cultural matters. As well as articles which examined war aims and addressed plans for post-war political and social reconstruction, the Socialist Party newsletter *Northern Star* regularly carried socialist reconsiderations of Irish history and pieces of cultural commentary, and took a particular interest in film releases during the war. The Communist Party weekly *Unity* similarly published reviews of books, exhibitions, and radio programmes as well as occasional poems, and encouraged its readers to attend concerts of classical music.

This chapter examines overlapping discourses in literary and political writing in the province, at a time when writers and publications that were ostensibly literary made significant interventions in political matters and when politicians and journalists made bold forays into literary territory. To this end, I explore the ways in which writers contested the overtly politicized issues of the place and status of Northern Ireland in relation to the Second World War across several genres, and show how the language and events of the war were incorporated into political arguments. Preceding chapters have been largely circumscribed by genre, but this chapter addresses a far more diverse body of work, including biographies, cartoons, historical writing, little magazines, pamphlets, plays, poems, short fiction, speeches, tourist guidebooks, travel writing, and other miscellaneous prose works.

As the various publications that were officially commissioned or sanctioned by the Stormont government sought to emphasize the strategic importance of the province to the British war effort as a means of strengthening ties between Northern Ireland and Britain, nationalist and republican writing of the war years was firmly anti-partitionist and attempted to downplay or deny the province's role in the war. Such publications often targeted the political corruption of the unionist elite and ongoing discrimination against the Catholic minority. To an extent, this fault-line mirrored existent divisions and was predicated on the sectarian identities that dominate the political culture of the province. The debate was not entirely determined by a conflict between pro-war unionists and anti-war nationalists, however, and the growth during the 1930s and 1940s of a vocal and diverse movement of Communist, socialist, and internationalist writers, poets, and pamphleteers, prolific in their production and distribution of printed matter, briefly challenged the province's sectarian political landscape and offered an escape route for those unwilling to become part of this. As John Wilson Foster has observed:

> Pre-war socialism was a way in which Northern Irish writers could overcome, however precariously, their prior and largely involuntary primary identities as either Protestant or Catholic, unionist or nationalist and take part, first and foremost, in an unpartitioned and recognizable intellectual and artistic community (or, at worst, coterie); as a bonus, it was a way too of defining oneself as an artist and dangerous . . . Socialism was a way in which such Protestant literati as Bell, Hewitt, Greacen and others could cock a snook at the prevailing atmosphere of Unionist Northern Ireland which starved artists of sufficient oxygen [...] Socialist views were a purchase on art and intellect and also a way of being anti-Unionist without being nationalistic and (to use an offensive phrase of the day) a 'Fenian lover'.[11]

The growth in the appeal of socialist ideas at this time, driven by a desire for domestic social reform and by the entry of the Soviet Union into the war in June 1941, modified Northern Irish literary and political responses to the war and to local affairs on both sides of the sectarian divide. Both unionist and anti-partitionist writers incorporated socialist ideas and rhetoric into their arguments in response to this growth in popularity, but socialists themselves found that the war presented them with difficulties. In a speech at the Cooperative Hall in Belfast in June 1942, later reprinted in pamphlet form by the Communist Party of Ireland, the Scottish Communist Westminster MP William Gallacher argued that 'In searching for unity here in Northern Ireland or in association with any contacts in the South, the richest soil for the growth of union is the new understanding the people are getting everywhere of the Soviet Union'.[12] As the Molotov–Ribbentrop pact had created difficulties for left-leaning activists and their publications, the entry of the Soviet Union into the war also proved problematic for socialists and Communists in Northern Ireland, many of whom were ideologically anti-partitionist but who found themselves drawn into supporting an Allied war effort in which the British Empire was a major force. Some circumvention of this was possible, as can be seen from W.H. McCullough's claim in another Communist Party pamphlet entitled

---

[11] Wilson Foster, 'Was There Ulster Literary Life before Heaney?', *Between Shadows*, pp. 213–214.
[12] William Gallacher, MP, *Freedom or Slavery?* (Belfast: Communist Party of Ireland, 1942), p. 5.

Changes are needed at Stormont that 'This is a real peoples' war. On the side of the democratic forces are included the Soviet Union, the first Socialist country in the world, China who has fought Japanese Imperialism for over a decade, and liberty-loving peoples thoughout the world'.[13] The pamphlet spends much energy lauding the bravery of the Soviet Union, and criticizes the Northern Ireland Government for failing to mobilize the people of the province sufficiently, calling for a representative government comprising members of all parties. On the question of the southern state, McCullough was reticent: a short and vague section entitled 'Attitude Towards Éire' claims only that the neutrality of the southern state was of grave concern to 'democratic opinion', and muses that 'it is indeed strange to find that part of Ireland out of step with the rest of mankind'.[14] A later McCullough pamphlet, *Ireland Looks to Labour* (1943), was more optimistic, and asked all anti-fascists in Ireland to fall in behind the war effort despite the continuance of partition, apparently in the hope that the projected rise of a powerful twenty-six county Labour movement could lead to the 'final and complete unification of Ireland and the establishment of Socialism'.[15] His subsequent call for the full implementation of the British government's Beveridge Report further illustrates the contradictions within the socialist movement in Northern Ireland at this time.

By 1945, in *For a Prosperous Ulster: An Explanation of the Communist Party's Policy for Northern Ireland*, McCullough had retreated from any talk of unity, and stated merely that the Labour movement should 'fight for a Government that will be a good neighbour of the Government of Southern Ireland'.[16] It should be noted that his admiration of the Soviet Union remained constant throughout these vacillations. The tortuous ideological trajectory of the maverick MP Harry Midgley, from advocate of Home Rule during the 1920s, through leading roles in the NILP during the 1930s and early 1940s, to his departure to form his own Commonwealth Labour Party in 1942, and to become the first non-unionist member of a Stormont cabinet the following year, before finally taking the Unionist party whip in 1947, offers the most striking illustration of the difficulties

[13] W.H. McCullough, *Changes are Needed at Stormont* (Belfast: Communist Party of Ireland, *c.*1940), p. 15.
[14] McCullough, *Changes are Needed at Stormont*, p. 14.
[15] W.H. McCullough, *Ireland Looks to Labour* (Belfast: Communist Party of Ireland, 1943), p. 16, pp. 20–21.
[16] W.H. McCullough, *For a Prosperous Ulster: An Explanation of the Communist Party's Policy for Northern Ireland* (Belfast: Communist Party, *c.*1945), p. 16.

in trying to pursue socialism with an international conscience in the rigidly circumscribed atmosphere of Belfast political life at this time.[17]

The post-war history of the NILP itself, riven by splits and unable to build on wartime socialist momentum, bears this out. However, the growth of socialist groups and publications in Belfast during the 1930s and 1940s did help to open up a political culture largely defined and determined by its insularity to some new and external pressures and influences. The impact of the Spanish Civil War on the Northern Ireland general election of 1938, thanks in no small part to Midgley's own controversial campaign in his Dock constituency in support of the defeated Republican forces, is demonstrative of this.[18] During this period, writers of all shades of opinion attempted to develop comparisons between the political situation in Northern Ireland and that of other countries, often using terms specifically associated with the Second World War, such as 'quisling'. These attempts demonstrate how, to use a term adopted by Bew, Gibbons, and Patterson, the war 'deinsulated' the political culture of the province at this time, and suggests that writers felt increasingly able to reconsider the province in an international context.[19] In a pamphlet published by the Belfast branch of the PEN in 1942, the historian D.A. Chart argued that historical writers were especially well placed to advance the aims of the International PEN, and encouraged the pursuit of comparative studies. Having outlined the lacunae he perceived in the study of Irish history, he concluded:

> International comparison is needed in all branches of history. The Continent often speaks of Great Britain as being insular in its outlook and thought, but we, being on the far side of that island barrier, are still more inclined to confine our studies to our own country and consider its experience unique and solely to be regarded. Before the history of a part of the world is attempted, there should be some knowledge and appreciation of the whole.[20]

Chart's entreaty might be compared with Seán Ó Faoláin's repeated attempts in *The Bell* to emphasize the interdependence of the wider world. An early editorial in May 1941 entitled 'Provincialism' argued that

---

[17] For an account of Midgley's career, see Graham S. Walker, *The Politics of Frustration: Harry Midgley and the Failure of Labour in Northern Ireland*, (Manchester: Manchester University Press, 1985).

[18] Walker, *The Politics of Frustration*, pp. 98–110. See also Sam McAughtry, *Hillman Street High Roller* (Belfast: Appletree, 1994), p. 99: 'In Dock Ward we talked of little else. We had hardly a rag on our backs . . . we'd hardly shoes to our feet, we were queuing up for stale loaves, and there we were worrying about the Spanish Civil War'.

[19] Paul Bew, Peter Gibbon, and Henry Patterson, *The State in Northern Ireland 1921–72* (Manchester: Manchester University Press, 1979), p. 103.

[20] *The P.E.N. In Ulster, Contributed by Well-Known Writers of Belfast Centre* (Belfast: Reid and Wright, 1942), p. 6.

'everywhere, and Everyman, nowadays, is indebted to somewhere and somebody else, related to somewhere else, inferior and superior in something or other to somewhere else. There are no longer any water-tight regions'.[21] This presented writers in Ireland with a specific dilemma, as Ó Faoláin acknowledged in the editorial introducing a 'Special Ulster Number' of the magazine two months later, which bemoaned the growing divide between culture north and south of the border:

> Unfortunately, however much there is to be said for those two modes of life—for that international way to the open sea of world-ideas, or for this national way of cultivating our own garden—it cannot be said that either is being at all as fruitful as that undivided Ireland of, say, forty years ago. The emphasis on inward and outward is possibly to blame, this passionate, and therefore almost always stupid, rivalry or hyper-nationalism and hyper-internationalism that has resulted from Partition.[22]

The 'two modes' here decried by Ó Faoláin determine much of the debate over Northern Ireland's place in the war, and feature prominently in the works of unionist and loyalist writers keen to emphasize the heightened international stature of the province during the war, generally at the expense of the southern state: to this end, St John Ervine's distinction in 1943 between Northern Ireland's 'outlook' and Éire's 'inlook' (probably unconsciously) echoed Ó Faoláin's analysis.[23]

The Second World War drew some writers in Northern Ireland into new and unfamiliar territory. Towards the end of this chapter a consideration of the ways in which writers of various hues approached Winston Churchill—a figure who was talismanic in the context of the British war effort but whose interventions in Irish affairs earlier in the twentieth century remained hugely contentious—reveals the extent to which the political culture in Northern Ireland during the war encouraged unexpected advocacy and further challenged established patterns of debate. The number of publications printing extracts from Churchill's speeches in support of their arguments (some pamphlets reprinted entire speeches) also highlight the crucial importance of the quotation and recontextualization of existing material to political discourse in the province during the war. Partly due to this, this chapter does not confine itself to material published in Northern Ireland. *The Bell* in particular was an important forum for debate on Northern Ireland in the 1940s, and I have treated relevant material published in Dublin and London as an integral part of the political

---

[21] 'Provincialism', *The Bell* 2, no. 2 (May 1941), pp. 5–8 (pp. 5–6).
[22] 'Ulster', *The Bell* 2, no. 4, p. 5.
[23] Quoted in 'Telegraph Plans', *Northern Star* 4, no. 1 (March 1943), pp. 12–14 (p. 13). Ervine's remarks had originally appeared in the *Belfast Telegraph* the previous month.

and literary culture of the province at this time. It is worth noting that one of the most strongly worded condemnations of Irish neutrality can be found in an English novel, Nicholas Monsarrat's *The Cruel Sea* (1951), which describes the lives of Royal Navy sailors during the Battle of the Atlantic. In a two-page-long polemical digression Monsarrat, who himself served in the Royal Navy Volunteer Reserve on the Western Approaches during the war, wrote that 'it was difficult to withhold one's contempt from a country such as Ireland, whose battle this was and whose chances of freedom and independence in the event of a German victory were nil'.[24]

Conclusions of historians regarding the impact of the Second World War on Northern Ireland have tended to focus on the status of the border following the conflict, and the resulting political and territorial implications for the province and for the island as a whole.[25] There is a general consensus that by the end of the war Northern Ireland lay more securely within the United Kingdom—a view that was anticipated by unionists at a very early stage. Prime Minister Lord Craigavon's broadcast in February 1940 set the tone for much subsequent rhetoric, concluding with these words:

> ... I am anxious that all my listeners across the Channel should realise that though Ulster be but a small link in the chain which encircles and binds the Empire, she is, by virtue of her strategical position and her hardy Northern stock, a strong link—a link that will neither break nor bend before the King's enemies. We are King's men. We will be with you to the end.[26]

When Craig's successor J.M. Andrews resigned in 1943, Churchill's letter of commiseration claimed that 'the bonds of affection between Great Britain and the people of Northern Ireland have been tempered by fire and are now, I firmly believe, unbreakable'.[27] The following year Hugh Shearman, later a writer of pro-union propaganda for the British government, argued in the one-off little magazine *Northern Harvest* that 'Ulster's ready participation in the war' had reinforced connections between Great Britain and Northern Ireland, and, with some smugness, observed that 'Ulster people have a vivid and pleasant sense of having thoroughly backed

---

[24] Monsarrat, *The Cruel Sea* (London: Cassell, 1951; repr. 1996), pp. 151–152.
[25] Brian Barton, 'The Impact of World War II on Northern Ireland and on Belfast–London Relations', in *The Northern Ireland Question in British Politics*, edited by Peter Catterall and Sean McDougall (Basingstoke: Macmillan and New York: St Martin's Press, 1996), pp. 47–70; Patrick Buckland, *A History of Northern Ireland* (Dublin: Gill and Macmillan, 1981), p. 89; Fisk, p. 470, p. 476; Thomas Hennessey, *A History of Northern Ireland, 1920–1996* (Dublin: Gill and Macmillan, 1997), p. 92; Sabine Wichert, *Northern Ireland Since 1945* (London and New York: Longman, 1999), p. 2.
[26] Craig, 'We Are King's Men', in *Field Day III*, p. 365.
[27] Quoted in Fisk, p. 470.

a very fine winner in the war'.[28] If, as Robert Fisk has written, 'The war created a strengthened bond between London and Belfast, a link that was accentuated and repeatedly emphasized throughout the war by Éire's refusal to stand by Britain in her hour of need', the Northern Ireland Government were certainly keen to emphasize both the 'strengthened bond' and the southern 'refusal' in the years after the war, and commissioned or supported several publications to make these arguments.[29]

Pre-eminent among these was John W. Blake's lengthy *Northern Ireland in the Second World War* (1956), commissioned by the Stormont administration in 1945 and published by the British state publishing company His Majesty's Stationery Office (HMSO). The title *Northern Ireland in the Second World War* is itself significant: the choice of 'in' rather than 'and' or 'during' is illustrative of the book's aim to emphasize the province's active participation in the war. The book was written with the cooperation of civil servants at Stormont, and provides a comprehensive survey of the agricultural, industrial, and military history of the province at war, as well as detailing the deployments of Ulster regiments and Belfast-built ships around the world. The text is accompanied by numerous statistical tables and several gatefold maps. Despite the arid nature of some of his material there was a clear ideological dimension to the content and tone of Blake's history, deriving from its official status: as Gillian McIntosh writes, it was 'intended to represent the Northern Irish state's part in the war in the way in which the unionist government wished it to be remembered' and was aimed 'at reinforcing in the minds of the British public and politicians the common bond which war had created between Northern Ireland and Britain . . . which unionists believed would ultimately prevent future Westminster administrations from abandoning them'.[30] Possibly as a result of Blake's emphasis on the debt owed by the British government for Ulster's contribution and loyalty during the war, the book did not meet with unalloyed approval in London. Brigadier H.B. Latham of the British Cabinet Office Historical Section complained that Blake's sole focus on Northern Ireland resulted in a distorted history, and that to describe the activities of ships simply because they were built in Belfast or of army units because they were based in Northern Ireland had led to 'complete nonsense'.[31] The *Times Literary Supplement* was also critical, writing that Blake's history, with its wealth of statistical information was 'not . . . a book for the ordinary reader' and that it was 'questionable whether a provincial history of the war [was] either necessary or dignified'.[32] Such comments

[28] Hugh Shearman, 'Ulster To-Day', in *Northern Harvest*, pp. 117–130 (p. 126, p. 127).
[29] Fisk, p. 470.   [30] McIntosh, *Force of Culture*, p. 157, p. 166.
[31] McIntosh, *Force of Culture*, p. 165.
[32] 'Books Received', *Times Literary Supplement*, 25 January 1957.

show a certain degree of resistance in Britain to the inclusion of Northern Ireland's anomalous story within the history of the British war effort, which obliged pro-union writers to write against both nationalist and British preconceptions of the war, and which may account for the extremities in tone and content of some of the works discussed in this chapter.

In addition to its almost overpowering barrage of factual information, Blake's history also promoted an essentialist and homogenous conception of the 'Ulster' character, described as an 'Anglo-Scottish planter stock, Protestant and alien in the first instance... Presbyterian Scots among them, dour, fervent, conscious of high destiny and taught self-reliance by many a grim experience [who] left their mark indelibly on the province'. The book presents the war as a test passed with merit by the people of Northern Ireland, which further separated the province from the southern state: 'Though the province was small, nevertheless it contained hidden strength; and its greatest strength derived from the character of the Ulster people. Geography, history, tradition and religion all in some way differentiated Northern Ireland from Eire [*sic*]'. Blake claimed that the people of Northern Ireland were 'less given to romantic fancies than the Southern Irish' and were thus more amenable to the presence of American soldiers in their midst. The final lines of the book claimed that 'Devotion and self-effacement gave fundamental worth to Northern Ireland's war effort. For the final assessment is of the spirit'.[33]

Published in London, clothed in an orange dust-jacket and violently polemical, St John Ervine's biographical study *Craigavon: Ulsterman* (1949) also sought to emphasize the sense of separation between Northern Ireland and the southern state engendered by the Second World War. Ervine himself admitted in the preface that the book, over 670 pages long, was no formal biography, but aimed to give the facts of the late prime minister's life and 'expound the beliefs and political faith of Ulster Unionists, of whom I am one'.[34] Though he had long resided in London, the novelist and playwright remained a frequent and irascible correspondent to various newspapers and periodicals in Belfast, making inflammatory contributions to several cultural and political debates. Much of *Craigavon: Ulsterman* is dedicated to attacking Irish neutrality. In his preface—a rambling and digressive amalgamation of statistical data and personal anecdote—Ervine claimed that Northern Ireland's involvement in the Second World War offered a pressing and contemporary justification for partition and, significantly, entitled the province to claim moral superiority over the southern state:

---

[33] Blake, p. 34, p. 298, p. 535.
[34] St John Ervine, *Craigavon: Ulsterman* (London: Allen and Unwin, 1949), p. vii.

The conviction held by many Southern Irishmen, and especially by Gaelic Leaguers, that Ireland, like an over-fastidious spinster, can draw her robes around her and avoid the contagion of the world's slow stain by pretending that she is totally detached from the rest of mankind and can live self-sufficiently by herself, muttering ancient incantations in an obsolete language and maintaining a far, far nobler life than is maintainable elsewhere, is one which Ulster Unionists, who have a high sense of reality, cannot share.[35]

Ervine emphasizes Northern Ireland's membership of the Commonwealth and willingness to play a part on the world stage against the southern state's relative isolation during the war. The repeated use of the self-coined term 'Eireans', deliberately casting those from south of the border as alien, aids this strategy. He continues to credit partition with sparing the whole of Ireland from the 'suffering and distress' of the Second World War, and argues that Craigavon and others who had fought for partition in the first place had thus helped to prevent the subsequent 'horrors of war' from breaking 'upon her unprotected body'.[36] Ervine is also keen to discredit and diminish the extent of southern participation in the war in terms of recruitment to the British armed forces, attacking a perceived tendency to overstate this. Conceding that there is a scarcity of accurate figures to settle the matter, he nonetheless deplores the idea that 'Accompanying these diverse and excessive estimates and forthright assertions was usually an insinuation or even a direct statement that Southern Ireland was doing far more for the Allies than Northern Ireland'.[37] Craigavon, indeed, remains a peripheral figure for much of the book, and on many pages makes no appearance at all: instead Ervine uses the book as an opportunity to write a highly partial history of Ireland over the life of its purported subject, pursuing a number of vendettas as he proceeds. The tone is frequently abusive, and no opportunity is lost to discredit 'Eireans', the Catholic Church, or the southern government (Eamon de Valera is variously described as 'black clad, as if perpetually attending funerals' and as a 'shoddy Torquemada').[38]

When Ervine does address Craigavon, however, it is with reverence, the depth of which may be gauged from the fact that the final part of the book, recounting Craigavon's last year as prime minister and death in office, is entitled 'He Goes Home'. The eccentricity of the book's composition and the importance Ervine accords to the war as part of his argument are equally apparent from the fact that the seventy-third section of this concluding part reads solely 'On September 3, war against Germany was declared'.[39] Although Ervine is clearly determined to emphasize the

---

[35] Ervine, *Craigavon*, pp. vii–viii.   [36] Ervine, *Craigavon*, pp. x–xi.
[37] Ervine, *Craigavon*, p. xvi.   [38] Ervine, *Craigavon*, p. 572.
[39] Ervine, *Craigavon*, p. 550.

involvement of the province in this war, his narrative certainly does not follow that of a People's War in part sketched by Blake. If reverence is accorded to Craigavon and the commercial and unionist elite, the workers of the province are granted a great deal less respect, as Ervine deplores the 'proletariat's infantility' in the face of war and argues that the 'greatest difficulty' in the organization of the war effort was posed by the 'apathy' of working people who believed the Germans could do them no harm. He refuses to countenance the idea that the government's preparations for civil defence had been in any way insufficient, and deals with this issue in fewer than nine lines, arguing that since Belfast had been built on piles it had proved impossible to build deep underground shelters in the city, and that 'Other complaints as stupid and shallow were made by the sort of people who always start to scream and panic when trouble comes'. These dismissals are contrasted with the assertion that it was 'lucky for the North of Ireland that Craigavon's head was very cool'.[40]

Grief at Craigavon's death in November 1940 was, according to Ervine, 'widespread and undisguised...Craigavon, more truly than any other man, personified his people...Merely to be in his company was to feel reassured'. Tributes paid by politicians and others of all shades of opinion are recounted over five pages, but the eighty-fifth section of 'He Goes Home' again consists of one line of text alone: 'There was no message of any kind, official or personal, perfunctory or sincere, from the hierarchy of the Roman Catholic Church in Ireland'.[41] Much of Ervine's subsequent assessment of Craigavon's legacy is given over to a bizarre attempt to refute the idea that Ulstermen could be characterized as 'dour', including a sustained personal comparison of Craigavon and de Valera over twenty-six lines:

> Craigavon liked functions: de Valera detests them. Craigavon smoked and drank and gave parties: de Valera neither smokes nor drinks, and he does not entertain, as he himself told the Dáil early in 1944. Craigavon was interested in men's worldly state: de Valera, like all men of unconvivial and monastic character, is indifferent to mortality.[42]

Over the following thirty pages that conclude the study, Ervine derides Éire's foolishness in leaving the Commonwealth, and expresses the hope that a united Ireland will one day join (significantly as 'King's men') a union with Great Britain and other parts of the Empire, including 'we dare to hope, Indians'.[43] A deliberately divisive and provocative appendix, occupying another thirty pages, provides a 'sectarian analysis' of illiteracy

---

[40] Ervine, *Craigavon*, p. 554, p. 555.   [41] Ervine, *Craigavon*, p. 561, p. 566.
[42] Ervine, *Craigavon*, p. 571.   [43] Ervine, *Craigavon*, p. 612.

in Ireland north and south, using tables which break down the populations of each province and county into religious categories: Roman Catholic, Episcopalian, Presbyterian, Methodist, and other denominations. Within these religious affiliations the respective numbers and percentages of literate individuals over the age of nine are given—statistics which purport to show that higher levels of literacy may be found amongst Protestants.

The main text of *Craigavon: Ulsterman* is frequently interrupted by tables of figures showing election results, salary scales, and army recruitment numbers by geographical area and religious affiliation, and by lengthy quotations taken from parliamentary debates, legal statutes, and from Craigavon's private correspondence, but Ervine also quotes liberally from works of literature. Recalling the traumatic effect on the city of Belfast of the sinking of the Titanic in 1912, he reproduces the whole of Thomas Hardy's poem 'The Convergence of the Twain'. Later in the book, in tribute to Craigavon's wife, Ervine quotes the final twelve-and-a-half lines of Shakespeare's 'Sonnet 116'.[44] The poetry of Robert Browning appears at length on several occasions: in a section describing Craigavon's resolve to put an end to civil disorder in Belfast in the last week of November 1921, seventeen lines of Browning's long poem 'Prince Hohenstiel-Schwangau' are quoted, beginning with the lines 'Heavily did he let his fist fall plumb/On each perturber of the public peace'. This quotation is contextualized with the assertion 'So Browning writes of Prince Hohenstiel-Schwangau, and might have written in anticipation of Craig'.[45] The study is also illustrated with photographic plates showing Craigavon and his family, as well as other scenes from recent history, including a parade of the Ulster Volunteer Force, the signing of the Ulster Covenant, the meeting of the first Stormont cabinet, and the visit of Winston Churchill to Belfast in 1926. As we shall see, the eccentric, digressive, and highly partial approach taken by Ervine in this book—a cross-generic mixture of selective history, personal attack, literary excerpts, and statistical information—is characteristic of political publications of all hues in Northern Ireland around the time of the Second World War.

Another study of Craigavon, Hugh Shearman's *Not an Inch: A Study of Northern Ireland and Lord Craigavon*, was published in 1942, seven years before Ervine's book, and less than two years after the prime minister had died in office.[46] Though far less intemperate than Ervine, Shearman

---

[44] Ervine, *Craigavon*, p. 217, p. 539.   [45] Ervine, *Craigavon*, p. 456.

[46] Shearman is notable for his conservative and unionist historical works, but also published two novels during the war: *The Bishop's Confession* (1943) and *A Bomb and a Girl* (1944). The latter was described by its author as a study in 'the psychology of crime' (p. 7). The action of the novel takes place around Queen's University Belfast in the years immediately before the Second World War, as a young man, Stanislaus McOstrich, builds and

similarly uses Craigavon's indelible association with the province, as head of its government from partition until his death, as the basis for a history of Northern Ireland. The titular subject is again monumentalized in reverential tones, as is apparent from chapter titles including 'The Northern Iron', 'The Forging of the Iron', and 'The Man and the Conflict'. *Not an Inch* largely avoids referring to the ongoing world war, but Shearman does praise Craigavon's foresight in apprehending the likelihood of war during the 1930s, and is keen to write Northern Ireland into a European context:

> [Craigavon's] anxiety about the foreign situation and about the future of the province emerged in various speeches. A phrase he used was, 'Ulster is nobody's Czechoslovakia', and he warned an English audience that outside interference with the balance of parties and interests in Ireland might easily produce a situation such as had arisen in the Spanish civil war. He seemed to envisage Belfast as the Barcelona of a fresh tragedy.[47]

Including *Not an Inch*, between 1942 and 1971 Shearman published six books of varying length under the auspices of the Northern Ireland Government. His post-war writings addressed the Second World War with increasing directness and, as McIntosh has observed, his attitude towards southern neutrality quickly became more hostile—a change in tone that Shearman himself later attributed to the discovery of the concentration camps.[48] A shift in his views can be observed between *Northern Ireland: Its History, Resources and People*, published by HMSO in 1946, and *Anglo-Irish Relations*, published by Faber and Faber in 1948. Both publications appear to have been produced for a British readership. Though the introduction to the earlier thirty-two-page booklet described the 'vital importance which Northern Ireland has had in the strategy of Britain and the United Nations in the Second World War', it expended just over two pages on the war, stating that 'While Éire declared herself to be neutral, Northern Ireland entered the war automatically as part of the United Kingdom but also by the will of its inhabitants'.[49] Two years later, in the lengthy historical study *Anglo-Irish Relations*, Shearman attacks Irish neutrality, arguing that the policy had made the southern state 'a burdensome passenger in the carrying out of Britain's defence arrangements', and that furthermore 'Northern Ireland was playing the part which Éire might

---

detonates a bomb, killing one of his lecturers (Shearman, *A Bomb and a Girl* [London: Faber and Faber, 1944]).

[47] Hugh Shearman, *Not an Inch: A Study of Northern Ireland and Lord Craigavon* (London: Faber and Faber, 1942), p. 179.

[48] McIntosh, *Force of Culture*, pp. 185–186.

[49] Hugh Shearman, *Northern Ireland: Its History, Resources and People* (Belfast: HMSO, 1946), p. 3, p. 18.

have played', given the enormous strategic and economic importance of the province to the British war effort.[50]

In *Anglo-Irish Relations* Shearman openly discusses the problems faced by the Labour movement in Northern Ireland. He suggests that the NILP has become paralysed by its failure to achieve a consistent post-war position on the matter of the border, but argues that the popularity of left-wing ideas has encouraged the Unionist party to pursue more progressive social policies and made it 'a much less conservative party'.[51] Shearman claims that Northern Ireland is in fact at the vanguard of such reforms, ahead of Britain and far ahead of the southern state, rejecting dogmatic socialism and steadily advancing public control at the expense of private enterprise.[52] Such assertions seem calculated to encourage a more favourable disposition towards the province amongst a left-wing readership in Britain, and indeed Shearman goes on to claim that the war has done much to change the attitude towards Ireland of the British Labour party, which had traditionally been sympathetic to the south 'at the expense of the north'. Concluding his study, Shearman attempts to invert a 'curious paradox', in what he identifies as the prevailing perception of Anglo-Irish relations. Rather than seeing Ireland as engaged in a struggle against a much larger country over many centuries, he suggests it is possible to see England instead as the minority 'small community fighting for its life and its ideals', noting that historically the Irish have been on the side of Spain, France, and (in 1916) Germany against England, and that again in 1940, when England stood alone against a mightier foe, Ireland (excepting Northern Ireland) 'remained a burdensome and embarrassing neutral'.[53]

None of Shearman's subsequent works would scale these heights of opprobrium. *Ulster* (1949), published in London by Robert Hale, was an anomalous addition to a series of guides to the history, landscape, and economy of a number of English counties (and the Isle of Man). Presumably due to the nature of the series in which it is published, Shearman does not attack southern neutrality in this volume, concentrating instead on the importance of the province in wartime as a centre of agricultural and industrial production, and emphasizing the positive social and cultural impact of the war. He suggests optimistically that the presence of service personnel and refugees of many nationalities had 'considerable repercussions on the social life and outlook of the people', and with reference to

[50] Hugh Shearman, *Anglo-Irish Relations* (London: Faber and Faber, 1948), p. 250, p. 252.
[51] Shearman, *Anglo-Irish Relations*, p. 266.
[52] Shearman, *Anglo-Irish Relations*, p. 267.
[53] Shearman, *Anglo-Irish Relations*, p. 270, pp. 273–274.

the Williamite War claims that 'during the war of 1939–45 one could hear a greater variety of languages and accents in the streets of Belfast than were to be heard even at the time when Schomberg's heterogeneous army was there 250 years before'.[54]

In *Northern Ireland*, a guidebook published by HMSO in 1968, Shearman was similarly upbeat, glossing over the matter of partition in a section entitled 'Troubled Times', observing that the Second World War 'brought new problems and new opportunities', whilst suggesting that 'The strategic importance of Northern Ireland—as a base covering the Atlantic shipping lines and a training ground for British and Allied troops—was emphasized by the neutrality of the Irish Free State to the South'.[55] Shearman highlighted what he perceived as the positive consequences of the war for the province:

> In spite of the evils and hardships imposed by the War, it also had the effect of giving a new impetus to social and economic reforms. Greatly assisted by the acceptance of the principle of 'parity' with Great Britain, the post-war Government of Northern Ireland initiated far-reaching measures of reform, in education, in the social services, in the stimulation of the economy and in other spheres.[56]

Three years later, in *Northern Ireland 1921–1971*, a heavily illustrated book published by HMSO to celebrate the fiftieth anniversary of partition, Shearman wrote that the war 'emphasised the contrasting and diverging destinies that had been chosen by the northern and southern communities in Ireland', and noted the 'cordial cooperation' between the Attlee government in London and Brooke's administration in implementing progressive policies proposed in the Beveridge report.[57] As in the 1968 guidebook, Shearman quotes from Churchill's broadcast of 13 May 1945, when, following victory in Europe, the British prime minister claimed that, but for the province's 'loyalty and friendship', the British people 'should have been confronted with slavery or death', perhaps the most emphatic assertion that the war had cemented partition and strengthened the political bond between Britain and Northern Ireland.[58]

---

[54] Hugh Shearman, *Ulster* (London: Robert Hale Limited, 1949), p. 135.

[55] Hugh Shearman, *Northern Ireland* (Belfast: HMSO, 1968), p. 23.

[56] Shearman, *Northern Ireland*, p. 24.

[57] Hugh Shearman, *Northern Ireland 1921–1971* (Belfast: WG Baird Limited for HMSO, 1971), p. 178, p. 181.

[58] Shearman, *Northern Ireland*, p. 23; Shearman, *Northern Ireland 1921–1971*, p. 179. See also Winston Churchill, 'Forward, Till the Whole Task Is Done', in *Blood, Toil, Tears and Sweat: Winston Churchill's Famous Speeches*, edited by David Cannadine (London: Cassell, 1989), pp. 257–266 (p. 259). Churchill's speech is particularly notable in this context for its attack on Irish neutrality and on de Valera personally.

Ervine's biographical study and Shearman's miscellaneous publications show their willingness to act on behalf of the government of Northern Ireland in the debate over the province's place and role in the Second World War after the war's end. Like the official historian Blake, both writers claimed that Northern Ireland's involvement in the war had boosted its international stature, and are bullish about the readiness of the province to contribute to future world events. They argue that this heightened international significance is entirely dependent on Northern Ireland remaining within the United Kingdom and continuing to define itself in ever more strident terms against the southern state.

Shearman's guide books also show how contentious political arguments were allowed to diffuse in non-confrontational, overtly innocuous publications, and more populist advocacy of these ideas may be found in less official sources. *Ulster Parade*, a little magazine founded by the playwright Ruddick Millar, was published during the war by the Quota Press in association with the Belfast *News Letter*, and carried work by local authors. For the most part this consisted of light-hearted prose entertainments with a local focus, along with some short playlets and poems. Quoting from a favourable review in the *Bangor Spectator*, the back cover of the fourth number suggested that its light and humorous nature and neat size made it ideal for travelling or as a gift for friends and relatives serving in the forces abroad, and recommended sending 'a copy to those Canadian and U.S.A. Friends who have so kindly been sending you parcels... You cannot send money— so here is your chance to send a little bit of Ulster'.[59] Contributors to *Ulster Parade* rarely addressed the war directly (the magazine seems intended to offer distraction from the ongoing conflict), but those that did so tended to support the war effort uncritically. Poems are populated by 'noble' soldiers, 'stern-faced' workers, and 'proud' labourers.[60] A piece by Gerald R. Lyttle entitled 'Yank in Ulster' consists of an imaginary exchange between an unnamed local man and an American GI of Ulster descent. The former takes it upon himself to explain the local political situation to the soldier, claiming that after twenty-one years since Northern Ireland 'assumed the status of a self governing unit within the Empire... we feel justly proud of our short history—a history of both Faith and Loyalty'. He continues to argue that Hitler 'would spell success' if the Germans were to occupy the province, emphasizes the strategic importance of Northern Ireland, arising from its location on the edge of the Atlantic, and is dismissive of 'the comparatively feeble state of Eire [*sic*] over the Border.' The unnamed man's

---

[59] *Ulster Parade 4*, (1943).
[60] Irene Turner, 'From the Cave Hill', *Ulster Parade 4*, pp. 70–71; Celia Randall, 'Dawn—Belfast Hills (April, 1941)', *Ulster Parade 7*, (n.d.), p. 84.

lengthy speech draws to a close by contrasting the smallness of the province on the map of the British Empire with the fact that the 'biggest shipbuilding yards, the biggest linen factory, the biggest tobacco factory' may be found in Belfast. Lyttle's piece ends on a saccharine note, with the GI's reply that the man forgot to include that 'Ulster possesses the biggest hearts in all the world'.[61] The messages conveyed here are familiar from unionist political discourse, as Northern Ireland's fidelity to Great Britain and the Empire, its newfound strategic significance, and its industrial prowess are all stressed. It is also significant that readers of *Ulster Parade* were encouraged to send the magazine to friends in Canada and the United States, and that the exchange recounted by Lyttle takes place between a local man and an American GI. The Second World War presented unionist writers with many opportunities to recast their allegiance to Britain, but they were also determined to secure Northern Ireland's place within the transatlantic Allied war effort.

A Yank from Ulster (1943), a play by the founder of *Ulster Parade* Ruddick Millar, reflects this desire more obliquely. Also published by the Quota Press, the play opens with the arrival of American soldiers in the fictional village of Kilbally, contrasting the delight of the younger female characters at this prospect with the hostility of the older, male generation of farmers, concerned at the potential damage to crops and irritated at being referred to as 'Pop'. One of the GIs, Jim Logan, is a Hollywood film star who acts under the name Willis Williams. He has an Ulster ring to his American accent, and turns out (somewhat implausibly) to have left the village only eleven or twelve years previously. Logan becomes romantically involved with Margaret, the daughter of John McMillan, the patriarchal farmer central to the play. The local magistrate William McWhirr is disgusted by the behaviour of the Americans, calling them 'a disgrace to Kilbally' and remarking of Logan that 'He and his kin' are a menace to our women folk'.[62] McWhirr intends to start a protest movement to force the Americans from the locality, but Margaret, having asked him why he thinks the soldiers were sent there in the first place, furiously answers her own question: 'Because they're ready to defend our country—to save your precious skin and mine. Because they're going to fight for us and maybe die for us'. The play ends with the discovery that McWhirr is Logan's uncle, and the marriage of Logan to Margaret. *A Yank from Ulster* is propagandist

---

[61] Gerald R. Lyttle, 'Yank in Ulster', *Ulster Parade 5*, (n.d.), pp. 103–108 (p. 105, p. 106, p. 107, p. 108). This issue is also undated, but it can be assumed that, like the fourth number, it dates from 1943.

[62] Millar's one-act comic play 'You Never Know Your Luck' also makes reference to a romance between a local girl and a GI (*Four New One-Act Plays*, edited by Patricia O'Connor [Belfast: Quota Press, 1948]).

in its resolution and its portrayal of the American influx, and seeks to emphasize the bonds between Northern Ireland and the United States, over and above the province's participation in the British war effort. The British armed forces are mentioned almost as an afterthought at the end of the play, when McMillan's other daughter Jean is married off to a local farmer, Ned Wilson, who joins the Royal Air Force.[63]

These ideas were also promoted in another Quota Press publication, Isobel Marshall's collection of short stories *A Jack and His Jill: A Romance of Modern Derry* (1944).[64] The story 'Miss Felicity Entertains the Americans' opens with the village of Alltandore being roused from 'its customary state of slumberous content' by the arrival of US forces: 'The little town hummed with excitement, curiosity and rumour, and the tall smartly-uniformed men with their handsome bronzed faces were regarded with admiration, tinged with a certain shyness by the inhabitants'. Although she had been born into a wealthy family, the now elderly Miss Felicity lives in poverty in a cottage on the outskirts of the village. As a young woman she had fallen in love with a draper, whom she was refused permission to marry and who subsequently left the village. Miss Felicity invites four of the American soldiers for a tea party at Christmas, and the company of the young men makes her thoughtful about the loss of her lover. Wishing to recapture her youth, she decides to buy some new clothes for herself and her maid, Susan, but balances this outlay by purchasing some Ulster Savings Certificates, being 'mindful of sundry warning posters regarding idle spending'. Her former lover, Peter, then reappears in the village, and it transpires that Will, one of the American soldiers who attended the tea party, is his son, after which discovery Peter and Miss Felicity marry.[65]

The title story of Marshall's collection follows a young orphaned woman, Jemima Jane, who leaves her cruel aunt in the country and moves to work in a drapery shop in Derry. She finds the wartime atmosphere of the city exciting, and is particularly intrigued by the 'various figures in uniform'. Like Miss Felicity, government propaganda posters encourage her to support the British war effort personally and practically:

> The very posters fired her with enthusiasm. Isolated as she had been in the country, she had never realised what war meant and had thought little about it. Now her whole desire was to help in any way she could. She became a

---

[63] Ruddick Millar, *A Yank from Ulster* (Belfast: Quota Press, 1943), p. 9, p. 10, p. 22, p. 37, pp. 57–58, p. 61. The play was first performed at the Clarence Place Hall, Belfast, on Christmas Night 1942 by the University Players (p. 76).

[64] Some of these had already been published in *Ulster Parade*.

[65] Isobel Marshall, 'Miss Felicity Entertains the Americans', in *A Jack and His Jill: A Romance of Modern Derry* (Belfast: Quota Press, 1944), pp. 51–65 (p. 51, p. 52, p. 55–58, p. 60, p. 62, p. 64).

diligent collector of salvage, a special box was kept for rags, another for rubber, while the smallest piece of bone was immediately carried to the nearest collection.[66]

Jemima Jane begins working in a military canteen, where she meets Jack Archer, a farmer's son from Antrim who has joined the Royal Navy. Their romance is cut short when he leaves on active service, first taking her to a local beauty spot where 'the mountains of Donegal lay purple on their left, and the Foyle crept below them—a ribbon of gleaming silver amongst fields of summer green'. She later hears that Archer's ship has been sunk, but at the end of the story he appears miraculously at the place where they had earlier parted.[67]

The weakness of Marshall's plotting can barely support the propagandist messages that she is keen to impart, but, like Millar's play, the fact that each of her stories concerns a woman becoming romantically involved with a serviceman advances the idea that Northern Ireland's role in the war is to support the American and British armed forces. The stories and plays published by the Quota Press are non-confrontational, and tend to avoid attacking the neutrality of the southern state or acknowledging the existence of nationalist dissent within the province. Nevertheless, in promoting close and positive relations between local people and service personnel, thereby emphasizing the place of Northern Ireland within the transatlantic war effort, this popular material can be seen to contribute indirectly to the contemporaneous unionist line.

The interpenetration of nationalist literary and political spheres can also be observed, exemplified by two pamphlets published by the MP Cahir Healy.[68] The front cover and title page of *The Mutilation of a Nation: The Story of the Partition of Ireland* (1945) promise 'many extracts from the records of the period, the speeches of public men, writers and Statesmen from 1920 onward. The gerrymandering of electoral areas, and persecutions of Nationalists, with statistics', and much of the pamphlet is indeed taken up by the selective reprinting of quotations. Some of these have been chosen to demonstrate the bigoted attitudes of unionist politicians towards the Catholic population, but other quotations taken from 'English Statesmen', including Andrew Bonar Law, Lord Robert Cecil,

---

[66] Marshall, 'A Jack and His Jill', in *A Jack and His Jill*, pp. 9–40 (p. 24).

[67] Marshall, 'A Jack and His Jill', p. 29, p. 34, p. 35, p. 40.

[68] Healy was elected to the Northern Ireland House of Commons for the South Fermanagh constituency in 1929 and retained the seat until 1965, though he boycotted the Stormont parliament until 1945. He was also elected to Westminster for the Fermanagh and Tyrone constituency on three occasions, serving from 1922–24, 1931–35, and 1950–55 (Eamon Phoenix, 'Healy, Cahir (1877–1970)', *DNB*, <http://www.oxforddnb.com/view/article/64467>).

and Earl Winterton, appear to favour a united Ireland.[69] Recruiting other unlikely personages to the anti-partitionist cause, Healy also quotes from Hugh Shearman's biography of Lord Craigavon, Winston Churchill's Bradford speech of 1914, and the third clause of the Atlantic Charter of 1941, where Churchill and US President Roosevelt sought to guarantee 'the right of all peoples to choose the form of government under which they will live, and... to see sovereign rights and self-government restored to those who have been forcibly deprived of them'.[70] The pamphlet also briefly explores the historical reasons for partition, and uses tables of figures to show the extent of gerrymandering and under-representation suffered by the minority Catholic population in Northern Ireland.[71] A final nineteen-page section, entitled 'A Peep into the News', is made up of short anecdotes describing the mistreatment of Catholics in the province, taken from newspapers, radio programmes, and speeches, followed by Healy's analysis of statistical data relating to employment and housing, again presented in tables.[72]

In 'A Peep into the News' Healy deliberately examines recent injustices in Northern Ireland in the context of the Second World War, thereby exposing hypocritical establishment and government behaviour. He contrasts the execution of the IRA bombers Peter Barnes and James Richards in Birmingham on 7 February 1940 with the handover to Japan that same day of nine German citizens taken from a Japanese liner, despite the fact that the prisoners had been captured under international law. Healy, who had himself been interned by the British authorities between July 1941 and December 1942, also compares the treatment of a Mrs Alice Graham, dismissed from the Post Office in early 1943 after one of her sons had been interned and another convicted of treason felony, with that of Leo Amery, who remained British Secretary of State for India while his son John made propaganda broadcasts for the Nazis from Germany.[73] Intent on drawing connections between local incidents and international affairs, Healy also reprints an extract from an article in the *Derry Journal* on 6 September 1939, which reported that 400 Catholic workers who had been told it was

---

[69] Cahir Healy MP, *The Mutilation of a Nation: The Story of the Partition of Ireland* (Derry: Derry Journal Ltd, 1945), p. 4.

[70] Healy, *Mutilation*, p. 3.   [71] Healy, *Mutilation*, pp. 11–22.

[72] Healy, *Mutilation*, pp. 23–44.

[73] Healy, *Mutilation*, p. 23, p. 27. Healy was interned under the Defence of the Realm Act for eighteen months in Brixton Prison in London, after a letter apparently containing his thoughts on the possibility of a German victory was intercepted. Whilst in prison he formed a lasting friendship with the leader of the British Union of Fascists, Sir Oswald Mosley (Phoenix, 'Healy, Cahir (1877–1970)', *DNB*). See also Christopher Norton, 'The Internment of Cahir Healy M.P., Brixton Prison July 1941– December 1942', *Twentieth Century British History* 18, no. 2 (2007), pp. 170–93, doi: 10.1093/tcbh/hwm007.

unsafe for them to continue work in a shipyard had assembled at St Mary's Hall, and elected to send telegrams to Churchill, Chamberlain, Mussolini, Roosevelt, de Valera, and Daladier, reading: 'Catholic workers of City of Belfast engaged in work of national importance have been brutally victimized and thrown out of work because of religion. Do you stand for this?'[74] They do not appear to have received any replies. On the penultimate page of the pamphlet Healy quotes without comment, contextualization, or explanation from St John Ervine's novel *Mrs Martin's Man* (1914), where a voice with an Ulster accent is heard talking about the iniquities of the Home Rule Bill in terms of 'them Cathliks havin'' the upper hand', before another is heard to say that they had suffered no interference as a result of being Catholic when in England, but 'in this place...'. The voice continues to relate being driven out of the shipyard, and describes workers writing 'To hell with the Pope' on the side of the ship under construction.[75] Healy's polemical collation of argument and anecdote, culled from a range of factual and fictional sources, which quotes freely from political opponents and seeks to compare the local situation with developments abroad, is an illustration in microcosm of the complex texture of published debate at the time.

The previous year, Cahir Healy had made a fictional intervention of his own with the short story *A Hired Boy on the Border* (1944), published in pamphlet form by the Dublin Catholic Truth Society. The story is related by a seventeen-year-old boy from rural County Donegal, who travels to a hiring fair in Strabane, where he is taken on by a Presbyterian farmer named Jonkins, whose farmhouse straddles the border. Jonkins explains that as a result of this location he finds himself pestered by customs officials from both jurisdictions, though he rejects the idea that any real hostility exists between the two forces: 'They call our place "Neutrality House", for both Sides lay claim to it, and search it—maybe together—odd whiles. The folks believe the two packs stan' scowlin' at wan another day and night, but I could open their eyes if I liked'. The ground for the allegory having been laid, the story continues to describe the boy's time working on the farm, and the frequent visits of customs officials attempting to recover smuggled goods. The focus on smuggling belies the wartime setting of the story, but the effects of the ongoing conflict are acknowledged only once, when after a breakfast of porridge, milk, bread, butter, and eggs the boy observes that 'We might hear a lot iv rationin' but we never met it'.[76] Unlike Healy's

---

[74] Healy, *Mutilation*, p. 29. I have not been able to establish whether 'City of Belfast' refers to the city itself or to a ship bearing this name.

[75] Healy, *Mutilation*, p. 43.

[76] Cahir Healy, *A Hired Boy on the Border* (Dublin: Catholic Truth Society, 1944), p. 7, p. 11.

later pamphlet, the story does not encourage the contemplation of a wider historical context to the matter of the border, and the vaguely whimsical narrative also requires a less forthright anti-partitionism, as is apparent from Jonkins' reply to the boy when he is asked why the house is continually searched:

> 'Oh, because we're on the Border—the first house on an unapproved road. I wish to heaven we could shift it to Athlone; they say that's the centre iv Irelan'. Maybe it's the Customs men from your side we'd hev later in the day. It's a mortal pity iv folks that hev this oul' Border at the back door', he added despondently.[77]

With such remarks Healy seeks to ridicule the very existence of the border, and Jonkins' mischievous desire to move the frontier to Athlone suggests that it should be regarded as no more than an arbitrary demarcation. In addition to the various allusions to smuggling, the story also suggests that the border is culturally and socially porous. The boy from Donegal is surprised by the frequent parties featuring music and dancing held at night in the farmhouse, which, due to the Presbyterian faith of his master, he had not expected. In this carnivalesque transgression Healy offers hope for a future in which Ireland is united by an enjoyment of culture and freed from religious strictures (Jonkins refuses to conform to Presbyterian stereotype, presiding over an untidy house and remaining in bed in the mornings, waking the boy in the room above by striking the ceiling with a long ash pole). The story builds to its climax when Jonkins asks the boy to escort two cows over the border from the southern state one night. He is caught on the northern side by patrolling Specials, who promise him 'a great time in Derry Jail', but is allowed out on bail the next day of court sitting, when Jonkins pays all fines owing. The boy subsequently discovers that his mission was a dummy, to distract the officials from the movement of an entire herd of cattle across the border half a mile away.[78] The story thus ends with the outwitting of the northern authorities and the implied message that Northern Ireland is under-resourced (in this regard it is significant that goods in the story travel one way only). Considered in its political context, Healy's short story is clearly less stridently anti-partitionist than the later pamphlet, and, indeed, the nature of his Dublin publisher suggests that it would probably be assured of a receptive audience. *A Hired Boy* uses gentle humour to ridicule, rather than attack, the existence of the border, and Healy does not seek to explore partition with reference to an international or colonial context. The divergent strategies of these pamphlets exemplify contrasting northern nationalist approaches towards the Second World

---

[77] Healy, *Hired Boy*, p. 11.   [78] Healy, *Hired Boy*, p. 13, p. 8, pp. 15–16.

War. Some publications addressed the war directly, comparing local injustices with recent events elsewhere in the world, and criticizing the Allied war effort on the basis that Britain's colonial record rendered the enterprise hypocritical, but others turned away from the war and pursued a strategy of selective blindness, often aided by a retreat to a rural hinterland.

The publication of the booklet *Orange Terror* in 1943 underlines the importance of Dublin publications to the debate. The seventy-two-page critique, published under the pseudonym 'Ultach', brought together two articles which had previously been published in the Dublin *Capuchin Annuals* of 1940 ('The Persecution of Catholics in Northern Ireland') and 1943 ('The Real Case against Partition'), where they had appeared alongside other polemical and fictional pieces which deplored unionist rule in Northern Ireland since partition.[79] The publication of *Orange Terror* as a separate booklet was announced by Father Senan, the editor of the *Capuchin Annual*, in the 1943 edition. He stated that proceeds from sales of the booklet would go into a fund 'to fight partition', and, like the publishers of *Ulster Parade*, encouraged readers to send the new thinner publication to friends and family members abroad.[80] *Orange Terror* constitutes a hugely significant indictment of unionist rule at the time: the booklet was banned by the Northern Ireland government but circulated in the southern state, provoking considerable debate in the pages of *The Bell* and in the chamber at Stormont over subsequent months. The *Capuchin Annual* was also banned in the province following this controversy.[81]

Like Healy and others, Ultach incorporates numerous quotations into his argument, drawing on speeches and statements by politicians and others, including the former and present prime ministers of Northern Ireland, to demonstrate the endemic anti-Catholic bias of the unionist establishment. Statistical information and tables of figures are deployed to show the extent of gerrymandering, and the imbalance in the distribution of education funding in the province.[82] *Orange Terror* is more overtly dialogic

[79] 'Ultach', 'The Persecution of Catholics in Northern Ireland', *The Capuchin Annual 1940* (Dublin: Capuchin Periodicals' Office, October 1939), pp. 161–175, and 'The Real Case against Partition', *Capuchin Annual 1943* (Dublin: Two, Capel Street, May 1943), pp. 283–361. Although the 1940 Annual states that it was published in October 1939, the 1943 edition apparently did not appear until May 1943. 'Ultach' was a pseudonym used by the Belfast-born writer, broadcaster, and educationalist James Joseph Campbell (1910–1979). (Arthur Green, 'Campbell, James Joseph (1910–1979)', *DNB*, <http://www.oxforddnb.com/view/article/64464>)

[80] Father Senan, 'Orange Terror', *Capuchin Annual 1943*, p. 643.

[81] Michael Farrell, *Northern Ireland: The Orange State* (London: Pluto Press, 1976), p. 94.

[82] 'Ultach', *Orange Terror: The Partition of Ireland, a reprint from The Capuchin Annual, 1943* (Dublin: Capuchin Annual Office, 1943), p. 13, p. 16, p. 17. All subsequent references to 'Ultach, *Orange Terror*' are to this original 1943 edition.

than other publications of this time, however: more than half of the booklet is taken up by a section entitled 'Comments', where interested parties were invited to contribute their views on partition and unionist rule, to which Ultach then responded.

The publication is particularly visually striking: the cover of the booklet features a flock of bats, suggesting that the fear inspired by unionist rule was almost supernatural (Fig. 4.1). Two illustrations that accompany the text—one in the 1943 *Capuchin Annual* and one in the booklet itself— are also dramatically symbolic and seem to betray the influence of Soviet didactic political art. The print which appears in the *Capuchin Annual* bears Ultach's name at its foot, and shows a vast, cruel-faced giant smashing a statue of Lady Justice onto a burning street of terraced houses with one hand, as the other turns the handle of a huge black press marked 'Pogrom', in which tiny figures are being crushed into an oozing pulp. Below this, a trio of top-hatted drummers beat their instruments in unison

Fig. 4.1 'Ultach', *Orange Terror: The Partition of Ireland, a reprint from The Capuchin Annual, 1943* (Dublin: Capuchin Annual Office, 1943)

By kind permission of the Irish Capuchin Franciscans.

as a fourth is in the process of writing 'To Hell With The P...' on the plinth on which the press rests (Fig. 4.2).[83] The second print is similarly forbidding. Here the same giant is dressed in robes, and a badge featuring a crown is pinned to his breast. He holds a whip in his left hand and a perfectly balanced pair of scales in his right. On one side of the scales is a solitary top-hatted drummer, but on the other stand six bare-headed figures of a similar size. A branding iron marked 'RC' lies next to a burning brazier on the ground, and the giant's feet rest on several identically shaped human bodies, whose faces are pressed into the ground.[84] *Orange Terror* also includes a photograph showing a brick wall on which the slogans 'Rebels Beware', 'To Hell With Popery', 'Where Popery Reigns Poverty Remains', 'Rem 1690, Down the IRA', and 'God Save Our King' have been daubed. This is accompanied by the caption 'In 1943, on your way to Mass in a Belfast church, this warning greets you at a street corner'. Copies of selected documents were also reprinted in the booklet. These included a resolution made by the County Grand Lodge of the Belfast Orange Order, stating that any member of the order found frequenting a Roman Catholic public house would be found guilty of 'unbecoming conduct' and dealt with accordingly, and an Introduction Card issued by the Northern Ireland Ministry of Labour in 1936, on which the reason given by one employer for refusing a man work is simply listed as 'Religion'.[85]

In addition to the visual and theoretical impact of *Orange Terror*, Ultach also shows a keen awareness of the importance of the use of language to the maintenance of the political status quo. Noting the pervasive and hypocritical use of the word 'loyal' in promoting the British war effort in the province, he observes that 'of course the Home Guard is another nice hideyhole for those good "loyalists" who would like to see the Papishes conscripted, but have no intention themselves of proving their "loyalty" in act', and later interrogates the historic political usage of the word 'loyal' in the maintenance of unionist rule, with reference to recent newspaper reports.[86] The booklet concludes with a poem, written by Ultach, entitled 'Belfast, 1942', which takes the form of a prayer from a father to his son that the younger man's heart will not be blackened by 'The fevered hate/Of men misled/By greed's envenoming word'.[87] The anti-partitionist aim of the booklet is clear, but formally and stylistically, and like Ervine's *Craigavon: Ulsterman* and Healy's *The Mutilation of a Nation*, *Orange Terror* is characterized by its diversity.

---

[83] Ultach, 'The Real Case against Partition', *Capuchin Annual 1943*, p. 283.
[84] Ultach, *Orange Terror*, p. 58.
[85] Ultach, *Orange Terror*, p. 28, p. 12, pp. 18–19.
[86] Ultach, *Orange Terror*, p. 5.   [87] Ultach, *Orange Terror*, p. 72.

283

Fig. 4.2 Illustration from 'Ultach', 'The Real Case against Partition', *Capuchin Annual 1943* (Dublin: Two, Capel Street, May 1943), pp. 283–361 (p. 283)
By kind permission of the Irish Capuchin Franciscans.

The booklet opens with a section entitled 'I Live There', in which Ultach describes how he has suffered at the hands of 'them', 'the people', and 'those people'—terms by which he refers to those who vote for and maintain unionist rule. Though he and his family have been beaten, witnessed the killing of family members, evicted from their home, and reduced to poverty, Ultach claims that he continues to view his persecutors as 'agreeable and obliging' on a personal level. Having outlined the wider patterns of discrimination and intimidation in the province, Ultach poses the question 'And how has the situation changed if at all since war began?' He answers that the war has simply provided the authorities in Northern Ireland with another excuse to intimidate the Catholic population, on the basis that 'All internal disturbance must be sacrificed in the wider interests of the Empire'. Arguing that anti-Catholic discrimination is an integral part of the Northern Irish war effort, he claims that workers from England and Scotland are invited to cross the Irish Sea to take up manufacturing jobs in Belfast when the native Catholic population is being offered war work in England.[88] With profound weariness, Ultach describes how many welfare and relief organizations avoided helping Catholics in the aftermath of the Blitz, whilst regulations hampered those organizations that did try to help:

> Even the war and its consequences for civilian life are turned to the benefit of the ascendancy clique and their followers. The spectacle of one man having a house half wrecked and getting no compensation while another actually has his house not only repaired but redecorated in a fashion it never knew before; the spectacle of vested interests being allowed to cut right across even air-raid welfare activities; the smug job-hunter holding forth about the war effort, the co-operation of all classes, the healing of sectarian wounds, and his not caring what a man is, etc., etc., and at the same time doing nothing for the war effort except such petty persecution of Catholics as comes within the scope of his job.[89]

Orange Terror begins as an exposé of discrimination and intimidation, but moves beyond this to a systematic critique of unionist rule, recasting partition and the treatment of the Catholic population in Northern Ireland in a European context. Claiming that 'Established twenty-two years ago, before Hitler's phenomenal rise to power, [Northern Ireland] nevertheless presents an almost perfect example, within its limitations, of what we know as the totalitarian state', Ultach draws on Waldemar Gurian's *The Future of Bolshevism* (1936), a study which aimed to show the essential similarity of the regimes of Soviet Russia and Nazi Germany. Ultach contends that Northern Ireland was also dominated by one party, which likewise maintained a front of democratic accountability through regular rigged elections. He suggests that intimidation of the nationalist press and use of the Special Powers Acts of 1922 and 1933 also constituted totalitarian

---

[88] Ultach, *Orange Terror*, p. 1, p. 5.   [89] Ultach, *Orange Terror*, p. 6.

measures, and argues that by continually stoking fears of Rome and per-
secuting Catholics, official and unofficial government agents ensured the
necessary state of high political tension that such regimes used to keep
the masses in movement. In support of this thesis Ultach quotes from
speeches by Craigavon, Brooke, Andrews, and other establishment figures, all discouraging people from employing Catholics, or were otherwise
demonstrative of anti-Catholic bias.[90]

Ultach's analysis had been preceded by a socialist outrider: in 1938
the Communist Party pamphlet *Craigavon in the Dock* claimed that the
1922 Special Powers Act had given the Northern Ireland authorities powers 'equalled in no country outside Fascist Italy and Germany'. It cited
an English Civil Liberties Committee report of 1936 which had argued
that such regulations contravened habeas corpus and that the status of the
unionist government in the province was 'paralleled only by Continental
dictatorships'.[91] In 'Ulster: a Reply', a response to *Orange Terror* published in *The Bell* in March 1944, Denis Ireland's Ulster Union Club
also favoured the analogy: referring to the internment of one of the club's
own members for the publication of subversive material, it claimed that
Northern Ireland could be seen as 'one of the earliest models of a police
state in Europe'.[92] The comparison was even drawn to comic and satirical effect: a cartoon published in the Queen's University undergraduate
magazine *PTQ* in 1940 entitled 'Secret Police of the Nations' depicted
caricatured figures of the Gestapo, the OVRA, and OGPU before a fourth
sketch showed three ungainly, confused, and vacant-looking B Specials,
one waving a gun towards a startled cat.[93]

The use of imagery and terminology relating to the Second World War
was widespread within nationalist and socialist print culture in the province at this time, and the search for reflections of the global in provincial life
is one way in which the war 'deinsulated' Northern Ireland. Responding
to Ultach's arguments in the 'Comments' section of *Orange Terror*, the
republican abstentionist Éamon Donnelly, introducing himself with the
words 'I am not a bigot', argued that descendants of planters 'have no
more right in Ireland than the Germans have in either Czecho-Slovakia or
Norway' and 'are the oldest Quisling Government in Europe'.[94] Donnelly's

---

[90] Ultach, *Orange Terror*, p. 8, pp. 9–11, pp. 13–14.
[91] *Craigavon in the Dock: An Indictment by the Communist Party of Ireland* (Belfast: Communist Party of Ireland, 1938), p. 23.
[92] Ulster Union Club, 'Ulster: a Reply', *The Bell* 7, no. 6 (March 1944), pp. 474–484(p. 479).
[93] John Killen, *The Unkindest Cut: A Cartoon History of Ulster 1900–2000* (Belfast: Blackstaff Press, 2000), p. 72.
[94] Ultach, *Orange Terror*, p. 56.

reference to the Nazi invasion of Czechoslovakia echoes Henry Harrison's repeated use of the term 'Sudeten Irische' in his anti-partitionist book *The Neutrality of Ireland: Why it was Inevitable* (1942). Harrison compared Neville Chamberlain's hypocritical expressions of concern for 'the liberties of the Sudeten Deutsche abroad [with] his stony indifference for the liberties of the Sudeten Irische at home'.[95] In a 1940 Left Book Club publication entitled *Churchill Can Unite Ireland* Jim Phelan described the plantation of Ulster as a kind of 'Sudeten-German affair', but claimed that republicans and socialists had no quarrel with the descendants of planters, who had been sold religious hatred in a 'Nazi trick'; similarly, in the Fabian pamphlet *The Irish Question Today* (1941) John Hawkins refers to Fermanagh, Tyrone, Derry City, South Down, and South Armagh as ' "Sudetenland" counties' and argued that a united Ireland 'would at any rate check the Quisling-breeding to which unnaturally divided nations are peculiarly subject'.[96] The analogies drawn between Northern Ireland and the Sudetenland are inexact and confusing, but aim to equate the Nazi invasion of the northern regions of Czechoslovakia with the British presence in Northern Ireland. Comparisons between the province and Czechoslovakia were not drawn solely by nationalist writers: in his study of Craigavon, *Not an Inch*, Hugh Shearman quoted the late prime minister using the phrase 'Ulster is nobody's Czechoslovakia', with entirely different implications.[97] With these words Craigavon attempted to stoke the threat of invasion by the southern state, and warned that any attempt by Britain to cede Northern Ireland to Éire would be resisted.

The term 'quisling' was also used on both sides of the debate during and after the war. In *The Mutilation of a Nation* Cahir Healy described the Northern Ireland government as 'Ulster Quislings [who] prefer the considerable emoluments and prestige which come from governing a corner of the Irish Nation to taking their place in a national assembly', whilst his fellow nationalist MP Eddie McAteer concluded his anti-partitionist pamphlet *New Thoughts on an Old Subject* (1948) with the words 'If I succeed in adding but one per cent to the cost of British or British quisling administration here I shall have succeeded beyond my best expectations'.[98] The term was a powerful piece of personal abuse. In a speech to the Northern

---

[95] Henry Harrison, *The Neutrality of Ireland: Why it was Inevitable* (London: Robert Hale Limited, 1942), p. 187.
[96] Jim Phelan, *Churchill Can Unite Ireland* (London: Victor Gollancz, 1940), p. 68, p. 69; John Hawkins, *The Irish Question Today* (London: Victor Gollancz and Fabian Society, 1941), p. 47, p. 49.
[97] Shearman, *Not an Inch*, p. 179.
[98] Healy, *Mutilation*, p. 6; Eddie McAteer, *New Thoughts on an Old Subject* (Donegal: Donegal Democrat, 1948), p. 6.

Ireland House of Commons, reprinted in pamphlet form as *The Stormont Cabinet: A Labour Indictment* (1943), the Labour MP Jack Beattie said of his former colleague Harry Midgley, who had taken a seat in the unionist cabinet, that 'the Quisling and the turncoat is the object of contempt in all countries—nowhere more so than in Northern Ireland.'[99]

These three uses of the word 'quisling' cast unionists as collaborators, and participants in a puppet regime on behalf of a totalitarian force of occupation. Nationalist usage of the word sought to suggest that Britain's war against the Axis powers is hypocritical given its own colonial history in Ireland, but also subverts the propagandist discourse of the British war effort in which the term was of common currency. An editorial in the London *Times* on 19 April 1940, ten days after the German invasion of Norway, opened with the lines 'We should all be profoundly grateful to Major Quisling. He has added a new word to the English language' and emphasized the speed with which the term had taken hold: 'During the past week... he has attained a swift notoriety. Not only has his name been heard or read by almost everybody, but twice already it has been used in these columns as a plain synonym for "traitor" '. The editorial highlighted the acoustic resonance of the word, described as a 'gift from the gods' for journalists and writers, that 'contrives to suggest something at once slippery and tortuous'.[100] Winston Churchill's references to 'filthy quislings' and 'squalid quislings' in broadcast speeches in the second half of 1941 further cemented the meaning of the term.[101] The word 'quisling' had become closely associated with the (British) war against Nazi Germany, and its usage by anti-partitionist writers in attacks on British or unionist rule in Northern Ireland was part of a growing movement to show that Britain's pursuit of the war was hypocritical, marking a significant departure from the idea that partition was wrong in and of itself. Subversion of language associated with a political opponent can also be observed in unionist rhetoric. Lord Craigavon's famous broadcast in February 1940 included the pledge that 'Britain's difficulty is Northern Ireland's opportunity to place all her resources, both human and material, at the disposal of

---

[99] Jack Beattie, *The Stormont Cabinet: A Labour Indictment* (Belfast: West Belfast Labour Party, 1943), p. 3.

[100] 'Quisling is as Quisling Does', *The Times*, 19 April 1940.

[101] 'Winston Churchill: broadcast' (24 August 1941), and 'speech' (to Joint Session of United States Congress, Washington D.C., 26 December 1941), in *The Churchill War Papers*, vol. 3, 'The Ever-Widening War', 1941, edited by Martin Gilbert (London: William Heinemann, 2000), pp. 1099–1106 (p. 1103) and pp. 1685–1690 (p. 1688). In the first of the speeches the term 'quisling' is applied to Norwegian collaborators alone, but in the address to the US Congress the word is used to describe all those in occupied Europe who had been 'suborned' by invading Nazi forces, suggesting that over the months the word had passed into more general usage.

the United Kingdom in this hour of crisis'—an ironic appropriation of the nationalist slogan 'England's difficulty is Ireland's opportunity' popularized during the First World War.[102]

The Second World War does seem to have provided a context within which nationalists and unionists could engage afresh with each other's contentions. In *New Thoughts on an Old Subject* Eddie McAteer appealed for a peaceful post-war campaign of non-cooperation with government and military forces in Northern Ireland, drawing particularly explicit analogies. He argued that:

> Irish people must not be spectators at military tattoos, parades or any functions under Occupation auspices. Our attitude must be the attitude of the French to the Germans whilst France was under German occupation . . . We have no personal antipathy to the human beings encased in British uniforms but we must make it clear that we have the very strongest objection to their uniforms in Ireland. Icelanders left the pavement when British soldiers approached.[103]

Given the extent of French collaboration with the Nazi forces of occupation, the provision of support by Britain for the French resistance movement during the war, and the subsequent liberation of France by Allied forces, McAteer's assertion in this regard is perhaps ill-advised, but his reference to Iceland is apposite. When occupied by British forces in 1940, Iceland remained neutral: like Northern Ireland, Iceland was strategically important to the Allies in terms of the Atlantic convoys, and like Northern Ireland was occupied by many thousands of American troops in the latter stages of the war. Relations between Icelanders and the occupiers were sometimes frosty, but there was no organized attempt to disrupt the activities of the Allied forces.[104] By referring to Iceland, McAteer engages with the proposition that Northern Ireland's status within the United Kingdom

---

[102] Craig, 'We Are King's Men', in *Field Day*, vol. 3, p. 363. St John Ervine adapted Craig's words for a voiceover for a wartime propaganda film entitled *Ulster*, which sought to emphasize Northern Ireland's industrial prowess:

> The Northern Ireland Parliament made this declaration at the outbreak of war. The people of loyal Ulster will share the burden of their kith and kin in every part of the Empire to the uttermost of their resources. Britain's difficulty is Northern Ireland's opportunity to place all her possessions, human and material, at the service of our King. The people of Ulster have long loved and have defended liberty. They will not fail to defend it now.

(Quoted in John Hill, *Cinema and Northern Ireland: Film, Culture and Politics* [London: British Film Institute, 2006], pp. 85–86.)

[103] McAteer, p. 3.

[104] James Miller, *The North Atlantic Front: Orkney, Shetland, Faroe and Iceland at War* (Edinburgh: Birlinn, 2003), pp. 87–88, pp. 101–111, pp. 120–132.

was vital to Allied success in the European war, which, as I have shown, was rapidly adopted as an article of faith by many unionist writers and politicians.

In the article for the socialist *New Statesman* that so incensed his congregation, W.R. Rodgers asked 'Have we in Ulster a "fascist" government?'[105] There were many nationalists, it seems, who would have answered in the affirmative. In his pamphlet *Ireland—can it remain neutral?* (1941), the Scottish Communist MP William Gallacher repeatedly referred to the Ulster Volunteers of 1912 as 'Storm Troopers'.[106] T.J. Campbell, a contributor to the 'Comments' section of *Orange Terror*, twice refers to the ruling orange elite as 'Herrenvolk', using the Nazi conception of the Germans as a master race born to rule and maintain order.[107] Likewise, in the 1943 *Capuchin Annual*, Benedict Kiely writes that the possibility of cross-community cooperation in Omagh is hindered by 'an unreasoning *Herrenvolk* mentality', and in March of that year the Socialist Party's *Northern Star* newsletter described a recent newspaper article by St John Ervine as a 'clarion call to the Ulster Herrenvolk'.[108] Like 'quisling', this word had been brought into common usage by the war against Germany, and can similarly be identified with the British war effort through its use in a broadcast by Churchill two years previously.[109] The imported terms 'quisling' and 'Herrenvolk' were used in British political discourse of the Second World War to condemn the treachery of the collaborator and the dictatorial nature of Nazi ideology, but the very foreignness of the words (which were frequently italicized) also helped to promote the idea that these tendencies were alien to the British character and to British

---

[105] Rodgers, 'Black North', *New Statesman*, 20 November 1943. O'Brien, *W. R. Rodgers*, p. 55. In an unpublished typescript (*c.*1941–44) Rodgers' friend Louis MacNeice suggested that, to an English spectator, Orange Order parades might appear reminiscent 'even of fascism' (MacNeice, 'Northern Ireland and Her People', in Heuser (ed.), *Selected Prose*, pp. 143–153 [p. 149]); Moya Woodside similarly refers to 'semi-Fascist Ulster' in a diary entry on 18 October 1940. Bernard Griffin, the Catholic Archbishop of Westminster from 1943 until his death in 1956, angered the Stormont Government when he compared the treatment of the Catholic minority in Northern Ireland with the Nazi persecution of Catholics in Germany and Poland (Donal Ó Drisceoil, *Censorship in Ireland 1939–1945: Neutrality, Politics and Society* [Cork: Cork University Press, 1996], p. 225).

[106] William Gallacher, *Ireland—can it remain neutral?* (London: Communist Party of Great Britain, 1941), p. 5.

[107] Ultach, *Orange Terror*, pp. 60–62.

[108] Benedict Kiely, 'Long After O'Neill', *Capuchin Annual 1943*, pp. 239–250 (p. 244); 'Telegraph Plans', *Northern Star 4*, no. 1 (March 1943), p. 13.

[109] In the broadcast on 24 August 1941, following a summit with American President Roosevelt at which the Atlantic Charter had been drafted, Churchill said 'It is the rule of the *Herrenvolk*—the master race—who are to put an end to democracy, to parliaments, to the fundamental freedoms and decencies of ordinary men and women' (Churchill, 'Broadcast' in Gilbert (ed.), *The Churchill War Papers*, vol. 3, p. 1103).

public life.[110] Anti-partitionist and nationalist writers used these terms in various attempts to equate the behaviour of the British and Northern Ireland governments and their forces with the recent actions of Nazi Germany, but with the unintended consequences of embedding their writings within the discourse of the war. This undoubtedly problematized their efforts to cast the province as an uninterested or unwilling participant in the conflict, aligned with neutral Éire.

Several contributors to the *Capuchin Annual* during the war pursued this approach. A series of Northern Irish travelogues either avoided acknowledging the effects of the Second World War on the province altogether, or suggested that the war was a false, alien, or immoral intrusion, incompatible with the idealized conception of Ireland on which the writers preferred to dwell. This course was also established visually: lengthy photographic sections in the 1940 and 1943 annuals were dedicated to Ulster, but privileged scenes of rural tranquillity and failed to show any of the physical effects of the conflict. Fifty pages of photographs in the 1943 annual do include some images of Belfast, including the view over the city from Cave Hill and shots of the City Hall, St Malachy's College, and the Falls Road, but in displaying no signs of bomb damage or wartime paraphernalia it must be presumed that these date from before the war.[111] Whatever the provenance of the photographs, the aim was to present a view of Ulster as unsullied by the effects of the war. Writers for the *Capuchin Annual* are reluctant to concede that the war might be of any real concern to Ireland, and contemplate the outsiders who have arrived in Northern Ireland as a result of the conflict with disdain. In the pages of the novel the war appears less as a matter of global consequence and more as a malign cultural phenomenon. In a piece entitled 'Ulster's Contribution to Anglo-Irish Literature' for the 1940 edition, the architect and poet Padraic Gregory wrote that

> ... it is pleasant to be able to record two facts, the first that Ulster writers are still, to-day—at a time when the simplicities of an agricultural people are in danger of being overwhelmed by the complexities of mechanisation—concerning themselves with simple elemental things and ably interpreting those experiences, emotions, and aspirations, which have been common to humanity since the beginning of time; and the second, that we know of no

---

[110] For example, in a 1940 broadcast on Hitler's imperial ambitions, the British Foreign Secretary Lord Halifax proclaimed that 'To this German ideal of vassal States dominated by the *Herrenvolk* Britain opposes the ideal of freedom—a community of nations, freely cooperating for the good of all, and animated by justice and good faith in their dealings with one another' ('Lord Halifax's Broadcast', *The Times*, 23 July 1940).

[111] 'Cuard Na hÉireann', *Capuchin Annual 1943*, pp. 89–138.

Ulster writer of the day who may be said to be deliberately assisting the decadence so apparent in modern English literature. [112]

The fear of 'decadence' and a deep-seated dislike of growing industrialization inform many contributions to the publication, along with a resentment of the transatlantic war effort on the grounds that it has accelerated these unwelcome intrusions. Most of the material that I examine in this chapter shows how the war 'deinsulated' Northern Ireland's political culture, but some nationalists deliberately resisted this process and strove to reinsulate the province, both from the effects of the war and from external, and specifically Anglo-American, cultural influences.

In an essay for the 1943 *Capuchin Annual* the Dublin-born lecturer and writer Máirín Allen described her memories of Belfast while at school there at the time of the First World War, before reflecting on the atmosphere in the city during the present war. In Allen's recollections the First World War appears to have been of little direct consequence to Belfast. A dull background subject discussed only by adults, the conflict was thoroughly overshadowed by the pressing immediacy of the events taking place around her: the activities of snipers on the Shankill Road, the intimidating presence of British soldiers, and the constant raids by A and B Specials. She does remember adult nationalist indignation over the question of conscription, however, and recalls that even at a young age she herself thought that the policy was 'very wicked indeed'.[113] Viewed through the lens of the ongoing conflict, Allen's recollections of the First World War are resonant of nationalist resistance to Belfast's involvement in the Second World War, and her piece closes with a description of her recent return to the city:

> There is not enough war work to employ all Belfast's workless. The tallest mill on York Street is a heap of bricks and mortar. One looks from Castle Junction down old High Street towards the Albert Memorial and great, gutted gaps confront the eye. The historic Whig offices in Bridge Street have a shaken look... This is blitzed Belfast.
>
> A boy goes by shouting the 'Tally,' Belfast's evening paper, the *Belfast Telegraph*, and easily the best evening paper in Ireland. But there is no news—nothing but war propaganda. The dimly-lit trams—blacked-out, of course, and criss-crossed with strips of paper—are bewildering. A 'phone call in a blacked-out and bulb-less telephone booth strains one's frayed temper. The Grand Central Hotel will surely provide matches. But the Grand Central Hotel is too full of uniformed girls and men to bother. American

---

[112] Padraic Gregory, 'Ulster's Contribution to Anglo-Irish Literature', *Capuchin Annual 1940*, pp. 218–221 (p. 221).

[113] Máirín Allen, 'Where Lagan Streams...', *Capuchin Annual 1943*, pp. 180–187 (p. 180).

accents are around one—and Belfast accents, unchanged by years of radio-standard-English. 'Coffee, miss?' 'No, thank-you.'[114]

The discombobulation she feels at the changes in Belfast is reflected in these concluding paragraphs, where the impact of the war is registered as a series of shattering and confusing effects detached from their causes, which she seemingly has little interest in exploring. The prose itself is disjointed: the trams are 'of course' blacked out and taped in case of air attack, but she still seems to find this 'bewildering', and the air of disconnection is compounded literally by the 'blacked-out and bulb-less telephone booth'. Her professed confusion enables her to describe the war in terms of a random affliction, alien to the city, whilst the claim that the *Belfast Telegraph* is 'easily the best evening paper in Ireland', and her dismissal of today's news as 'nothing but war propaganda' voice resentment at the idea that Irish and local news has been overtaken or displaced by international events. Allen's reference to the pervasiveness of American accents implies that Belfast faces a new cultural threat at this time, but her observation that the native accent remains unchanged following 'years of radio-standard English' and final 'No, thank-you' (to coffee, the drink of intellectuals and foreigners) are illustrative of a determination to resist this new influx.

Allen continued in this vein in 'Ulster Sketch Book', published in the *Capuchin Annual* the following year. This short travelogue focused on the religious history and architecture of the ancient province, and this devotional context amplified the incongruities of the ongoing conflict. She seemed particularly troubled by the influx of foreign military personnel. Derry is described as 'busy catering for the amusement of British and Canadian and American soldiers and airmen and marines, white and coloured', and Armagh appears 'strangely cosmopolitan'.[115] Allen is again concerned by the intrusion of non-native accents:

> At a street corner American coloured troops stopped their jeep to ask the way. And the hotel bars were filled with the accents of Boston and Philadelphia and San Francisco: you might have closed your eyes and thought you were at an American talkie film. But all this super-imposed outer-world faded and became unreal before the Armagh that centres round Patrick's hill of the white doe, where the Cathedral on the site of his church now stands.[116]

The unpalatable contrast between 'coloured troops' and 'the white doe' dramatizes her refusal to allow ancient myths to be displaced by current

---

[114] Máirín Allen, 'Where Lagan Streams...', *Capuchin Annual 1943*, p. 187.

[115] Máirín Allen, 'Ulster Sketch Book', *Capuchin Annual 1944* (Dublin: Two, Capel Street, August 1944), pp. 363–377 (p. 367).

[116] Máirín Allen, 'Ulster Sketch Book', *Capuchin Annual 1944*, p. 373.

events. Allen is typically resistant to the urbanized areas of the province, writing in an 'Afterword' that, in attempting to sketch rapidly Ulster's main features, she has chosen to concentrate on the rural because 'what is most enduring in the northern province, what is fruitful and what is traditional has survived best in the countryside'.[117]

Other contributors to the *Capuchin Annual* were also seriously dismayed by the 'cosmopolitan' impact of foreign voices. In a piece entitled 'Armagh City—First Impressions' for the 1943 edition, the Cork poet D.L. Kelleher described visiting the city for the first time in 1941, having previously known it only from a woodcut in a school textbook. Like Allen, his romantic conception of the city is troubled by the presence of soldiers:

> ... there was a difference. I was seeing Armagh under war conditions with troops from the ends of the earth in the streets. The accents of far countries made a strange contrast with the mellow, muffled bark of the native Armagh. The old place sloping down from its two cathedrals to that piece of the English scene that is the Mall still kept the gracious air of the book-plate, but every passing soldier was a reminder that we are living in a new age and that now it is more than ever true that only the violent can hope to carry away the kingdom of earth as well as the kingdom of heaven.[118]

As Terence Brown has observed, the preoccupation of nineteenth-century writers of the Irish Literary Revival with the image of Ireland as a rural or pastoral nation maintained its hold over artists and writers in the newly independent southern state. Retreats to the Ulster countryside in the pages of the *Capuchin Annual* may be read in the context of this often politicized tendency, where 'rural life was a condition of virtue inasmuch as it remained an expression of an ancient civilization, uncontaminated by commercialism and progress'. Brown also notes that 'When Irish writers turned to rural Ireland to discern there an unsullied tradition, they naturally highlighted those aspects of that life which suggested an undying continuity, an imperviousness to change, an almost hermetic stasis that transcended history'.[119] In the *Capuchin Annual* travelogues we see this version of the Irish pastoral coming under considerable strain, when its ability to transcend history is questioned by the enormity of the world war, the presence of large numbers of outsiders, and the intrusion of the physical paraphernalia of the conflict.

---

[117] Máirín Allen, 'Ulster Sketch Book', *Capuchin Annual 1944*, p. 377.

[118] D.L. Kelleher 'Armagh City—First Impressions', *Capuchin Annual 1943*, pp. 451–452 (p. 451).

[119] Terence Brown, *Ireland: A Social and Cultural History 1922–2002* (London: Harper Perennial, 2004), p. 73.

The short-form travelogue was pervasive at this time. In 'Journey in Ulster', which also appeared in the 1943 *Capuchin Annual*, Conal Casey made a tour of all nine counties of the ancient province, and like Allen and Kelleher contrasted the mythical past with the intrusions of the present. In Enniskillen, Casey detects an air of repression and the sense that there is 'No freedom now'.

> In the hotel, Government officials and commercial travellers meet at breakfast, Belfast accents and English accents, naively discuss war propaganda and war films. The town comes slowly, watchfully to wakefulness, blinds rising like lifting eyelids, carts rattling in from the country, men and women going to Mass. Fort Hill lifts one suddenly to a vision of the long lake stretching to the quiet mountains, the loveliness of Fermanagh, detached and apart from all wars and human change, as beautiful as it was when the poet was welcomed to the chieftain's house.[120]

Rural Ulster is presented here as a refuge from contemporary troubles, as Fermanagh's pastoral 'loveliness' is contrasted with the alien falsity of a war promulgated through ephemeral 'propaganda' and 'films', and discussed 'naively' in accents alien to the locality. For Casey and Allen, urban areas were more susceptible to the corrupting influences of the war, and Casey argues that Derry's involvement in the conflict was only part of a long-running programme of cultural and historical adulteration of the city:

> Deep down, Londonderry should be part of Ireland, but its vision has been twisted by centuries of misrepresented and misunderstood history; has in the last thirty years been given a new manufactured loyalty, in the last four years been invigorated by a hectic and artificial war-time activity. Derry as I saw it had been swamped by Londonderry. Streets were beflagged, shop windows filled with models of military aeroplanes, footwalks crowded with American and English soldiers, sailors, airmen. Military lorries streamed past under the shadow of the walls. Two black soldiers walked rollingly down Lawrence Hill . . .
>
> Londonderry could not between 1939 and 1943 (when the ban was lifted), march in procession. War-time conditions had silenced the drums, scattered the files of sashed men, folded the banners. In time the present war will become part of this strange tradition, falsified history, ignorance of the things that went into the making of the city. That is an unpleasant prospect for one who loves Derry of the oak grove, the quiet dark church and the kneeling children, the singing and the music and the Gaelic Feis. Derry found its economic and industrial power in the Donegal hinterland, now cut from it. Londonderry when the shouting of the captains ends will have

---

[120] Conal Casey, 'Journey in Ulster', *Capuchin Annual 1943*, pp. 495–501 (p. 496).

memories of white ships on the Lough, swaggering sailors on the street; thin porridge, when compared with the farm produce of Donegal. A man I knew spoke to me on the street. He said: 'The nations of the world are here.'

Well, the nations will go. There will again be closed factories, men without work, a city dying economically after political execution. Londonderry should raise another pillar to Carson and write under it: *By this hand we fell.*[121]

Brash, noisy, and false, the war is incompatible with an ancient, peaceful, primarily rural and devotional culture, characterized by the oak grove and the quiet church. The model planes in the shop window shrink the significance of the war to a childish diversion. Later on the train, as a Spitfire dives to the level of his carriage, Casey bemoans the fields at Limavady 'scarred' with the concrete of an aerodrome.[122] Like his fellow *Capuchin Annual* contributors Casey describes the coming of war as an imposition of alien sights and sounds (along with Allen, he appears to be particularly disturbed by the presence of black American troops), but his response to these intrusions differs significantly from the disconnected impressions of Belfast conjured by Allen's autobiographical essay, and from Kelleher's pessimistic apprehension of a 'new era' in Armagh. Casey sees Derry's involvement in the war as merely another stage in an ongoing project to pervert history and manufacture loyalty, a sustained plot to sever the city from neighbouring Donegal administratively and psychologically. Conceding that the city has benefited economically from the war, he contends that such material prosperity will be fleeting, and suggests that the positive legacy of the war in the province will be quickly subsumed by the 'normal life' of continuing cultural, economic, and political repression. Casey's response to the man who tells him 'The nations of the world are here' resists the idea that Northern Ireland might be reconfigured by the influx of outsiders and its role in the global conflict. Whereas the anti-partitionist arguments of Healy and Ultach drew imaginative analogies and comparisons between the recent history of Northern Ireland and international developments, many contributors to the *Capuchin Annual* sought to withdraw from a global context through strategies of wilful isolationism.

It is possible that these journeys through wartime Ulster were inspired by Seán Ó Faoláin's *An Irish Journey* (1940)—a travel book illustrated by Paul Henry. Like Allen and Kelleher, Ó Faoláin was disturbed by the impact of the war on the ecclesiastical city of Armagh, where 'The War, as the cinema says, featured prominently in the town—British soldiers coming and going, the lovely eighteenth century Rokeby Green desecrated by

---

[121] Casey, 'Journey in Ulster', *Capuchin Annual 1943*, pp. 497–498.
[122] Casey, 'Journey in Ulster', *Capuchin Annual 1943*, p. 498.

tramping feet, soaking tents, and old bricks flung down to make roadways across it'.[123] Like Casey, Ó Faoláin is distrustful of cinematic propaganda and is dismayed at the defilement of an historic landscape. But unlike the contributions to the *Capuchin Annual*, *An Irish Journey* makes no attempt to downplay the scale of the impact of the war, the effects of which are presented as deadening and horrifying. Condemning Omagh as 'one of the dullest, flattest towns in the whole country', Ó Faoláin then travels through Derry and Strabane to Belfast:

> [The city] had begun to seem less and less desirable the nearer I came to it. I think I saw it, this time, under the worst possible conditions—war-conditions; sandbags; concrete shelters—pathetically futile; general gloom. Only at night, in the black-out, when every street was a gully of darkness, and a sense of eerie mystery lurked at every corner, did I feel the least stir of my imagination. Donegall Place suggested *The Murders of the Rue Morgue*. Grosvenor Road might have been a brothel quarter.[124]

The reference to Edgar Allan Poe is entirely appropriate, as Ó Faoláin goes on to describe Belfast's 'blackness' and 'ruthlessness' with fear and horror, as though the war has cast a peculiarly macabre and supernatural pall over the city (the bats of *Orange Terror* certainly have their place in this context). He suggests that Goya would have enjoyed the Falls Road during blackout, and a description of RUC officers on patrol proceeds in this gothic vein:

> [they] hulked out of the dark, like mountains, before us, and bruised into one of those slits of light to warn Mrs Murphy that the Germans mustn't be guided to Belfast by her tuppenny tallow candles. There they leaned, great ominous figures, threatening a brutality which their poor country hearts never bred, clothed in the midnight of uniforms, with their gasmasks in bags bulging their backsides, and there was pity and horror in this brutalization by the North of Southern softness. (I wonder how many of these policemen come from Kerry and Clare and Tipperary?)[125]

These officers, formerly of the Royal Irish Constabulary, but relocated to Belfast following partition, dominate a cartoonish tableau that ridicules the zealous enforcement of blackout restrictions (*An Irish Journey* was published in 1940, the year before the Belfast Blitz) and highlights an anomalous and discordant by-product of partition: the presence of officers from the south in crown forces north of the border. Ó Faoláin then

---

[123] Seán Ó Faoláin, *An Irish Journey* (London, New York, Toronto: Longman, 1940) p. 274.
[124] Ó Faoláin, *Irish Journey*, p. 240, pp. 263–264.
[125] Ó Faoláin, *Irish Journey*, p. 265.

moves into the sociological territory explored by Ultach's article for the *Capuchin Annual* the same year, investigating the matter of Catholic 'disloyalty', and similarly quoting from anti-Catholic speeches of Craigavon and other members of the unionist establishment. He also cites an *Irish News* inquiry into the recruitment of Catholic working-class men by the Ulster regiments during the First World War, which compared the numbers who were killed in action during the war with the subsequent loss of life during the Belfast 'pogroms' of 1920–22.[126] Ó Faoláin's shift in emphasis and tone shows how the impressionistic, non-systematic mode of the travelogue co-existed within the same polemical anti-partitionist discourse as the journalistic approach of Ultach, similarly incorporating quotation and statistical analysis.

More nuanced and equivocal is Benedict Kiely's 'Long After O'Neill', an article published in the 1943 *Capuchin Annual* which describes the changes to rural life on the Tyrone side of Lough Neagh since the outbreak of war. Kiely's post-war novel *Land Without Stars* showed how the Second World War presented considerable difficulties for nationalists, and 'Long After O'Neill' presents a similarly ambiguous appraisal of the effects of the war on Northern Ireland. Far less politically inflected than other contributions to the *Capuchin Annual*, Kiely's essay openly acknowledges the involvement of the Catholic population in the war. Visiting the village of Pomeroy, where, he writes, locals used to play association football with British soldiers before the war, Kiely meets a man who has started playing Gaelic football instead. Kiely asks where the other local footballers are, and the man tells him that most members of the team have joined the British army and are fighting in Egypt, saying 'Nothing else for them to do. Tell me now what outlook is there for any young fellow with ambition? You're O.K. If you belong to the other side, you know. But if your colour is Irish green...'[127] In contrast with Kelleher's vague fear of a 'new era' and Allen's disconnected impressions of Belfast, which both appeared in the same edition, Kiely draws a clear line here between the global progress of the war and the parochial life of the village, and notes that the effects of the war were felt differently by nationalist and unionist populations. Unlike Ultach, whose article 'The Real Case Against Partition' was also published in the 1943 annual, Kiely is even-handed when apportioning blame for the civic paralysis. Of his home town of Omagh he writes:

> ... neither the Nationalist council nor the Unionist council showed any great desire to do anything sweeping for the social or sanitary development of the

[126] Ó Faoláin, *Irish Journey*, p. 268.
[127] Kiely, 'Long After O'Neill', *Capuchin Annual 1943*, p. 243.

town. And that is extremely interesting at a time when a European war has given a sudden, almost frenzied, life to local administration and social work in other parts of Ireland.[128]

Casey saw the city of Derry 'invigorated' by merely fleeting 'hectic and artificial war-time activity', but Kiely suggests that whilst Omagh remains riven by sectarian division, elsewhere in Ireland the war has effected positive change, in the provision of 'local administration and social work'. It is frustrating that Kiely does not elaborate on what he means here, but in appearing disheartened by the lack of change, rather than repelled by the extent of it, he diverges once more from the path taken by fellow contributors.

Kiely seems disappointed by the very nature of the ongoing war. Historically, he claims, young men arrived in the garrison town of Omagh from all over the north-west of Ireland, in the romantic hope of an adventurous life in the Ulster regiments. The present war, it seems, offers no chance of adventure, as Kiely writes that 'The garrison is bigger than ever but it has lost all that colour that was its one poor merit, the yellow blare of brass, the wild promise of great horizons'. He proceeds to recall three very different men he encountered in Omagh who had all recently joined the British armed forces. The first is a young local boy—an orphan raised by neighbours and in Borstal. A month after their meeting he is seen by Kiely being arrested for desertion, waving a hand and 'laughing in salutation and farewell'. The second is English—an airman who he finds sitting with his head in his hands beside a salmon leap, and who tells Kiely of his Irish ancestry. The third is a Belfast theologian and member of the Plymouth Brethren movement, who laughingly takes a Catholic tract from Kiely:

> The war may have swallowed them up; some wild tornado of bursting shells, falling bombs, maddened struggling men, in any place between Ostend and Mandalay. The poor Irish lad, intensely uncomfortable in his uniform; the seasoned man with his good habit of introducing himself to chaplains; the theologian with his tracts; dozens, hundreds of others, marching past, swallowed up in a terrible tide.[129]

As in *Land Without Stars*, the powerlessness of the individual is set against the immensity of the war, figured once again as a barely comprehensible global phenomenon. As with Gavin Burke's ARP uniform in *The Emperor of Ice Cream*, the allusion to ill-fitting clothes is salient, and is once again illustrative of nationalist awkwardness in the face of this global conflict.

---

[128] Kiely, 'Long After O'Neill', *Capuchin Annual 1943*, p. 244.
[129] Kiely, 'Long After O'Neill', *Capuchin Annual 1943*, p. 248.

If Kiely's writings are characterized by equivocation and uncertainty, disquiet and unease over Northern Ireland's place in the war also lurk beneath the prose of the Protestant nationalist Denis Ireland. 'The Road to the Isles', which appeared in *Northern Harvest* in 1944, was another Ulster travelogue, in which Ireland explored the impact of the war on rural life and landscape. The bus tour takes him out along the Antrim coast road where the 'only sign of war is a motor torpedo boat, droning like a mechanical beetle, so far out as to be invisible'. On reaching Portrush, however, he finds the town 'full of British troops suffering the pains of exile in a foreign land. Which is strange, seeing that Portrush is the nearest thing to an English seaside town that Ireland has to show, a corner of a foreign field that is forever Blackpool'.[130] The facetious reworking of Rupert Brooke's 'The Soldier' indicates that the war has engendered a sense of geographical uncertainty.[131] Moving on, Ireland suggests that the city of Derry is more secure in its Irishness, despite the seaplanes over the Foyle and the warships in the Atlantic, as he describes it in *Capuchin Annual*-esque terms as the city 'of the leafy oak shade, the spires and pinnacles against the sunset, the rusty key that must be turned, not forced, before Ireland is a nation once again'.[132] Again, however, the presence of military personnel complicates matters:

> In the bar of the hotel the hawk-men are relaxing after their patrols over the grey wastes of the Atlantic; the atmosphere is pure tin-shanty West translated into terms of the flying services, with machine guns substituted for six-shooters and quickness at the bomb lever the mark of a living man. The frontier has rolled back from North America, eastwards in time and space to Europe, then westwards again to this city on the Foyle where Irish Protestantism first issued its battle cry of 'No Surrender'.[133]

The implications of 'hawk-men' are diverse. Casting the airmen as alien or extra-human, predatory, and threatening, the word also recalls W.H. Auden's poem 'Consider this and in our time' (1930), which opens with an invitation to 'Consider this and in our time/As the hawk sees it or the helmeted airman', and, significantly, roves in its first stanza over a scene of military personnel in a hotel bar.[134] The poem's initial invitation

---

[130] Denis Ireland, 'The Road to the Isles', *Northern Harvest*, pp. 131–139 (p. 131).

[131] Rupert Brooke's poem 'The Soldier' (1914) opens with the lines: 'If I should die, think only this of me:/That there's some corner of a foreign field/That is for ever England' (*Rupert Brooke: The Collected Poems, with a Memoir by Edward Marsh* [London: Sidgwick, 1918; 3rd rev. edn. 1942, reprinted 1979], p. 302).

[132] Ireland, 'The Road to the Isles', *Northern Harvest*, p. 133.

[133] Ireland, 'The Road to the Isles', *Northern Harvest*, pp. 133–134.

[134] W.H. Auden, 'Consider this and in our time', *Selected Poems*, edited by Edward Mendelson (London: Faber and Faber, 1979), pp. 14–16 (p. 14).

to make sense of 'our time' from the detached and elevated viewpoint of the ancient or modern flyers quickly unravels in a confused series of accusations, observations, and sketches, vaguely premonitory of impending apocalypse. Similarly unbound by borders, Denis Ireland's hawk-men illustrate the difficulty in trying to determine the place of Northern Ireland in the war. In this passage frontiers shift with rapidity, leaving Derry in an uncertain, transcontinental, and transcultural location, unmoored from a clear sense of time or historical context, where the European war is overlaid with the jargon of the cinematic American Wild West. As in Auden's poem, register and tone are unfixed and fluid. Ambiguities proliferate, and as with Kiely's writings on and around the war, Denis Ireland's flippant humour enables a certain amount of evasion, as cultural, historical, and literary references are scattered like chaff. In this essay his preoccupation with frontiers and concern for Ulster's physical geography reflect his deeply held anti-partitionist convictions, but also betray his interest in the debate over Northern Ireland's place and role in the war, to which he would be a vocal contributor over the coming decades.

Denis Ireland was certainly politically active at this time. In 1941 he founded the Ulster Union Club, a confusingly named anti-partitionist movement 'to recapture for Ulster Protestants their true tradition as Irishmen'.[135] Several pamphlets were published under its auspices, and Ireland also contributed to numerous little magazines, newspapers, and radio programmes in Belfast and Dublin throughout the war. A captain in the Royal Irish Fusiliers during the First World War, in 1948 he became the first resident of Northern Ireland to take a seat in Seanad Éireann. His career is illustrative both of the cultural gravitational pull of Dublin and of the interpenetration of literary and political spheres at this time.[136] The Ulster Union Club was itself enthusiastically didactic in both the arts and anti-partitionist politics, advertising in its first manifesto activities including weekly discussions and lectures on current affairs, economics, history, and the Irish language, as well as dancing and music classes.[137] As a Protestant nationalist who remained hugely proud of his service in the First World War, Denis Ireland's life and writings exemplify the maverick tendency that managed to prosper during the war years.[138]

---

[135] 'Ulster Union Club. A New Protestant Movement', *Irish Times*, 19 February 1941.

[136] Anthony Powell was stationed next door to Denis Ireland in Belfast during the Second World War (Risteárd Ó Glaisne, *Denis Ireland* [Baile Átha Cliath: Coiscéim, 2000], p. 165).

[137] Ulster Union Club, *What is the Ulster Union Club?* (Belfast: Ulster Union Club, 1941), p. 6.

[138] Robert Greacen, 'Denis Ireland: a Memoir', *Honest Ulsterman 44/45* (August/October 1974), pp. 50–52 (p. 50).

The Second World War is a significant preoccupation in Denis Ireland's post-war writings, and, as a nationalist, his continued willingness to revisit the war years is notable. Radios and gramophones are a recurring presence in his recollections of the period. Symbolic, perhaps, of a sense that Northern Ireland was at one remove from the war, they offer a way of tuning in to events in Europe, or a means of drowning these out with music. 'Notes Taken on the Eve of War', published in *From the Jungle of Belfast* (1973) describes a scene in late September 1938, in the lounge of a hotel beside Carlingford Lough, as elderly ladies knit in time to the music playing on the wireless. As the tune comes to an end, everyone in the room becomes still. The voice of an announcer in London is heard, reporting that the Munich conference has ended in agreement, and the knitting resumes:

> Like mice emerging from the wainscoting, all slip back into safe suburban slots—back to tea-time tinklings from The Geisha; back to smut from the circulating libraries; back to English leg-papers made flesh at the Belfast Opera House; clockwork adultery simulated beneath the gilt fronts of empty, lorgnette-presuming stage-boxes.
>
> For a moment, threatening the clockwork, back-numbering even smutty novels and *Gone With the Wind*, the grinning skeleton of reality in Europe beckoned at the door of our provincial Irish woodshed. Then drops and lotions from the B.B.C. faded the frosty spectacle beyond the hotel windows where in the golden haze of a glorious September afternoon, against the forested background of dark-blue Carlingford mountains, there had glimmered for a moment, like icebergs on a summer sea, the ghosts of the new Ice Age in Europe, the skeleton horsemen of the now-postponed Apocalypse, the ghastly arc-lit abattoirs of the Third Reich, the greasily-smoking chimneys of Auschwitz, and all the horrors still to come.[139]

At a time of collapsing borders in Europe, Carlingford Lough is an apposite scenic backdrop, since the lake forms part of the partition between Northern Ireland and the southern state and opens onto the Irish Sea. As in Derry, Denis Ireland finds the tensions of cultural and geographical uncertainty in an Irish border region reverberating with new urgency in the context of the European war. In Derry the war appeared through the phoney cinematic lens of the American Wild West, but here it is local culture that is found wanting, as the 'provincial Irish woodshed' and the cultural mores of geriatric and suburban Belfast are set against the vast scale of the horrors to come. His implication that the moribund cultural atmosphere in Northern Ireland was incapable of addressing events of

---

[139] Denis Ireland, 'Notes Taken on the Eve of War', in *From the Jungle of Belfast* (Belfast: Blackstaff Press, 1973), pp. 67–69 (p. 68).

such magnitude should be read in the context of his desire for Irish unity and vain hope that the war might enable this.

Rather than joining the southern state in following a policy of neutrality, Denis Ireland proposed instead a detailed and convoluted anti-partitionist plan for the involvement of the whole island in the war. This he outlined in *The Bell*, following a lengthy debate on the matter of Northern Ireland in that magazine over the winter of 1943–44. Following the publication of *Orange Terror*, in November 1943 *The Bell* published a reply to Ultach's booklet. ' "Orange Terror" A Demurrer', appeared under the pseudonym 'Ultach Eile' and argued that the basis of partition, sectarian discrimination, and civil unrest was economic rather than religious, claiming that 'The persecution of the Catholics in the Six Counties arises from the scarcity of jobs and the system of Orange foremen under a government which derives its support from the conflict thus engendered'. Ultach Eile conceded that Protestants lagged behind Catholic workers in political development, but criticized the tendency to cast Protestants as foreign and alien, asking that the term 'Planter stock' be retired. He reserved his strongest words for the 'Six County Bosses', however, and suggested that their attitude had had a direct bearing on Ireland's place in the war:

> Had it not been for them an Independent Ireland would have arisen long ago, and the relations between the two free peoples would have been such good neighbour relations, that in the opinion of many people, including the writer, we should, whether wisely or not, have been in this war, whereas the mischief-makers have not been able to carry even their own followers into it. The flares of war have revealed them to people on both sides of the Channel as an anachronism.[140]

Orange Terror and Ultach Eile's response provoked considerable reaction. The following month a piece by a student from Trinity College Dublin was published, entitled 'A Protestant Visits Belfast'. From a northern family who had moved to Munster before his birth, Harry Craig wrote of reading *Orange Terror* that 'The whole record filled me with humiliation'.[141] Deputed by college friends to travel north, he assembled a collection of anecdotal evidence from a variety of informants which tended to support Ultach Eile's economic analysis of the situation, and suggested that the lower level of political violence during the war was a result of the fall in unemployment. For Craig the war had offered the potential for cross-sectarian and cross-border cooperation, but this had been quickly

---

[140] 'Ultach Eile', ' "Orange Terror" A Demurrer', *The Bell* 7, no. 2 (November 1943), pp. 137–142 (pp. 139–140, pp. 141–142, p. 142).
[141] Craig, 'A Protestant Visits Belfast', *The Bell* 7, no. 3, p. 236.

snuffed out by a Stormont administration which liked 'neither a shaking border nor a united people':

> A shipyard worker told me that: 'When a large section of the Catholic population were carrying wreaths for the graves of their dead a Crossley tender pulled out in front.' The bully-tactics again, as old as the Mournes, still yielding results. Other minor incidents, cleverly stimulated, renewed the friction and Stormont began to sleep more happily on the hatred it engendered.[142]

The following February the Dean of Belfast waded into the fray, with ' "Orange Terror": A Rebuttal', which excoriated the original booklet's 'evil misrepresentations', dismissed the idea that Catholics were being persecuted or excluded from the workplace, and mocked Craig's piece, sarcastically inquiring as to whether he had spent a whole weekend in the city.[143] In a letter published in the same issue Robert Greacen was also critical of Craig, writing that visitors who spent mere brief spells in Belfast were unqualified to attempt an analysis of the situation, and claiming that well-intentioned left-wing journalists were causing 'incalculable damage to the cause of reconciliation which they so blatantly profess'.[144]

In March 1944 *The Bell* carried an article under the name of the Ulster Union Club, giving the movement's own reaction to this ongoing debate. Given that Denis Ireland had already contributed to the magazine, and was President of the club, it is likely that he was the writer of this response, entitled 'Ulster: a Reply. The Strings, My Lord, Are False'. Describing the argument between *Orange Terror* and the Dean as 'atrocity swapping', Ireland complained that the exchange had contributed to the common misapprehension that all nationalists were Catholic.[145] He dismissed the Dean's claims that the Catholic minority found it easy to find work in Belfast since these had not taken account of 'abnormal circumstances of present war', and on behalf of the club proceeded to address the prospects for Irish unity in the context of the war:

> As an example of the difference between our constructive way of thinking and that unprogressive mentality behind and supporting the Dean of Belfast, it is only necessary to mention the war, since in war-time all policies necessarily issue in terms of military strategy. From the moment the French Republic collapsed in June, 1940, all our thinking was directed towards

[142] Craig, 'A Protestant Visits Belfast', *The Bell* 7, no. 3, p. 238, p. 241.

[143] Dean of Belfast, '"Orange Terror": A Rebuttal', *The Bell* 7, no. 5 (February 1944), pp. 382–393(p. 389).

[144] 'Public Opinion', *The Bell* 7, no. 5, p. 454. Cahir Healy also quoted from Craig's article in *The Mutilation of a Nation*, p. 27.

[145] Ulster Union Club, 'Ulster: a Reply', *The Bell* 7, no. 6 (March 1944), pp. 474–484(p. 475, p. 477).

a plan whereby at any rate functional military unity could be secured in Ireland. Our attitude was that of standing on what Professor Savory calls our 'nobility', that is, remaining for the most part at home and withdrawing British and American forces, we Protestants of Northern Ireland should have said to our Catholic fellow-countrymen:—'We do not share many of your opinions about this war. But since, so long as Partition lasts, Ireland cannot be in it as a whole, or to any full degree—since, beyond making money out of war industry, we ourselves are playing only a minute fraction of a part in it, then we too will become neutral—on three conditions. First, that for an agreed period Northern Ireland remains a Federal State within an Irish national framework; second, unity of Defence having been achieved, the question of continuing the present policy of neutrality or of entering upon a defensive alliance with Great Britain to be decided by a united Irish parliament; third, that you introduce conscription for a National Army of Defence in the Twenty Six Counties at the same moment as we do in the Six.[146]

Following Irish unity on these lines, Denis Ireland argued, British and American forces would have been 'released for service elsewhere', a unified Ireland would voluntarily have entered the war, and the northern province would then have been able to play a major role in the war, rather than remaining 'at home without even making a large scale effort to defend her corner of the island'.[147] From this extended hypothesis, one may draw the conclusion that Denis Ireland believed Northern Ireland should have been playing a greater role in the war. This belief clearly indicates his eccentricity to most nationalist opinion.

Denis Ireland continued to dwell on Northern Ireland's role in the Second World War in post-war writings. In the punningly titled pamphlet *Letters from Ireland* (1945) he published a series of open letters to five real and symbolic figures: Winston Churchill, 'The Shade of William III', 'A Fellow-Protestant', 'John Bull', and 'John Bull's New Manager'. The letter to Churchill, signed 'Late Captain, Royal Irish Fusiliers', opened with the ominous sound of Orange drums, sounded to celebrate 'Peace' in Europe. Ireland went on to take issue with the British prime minister's famous victory broadcast hailing the fidelity of Northern Ireland during the war, arguing that had partition not existed, a united Ireland could have entered the war on the side of the Allies. Denis Ireland ridiculed the idea of defending a country by dividing it, and, in a sharply inflected parody of another of Churchill's speeches, argued that:

... the Irish are only more British than the British themselves in defence of their individual and national liberties. We, too, not only would fight, but have fought

---

[146] Ulster Union Club, 'Ulster: a Reply', *The Bell* 7, no. 6, p. 480, p. 481.
[147] Ulster Union Club, 'Ulster: a Reply', *The Bell* 7, no. 6, p. 482.

before now, on the beaches, in the streets, and on the mountains—particularly on the mountains, as you sir, as an English statesman, must well remember.[148]

In the letter to 'John Bull's New Manager' (Clement Attlee, presumably) he was again dismissive of the idea that the maintenance of partition was key to British security in the event of another war, betraying a nationalist fear that in the immediate aftermath of war the unionist claim on Northern Ireland had been strengthened by Churchill's victory speech.

Winston Churchill was, unsurprisingly, a pivotal presence in writing which addressed partition in the context of the Second World War. The strikingly titled *Churchill Can Unite Ireland*, by Dublin-born republican activist, novelist, and memoirist Jim Phelan, was published in London in 1940 as part of the Left Book Club's 'Victory Books' series: other titles included *Enlist India for Freedom!*, *Learn From France*, *The People's War*, and *Guilty Men*, the hugely popular polemical indictment of appeasement which appeared the same year. *Churchill Can Unite Ireland* is illustrative of the complex position occupied by Churchill at the intersection of debates over neutrality, partition, and Anglo-Irish relations.

Phelan assumes almost total ignorance of Irish matters on the part of his intended British audience. He addresses readers in semi-humorous, gently patronizing, and sometimes overtly hostile tones, drawing frequent comparisons between the present actions of the Nazis in Europe with those past of the British in Ireland. Recalling such brutalities in the first half of the book, Phelan argues that the British people in their ignorance 'did allow a man to do things in their name which Hitler has not yet surpassed', and claims that 'It is a cruel and terrible jest to make at this time—but when a speaker tries to tell the peasants of Galway or Tipperary of Nazi horrors the sincere and deeply-moved person generally exclaims that the murdering blanks are as bad as the English!' He also attacks the pro-treaty forces during the Irish Civil War as 'cunning fore-runners of the Nazi "persecuted minority racket"' and a 'Fascist mob—in emerald green uniforms', and is dismissive of hostile British press coverage of Irish neutrality and potential collaboration with Germany.[149] The figure of Churchill dominates the second half of the volume and is introduced at the opening of the chapter 'Our Enemy the Friends', the title of which exemplifies the paradoxical and unorthodox turn taken by the book:

Twenty-six years ago, in 1914, an Irish politico-financial gang ran a British politician out of town. No one who has read much about Ireland in the

British press will be greatly surprised at that. What might be a little more surprising is that the leader of the Party responsible is now Lord Craigavon, that the town was not Tipperary but Belfast, that the British politician was one Winston Churchill.[150]

Phelan's erroneous reference here is to Churchill's infamous visit to Belfast in January 1912, when, as First Lord of the Admiralty in the British Liberal government he was booed on arrival, before his car was attacked and his effigy brandished by a mob of loyalist demonstrators. Later that day he shared a platform with John Redmond at the Belfast Celtic Football Ground and was cheered by a crowd of 5,000 as he spoke in favour of Home Rule. Churchill was not sympathetic to the nationalist cause but believed that Home Rule would strengthen the Empire and the bond between Great Britain and Ireland: at this early stage he saw this alliance as vital to the defence of the United Kingdom. Angry dockers hurled rotten fish at Churchill and his wife as they left Belfast.[151] Hugh Shearman reports that Churchill's car had to make a detour on the way to the station, to avoid thousands of shipyard workers who had lined the route, their pockets filled with 'Queen's Island confetti' (rivet heads).[152] Phelan's mistaken date of 1914 is also important. On 14 March of that year Churchill made a strongly anti-unionist speech in Bradford in England, calling for a peaceful solution to the escalating situation in Ulster, taking the Tory party to task for their indiscriminate use of military force and their hypocritical support for the Boers, and arguing that the law in Ireland should be applied equally to nationalists and unionists without preference. As Phelan notes, Churchill was met with incomprehension 'when he tried to talk *much the same stuff as is in this book*' (Phelan's italics).[153] The Bradford speech seems to have been in wide circulation during the war: the fact that it was reprinted in full in the 1943 *Capuchin Annual*, without introduction and immediately following Conal Casey's anti-partitionist travel piece 'Journey in Ulster', is telling in itself.[154] Under the heading 'A Statesman's View of Northern Ireland' Cahir Healy used an extract from the speech to open the pamphlet *The Mutilation of a Nation*, whilst the speech was also reprinted in full in *Churchill on Ulster*, a pamphlet published by the Socialist Party in Belfast in 1943, the foreword of which stated that it

---

[150] Phelan, *Churchill*, p. 67.
[151] Mary C. Bromage, *Churchill and Ireland* (Notre Dame, Indiana: University of Notre Dame Press, 1964), pp. 20–24.
[152] Shearman, *Not an Inch*, p. 100. Shearman adds that when Churchill visited Belfast many years later, however, 'he got a thoroughly friendly reception' (p. 101).
[153] Phelan, *Churchill*, p. 67.
[154] 'Twenty Nine Years Ago', *Capuchin Annual 1943*, pp. 502–512.

was expressly intended as a riposte to a recent broadcast by the Northern Ireland prime minister, Sir Basil Brooke.[155]

Reprinting the Bradford speech in these ways aimed to embarrass the unionist establishment by highlighting their erstwhile hostility to the now hugely popular British prime minister, and probably the single most important icon of the British war effort: in 1943 the West Belfast Labour Party published a pamphlet entitled *The Stormont Government: A Labour Indictment*, printing a speech made by Jack Beattie, Labour member for Pottinger, to the Northern Ireland House of Commons on 11 May of that year, in which Beattie opposed a government motion of confidence in the cabinet of newly installed Prime Minister Brooke and feigned mock sympathy for the departed old guard:

> Hardly one of the new government was to be seen in the bad old days when there was dirty work to be done. I don't believe that one of them, with the exception of the new Minister of Labour, even threw a stone or attempted to crack Churchill's skull when he came here in 1912![156]

The Socialist Party pamphlet *Churchill on Ulster* also attempted to capitalize on the unionist hostility to Churchill in 1912, claiming of that year's visit that 'The Party which denied freedom of speech to a member of the British Government before it became the Government of Northern Ireland is not likely to worry overmuch about free speech for its political opponents after it became the Government'. The pamphlet then quoted from a speech made by Beattie in 1942, in which he attacked the Northern Ireland government for having 'played the part of a willing tool to that despicable element in England—the diehard Imperialists, who hated everything Irish, just as they hated everything Indian', and indicted the Northern Ireland House of Commons as totalitarian, for bearing 'more relation to Hitler's Reichstag, with its membership of Storm-troopers, than to the Mother of Parliaments'.[157]

Cahir Healy's pamphlet *The Mutilation of a Nation* also highlighted the 1912 visit, in a section entitled 'How Belfast Received Churchill', which contrasted the recent invitation extended to Churchill by the Unionist Corporation of Belfast to become an 'honorary burgess' of the city with the threats made to his life three decades earlier. Healy then quotes from Hugh Shearman's biography of Craigavon, *Not an Inch*, in which Shearman had claimed that 'If Mr. Churchill had not been accompanied by his wife, he

---

[155] Healy, *Mutilation*, p. 3; *Churchill on Ulster* (Belfast: Socialist Party, 1943), p. 3.

[156] Jack Beattie, *The Stormont Cabinet: A Labour Indictment* (Belfast: West Belfast Labour Party, 1943), pp. 3–4. Beattie refers here to William Grant, then MP for Belfast, Duncairn, and Minister for Labour from May 1943 to May 1944.

[157] *Churchill on Ulster*, p. 3, p. 4.

would have been spilled out of his car and would have had his entrails kicked out on the stones of Royal Avenue', thereby turning the words of a government propagandist against the unionist establishment itself.[158] Notwithstanding Churchill's interventions in Irish affairs in the three decades since the Bradford speech, the troubled visit of 1912 and the speech of 1914 were gleefully appropriated by nationalist and socialist pamphleteers, who sought to highlight and exploit a perceived hypocrisy in the unionist government's professed support for the British war effort.[159]

In *Churchill Can Unite Ireland* Phelan took matters further, and expressed a hope that Churchill's personality itself could effect positive change in Ireland. He saw Churchill as the only figure who could challenge what Phelan called the policy of 'punctilio', an attachment to deferential attitudes that kept vested interests in control of the British establishment, and identified a cultural shift in Britain, resulting from Churchill's recent replacement of Chamberlain as prime minister. Phelan cited an article by H.G. Wells in *Reynolds News*, in which the writer had:

> ... scattered a few more frills behind which the English few have been hiding ... *He wrote like Fintan Lawlor.* [*sic*]
>
> Now *there* is language at last that the people of Austria and Czechoslovakia and Ireland can understand. It may be that part at least of the change is due to the personal example of Winston Churchill.[160]

The remarkable hyperbolic equation of Wells and Lalor is demonstrative of the extraordinary leaps in thought seemingly possible at this time, but what excited Phelan here was the loosening of British political discourse, the idea in fact that 'the British are talking like the Irish at last'. As one of the 'worst offenders' in plain speaking he held Churchill largely responsible for this change in tone and approach. Having implied, with another extraordinary leap, that Churchill was in some way 'Irish' in character if not in nationality, Phelan belatedly began to work through the claim made

---

[158] Healy, *Mutilation*, p. 4. Shearman, *Not an Inch*, p. 100.

[159] St John Ervine admired Churchill's role in the Second World War but remained critical of his visit to Belfast in 1912. Recalling how demonstrators held back from upending Churchill's car when they spotted his wife sitting beside him, Ervine wrote in 1949 that: 'It is appalling to think of what our fate might have been twenty-eight years later if Mrs Churchill had not accompanied her husband. For those angry men would certainly have turned the car over, and the great orator who rallied his country in a day of dire disaster might have perished in a fatuous adventure' (Ervine, *Craigavon: Ulsterman*, p. 214).

[160] Phelan, *Churchill*, p. 97, p. 99. James Fintan Lalor (1807–1849) advocated radical reform of the landholding system in Ireland in the mid-nineteenth century. He contributed to *The Nation* and later founded the *Irish Felon* newspaper. Half a century after his death his ideas were to prove influential on the leaders of the 1916 Easter Rising. (R.V. Comerford, 'Lalor, James Fintan (1807–1849)', *DNB*, <http://www.oxforddnb.com/view/article/15906>).

in the title of his book. He suggested that if Irish talks were scheduled
between Churchill, de Valera, Peadar O'Donnell, Craigavon, Jake Kilroy
(or another representative of the IRA), Cathal O'Shannon (to represent
Labour in Éire), Pat Fox (to represent Labour in Northern Ireland), Sean
O'Casey (to speak for the Irish Citizen Army and other adherents of James
Connolly), and a random peasant (to represent himself), the result would
be Irish unity. In Phelan's hypothesis, Churchill would offer British and
French troops to defend a united Ireland, and in answer to Craigavon's
inevitable protestations would ask the northern prime minister to prove
his ultimate loyalty by acquiescing. 'The abolition of the border', Phelan
suggests satirically, 'will be dangerously complex and long-drawn out and
generally difficult. It might even need three hours' work and a dozen type-
written forms'.[161]

There is no point in commenting on the historical accuracy or otherwise
of Phelan's argument: it is by turns deliberately hyperbolic and provocative,
and his hypothetical flights of conjecture and imagination are at times as
baffling as those of Denis Ireland. Like Ireland's writings, *Churchill Can
Unite Ireland* is illustrative of the curious and eccentric lines of reasoning
made possible by the wartime context, whereby a confirmed republican
could assert his faith in a Conservative and Unionist British prime minister
as part of a wider argument in favour of Irish unity. Like the reprints of
the Bradford speech, Phelan's book also highlights the problematic relationship between the unionist establishment and Winston Churchill. Despite
repeated expressions of loyalty to the British war effort, unionist mistrust of
the British government in London continued to percolate over the course of
the war, partly due to Churchill's perceived willingness to deal with de Valera.
Eerily, the final lines of Phelan's book (published in 1940), read: 'Liberty
does not grow on trees; it must be fought for. Not "now or never". Now'.[162]
These foreshadow the words of the infamous telegram from Churchill to de
Valera following the bombing of Pearl Harbor in 1941, which, it is implied,
offered Irish unity in return for Éire's entry into the war on the side of Allies,
and read in part 'Now is your chance. Now or never. A Nation once again'.[163]

* * *

To draw together the arguments and concerns expressed in the diverse
range of publications explored in this chapter, we might consider the
various cultural and political uses of one highly malleable word, 'bridgehead', in works by writers of all shades of opinion in relation to Northern

---

[161] Phelan, *Churchill*, p. 103, p. 112, p. 115.   [162] Phelan, *Churchill*, p. 120.
[163] John Bowman, *De Valera and the Ulster Question 1917–1973* (Oxford: Clarendon
Press, 1982), p. 246.

Ireland and the Second World War. As I noted in the second chapter of this book, Robert Greacen expressed a hope in the *New Northman* in 1942 that Northern Ireland could 'act as the bridgehead between Ireland and Great Britain and ... suck the best out of the English, the Gaelic and the Anglo-Irish cultures', suggesting that the province might benefit from its singular geographical location.[164] More equivocally, the historian J.C. Beckett wrote in 1943 that 'Ulster's highest duty is to maintain an Anglo-Irish bridgehead, or at least stronghold, a place where the typical Anglo-Irish virtues, not very attractive virtues, can be bred'.[165]

For others the word had more negative connotations. Greacen reused his own optimistic sentiments in an article on 'Drama Up North' for *The Bell* in February 1947, but in the same issue Peadar O'Donnell's editorial 'Whose Bridgehead?' argued that if the British government were to renounce the idea that Northern Ireland was a 'bridgehead' for the British Empire then Irish unity would quickly follow.[166] Using the word in its original military sense, O'Donnell thereby argued that the partition of Ireland was deliberately strategic. A subsequent article by the secretary of the Ulster Unionist Association, W. Douglas, responded angrily to the editorial. Douglas was keen to emphasize the critical role of the province in the Allied invasion of Europe:

> It will be as the Bridgehead—that vital stepping stone between the great American Democracy and Europe—that Ulster's name will go down in the history of the conflict. Across that stepping stone fully 400,000 American troops passed and with them came thousands of tons of war material—guns, tanks, aircraft, equipment of every kind.[167]

The capitalized appearance of 'Bridgehead' here differs again from Greacen's conception, and credits the province with a greater role than is permitted by O'Donnell. In addition to its function as a staging post for this panoply of military hardware, it is implied that Northern Ireland is newly ideologically important as a 'vital' conduit for the flow of democratic ideas between America and Western Europe.

In *The Bell* of March 1951 Peadar O'Donnell again used the term, in an editorial 'Pointer to an Article' introducing Seán Ó Faoláin's essay 'Autoantiamericanism', which warned against kneejerk resistance to the growing influence of American culture in Ireland. O'Donnell writes of Ireland sending its youth to join the expanding population of the United

---

[164] Greacen, 'A Survey of Ulster Writing'. *The Northman XI*, no. 2, p. 10.
[165] Letter from J.C. Beckett to John Boyd, 8 November 1943, John Boyd Collection.
[166] 'Whose Bridgehead', *The Bell* 13, no. 5 (February 1947), pp. 1–2.
[167] W. Douglas, 'Impossibility of Irish Union', *The Bell* 14, no. 1 (April 1947), pp. 33–40(p. 38).

States, via the underworlds of the poorest parts of cities. 'From those early squalid bridgeheads Irish exiles won their way onto the level of normal American work-a-day life'.[168] In the following issue the word appeared again, in 'Fears of Ulster Protestants'—a combative dialogue between Revered F.S. Leahy of the Irish Evangelical Church and the republican activist and writer George Gilmore, in which the latter refers to Northern Ireland as 'a Tory bridgehead statelet'.[169]

The word clearly has many applications in relation to Northern Ireland. It is used approvingly and theoretically by the liberal poet Greacen, keen to encourage cultural exchange, as an anti-colonial term of opprobrium by nationalists and republicans, but is also favoured by unionist writers keen to secure the status of Northern Ireland as a British military necessity. In his 1949 study of Craigavon St John Ervine wrote that 'No sensible person can, or does, deny that the maintenance of the bridgehead in Northern Ireland was a vital necessity of that war', whilst in a speech to the Northern Ireland House of Commons in October 1946 Prime Minister Basil Brooke twice referred to Northern Ireland as a 'bridgehead'.[170] In the first instance he used the term in a strategic context, crediting partition with ensuring the safety of the whole island of Ireland:

> It was a fact—and perhaps hon. Members do not know this—that this was the bridgehead, and that the British army was standing ready to move to the rescue of the free state, should they have been invaded. That is what prevented these islands from suffering the horrors of war.[171]

Brooke also used the word more symbolically, describing the province as the 'bridgehead, the Rock of Gibraltar as it was called...the mainstay in the Battle of the Atlantic'.[172] John W. Blake similarly deployed the term, claiming that, following the entry of the United States into the European war, Northern Ireland 'provided a natural bridgehead between the Atlantic ports of North America and the western seaboard of Great Britain', and that, as the first troops arrived:

> Northern Ireland was now, so to speak, a bridgehead between the parts of the English speaking world. Whilst Eire [*sic*] was engaged in issuing a formal protest against the occupation of Irish soil by United States troops, Northern

---

[168] 'Pointer to an Article', *The Bell* 16, no. 6 (March 1951), pp. 5–7 (p. 6).

[169] Leahy and Gilmore, 'Fears of Ulster Protestants', *The Bell*, 17, no. 1 (April 1951), 19–25 (p. 23).

[170] Ervine, *Craigavon*, p. 578.

[171] *Parliamentary Debates: Northern Ireland House of Commons Official Report*, XXX (Belfast: HMSO, 1947), 5 March 1946–31 March 1947, column 1965.

[172] *Parliamentary Debates: Northern Ireland House of Commons*, XXX, 5 March 1946–31, March 1947, column 1971.

Ireland, full partner with Great Britain and the U.S.A. in war, was setting about the task of making the soldier from the New World feel at home.[173]

He also reported that in June 1940 a brigade of Royal Marines was stationed at Milford Haven in Wales, ready in the event of a German invasion of Ireland 'to seize a bridgehead in Eire [*sic*] through which reinforcements could be introduced from Great Britain'.[174] Blake, indeed, seems to have dwelt on the polyvalent practical and theoretical significance of the word, claiming with some hubris in the conclusion of his account of the American influx, that Northern Ireland:

> ... might in the light of history conceive herself to be a meeting place of east and west. It was not wholly fanciful to think of Northern Ireland in this war as a land where the divergent ways of the eastern and western parts of the North Atlantic civilisation, which time, distance and environment had produced, could be brought together and perhaps become in some measure reconciled . . . Geography and history, high strategy and current politics, had thus combined to enable Northern Ireland to come into her own as the Atlantic bridgehead.[175]

It is striking how closely Blake's conception resembles Denis Ireland's hopes for a united Ireland: in *Eamon de Valera Doesn't See it Through: A Study of Irish Politics in the Machine Age* (1941) he argued that 'we should remember the location of those four green fields in the Atlantic, not only as an outpost of European civilization but also, and to an increasing extent, as the stepping-stone and connecting link between Britain and America'. Denis Ireland does not use the word 'bridgehead', but also sought to exploit a geographical fortuity, claiming that:

> ... the facts of geography and invention already unmistakably demonstrate that Ireland's real national destiny in the twentieth century is to become neither a museum piece nor a temporary lodging for exiles, but the link and intermediary between the Old World and the New.[176]

The historian Trevor Allen has noted that the codenames given to British and Irish cities during the war by German intelligence forces were often appropriate to the nature of the places they described: the steel-producing city of Sheffield, for instance, was known as 'Schmelztiegel' or 'crucible'. Belfast was given the name 'Etappe', which in the context in which it was used meant 'stage, or staging post in lines of communication'. Allen suggests that such a description 'clearly fitted the entrance to Belfast Lough

---

[173] Blake, p. 46, p. 271.   [174] Blake, p. 157.   [175] Blake, pp. 298–299.
[176] Denis Ireland, *Eamon de Valera Doesn't See it Through: A Study of Irish Politics in the Machine Age* (Cork: Forum Press, 1941), p. 55, p. 61.

with its busy anchorages', but the idea of such a 'staging post' also reflects the various attempts to fix Northern Ireland's place in relation to the war.[177]

The terms 'bridgehead' and 'staging post' are illustrative of Northern Ireland's political culture during the war years, emphasizing the prevailing sense of uncertainty at this time. If the province existed in a state of inter-regnum between 1939 and 1945, this was particularly visible in the written political culture of the time. Hostilities between nationalists and unionists may have subsided for the duration of the war, but the ongoing debate over partition and the treatment of the Catholic population was undoubt-edly altered and complicated by the practical, ideological, and psycho-logical external pressures that were brought to bear on the province at this time. The role of Northern Ireland in the Allied war effort would seem to have cemented its place within the United Kingdom and strengthened the position of the unionist establishment, but officially commissioned works by Blake and Shearman which aimed to burnish the province's war record suggest that the highly contingent nature of this newfound international stature had not gone unnoticed. The sheer enormity of the war and the pervasiveness of its effects in Northern Ireland posed a severe challenge to idealistic and isolationist nationalism in the province, demonstrated by the strained nature of the Ulster travelogues which appeared in the *Capuchin Annual*. The war years fostered a cross-generic and intertextual approach, exemplified by Ultach's *Orange Terror*, which addressed the problems of the present by drawing together statistical data, polemical argument, and visual material, and quoted at length from political oppo-nents. This strategy is reflected in the works of nationalist, socialist, and unionist writers: the use of quotation was particularly widespread at this time, sometimes to surprising effect. The adoption of Winston Churchill's 1914 Bradford speech by nationalist and socialist pamphleteers is demon-strative of the curious patterns of debate during the war, whereby Paddy Devlin, interned in Crumlin Road Gaol during the later years of the war, was surprised to hear fellow republican prisoners praising the British for their part in the war against Hitler and Mussolini.[178] The wartime pub-lications of Denis Ireland and Jim Phelan show how the wartime con-text encouraged such extraordinary leaps in thought, as local issues were re-examined in light of international developments.

The multifarious uses of the term 'bridgehead' reflects the nature of the debate, whereby terms such as 'quisling' or 'Sudetenland', indelibly associ-ated with the European conflict, were appropriated for use in very differ-ent arguments. The tendency of writers of all shades of political opinion

---

[177] Trevor Allen, *Storm Passed By*, p. 111.   [178] Devlin, *Straight Left*, p. 49.

to draw comparisons between the specific situation at home and newly febrile arenas of conflict elsewhere in Europe and further afield shows how the political geography of the province was reconfigured: whilst Bew, Gibbons, and Patterson focus on the economic and political 'deinsulation' of Northern Ireland during and immediately after the Second World War, this was very much a cultural process as well.

Afterword: 'We had met people very different from ourselves'

Victory in Europe was celebrated in Northern Ireland on 8 May 1945. The war in the Far East would continue for another three months, and James Magennis's night mission did not take place until the end of July 1945. On VE day the sun shone, as services of thanksgiving were held and masses were offered to future peace.[1] Bunting appeared, flags were waved, and bonfires were lit. Huge crowds gathered outside Belfast City Hall to listen to Churchill's Victory broadcast, relayed via loudspeaker at 3 p.m. In Newtownbutler both Catholic and Protestant bands led a procession of servicemen through the village, but many nationalists took no part in the celebrations.[2] An unnamed local historian describes the mixed reaction to the end of the war in the city of Derry:

> Opinion tends to be that Derry nationalists, while relieved that the war was over, found the sort of jingoistic patriotism that such occasions inspired to be alien. In a way too, it marked the end of an era during which Derry had enjoyed unprecedented activity and experienced a diversity of cultures from around the world. With the war over, Derry returned to anonymity and was once again relegated to the history books.[3]

In retrospect, given the central place of Derry in Northern Ireland's turbulent post-war history, the writer's references to 'anonymity' and 'the history books' seem grimly ironic, since the city is now more readily and indelibly associated with the Troubles.

Dennis Kennedy, eight years old at the time of VE day, recalls in his memoir *Climbing Slemish* that at the end of his street in Lisburn a bonfire was built on which an effigy of Hitler was burned. With his mother, Kennedy travelled into Belfast the following day to witness raucous celebrations in the centre of the city. On the way home they heard the local RUC sergeant ordering people to 'Put up that bunting'. Kennedy observes that 'Only one war was over'.[4] Clair

---

[1] *The War Years: Derry 1939–45*, p. 53.
[2] McCusker, *Castle Archdale and Fermanagh in World War II*, 146.
[3] *The War Years: Derry 1939–45*, p. 53.   [4] Dennis Kennedy, *Slemish*, p. 222.

Wills has written of her sense, when writing a cultural history of Ireland during the war, that she was measuring the country 'against a chronology which isn't really its own', and anecdotes such as Kennedy's illustrate the difficulties of incorporating the six-year-long Second World War into the open-ended, endlessly fraught, and contested history of Ireland, or indeed of incorporating Ireland into narratives of the war.[5] Whilst acknowledging these difficulties, it is also clear that it is no longer possible or credible to ignore the impact of the war on the course of twentieth-century Irish history, north or south of the border.

This book has explored the works of writers and artists who have tried to register the impact of the Second World War on their lives and localities. In this respect, Kennedy's view of the significance of the war to his life and those of his contemporaries is illuminating:

> We were children of the war, and had lived through one of the most appalling periods in human history. Millions had died in conflict and in air-raids on civilian targets and in the systematic extermination of the Holocaust. Cities across Europe had been destroyed, and in Japan the atom-bombs had taken devastation to a new level of awfulness.
>
> Yet we remained almost untouched by it. We had seen one or two nights of blitz from our bedroom window, and had wandered around smouldering ruins in Belfast, but there were no bombs in Causeway End.
> ...
> The war taught us a lot. We knew all about Hitler and Mussolini, about Roosevelt and Stalin. We could show you Tripoli and Murmansk on the map, and Stalingrad and Caen, and Tokyo and Hiroshima.
>
> We had met people very different from ourselves.[6]

These recollections summarize the unresolved contradiction between the idea that the war exposed the province to new external influences ('The war taught us a lot', 'We had met people very different from ourselves'), and the sense of literal and cultural isolation at this time ('Yet we remained almost untouched by it'). Kennedy's observations show how the historical importance and global scale of the war were felt in the province, whilst (for those outside Belfast and Derry, at least) its direct, destructive, and fatal effects were muted.

The very magnitude of the conflict, and the moral imperative (often retrospectively) attached to the campaign against Nazi Germany, have undoubtedly complicated the ways in which the war has been debated in Ireland. During and immediately after the conflict both nationalist and unionist writers addressed the question of what the Second World War could mean for Northern Ireland with vigour and imagination, but since then, it seems, sectarian divisions have determined political attitudes

---

[5] Wills, *That Neutral Island*, p. 11.   [6] Dennis Kennedy, *Slemish*, p. 223.

towards the events of 1939–45. For unionists and loyalists, the battles of the Second World War have never attained the same mythical status as the Somme, but some attempts were made to draw Northern Ireland's role in the Second World War into unionist rhetoric. In 1981 the leader of the Democratic Unionist Party Ian Paisley (who did not serve in the British armed forces during the war) berated the then Taoiseach Charles Haughey as a 'green aggressor and conspirator', and claimed that 'When our forefathers donned the British uniform and fought for King and Country, Mr Haughey's fellow countrymen used their lights to guide enemy bombers to their targets in Northern Ireland'.[7] In 1989 the leader of the Ulster Unionist Party James Molyneaux, who served in the RAF during the war, took part in the D-Day landings, and arrived at Belsen three days after it had been liberated by the Allied Second Army, seemed keen, in his authorized biography, to draw parallels between his experiences during the war and his post-war political career. Most contentiously he compared working with the existing Nazi leadership at local level in Germany following surrender with his attempts to cooperate with nationalists during his time as a local councillor in Antrim: 'It went hard with us as it sometimes goes hard with us nowadays when you see people who are in line with violence—Sinn Fein—and you have to sit in councils and work with them. It was the same feeling then'.[8] Another Unionist Party leader, Brian Faulkner, who worked in the family shirt factory during the war, admitted in his *Memoirs of a Statesman* (1978) that in retrospect it had been 'foolish' not to enlist in the armed forces, claiming that 'medals and a military rank were valuable assets for political advancement in the post-war world, and lack of either was a serious obstacle to overcome'.[9] Since the events of the late 1960s, and the escalation of political violence throughout the 1970s and 1980s, the significance of the Second World War to the social, political, and cultural life of Northern Ireland has become less and less apparent, however.

Such uncertainty is vividly sketched in an exchange in Glenn Patterson's Belfast-set *Burning Your Own* (1988), in which a boy explains to the novel's young protagonist why the fictional Larkview housing estate on which they both live was built:

> 'Well, look, they grew up in the war, most of the people that bought houses on this estate. In the war or in the thirties. Not that much to fucking choose between the two if you're from Northern Ireland. There were riots in the

---

[7] John D. Brewer with Gareth I. Higgins, *Anti Catholicism in Northern Ireland, 1600–1998: The Mote and the Beam* (Basingstoke: Macmillan, 1998), p. 109, p. 114.

[8] Ann Purdy, *Molyneaux: the Long View* (Antrim: Greystone, 1989), p. 33.

[9] Brian Faulkner, *Memoirs of a Statesman*, edited by John Houston (London: Weidenfield and Nicholson, 1978), p. 14.

thirties, you know, things that make the stuff today look normal—house-burnings, killings, the lot. Bit like the war, only without the uniforms and on your own doorstep. The war had that going for it: by and by it happened somewhere else. And then, it wasn't as bad as the first one—no trenches, or any of that shit, not the same danger of the men coming home all packed up in their old kitbags . . .

'But after the celebrations, when the rationing continued and the work didn't, people started to catch themselves on. Whole areas had gone'—he snapped his fingers—'phut! And there they were having to live in prefabs or with their relatives . . . Suddenly just winning didn't seem to be enough. And it wasn't only the usual sort complained. D'you see what I'm getting at?'[10]

Satirizing the narrative of the People's War, Patterson also offers an earthy illustration of some of the ironies and inconsistencies in Northern Ireland's experience of the Second World War: though Francy flippantly claims that 'by and by it happened somewhere else' he also emphasizes the scale of destruction in Belfast resulting from aerial bombardment, saying that 'Whole areas had gone'. This passage also questions how the significance for Northern Ireland of a series of local and international conflicts might be established and compared. Any sense of the estate as a product of the progressive programme of social change effected by the Second World War is undercut by the semi-humorous dismissal of the war as just another episode in the troubled history of the province ('Not that much to fuck-ing choose between the two if you're from Northern Ireland'), whilst it is suggested that the violence of the late 1980s is of a lesser order than the sectarian riots of the 1930s ('things that make the stuff today look nor-mal'). Patterson also notes the lesser status of the Second World War in the province, when set against sacrifices made during the First World War. Like Frank Ormsby in his poem 'Some of Us Stayed Forever', Patterson suggests that the history of the province is more complex and extensive than the events of the late twentieth century have allowed.

Some of the writers and artists whose works I have examined detected echoes of their experience of Northern Ireland during the Second World War in the years of the Troubles. Colin Middleton claimed that the 'ten-sion, the repressed anxiety' he felt in the early 1970s was reminiscent of the war years, whilst Roy McFadden wrote of the fires and petrol bombs in Belfast in August 1969 that 'It's almost like wartime again. One measures food and remembers that rationed but keyed-up existence'.[11] Given the awkward position of the Second World War in relation to the

---

[10] Glenn Patterson, *Burning Your Own* (London: Chatto and Windus, 1988) pp. 18–19.
[11] Harriet Cooke, 'Colin Middleton', *Irish Times*, 1 January 1973; Letter from McFadden to Greacen, 17 August 1969, Greacen Collection, Box 4, File 3.

ongoing sectarian conflict, and the fact that the engagements were so different in nature, it is perhaps unsurprising that such comparisons are not more common. The Waterford-born travel writer Dervla Murphy explored some connections between the Troubles and the Second World War in *A Place Apart* (1978), an account of a journey by bicycle around the province. She notes that in Belfast at this time references to 'the war' are made 'quite unselfconsciously, just as the British might refer to their world wars', and writes that the city 'today is often compared with London during the Blitz. But at least the Londoners were united against an identifiable foreign foe and not exposed to the furtive exploits of their own society'.[12] Murphy later cites a report published by the Northern Ireland Community Relations Commission, stating that between 1969 and 1972 the province experienced the most widespread forced movement of populations to take place in Western Europe since the Second World War, as 60,000 people (eighty per cent of whom were Catholic) had to leave their homes.[13]

Outsiders may find it easier to draw links between the Second World War and the Troubles. John Depol, an artist and engraver who was stationed with the United States Army Air Force at Toomebridge Aerodrome in County Antrim during the war, returned to Northern Ireland in 1978 with his wife, and was dismayed by the changes in the physical environment that he saw:

> The road past our former headquarters near the ancient stone bridge was now a highway. HQ and the rest of the aerodrome had disappeared except for a few Thorne huts and some brick remnants, and the concrete foundations, on which had stood the mess hall and Aero club. Brush and trees grew at the edge of these foundations, and several houses were built on the concrete slabs . . .
>
> As we entered and left the larger towns, there were concrete forts out of the ports of which we saw scrutinizing eyes of soldiers and their automatic rifles aimed at us as we passed slowly by. We arrived in Belfast, but I did not recognize it. There were reels of barbed wire and rubble in the streets with armed patrols passing us on foot and others stationed in doorways. The inner city was cordoned off and passes were examined at checkpoints. How strange, and sad, for we could not see the city we had so well remembered in wartime.[14]

---

[12] Dervla Murphy, *A Place Apart* (Harmondsworth: Penguin, 1979), p. 132, p. 134.

[13] Murphy, *A Place Apart*, p. 182.

[14] John Depol, *Ireland Remembered* (Madison, NJ: Fairleigh Dickinson University, 1982), pp. 29–30.

This book has attempted to open up these matters for discussion. American literature and military archives lie beyond its scope, but Depol's drawings and writings suggest that the experiences of US service personnel and of soldiers and refugees from other countries in Northern Ireland during the war deserve full cultural and sociological study.

The war brought new figures into Northern Ireland but also prevented people from leaving. In *Ireland: A Social and Cultural History*, Terence Brown draws on the work of Clifford Geertz, who argued in the essay 'After the Revolution: The Fate of Nationalism in the New States' that newly independent states in the twentieth century exhibited a tension between epochalism and essentialism—impulses which encouraged states either 'to move with the tide of the present [or] to hold on to an inherited course'. Brown argues that these terms are 'highly illuminatory of the Irish experience since independence', and Geertz's distinction is certainly relevant to Northern Ireland's experience of the Second World War.[15] The tension between the two impulses can be observed in all the chapters of this study: in Kiely's fuzzy topography, in John Hewitt's regionalist vacillations, in Middleton's Belfast surrealism, but perhaps most clearly in the political debate between those who believed in adhering to the neutral policy of the southern state and those who wished to show that Northern Ireland was fully involved in the British war effort, and was an active and morally righteous participant in the global war.

As I suggested in the first chapter of this book, in relation to the involvement of the southern fire brigades in fighting fires in Belfast following the Easter Tuesday raid of 15 April 1941, it is possible that the Second World War will be increasingly explored as a way of establishing a semi-official shared history in Northern Ireland. Narratives of the war have the ability to cut across sectarian boundaries, by emphasizing the cross-community experience of destruction that, crucially, derived from an external source. In September 2005, to mark the sixtieth anniversary of VJ day, and six years after the memorial outside the City Hall had been unveiled, a mural of the Catholic seaman James Magennis appeared in the loyalist estate of Tullycarnet, East Belfast. It replaced an Ulster Freedom Fighters mural, which had depicted a soldier with a skull's head, and had included a silhouette of the grim reaper in the background.[16] The new mural was unveiled by local MP and MLA, and future First Minister of Northern Ireland, Peter Robinson. Speaking at the time, the loyalist activist and politician Frankie Gallagher commented that:

> When you know local history, it is not such a strange thing to happen. One of the challenges of this mural is education, it's about learning local

[15] Brown, *Ireland: A Social and Cultural History 1922–2002*, p. 169.
[16] 'Catholic Face in Loyalist Estate', BBC News website, 19 September 2005, <http://news.bbc.co.uk/2/hi/uk_news/northern_ireland/4259524.stm>.

history. We spend all our years learning about English Tudors and all the rest of it and we don't actually know what happened to each other across the divides. With taking this type of approach we are going to end up with a better understanding of each others' perspectives within each others' communities.[17]

[17] 'Catholic Face in Loyalist Estate', BBC News website, 19 September 2005.

Bibliography

Allen, Nicholas, and Aaron Kelly, eds. *The Cities of Belfast* (Belfast: Four Courts, 2003).

Allen, Trevor. *The Storm Passed By: Ireland and the Battle of the Atlantic* (Blackrock, Dublin: Irish Academic Press, 1996).

Appleyard, Brian. *The Pleasures of Peace: Art and Imagination in Post War Britain* (London: Faber and Faber, 1989).

Bardon, Jonathan. *Belfast: An Illustrated History* (Belfast: Blackstaff Press, 1982).

Barton, Brian. *The Blitz: Belfast in the War Years* (Belfast: Blackstaff Press, 1989).

Barton, Brian. *Northern Ireland in the Second World War* (Belfast: Ulster Historical Foundation, 1995).

Beattie, Jack. *The Stormont Cabinet: A Labour Indictment* (Belfast: West Belfast Labour Party, 1943).

Belfast Telegraph. Bombs over Belfast (Belfast: Belfast Telegraph, 2001).

Bell, Sam Hanna. *The Theatre in Ulster: A Survey of the Dramatic Movement in Ulster from 1902 until the Present Day* (Dublin: Gill and Macmillan, 1972).

Bell, Sam Hanna, Nesca Robb and John Hewitt, eds. *The Arts in Ulster: A Symposium* (London: Harrap, 1971).

Bew, Paul, Peter Gibbon and Henry Patterson. *The State in Northern Ireland 1921–72* (Manchester: Manchester University Press, 1979).

Black, Eileen. 'Scenes of Ulster Life: The Paintings and Drawings of William Conor', *Irish Arts Review Yearbook*, 18 (2002), pp. 146–152.

Blake, John W. *Northern Ireland in the Second World War* (London: HMSO, 1956, repr. Belfast: Blackstaff Press, 2000, ed. by Brian Barton).

Blythe, Ronald, ed. *Components of the Scene: Stories, Poems and Essays of the Second World War* (Harmondsworth: Penguin, 1966).

Boorman, John. *Hope and Glory* (United Kingdom: Columbia Pictures Corporation, Nelson Entertainment, Goldcrest Films International, 1987).

Bowen, Elizabeth. *The Heat of the Day* (London: Jonathan Cape, 1949).

Bowman, John. *De Valera and the Ulster Question, 1917–1973* (Oxford: Clarendon Press, 1982).

Bradbury, Malcolm. *No, Not Bloomsbury* (London: Andre Deutsch, 1987).

Brearton, Fran, and Alan Gillis, eds. *The Oxford Handbook of Modern Irish Poetry* (Oxford: Oxford University Press, 2012).

Brett, C.E.B. *Long Shadows Cast Before: Nine Lives in Ulster, 1625–1977* (Edinburgh and London: John Bartholomew & Son Ltd, 1978).

Brewer, John D., and Gareth I. Higgins. *Anti Catholicism in Northern Ireland, 1600–1998: The Mote and The Beam* (Basingstoke: Macmillan, 1998).

Bromage, Mary C. *Churchill and Ireland* (Notre Dame, IN: University of Notre Dame Press, 1964).

Brooke, Rupert. *Rupert Brooke: The Collected Poems, with a Memoir by Edward Marsh* (London: Sidgwick, 1918; 3rd rev. edn. 1942, repr. 1979).

Brown, Terence. *Ireland: A Social and Cultural History, 1922–2002* (London: Fontana, 1981; 3rd rev. edn. London: Harper Perennial, 2004).

Brown, Terence. *Northern Voices: Some Poets from Ulster* (Dublin: Gill and Macmillan, 1975).

Brown, Tony, and Russell Stephens, eds. *Nations and Relations: Writing Across the British Isles* (Cardiff: New Welsh Review, 2000).

Buckland, Patrick. *A History of Northern Ireland* (Dublin: Gill and Macmillan, 1981).

Calder, Angus. *The Myth of the Blitz*, (London: Pimlico, 1991).

Calder, Angus. *The People's War: Britain 1939–1945*, (London: Jonathan Cape, 1969; rev. edn. London: Pimlico, 1992).

Campbell, Arthur, and George Campbell. *Ulster in Black and White* (Belfast: WG Baird, 1943).

Campbell, Matthew J.B., ed. *The Cambridge Companion to Contemporary Irish Poetry* (Cambridge: Cambridge University Press, 2003).

Cannadine, David, ed. *Blood, Toil, Tears and Sweat: Winston Churchill's Famous Speeches* (London: Cassell, 1989).

Carnduff, Thomas. *Life and Writings*, ed. and introduced by John Gray (Belfast: Lagan Press/Fortnight Educational Trust, 1994).

Carroll, J.T. *Ireland in the War Years, 1939–1945* (Newton Abbot: David and Charles, 1975).

Carson, Ciaran. *Collected Poems* (Oldcastle, Co. Meath: Gallery Press, 2008).

Carson, Ciaran. *The Irish for No* (Dublin: Gallery; Winston Salem, NC: Wake Forest University Press, 1987).

Casey, Daniel J. *Benedict Kiely* (Cranbury, NJ: Associated University Presses Ltd, 1974).

Cathcart, Rex. *The Most Contrary Region: The BBC in Northern Ireland 1924–1984* (Belfast: Blackstaff Press, 1984).

Catterall, Peter, and Sean McDougall, eds. *The Northern Ireland Question in British Politics* (Basingstoke: Macmillan, and New York: St Martin's Press, 1996).

Catto, Mike. *Art in Ulster: a History of Painting, Sculpture and Printmaking*, 1957–1977 (Belfast: Blackstaff Press, 1977).

Churchill, Winston S. *The World Crisis. The Aftermath* (London: Thornton Butterworth, 1929).

Comfort, Alex, and Robert Greacen, eds. *Lyra: An Anthology of New Lyric* (Billericay, Essex: The Grey Walls Press, 1942).

Communist Party of Ireland. *Craigavon in the Dock: An Indictment by the Communist Party of Ireland* (Belfast: Communist Party of Ireland, 1938).

Conor, William. *The Irish Scene* (Belfast: Derrick Maccord, 1944).

Coughlan, Patricia, and Alex Davis. *Modernism and Ireland: Poetry of the 1930s* (Cork: Cork University Press, 1995).

Coulter, Ríann. '"An Amazing Anthology of Modern Art": Place, Archetype and Identity in the Art of Colin Middleton', *Visual Culture in Britain*, 9.1 (Summer 2008), pp. 1–26.

Coulton, Barbara. *Louis MacNeice in the BBC* (London, Boston: Faber and Faber, 1980).

Craig, Patricia. *Brian Moore: A Biography* (London: Bloomsbury, 2002).

Darracott, Joseph, and Belinda Loftus. *Second World War Posters* (London: Imperial War Museum, 1972).

Davidson, Mildred. *The Poetry is in the Pity* (London: Chatto and Windus, 1972).

Dawe, Gerald. *My Mother-City* (Belfast: Lagan Press, 2007).

Dawe, Gerald, ed. *Earth Voices Whispering: An Anthology of Irish War Poetry 1914–1945* (Belfast: Blackstaff Press, 2008).

Dawe, Gerald, and Edna Longley, eds. *Across a Roaring Hill: The Protestant Imagination in Modern Ireland* (Belfast: Blackstaff Press, 1985).

Dawe, Gerald and John Wilson Foster, eds. *The Poet's Place: Ulster Literature and Society Essays in honour of John Hewitt, 1907–87* (Belfast: Institute of Irish Studies, 1991).

Deane, Seamus, ed. *The Field Day Anthology of Irish Writing, Volume III* (Cork: Cork University Press, 1991).

Deer, Patrick. *Culture in Camouflage: War, Empire, and Modern British Literature* (Oxford: Oxford University Press, 2009).

Depol, John. *Ireland Remembered* (Madison, NJ: Fairleigh Dickinson University, 1982).

Derry Heritage Library Oral History Department. *The War Years: Derry 1939–45* (Derry: Guildhall Press, 1992).

Devlin, Paddy. *Straight Left: An Autobiography* (Belfast: Blackstaff Press, 1993).

Doherty, James. *Post 381: Memoirs of a Belfast Air Raid Warden* (Belfast: Friar's Bush Press, 1989).

Doherty, Richard. *Irish Men and Women in the Second World War* (Dublin: Four Courts Press, 1999).

Doherty, Richard. *Key to Victory: the Maiden City in the Second World War* (Antrim: Greystone Books, 1995).

Donoghue, Denis. *Warrenpoint* (London: Jonathan Cape, 1991).

Eckley, Grace. *Benedict Kiely* (New York: Twayne Publishers Inc., 1972).

Eliot, T.S. *Four Quartets* (New York: Harcourt, Brace and Company, 1943).

Ervine, St John. *Boyd's Shop: A Comedy in Four Acts* (London and New York: Allen and Unwin, 1936).

Ervine, St John. *Craigavon: Ulsterman* (London: Allen and Unwin, 1949).

Ervine, St John. *Mrs Martin's Man* (London; Dublin: Maunsel & Company Limited, 1914).

Farrell, Michael. *Northern Ireland: The Orange State* (London: Pluto Press, 1976).

Faulkner, Brian. *Memoirs of a Statesman*, ed. by John Houston (London: Weidenfield and Nicholson, 1978).

Fiacc, Padraic. *Ruined Pages: Selected Poems*, ed. by Gerald Dawe and Aodán Mac Póilin (Belfast: Blackstaff Press, 1994).

Fisk, Robert. *In Time of War: Ireland, Ulster and the Price of Neutrality 1939–45* (London: André Deutsch; Dingle: Brandon, 1983).

Fitz-Simon, Christopher. *Eleven Houses: A Memoir of Childhood* (Dublin: Penguin Ireland, 2007).

Fleming, George. *Magennis VC* (Dublin: History Ireland, 1998).

Flood, Jeanne. *Brian Moore* (Lewisburg: Bucknell University Press; London: Associated University Press, 1974).

Francis, Dermot, Brian Lacey and Jim Mullen. *Atlantic Memorial: The Foyle and the Western Approaches 1939–1945* (Derry: Derry City Council, Heritage and Museum Service, 2005).

Fussell, Paul. *Wartime: Understanding and Behaviour in the Second World War* (New York, Oxford: Oxford University Press, 1989).

Gallacher, William. *Freedom or Slavery?* (Belfast: Communist Party of Ireland, 1942).

Gallacher, William. *Ireland—can it remain neutral?* (London: Communist Party of Great Britain, 1941).

Gardiner, Juliet. *The Blitz: The British Under Attack* (London: HarperPress, 2010).

Gardiner, Juliet. *Wartime: Britain 1939–1945* (London: Headline, 2004, repr. London: Headline Review, 2005).

Garlake, Margaret. *New Art, New World: British Art in Postwar Society* (New Haven and London: Yale University Press, 1998).

Gearon, Liam. *Landscapes of Encounter: The Portrayal of Catholicism in the Novels of Brian Moore* (Calgary: University of Calgary Press, 2002).

Gibson-Harries, Derrick. *Life-Line to Freedom: Ulster in the Second World War* (Lagan: Ulster Society Publications, 1990).

Gilbert, Martin, ed. *The Churchill War Papers, Volume 3: The Ever-Widening War 1941* (London: William Heinemann, 2000).

Gilbert, Stephen. *Bombardier* (London: Faber and Faber, 1944).

Gillis, Alan. *Irish Poetry of the 1930s* (Oxford: Oxford University Press, 2005).

Gray, Tony. *The Lost Years: The Emergency in Ireland, 1939–45* (London: Little, Brown, 1997).

Greacen, Robert. *Brief Encounters: Literary Dublin and Belfast in the 1940s* (Dublin: Cathair Books, 1991).

Greacen, Robert. *Collected Poems 1944–1994* (Belfast: Lagan Press, 1995).

Greacen, Robert. 'Denis Ireland: a Memoir', *Honest Ulsterman*, 44/45 (August/October 1974), pp. 50–52.

Greacen, Robert. *Even Without Irene* (Dublin: Dolmen Press, 1969).

Greacen, Robert. *The Only Emperor* (Belfast: Lapwing, 1994).

Greacen, Robert. *Rooted in Ulster* (Belfast: Lagan Press, 2000).

Greacen, Robert. *The Sash My Father Wore* (Edinburgh: Mainstream, 1997).

Greacen, Robert, Bruce Williamson and Valentin Iremonger. *On the Barricades* (Dublin: New Frontiers, 1944).

Greacen, Robert, ed. *Poems from Ulster* (Belfast: W. Erskine Mayne, 1942).

Greeley, Robin Adèle. *Surrealism and the Spanish Civil War* (New Haven, CN, and London: Yale University Press, 2006).

Green, Henry. *Caught* (London: Hogarth Press, 1943).

Gurian, Waldemar. *The Future of Bolshevism*, translated by E. I. Watkin (New York: Sheed & Ward Inc., 1936).

Hall, Dickon. *Colin Middleton: A Study* (Joga Press, 2001).

Hammer, Martin. *Graham Sutherland: Landscapes, War Scenes, Portraits 1924–1950* (London: Scala and Dulwich Picture Gallery, 2005).

Hanna, Ronnie. *Pardon Me Boy: The Americans in Ulster 1942–45, a Pictorial Record* (Lurgan: Ulster Society (Publications) Limited, 1991).

Harbinson, Robert. *No Surrender: An Ulster Childhood* (London: Faber and Faber, 1960; repr. Belfast: Blackstaff Press, 1987).

Harbinson, Robert. *Selected Stories* (Belfast: Lagan Press, 1996).

Harbinson, Robert. *Song of Erne* (Belfast: Blackstaff Press, 1987).

Harbinson, Robert. *Up Spake the Cabin Boy* (Belfast: Blackstaff Press, 1989).

Harries, Meirion, and Susie Harries. *The War Artists* (London: Michael Joseph in association with the Imperial War Museum and the Tate Gallery, 1983).

Harrison, Henry. *The Neutrality of Ireland: Why It Was Inevitable* (London: Robert Hale Limited, 1942).

Harrisson, Tom. 'Ulster Outlooks', *The Cornhill Magazine*, 962 (London: John Murray, May 1944), pp. 80–91; 'Ulster Outlooks', *Cornhill*, 963 (November 1944), pp. 210–223.

Harte, Liam, ed. *Modern Irish Autobiography: Self, Nation and Society* (Basingstoke: Palgrave Macmillan, 2007).

Hawkins, John. *The Irish Question Today* (London: Victor Gollancz and Fabian Society, 1941).

Hayes, Maurice. *Minority Verdict: Experiences of a Catholic Public Servant* (Belfast: Blackstaff Press, 1995).

Healy, Cahir. *A Hired Boy on the Border* (Dublin: Catholic Truth Society, 1944).

Healy, Cahir. *The Mutilation of a Nation: The Story of the Partition of Ireland* (Derry: Derry Journal Ltd, 1945).

Heaney, Seamus. *District and Circle* (London: Faber and Faber, 2006).

Heaney, Seamus. *Opened Ground: Poems 1966–1996* (London: Faber and Faber, 1998).

Heaney, Seamus. *Preoccupations: Selected Prose 1968–1978* (London: Faber and Faber, 1984).

Hennessey, Thomas. *A History of Northern Ireland, 1920–1996* (Dublin: Gill and Macmillan, 1997).

Hewison, Robert. *Under Siege: Literary Life in London 1939–45* (London: Weidenfeld and Nicolson, 1977; repr. London: Methuen, 1988).

Hewitt, John. *Ancestral Voices: The Selected Prose of John Hewitt*, ed. by Tom Clyde (Belfast: Blackstaff Press, 1987).

Hewitt, John. *Art in Ulster: Paintings, Drawings, Prints and Sculpture for the Last 400 Years to 1957* (Belfast: Blackstaff Press, 1977).

Hewitt, John. *Belfast Art Gallery* (Museum Guide, pub. date unknown, repr. from *The Studio*, January 1947).

Hewitt, John. *Colin Middleton* (Belfast and Dublin: Arts Council of Northern Ireland, and An Chormhairle Ealaion, 1976).

Hewitt, John. *The Collected Poems of John Hewitt*, ed. by Frank Ormsby (Belfast: Blackstaff Press, 1991).

Hewitt, John. *John Luke 1906–1975* (Belfast and Dublin: Arts Councils of Ireland, 1978).

Hewitt, John. *A North Light: Twenty-five Years in a Municipal Art Gallery* (unpublished autobiography, John Hewitt Collection, University of Ulster, Coleraine).

Hewitt, John. *A North Light: Twenty-five Years in a Municipal Art Gallery*, ed. by Frank Ferguson and Kathryn White (Dublin: Four Courts Press, 2013).

Hicks, Patricks. 'History and Masculinity in Brian Moore's *The Emperor of Ice Cream*', *Canadian Journal of Irish Studies*, 25 (1999), pp. 400–413

Hill, John. *Cinema and Northern Ireland: Film, Culture and Politics* (London: British Film Institute, 2006).

Hyman, Timothy, and Patrick Wright, eds. *Stanley Spencer* (London: Tate Publishing, 2001).

Hynes, Samuel. *The Auden Generation: Literature and Politics in England in the 1930s* (London: Bodley Head, 1976).

Ireland, Denis. *Eamon de Valera Doesn't See it Through* (Cork: Forum Press, 1941).

Ireland, Denis. *From the Jungle of Belfast* (Belfast: Blackstaff Press, 1973).

Ireland, Denis. *Letters from Ireland* (Belfast: Ulster Union Club, 1945).

Jamison, Kenneth. *The Art of Colin Middleton* (Belfast: Arts Council of Northern Ireland, 1965).

Johnson, Nevill. *The Other Side of Six* (Dublin: Academy Press, 1983).

Johnstone, Robert, and Dennis Kirk. *Images of Belfast* (Belfast: Blackstaff Press, 1983).

Joyce, James. *Ulysses*, ed. by Hans Walter Gabler (New York: Random House, 1986).

Kavanagh, Patrick. *Collected Poems* (London: Penguin Classics, 2005).

Kavanagh, Patrick. *Collected Pruse* (London: MacGibbon & Kee, 1967).

Kearns, Kevin. *The Bombing of Dublin's North Strand, 1941: The Untold Story* (Dublin: Gill and Macmillan, 2009).

Kelly, James. *Bonfires on the Hillside: An Eyewitness Account of Political Upheaval in Northern Ireland* (Belfast: Fountain Publishing, 1995).

Kennedy, Brian. *Ulster Museum. A Catalogue of the Permanent Collection: 1, British Art 1900–1937 Robert Lloyd Patterson Collection* (Belfast: Friends of the Ulster Museum, 1982).

Kennedy, Dennis. *Climbing Slemish* (Victoria, British Columbia: Trafford Publishing, 2006).

Kennedy, S.B. *Irish Art and Modernism: 1880–1950* (Belfast: Institute of Irish Studies, The Queen's University of Belfast, 1991).

Kennedy, S.B. *The White Stag Group* (Dublin: Irish Museum of Modern Art, 2005).

Kennelly, Brendan, ed. *Penguin Book of Irish Verse* (Harmondsworth: Penguin, 1970).

Keogh, Dermot, and Mervyn O'Driscoll. *Ireland in World War Two: Neutrality and Survival* (Cork: Mercier Press, 2000).

Kiely, Benedict. *Drink to the Bird: A Memoir* (London: Methuen, 1991).

Kiely, Benedict. *Land Without Stars* (London: Christopher Johnson, 1946; repr. Dublin: Moytura Press, 1990).

Kiely, Benedict. *The Waves Behind Us: Further Memoirs* (London: Methuen, 1999).

Killen, John. *The Unkindest Cut: A Cartoon History of Ulster 1900–2000* (Belfast: Blackstaff Press, 2000).

Kinsella, Thomas. *The New Oxford Book of Irish Verse* (Oxford: Oxford University Press, 1986, rev. edn. 2001).

Kirkland, Richard. *Literature and Culture in Northern Ireland Since 1965: Moments of Danger* (Harlow: Longman, 1996).

Klein, Holger, ed. *The Second World War in Fiction* (London and Basingstoke: Macmillan, 1984).

Lambkin, Romie. *My Time in the War: An Irishwoman's Diary* (Dublin: Wolfhound Press, 1992).

Lampe, David. *Pyke: The Unknown Genius* (London: Evans Brothers, 1959).

Laughton, Freda. *A Transitory House* (London: Jonathan Cape, 1945).

Litton, Helen. *The World War II Years: The Irish Emergency: An Illustrated History* (Dublin: Wolfhound Press, 2001).

Longley, Edna. *The Living Stream: Literature and Revisionism in Ireland* (Newcastle Upon Tyne: Bloodaxe Books, 1994).

Longley, Edna. *Poetry in the Wars* (Newcastle upon Tyne: Bloodaxe Books, 1986).

Longley, Michael. *Gorse Fires* (London: Secker and Warburg, 1991).

Longley, Michael. *Tuppenny Stung: Autobiographical Chapters* (Belfast: Lagan Press, 1994).

Longley, Michael. *The Weather in Japan* (London: Jonathan Cape, 2000).

Lyons, F.S.L. *Ireland Since the Famine* (London: Collins/Fontana, 1971).

McAteer, Eddie. *New Thoughts on an Old Subject* (Donegal: Donegal Democrat, 1948).

McAughtry, Sam. *Hillman Street High Roller* (Belfast: Appletree, 1994).

McAughtry, Sam. *McAughtry's War* (Belfast: Blackstaff Press, 1985).

McAughtry, Sam. *On the Outside Looking In: A Memoir* (Belfast: Blackstaff Press, 2003).

McAughtry, Sam. *The Sinking of the Kenbane Head* (Belfast: Blackstaff Press, 1977; rev. edn., 2004).

McAvera, Brian, ed. *Post War Pre Troubles: Collective Histories of Northern Irish Art* (Belfast: Golden Thread Gallery, 2005).

McCullough, Elizabeth. *A Square Peg: An Ulster Childhood* (Dublin: Marino Books, 1997).

McCullough, W.H. *But Victory Sooner…* (Belfast: Communist Party of Ireland, c.1943).

McCullough, W.H. *Changes are Needed at Stormont* (Belfast, Communist Party of Ireland, c. 1940).

McCullough, W.H. *For a Prosperous Ulster: An Explanation of the Communist Party's Policy for Northern Ireland* (Belfast: Communist Party, c.1945).

McCullough, W.H. *Ireland Looks to Labour* (Belfast: Communist Party of Ireland, 1943).

McCusker, Breege. *Castle Archdale and Fermanagh in World War II* (Irvinestown: Necarne, 1993).

McDonald, Peter. *Mistaken Identities: Poetry and Northern Ireland* (Oxford: Clarendon Press, 1997).

McFadden, Roy. *Collected Poems 1943–1995* (Belfast: Lagan Press, 1996).

McFadden, Roy. *Flowers for a Lady* (London: Routledge, 1945).

McFadden, Roy. *Swords and Ploughshares* (London: Routledge, 1943).

McFadden, Roy. 'The Belfast Forties', *Force 10* (Autumn 1994), pp. 68–73.

McFadden, Roy. 'Corrigibly Plural', *Fortnight* 337 (March 1995), pp. 41–42.

McFadden, Roy. 'Reflections on Megarrity', *Threshold* 5, no. 1 (Spring/Summer 1961), pp. 25–34.

McIntosh, Gillian. *The Force of Culture: Unionist Identities in Twentieth Century Ireland* (Cork: Cork University Press, 1999).

McIntosh, Gillian. 'CEMA and the National Anthem: The Arts and the State in Postwar Northern Ireland', *New Hibernia Review* 5, no. 3 (2001), pp. 22–31.

MacIntyre, James. *Making My Mark: An Artist's Early Life* (Belfast: Blackstaff Press, 2001).

MacKay, Marina. *Modernism and World War II* (Cambridge: Cambridge University Press, 2007).

MacKay, Marina, ed. *The Cambridge Companion to the Literature of World War II* (Cambridge: Cambridge University Press, 2009).

MacKay, Marina, and Lyndsey Stonebridge, eds. *British Fiction After Modernism: The Novel at Mid-Century* (Basingstoke and New York: Palgrave Macmillan, 2007).

Mackay, Peter, Edna Longley, and Fran Brearton, eds. *Modern Irish and Scottish Poetry* (Cambridge: Cambridge University Press, 2011).

McMahon, Sean. *The Belfast Blitz: Luftwaffe Raids in Northern Ireland, 1941* (Belfast: Brehon Press, 2010).

MacNeice, Louis. *Collected Poems*, ed. by Peter McDonald (London: Faber and Faber, 2007).

MacNeice, Louis. *Letters of Louis MacNeice*, ed. by Jonathan Allison (London: Faber and Faber, 2010).

MacNeice, Louis. *Meet the U.S. Army* (London: HMSO, 1943).

MacNeice, Louis. *The Poetry of W.B. Yeats* (London: Oxford University Press, 1941).

MacNeice, Louis. *Selected Plays of Louis MacNeice*, ed. by Alan Heuser and Peter McDonald (Oxford: Oxford University Press, 1993).

MacNeice, Louis. *Selected Prose of Louis MacNeice*, ed. Alan Heuser (Oxford: Oxford University Press, 1990).

MacNeice, Louis. *The Strings are False: An Unfinished Autobiography* (London: Faber and Faber, 1965).

Maguire, W.A. *Belfast* (Keele, Staffordshire: Ryburn Publishing, Keele University Press, 1993).

Maher, Eamon. 'Belfast the Far From Sublime City in Brian Moore's Early Novels', *Studies* 90, no. 360 (2001), pp. 422–431.

Mahon, Derek. *Journalism* (Oldcastle, Co. Meath: Gallery Press, 1996).

Mahon, Derek. *New Collected Poems* (Oldcastle, Co. Meath: Gallery Press, 2011).

Marshall, Catherine, ed. *The Hunter Gatherer, the Collection of George and Maura McClelland at the Irish Museum of Modern Art* (Dublin: IMMA, 2004).

Marshall, Isobel. *A Jack and His Jill: A Romance of Modern Derry* (Belfast: Quota Press, 1944).

Marvell, Andrew. *The Poems and Letters of Andrew Marvell (Volume 1: Poems)* ed. by H.M. Margoliouth, rev. by Pierre Legouis with the collaboration of E.E. Duncan-Jones (Oxford: Oxford University Press, 1971).

Marwick, Arthur. *The Home Front: The British and the Second World War* (London: Thames and Hudson, 1976).

Mengham, Rod, and N.H. Reeve, eds. *The Fiction of the 1940s: Stories of Survival* (Basingstoke and New York: Palgrave Macmillan, 2001).

Millar, Ruddick. *A Yank from Ulster* (Belfast: Quota Press, 1943).

Miller, James. *The North Atlantic Front: Orkney, Shetland, Faroe and Iceland at War* (Edinburgh: Birlinn, 2003).

Miller, Kristine A. *British Literature of the Blitz: Fighting the People's War* (Basingstoke and New York: Palgrave Macmillan, 2009).

Monsarrat, Nicholas. *The Cruel Sea* (London: Cassell, 1951; repr. 1996).

Montague, John. *The Figure in the Cave and Other Essays* (Dublin: Lilliput Press, 1989).

Montague, John, ed. *The Faber Book of Irish Verse* (London: Faber and Faber, 1974).

Moore, Brian. *The Emperor Of Ice Cream* (London: Andre Deutsch, 1965; repr. London: Paladin, 1987).

Moore, Brian. *The Lonely Passion of Judith Hearne* (London: Andre Deutsch, 1955).

Muldoon, Paul, ed. *The Faber Book of Contemporary Irish Poetry* (London: Faber and Faber, 1984)

Mumford, Lewis. *The Culture of Cities* (London: Secker and Warburg, 1938).

Munton, Alan. *English Fiction of the Second World War* (London: Faber and Faber, 1989).

Murphy, Dervla. *A Place Apart* (Harmondsworth: Penguin, 1979).

Nesbitt, Noel. *A Museum in Belfast* (Belfast: Ulster Museum, 1979).

Norton, Christopher. 'The Internment of Cahir Healy M.P., Brixton Prison July 1941–December 1942', *Twentieth Century British History* 18, no. 2 (2007), pp. 170–93. doi: 10.1093/tcbh/hwm007.

Nowlan, Kevin B., and T. Desmond Williams. *Ireland in the War Years and After, 1939–51.* (Dublin: Gill and Macmillan, 1969).

O'Brien, Darcy. *W. R. Rodgers* (Cranbury, NJ: Associated University Presses, 1970).

O'Connor, Patricia, ed. *Four New One-Act Plays* (Belfast: Quota Press, 1948).

Ó Drisceoil, Denis. *Censorship in Ireland 1939–1945: Neutrality, Politics and Society* (Cork: Cork University Press, 1996).

O'Driscoll, Dennis. *Stepping Stones: Interviews with Seamus Heaney* (London: Faber and Faber, 2008).

Ó Faoláin, Seán. *An Irish Journey* (London, New York, Toronto: Longman, 1940).

Ó Glaisne, Risteárd. *Denis Ireland* (Baile Átha Cliath: Coiscéim, 2000).

O'Grady, Thomas. 'Provincial Life: The Early Novels of Benedict Kiely', *Irish University Review* 38, no. 1 (2008), pp. 20–37.

O'Neill, Terence. *The Autobiography of Terence O'Neill* (London: Rupert Hart-Davis Ltd, 1972).

Oliver, John A. *Working at Stormont: Memoirs* (Dublin: Institute of Public Administration, 1978).

Ormsby, Frank. *A Northern Spring* (London: Secker and Warburg; Dublin: Gallery Press, 1986).

Ormsby, Frank, ed. *Poets from the North of Ireland* (Belfast: Blackstaff Press, 1979, rev. edn. 1990).

Orwell, George. *The Lion and the Unicorn: Socialism and the English Genius* (London: Secker and Warburg, 1941).

Orwell, George. 'The Lion and the Unicorn: Socialism and the English Genius', *The Complete Works of George Orwell*, vol. 12, 'A Patriot After All', ed. by Peter Davison assisted by Ian Angus and Sheila Davison (London: Secker and Warburg, 1998), pp. 391–434.

Patrizio, Andrew, and Frank Little. *Canvassing the Clyde: Stanley Spencer and the Shipyards* (Glasgow: Glasgow Museums, 1994).

Patten, Eve, ed. *Returning to Ourselves: Second Volume of Papers from the John Hewitt International Summer School* (Belfast: Lagan Press, 1995).

Patterson, Glenn. *Burning Your Own* (London: Chatto and Windus, 1988).

Patterson, Glenn. *FAT LAD* (London: Minerva, 1993).

Paulin, Tom. *Fivemiletown* (London: Faber and Faber, 1987).

Phelan, Jim. *Churchill Can Unite Ireland* (London: Victor Gollancz, 1940).

Piette, Adam. *Imagination at War: British Fiction and Poetry 1939–1945* (London: Papermac, 1995).

Powell, Anthony. *The Soldier's Art* (London: Heinemann, 1966; repr. London: Arrow, 2005).

Powell, Anthony. *To Keep the Ball Rolling: The Memoirs of Anthony Powell, Volume III, Faces in My Time* (London: Heinemann, 1980).

Purdy, Ann. *Molyneaux: the Long View* (Antrim: Greystone, 1989).

Rawlinson, Mark. *British Writing of the Second World War* (Oxford: Clarendon Press, 2000).

Rawlinson, Mark. 'Review of Patrick Deer', *Culture and Camouflage: War, Empire and Modern British Culture, Review of English Studies* 62, no. 253 (February 2011), pp. 158–160. doi:10.1093/res/hgq073.

Redmond, Sean. *Belfast is Burning 1941* (Dublin: IMPACT, Municipal Employees Division, 2002).

Reynolds, David. *Rich Relations: The American Occupation of Britain 1942–1945* (London: Harper Collins, 1995).

Roberts, Michael, ed. *The Faber Book of Modern Verse* (London: Faber and Faber, 1936).

Robb, Nesca. *An Ulsterwoman in England* (Cambridge: Cambridge University Press, 1942).

Roche, Anthony. 'A Reading of Autumn Journal: The Question of Louis MacNeice's Irishness', *Text and Context* 3 (Autumn 1988), pp. 71–90.

Rodgers, W.R. *Awake! and Other Poems* (London: Secker and Warburg, 1941).

Rodgers, W.R. *Collected Poems* (London, New York, Toronto: Oxford University Press, 1971).

Rodgers, W.R. *Poems*, ed. by Michael Longley (Oldcastle, Co. Meath: Gallery Press, 1993).

Rolston, Bill. *Politics and Painting: Murals and Conflict in Northern Ireland* (Cranbury, New Jersey; London; Mississauga, Ontario: Associated University Press, 1991).

Rose, Sonya O. *Which People's War: National Identity and Citizenship in Britain 1939–1945* (Oxford: Oxford University Press, 2003).

Sage, Lorna, ed. *The Cambridge Guide to Women's Writing* (Cambridge: Cambridge University Press, 1999).

Sampson, Denis. *Brian Moore: The Chameleon Novelist* (Dublin: Marino, 1998).

Schneede, Uwe M. *The Essential Max Ernst*, trans. by R.W. Last (London: Thames and Hudson, 1972).

Seidenberg, Stephen, Maurice Sellar and Lou Jones. *You Must Remember This…Songs At The Heart Of The War* (London: Boxtree, 1995).

Shea, Patrick. *Voices and the Sound of Drums: An Irish Autobiography* (Belfast: Blackstaff Press, 1981).

Shearman, Hugh. *Anglo-Irish Relations* (London: Faber and Faber, 1948).

Shearman, Hugh. *A Bomb and a Girl* (London: Faber and Faber, 1944).

Shearman, Hugh. *Northern Ireland* (Belfast: HMSO, 1968).

Shearman, Hugh. *Northern Ireland 1921–1971*(Belfast: WG Baird Limited for HMSO, 1971).

Shearman, Hugh. *Northern Ireland: Its History, Resources and People* (Belfast: HMSO, 1946).

Shearman, Hugh. *Not an Inch: A Study of Northern Ireland and Lord Craigavon* (London: Faber and Faber, 1942).

Shearman, Hugh. *Ulster* (London: Robert Hale Limited, 1949).

Shelley, Percy Bysshe. *Shelley: Poetical Works*, ed. by Thomas Hutchinson, new edition corrected by G.M. Matthews (London, New York, Toronto: Oxford University Press, 1970).

Shires, Linda. *British Poetry of the Second World War* (London and Basingstoke: Macmillan, 1985).

Sillars, Stuart. *British Romantic Art and the Second World War* (Basingstoke: Macmillan, 1991).

Skelton, Robin, ed. *Poetry of the Forties* (Harmondsworth: Penguin, 1968).

Special Services Division, Services of Supply, United States Army. *A Pocket Guide to Northern Ireland* (Washington, DC: United States Government Printing Office, 1942).

Stanford, Derek. *Inside the Forties: Literary Memoirs 1937–1957*(London: Sidgwick and Jackson, 1977).

Stansky, Peter, and William Abrahams. *London's Burning: Life, Death and Art in the Second World War* (London: Constable, 1994).

Steward, James Christen, ed. *When Time Began to Rant and Rage: Figurative Painting from Twentieth-Century Ireland* (London: Merrell Holberton, 1998).

Stewart, Victoria. *Narratives of Memory: British Writing of the 1940s* (Basingstoke and New York: Palgrave Macmillan, 2006).

Stokes, Adrian. *The Critical Writings of Adrian Stokes* (London: Thames and Hudson, 1978).

Stonebridge, Lyndsey. *The Writing of Anxiety: Imagining Wartime in Mid-Century British Culture* (Basingstoke: Palgrave Macmillan, 2007).

Tolley, A. Trevor. *The Poetry of the Forties* (Manchester: Manchester University Press, 1985).

Ulster Union Club. *The Defence of Ireland* (Belfast: Ulster Union Club, 1942).

Ulster Union Club. *What is the Ulster Union Club?* (Belfast: Ulster Union Club, 1941).

Ultach. *Orange Terror: The Partition of Ireland, a Reprint from The Capuchin Annual, 1943* (Dublin: Capuchin Annual Office, 1943).

Various. *15 Poems* (Belfast: Socialist Party, 1942).

Various. *The P.E.N. In Ulster*, Contributed by Well-Known Writers of Belfast Centre (Belfast: Reid and Wright, 1942).

Various. *War Pictures by British Artists No. 2: Blitz*, introduced by J.B. Morton (London: Oxford University Press, 1942).

Various. 'The War Years in Ulster (1939–45): A Symposium', *The Honest Ulsterman* 64 (1979–80), pp. 11–62.

Walker, Graham S. *The Politics of Frustration: Harry Midgley and the Failure of Labour in Northern Ireland* (Manchester: Manchester University Press, 1985).

White, James. *Gerard Dillon: An Illustrated Biography* (Dublin: Wolfhound Press, 1994).

White, James. *The Watch Below* (London: Ronald Whiting and Wheaton, 1966).

Wichert, Sabine. *Northern Ireland Since 1945* (London and New York: Longman, 1999).

Wills, Clair. *That Neutral Island: A Cultural History of Ireland During the Second World War* (London: Faber and Faber, 2007).

Wills, Clair. 'The Aesthetics of Irish Neutrality During World War Two', *boundary 2* 31, no. 1 (Spring 2004), pp. 119–145. doi:10.1215/01903659-31-1-119.

Wilson, Judith C. *Conor 1881–1968: The Life and Work of an Ulster Artist* (Dundonald: Blackstaff Press, 1981).

Wilson Foster, John. *Between Shadows: Modern Irish Writing and Culture* (Dublin, Portland, Oregon: Irish Academic Press, 2009).

Wilson Foster, John, ed. *The Cambridge Companion to the Irish Novel* (Cambridge: Cambridge University Press, 2006).

Woolf, Virginia. *Between the Acts* (New York: Harcourt, Brace and Company, 1941).

Wyatt, Woodrow, ed. *The Way We Lived Then: The English Story in the 1940s* (London: Flamingo, 1990).

PERIODICALS AND LITTLE MAGAZINES

The Bell, ed. by Seán Ó Faoláin (1940–46) and Peadar O'Donnell (1946–54) (Dublin: 1940–54).

The Capuchin Annual (Dublin: Capuchin Periodicals' Office/Two, Capel Street, 1939–44).

Causeway: The Arts in Ulster, ed. by Michael Longley (Belfast: Arts Council of Northern Ireland, and Dublin: Gill and Macmillan, 1971).

Horizon 5(25), ed. by Cyril Connolly (London: January 1942).

Irish Bookman, ed. by Seamus Campbell (Dublin: 1946–48).

Lagan, ed. by John Boyd (Belfast: 1943–45).

The North: A Collection of Short Stories, Articles and Poems (Belfast: Ulster Union Club, 1944–45).

The Northman and *New Northman* (Belfast: Queen's University, 1935–47).

Northern Harvest: Anthology of Ulster Writing, ed. by Robert Greacen (Belfast: Derrick MacCord, 1944).

Northern Star (Belfast: Socialist Party, 1940–43).

Now in Ulster, ed. by Arthur and George Campbell (Belfast: Campbell Bros. and WG Baird, 1944).

Rann, ed. by Roy McFadden and Barbara Hunter (Lisburn: 1948–53).

Threshold (Belfast: Lyric Players Theatre, 1957–86).

Ulster Parade (Belfast: Quota Press, 1941–46).

Unity (Belfast: Workers Weekly Committee, 1942–45).

NEWSPAPERS

Daily Telegraph
London *Independent*
Irish Independent
Irish Times
Belfast *News Letter*
Northern Whig
Belfast Telegraph
London *Times*
The Standard

EXHIBITION CATALOGUES

John Armstrong 1893–1973 (London: Arts Council of Great Britain, 1975).

George Campbell 1917–1979: A Retrospective Exhibition June 5th to July 5th (exhibition catalogue, Drogheda: The Droichead Arts Centre, 1979).

William Conor 1881–1968 (Belfast: Arts Council of Northern Ireland, 1968).

Arne Ekeland, Paintings: 1937–85, introduced by Ole Henrik Moe (Newcastle upon Tyne: Polytechnic Gallery, 1986).

Paintings, Drawings and Watercolours from the Studio of the Late Colin Middleton MBE, RHA (London: Christie, Manson and Woods, Ltd, 1985).
Ulster Unit (Belfast: 1934).

THESIS

Coulter, Ríann. 'Nationalism, Regionalism and Internationalism: Cultural Identity in Irish Art, 1943–1960' (unpublished doctoral thesis, Courtauld Institute of Art, University of London, 2006).

REFERENCE WORK

Parliamentary Debates: Northern Ireland House of Commons Official Report, XXX (Belfast: HMSO, 1947).

SPECIAL COLLECTIONS

Linen Hall Library, Belfast
John Boyd Collection
Robert Greacen Collection
Denis Ireland Collection
Jack Loudan Collection

Public Records Office of Northern Ireland
Arts Council of Northern Ireland Archive
Diary of Emma Duffin
John Hewitt Papers
W.R. Rodgers Papers

Queen's University Belfast, McClay Library, Special Collections Department
Thomas Carnduff Archive
Stephen Gilbert Collection
Roy McFadden Papers

Ulster Folk and Transport Museum, Cultra, Co. Down
BBC Northern Ireland Archive
Colin Middleton Archive

University of Sussex, Library, Special Collections Department
Mass-Observation Archive

University of Ulster, Coleraine, Library, Special Collections Department
John Hewitt Collection

Index

Index